SLAYING THE NUCLEAR DRAGON

STUDIES IN SECURITY AND INTERNATIONAL AFFAIRS

SERIES EDITORS

Gary K. Bertsch
University Professor of Public and International Affairs and Director of the Center for International Trade and Security, University of Georgia

Howard J. Wiarda
Dean Rusk Professor of International Relations and Head of the Department of International Affairs, University of Georgia

SERIES ADVISORY BOARD

Pauline H. Baker
The Fund for Peace

Eliot Cohen
Paul H. Nitze School of Advanced International Studies, Johns Hopkins University

Eric Einhorn
Center for Public Policy and Administration, University of Massachusetts, Amherst

John J. Hamre
The Center for Strategic and International Studies

Josef Joffe
Hoover Institution, Institute for International Studies, Stanford University

Lawrence J. Korb
Center for American Progress

William J. Long
Sam Nunn School of International Affairs, Georgia Institute of Technology

Jessica Tuchman Mathews
Carnegie Endowment for International Peace

Scott D. Sagan
Center for International Security and Cooperation, Stanford University

Lawrence Scheinman
Monterey Institute of International Studies, CNS-WDC

David Shambaugh
The Elliott School of International Affairs, George Washington University

Jessica Stern
John F. Kennedy School of Government, Harvard University

SLAYING THE NUCLEAR DRAGON

Disarmament Dynamics in the Twenty-First Century

Edited by Tanya Ogilvie-White and David Santoro

The University of Georgia Press
Athens and London

© 2012 by the University of Georgia Press
Athens, Georgia 30602
www.ugapress.org
All rights reserved
Set in 10/14 Minion Pro by Graphic Composition, Inc.

Printed digitally in the United States of America

Library of Congress Cataloging-in-Publication Data
Slaying the nuclear dragon : disarmament dynamics in the
twenty-first century / edited by Tanya Ogilvie-White and
David Santoro.
     p. cm. — (Studies in security and international affairs)
   Includes index.
   ISBN-13: 978-0-8203-3689-3 (cloth : alk. paper)
   ISBN-10: 0-8203-3689-0 (cloth : alk. paper)
   ISBN-13: 978-0-8203-4246-7 (pbk. : alk. paper)
   ISBN-10: 0-8203-4246-7 (pbk. : alk. paper)
  1. Nuclear disarmament—History—21st century.
I. Ogilvie-White, Tanya. II. Santoro, David.
   JZ5675.S63 2012
   7.1'7472—dc33   2011037766

British Library Cataloging-in-Publication Data available

To all nuclear dragon slayers, everywhere

The nuclear dragon may be sleeping, but it is certainly not dead.
   Michael Howard

>

CONTENTS

Foreword   xiii
Mark Fitzpatrick

Acknowledgments   xix
Tanya Ogilvie-White and David Santoro

INTRODUCTION. The Nuclear Dragon: No Longer out on the Prowl   1
Tanya Ogilvie-White and David Santoro

CHAPTER ONE. The Optimistic Nuclear Weapon States: The United States and the United Kingdom   11
David Santoro

CHAPTER TWO. Advocating the Elimination of Nuclear Weapons: The Role of Key Individual and Coalition States   56
Marianne Hanson

CHAPTER THREE. The Rollback States: South Africa and Kazakhstan   85
Stephen F. Burgess and Togzhan Kassenova

CHAPTER FOUR. The Pessimistic Nuclear Weapon States: France, Russia, and China   118
David Santoro

CHAPTER FIVE. The Threshold States: Japan and Brazil   151
Maria Rost Rublee

CHAPTER SIX. The Nuclear Energy Aspirants: Egypt and Vietnam   188
Tanya Ogilvie-White and Maria Rost Rublee

CHAPTER SEVEN. The Nuclear Holdouts: India, Israel, and Pakistan   219
Devin T. Hagerty

CHAPTER EIGHT. The Defiant States: North Korea and Iran   249
Tanya Ogilvie-White

CHAPTER NINE. The Silent Proliferators: Syria and Myanmar   279
Jacqueline Shire

CONCLUSION. The Nuclear Dragon: One Eye Open, One Eye Closed   304
Tanya Ogilvie-White and David Santoro

Contributors   325

Index   329

FOREWORD

In the recent rekindling of the quest for a nuclear-weapon-free world, and in the inevitable pushback by nuclear "realists," there is a strong sense of déjà vu. As in the past, nuclear anti-activists often make their case in moralistic terms: because nuclear weapons pose the threat of global annihilation they must be abolished, and soon, by fiat. Deterrence advocates counter, as before, that nuclear weapons have kept the peace between major powers and in any case cannot be dis-invented.

The International Institute for Strategic Studies (IISS), where good fortune finds me heading the Non-Proliferation and Disarmament Programme, encourages a middle path between these two poles. Our perspective has been guided by the luminance of the late Sir Michael Quinlan, who, at the end of his sterling career and up until the time of his passing in February 2009, was a consulting fellow for the institute. He was a firm believer in the value of nuclear deterrence; indeed, he was an architect of the British variant of the deterrence posture. Yet his arguments always rested on a strong foundation of ethical responsibility.

In spring 2007, Sir Michael inspired us to ask if there was not a way forward between the two protagonist camps in the nuclear debate. His question prompted an intense study on the requirements for a nuclear-weapon-free world that culminated in 2008 in the seminal Adelphi Paper on *Abolishing Nuclear Weapons* by George Perkovich and James Acton. In assessing the technical and political hurdles to a world free of nuclear weapons, the two authors were cautiously optimistic that solutions can be found to the daunting technical issues of transparency, verification, and the structure of the nuclear industry. They also probed solutions to the set of political impediments to disarmament. These hurdles are even more daunting than the technical challenges.

In the pages that follow, Tanya Ogilvie-White and David Santoro have developed the analysis further, in assessing the security, psychological, and political dynamics of the impediments to the goal of nuclear disarmament. Their categorization of states in terms of capabilities and attitudes toward nuclear weapons is a distinctive and instructive framework for analysis. Lest readers are left hopeless by the discussion of obstacles, however, the editors and their coauthors also discuss tentative ways to overcome the roadblocks. This is a volume about the political challenges and opportunities on the way to a nuclear-weapon-free world.

Tanya and David are well suited, and in many ways uniquely qualified, to carry out this analysis. Both are spending the 2010–11 academic year at IISS, as fellows under the Stanton Nuclear Security fellowship programme. For her fellowship project, Tanya is authoring a book on the ideas about nuclear deterrence and disarmament developed and promoted by Sir Michael Quinlan in his voluminous private correspondence. Her research into Quinlan's letters gives her a clear window from which to explain the nuclear debates of the past four decades. David, for his fellowship project, is focusing on major power relations in the nuclear field. In particular, he is examining the responsibilities of the permanent members of the Security Council in stemming the spread of nuclear weapons, including how to define noncompliance and how to respond after it is detected. The work being undertaken by both authors constitutes key areas in the broad field of nuclear security for which the Stanton Foundation programme seeks to foster a cadre of new thought leaders.

The authors are well-regarded young scholars who each achieved academic success in their respective works explaining proliferation dynamics: Tanya, initially in her fall 1996 *Nonproliferation Review* article "Is There a Theory of Nuclear Proliferation?" and in follow-on work on South Africa, the nuclear holdouts, Iran, and other potential proliferators; and David, in his 2010 debut book *Treating Weapons Proliferation—An Oncological Approach to the Spread of Nuclear, Biological, and Chemical Technology*.

The study of disarmament dynamics is particularly relevant now that the connection between nonproliferation and disarmament has been reaffirmed. President Barack Obama led this reaffirmation in his April 5, 2009, Prague speech that aimed to restore the consensus undergirding the Nuclear Nonproliferation Treaty (NPT). He laid out an ambitious agenda of arms control steps, each of which is meaningful in its own right. As argued by Perkovich and Acton, allowing the nonthreatening expansion of nuclear power, reducing the possibilities for nuclear terrorism, preempting the proliferation temptation, and removing the risk of nuclear annihilation are all reasons to take disarmament seriously. Obama's arms control agenda also serves what might be called a "hidden agenda" of nonproliferation. By addressing disarmament head-on, Obama sought to focus global attention on the proliferation problem. In pledging to take the disarmament goal seriously and in taking concrete steps in that direction, he disarmed the charge of double standards. His message is that all responsible nations must undertake and fulfill obligations if the world is to be protected from the threat of nuclear weapons.

Critics have countered that talking about disarmament distracts attention from nonproliferation. This contention is demonstrably false. Rather, the opposite appears to hold. The more that powerful nations downplayed their disarmament obligations in the earlier years of this century, the more that Non-Aligned Movement members decried the discrimination of double standards and resisted steps to strengthen nonproliferation.

Nobody expected that agreement between the United States and Russia on modestly reducing the numbers of strategically deployed nuclear forces as ordained by New Strategic Arms Reduction Treaty would produce an immediate nonproliferation gain in giving North Korea and Iran reason to rein in their nuclear ambitions. The Obama administration did hope, however, that renewed recognition of the connection between disarmament and nonproliferation would help to persuade other countries to strengthen the global nonproliferation regime.

The linkage is intrinsic and mutually reinforcing, not simply a matter of political trade-offs. The steps needed now to strengthen the nonproliferation regime—enhanced transparency, enforcement of standards, and irreversibility of commitments—will also be essential to any future nuclear-weapon-free world. But strengthening nonproliferation is not perceived as cost-free. States will have to accept additional constraints on their security options and potential pursuit of nuclear fuel-cycle technologies. As the nuclear weapon states limit their arsenals, however, it is still an open question whether states that are non-aligned, and thus outside the explicit security assurance offered by nuclear powers, will be willing to accept such constraints.

Some of the early signals are not promising. The 2010 NPT Review Conference produced a lengthy outcome document that modestly succeeded in restoring international consensus on the goals of the treaty, but it did little to significantly strengthen nonproliferation measures. It is regrettable that the review conference did not use the occasion to strengthen the verification instruments of the International Atomic Energy Agency, enhance the enforcement measures of the nonproliferation regime, or tighten the withdrawal provisions of the treaty so that that it cannot be abused by states that are found in noncompliance. Efforts to strengthen the treaty in these ways were blocked by a group of nations led, in part, by some of the very states whose nuclear activities have raised concerns.

An unintended consequence of Obama's Prague speech was the weighty set of expectations it created about how far the United States could move toward nuclear disarmament. Obama has not had the domestic support necessary to do more, and he has not been helped by the uncompromising stance of his foreign adversaries and the global divisions that block progress. One of the key steps on his arms control agenda, for example, was the adoption of a treaty capping the production of fissile material for weapons purposes. Unfortunately, this goal remains blocked by forces beyond Obama's control. The Conference on Disarmament, the venue in Geneva that by name is exclusively devoted to conferring on disarmament, is still hopelessly deadlocked. This is not because of intransigence by any of the major powers, but because of the insecurities of a single regional player, which does not want to go down any road that could restrict a nuclear equalizer that gives it strategic parity with its larger neighbor. Although Pakistan and India today have roughly equivalent fissile material stockpiles and production capabilities, Pakistan worries that India's much larger holding of reactor-grade plutonium, if put to weapons use, would put Pakistan at a disadvantage.

The South Asia–based dynamics that have prevented discussion at the Conference on Disarmament of a fissile material cut-off treaty is but one of the state-level factors assessed in the pages of this volume. Raising this example does not diminish the responsibility of Russia and the United States, as the holders of the vast majority of the world's nuclear weapons, to lead the way in reducing these arsenals. But the Pakistan factor is instructive of the kind of political and security dynamics that affect nuclear decision making in many of the countries assessed in this volume. Slaying the nuclear dragon will require a multifront battle plan that is well informed by the political dynamics of all the nuclear players.

The goal of disarmament, as Sir Michael frequently reminded us, is not just the abolition of nuclear weapons. Rather, the goal must be the establishment of a nuclear-weapon-free world that is stable and secure. The architecture for such a world would have to make it at least as secure as the world as we know it in the last sixty-five years since the atomic bomb was first, and last, used, and far more secure than the thirty-one years that preceded it. There is no guarantee, of course, that the sixty-five-year record of non-use will continue, especially as more states acquire nuclear weapons and nonstate actors newly express an interest in also acquiring these uniquely powerful weapons of mass destruction. As long as nuclear weapons exist, there is a chance they will be used. And as long as nuclear weapons are seen as the ultimate deterrent, they will remain attractive to states that seek a security guarantee and the prestige of the nuclear weapons club. There is every need, then, to continue efforts to abolish nuclear weapons.

Mark Fitzpatrick
Director, Non-Proliferation and Disarmament Programme
The International Institute for Strategic Studies

ACKNOWLEDGMENTS

As with any ambitious project, this volume has benefited enormously from the guidance, insight, and kindness of many people, and from the generous support of several organizations. We, as editors, would like to express our sincere gratitude to them.

At the top of the list are our coauthors, Stephen Burgess, Devin Hagerty, Marianne Hanson, Togzhan Kassenova, Maria Rost Rublee, and Jacqueline Shire. Each of them offers a unique and original contribution to this volume. We thank them all for their excellent work.

We are indebted to the International Institute for Strategic Studies (IISS), which has provided us with a home where much of this project has been completed. We are also grateful to the Stanton Foundation, which has funded our positions at IISS under its newly established Nuclear Security Fellowship Program—a program aimed to stimulate the development of the next generation of thought leaders on nuclear issues. It is our earnest hope that this volume will make a modest contribution toward the realization of this goal.

Likewise, a special thank-you goes to the University of Canterbury, which granted Tanya study leave in 2010–11. A similarly warm acknowledgment goes to the Simons Centre for Disarmament and Nonproliferation Research, where David was based when this project was initiated. His visiting fellowship at New York University's Center on International Cooperation in the spring of 2010 also contributed to the completion of this volume.

We have benefited from many critical reviews from numerous informed and thoughtful readers. Our preliminary work, which was published by Stephen Schwartz in a March 2010 special section of the *Nonproliferation Review*, was reviewed by Christophe Carle, Lewis Dunn, Devin Hagerty, Michael Keifer, Mark Smith, and Christine Wing. Although it would be tedious to name all the people who have provided valuable insights and comments on this expanded and updated volume, our special thanks go to Mark Fitzpatrick for his incisive, judicious, and knowledgeable suggestions.

Lastly, and most importantly, a heartfelt thank-you to our respective spouses,

Al and Laëtitia, who have kindly born our obsession with this project (another one!) and, in fact, strongly encouraged us to keep going. Our debt to them is immense.

Tanya Ogilvie-White and David Santoro
2010–11 Stanton Nuclear Security Fellows
The International Institute for Strategic Studies

SLAYING THE NUCLEAR DRAGON

INTRODUCTION
The Nuclear Dragon
No Longer out on the Prowl

Tanya Ogilvie-White and David Santoro

ANYONE WHO HAS BEEN KEEPING UP with the news headlines over the past few years will know that nuclear disarmament is back on the international security agenda. Since former U.S. statesmen George Shultz, William Perry, Henry Kissinger, and Sam Nunn called on governments to rid the world of nuclear weapons in their now famous January 2007 and follow-on January 2008 *Wall Street Journal* articles, nuclear disarmament momentum has been building, after nearly a decade of absence.[1] Most importantly, the goal of a nuclear-weapon-free world has been taken up at the political level by U.S. president Barack Obama and other leading political figures in the U.S. Republican and Democratic Parties, as well as by other influential people and leaders in countries around the world. Rather than being viewed as a distant pipedream advocated by starry-eyed idealists who will not acknowledge strategic realities, nuclear disarmament has now become part of mainstream political discourse.

In the past, in discussions on the pros and cons of nuclear weapon possession, hard-nosed realists nearly always gained the upper hand. "Nuclear deterrence is responsible for the absence of major war between the major powers since the Second World War," they would argue. "And anyways, nuclear weapons cannot be dis-invented, so we have no choice but to learn to live with them." But arguments in favor of nuclear weapon retention are no longer as compelling as they once were: although dangers of mass destruction remain, the threat of global nuclear annihilation (which characterized the Cold War period and gave deterrence theory its centrality) no longer exists. Moreover, proliferation dangers have grown: nuclear technology has become cheaper and more accessible; nuclear capabilities have spread via legitimate and illegitimate means; and proliferation threats are beginning to tip the balance against the "nuclear optimists" (i.e., against those who have long advocated that nuclear weapons play a stabilizing role in international affairs).[2] Chief among the threats is the prospect of nuclear terrorism, which has always been acknowledged as a possibility but has become a serious preoccupation since the events of September 11, 2001 (9/11), brought home to a stunned world the limitless horrors of global terrorism.

Today, ridding the world of nuclear weapons has become the shared goal of many different countries, from the microstate to superpowers.[3] But that is not to pretend that a nuclear-weapon-free world is guaranteed or even on the horizon. Since Barack Obama delivered his visionary speech in Prague in April 2009, in which he notably stated U.S. support for the peace and security of a world free of nuclear weapons, a string of events has provided a dose of reality to anyone who needed reminding that the nuclear disarmament agenda is beset with difficulties. The list of disappointments is long and sobering, from the continuing paralysis in the Conference on Disarmament to the escalation of nuclear tensions with Iran and on the Korean peninsula. In fact, even the recent nuclear disarmament "successes" have been colored by a degree of discord that has taken the shine off Obama's vision. For example, the May 2010 Review Conference of the Nuclear Nonproliferation Treaty (NPT), which was seen as an opportunity to unite the international community behind an ambitious nonproliferation and disarmament agenda, ended with a fragile consensus that can at best be described as a lowest common denominator approach to nuclear disarmament diplomacy. Seven months later, U.S. ratification of the New Strategic Arms Reduction Treaty (New START) limped home after a bruising at the hands of a number of influential Republican senators.

These events are a foretaste of what is to come, as even in the shadow of 9/11 many still cling to the belief that nuclear weapons enhance security and that relinquishing them is far more dangerous than keeping them. This has led British military historian Michael Howard to argue that "the nuclear dragon may be sleeping, but it is certainly not dead."[4] We would go one step further and argue that the nuclear dragon might not even be asleep yet—he could just be resting, with one eye open. The persistence of nuclear myths and adversarial patterns of thinking in international politics means that the nuclear dragon could easily become reinvigorated, energized by doubts over the strength and endurance of global governance mechanisms, including the nuclear nonproliferation and nuclear security regimes; fears over the potential for nuclear breakout and nuclear blackmail in disarming and disarmed worlds; and dread of a return to an international system in which major conventional war is no longer held at bay by the threat of a nuclear exchange. These and a myriad of similar fears mean that the nuclear disarmament agenda faces serious obstacles even though the nuclear dragon is no longer out on the prowl, as it was during the Cold War.

While it is important to acknowledge that the challenges are immense, the world may nevertheless be in a position to make significant progress on nuclear disarmament and, in doing so, help reduce nuclear dangers. Although this is not the first time that a nuclear abolitionist movement has built up in nuclear history, the way the current movement has been developing is in many ways unique. In the past, nuclear abolitionist waves swelled either as a result of great fears or great opportunities, and mostly under the leadership of middle power states and civil society movements that are predominantly motivated by idealistic and moral goals, or members of the Non-Aligned Movement (NAM), which is motivated by a variety of goals.[5] For instance, at the end of the Second World War, the advent of the nuclear age, which was characterized by the nuclear bombings of Hiroshima and Nagasaki, provoked such horror around the world that nuclear disarmament quickly came to be seen as the only solution to avoid global nuclear annihilation. As Bernard Baruch, the U.S. delegate to the inaugural meeting of the United Nations Atomic Energy Commission, explained on June 14, 1946, "we are here to make a choice between the quick and the dead [...], if we fail, then we have damned every man to be the slave of Fear [...] we must elect world peace or world destruction."[6] But these efforts rapidly dissipated as obstacles were strewn in the abolitionists' path, and it was not until the early 1980s that a new abolition movement emerged, in response to fears that a serious downturn in U.S.-Soviet relations could lead to a nuclear showdown between the superpowers. The idea of nuclear disarmament then gained considerable momentum again in the early 1990s, in response to high hopes that the collapse of the Soviet Union and the end of the Cold War could rapidly phase out the role of nuclear weapons in the international system. By the mid-1990s, however, these hopes receded again, as what Yale University professor Paul Bracken described as a "second nuclear age" spawned a new generation of deterrence theories that attempted to legitimize nuclear weapon retention as an insurance policy against the rise of new nuclear threats.[7]

Today's push for nuclear disarmament is exceptional because it is being led by influential members of the American elite and, emulating them, counterparts in allied countries. They have reached the conclusion that the elimination of nuclear weapons is possible and, most importantly, is in the interests of the United States and the world, at least if it is pursued and implemented properly. This is highly significant because for the first time in decades, nuclear disarmament advocacy is developing at the elite level within key nuclear weapon states (NWS), and not only at the grassroots level or within the middle power states or the NAM. One of the central arguments that the new nuclear disarmament elites put forward is that progress toward a nuclear-weapon-free world is the only way to overcome long-standing bottlenecks in the nuclear nonproliferation and nuclear security regimes—regimes that have been plagued by divisions but that have become more important than ever in the post–Cold War international order.

Turning the nuclear disarmament vision into a reality requires a deep understanding of complex nuclear disarmament dynamics, both the forces driving it forward and those holding it back—an analysis that is often superficial or missing entirely in the existing scholarly literature. The urgent need for a fresh examination of the subject was clearly recognized by British defense strategist Michael Quinlan, who lamented what he regarded as an unhealthy divide between "righteous abolitionists" (those who on moral grounds demand that nuclear-armed states immediately dispose of their weapons) and "dismissive realists" (those who assert that the abolition of nuclear weapons is impossible short of a considerably different international security environment and therefore argue that it is preferable to focus on managing their existence).[8] As Quinlan argued, both traditional viewpoints are wrong. Despite the urgings of many "righteous abolitionists," nuclear disarmament cannot happen overnight: there are complex technical, financial, and, most importantly, politico-strategic considerations involved. At the same time, the arguments put forward by the "dismissive realists" are unsustainable because nuclear disarmament is—and always has been—a goal clearly accepted by the international community and one of the keys to the health of the nuclear nonproliferation and nuclear security regimes. This highlights the need to think creatively about how a world free of nuclear weapons could become more acceptable to all. King's College professor and leading nuclear strategist Lawrence Freedman hit the nail on the head when he stated in 2009 that we need "a new theory for nuclear disarmament."[9]

According to Quinlan, the nuclear disarmament scholarship that is required falls into two categories: (1) studies that examine the technical aspects of nuclear disarmament, which he calls the "disarmament mechanics"; and (2) studies that analyze the political conditions necessary for a nuclear disarming and disarmed world.[10] In fact, as its authors are quick to point out, it was Quinlan who inspired the 2008 *Adelphi Paper* by George Perkovich and James Acton on the technical (transparency and verification) and political requirements of a nuclear disarmed world—the most noteworthy scholarly study to date to tackle both of Quinlan's categories.[11] That study inspired scholars to probe the dynamics of nuclear disarmament in more depth, including the obstacles that are impacting current nuclear disarmament momentum.[12]

This volume makes a contribution to that body of new scholarship. Its main goal is to provide a comprehensive analytical study of the political, state-level factors that are driving and stalling today's nuclear disarmament agenda, followed by a discussion of tentative proposals for overcoming roadblocks. It does not analyze the political conditions that would allow for a nuclear-weapon-free world but rather the political opportunities and challenges affecting current disarmament momentum.

This volume expands and develops upon a collection of articles originally published in a March 2010 special section of the *Nonproliferation Review*.[13] It retains the country-based approach adopted in the first instance, with states divided into different groups. (In this volume, for the sake of providing a comprehensive analysis, we have added more groups of states to the five we originally chose, drawing on the expertise of additional scholars.) We have chosen this state-centric organizing device because, although the appreciation, management, and implications of current nuclear disarmament dynamics vary greatly for each country, strong similarities exist among some states, and it therefore makes sense to examine them as a group. We continue to believe that this approach is the most appropriate to provide a clear picture of today's key global nuclear disarmament developments.

In total, nine groups of states are examined in this volume, covering all the most important "state types" in the nuclear disarmament nexus. The first three groups comprise states whose policies tend to be mainly favorable to progress toward a world free of nuclear weapons. They include the "optimistic nuclear weapon states," the "advocacy states," and the "rollback states." Although there are five de jure NWS or recognized nuclear-armed states by the NPT (China, France, Russia, the United Kingdom, and the United States), only the latter two have arguably been truly active engines of the current nuclear abolitionist movement. As a result, while acknowledging fully that the reality is much more complex, this volume has chosen to distinguish between "optimistic nuclear weapon states" and "pessimistic nuclear weapon states" for the sake of brevity.

The "optimistic nuclear weapon states," therefore, are the first group of states analyzed in this volume (chapter 1). We refer to the second group of states as the "advocacy states": individual or coalitions of non-nuclear-armed states that are making a point of promoting the merits of nuclear disarmament through a range of activities and initiatives (chapter 2). The third group of nations comprises the "rollback states" or countries such as Belarus, Libya, Kazakhstan, South Africa, Ukraine, and arguably others that had active nuclear weapon programs in the past but chose to abandon them (chapter 3).

The next three groups of states examined in the volume include states whose policies may be potentially problematic for nuclear disarmament. These groups are labeled the "pessimistic nuclear weapon states," the "threshold states," and the "new nuclear energy aspirants." The volume's fourth group of states, the "pessimistic nuclear weapon states," comprises France, Russia, and China, the three NWS that have been much less sanguine, at least in practice, about the desirability and feasibility of a world without nuclear weapons (chapter 4). The fifth group consists of such states as Brazil, Japan, and others that have the building blocks in place to develop nuclear weapons but, to date, have refrained from crossing the "nuclear threshold" (chapter 5). We refer to the sixth group of states as the "new nuclear energy aspirants," that is, those states (such as Egypt in the Middle East and Vietnam in Southeast Asia) that could be tempted or suspected of harboring ambitions to develop nuclear weapons as spin-offs from the peaceful nuclear energy programs that they are in the process of launching (chapter 6).[14]

The final three groups of states comprise those whose policies are openly or secretly, deliberately or inadvertently, hindering progress toward nuclear disarmament. These are the "holdout states," the "defiant states," and the "silent proliferators." The chapter on the "holdout states" analyzes the policies of India, Israel, and Pakistan, the three states that have opted to remain outside the NPT framework and develop nuclear weapons despite widespread international condemnation (chapter 7). We refer to the eighth group of states as the "defiant states" because these states have enjoyed the many benefits of NPT membership but have deliberately and repeatedly flouted nonproliferation norms, either by developing nuclear weapons and withdrawing from the NPT (North Korea) or by adopting a confrontational stance toward the nuclear nonproliferation regime and defying UN Security Council resolutions (Iran) (chapter 8). Finally, states in the ninth group are labeled the "silent proliferators": states such as Myanmar or Syria that are strongly suspected of being active proliferators (or of collaborating with them), but that forcefully deny those allegations (chapter 9).

Organizing framework

States that are the drivers of current momentum	States with possible stalling effect on momentum	States with a primarily negative impact on momentum
Optimistic NWS	Pessimistic NWS	Holdout States
Advocacy states	Threshold States	Defiant States
Rollback states	Nuclear Energy Aspirants	Silent Proliferators

The authors who have contributed to this volume include international security scholars hailing from three continents. David Santoro begins with an examination of the current nuclear doctrines, postures, and disarmament policies of the United States and the United Kingdom, the two "optimistic nuclear weapon states." He argues that these states are key drivers of the current nuclear abolitionist momentum; they share the same approach (in a different role) to nuclear disarmament, which they are pursuing cautiously (regardless of criticisms at the domestic level, notably in the United States). Marianne Hanson then moves on to examine the recent disarmament diplomacy efforts of Western states such as Australia, Canada, Ireland, New Zealand, Norway, and Sweden, as well as efforts by disarmament coalitions such as the New Agenda Coalition (NAC) and the Seven Nation Initiative (7NI). She argues that the activities of these "advocacy states" have provided an important context for the current U.S.-driven push toward a world free of nuclear weapons. This is followed by a coauthored chapter on the third group, the "rollback states," written by Stephen F. Burgess and Togzhan Kassenova. Burgess and Kassenova focus their analysis on the nuclear policies and disarmament diplomacy of South Africa and Kazakhstan—two states that have made a strong practical contribution to the nuclear nonproliferation regime and global nuclear disarmament, but that have responded in different ways to recent U.S. disarmament leadership.

Opening the examination of the next three groups of states, David Santoro analyzes the "pessimistic nuclear weapon states," arguing that despite some steps forward, nuclear disarmament is not a priority for France, Russia, and China—quite the contrary—and that further progress toward nuclear disarmament in these states is largely uncertain. Maria Rost Rublee then analyzes the opportunities and challenges posed by the "threshold states" to current nuclear disarmament agendas, with a specific focus on Brazil and Japan. She argues that in both cases, while the future remains uncertain and challenges are numerous, the U.S.-driven push for nuclear disarmament as well as other factors may open the door to sustained, proactive nuclear disarmament diplomacy on their part. Next Maria Rost Rublee and Tanya Ogilvie-White examine the "new nuclear energy aspirants," focusing on the nuclear energy programs launched by Egypt and Vietnam. They argue that although the intentions of both states are entirely peaceful, questions may arise over whether they are trying to keep their nuclear-weapon options open for the future, especially if they decide to develop the sensitive parts of the nuclear fuel cycle. Suspicions of this nature would be detrimental to nuclear disarmament momentum, which highlights the need for maximum transparency as the nuclear renaissance gets underway.

The final section of the volume opens with an analysis of the nuclear policies and disarmament diplomacy of the "holdout states," in a chapter provided by Devin T. Hagerty. He explores the cases of India, Israel, and Pakistan and argues that there is little optimism that these states will be incited into advancing nuclear disarmament in the near to medium term. Tanya Ogilvie-White then examines the confrontational nuclear policies of North Korea and Iran (the "defiant states"). She argues that one of the unintended consequences of U.S. nonproliferation policy and disarmament agenda is that North Korea and Iran may engage in increasingly defiant behavior in order to undermine the growing international consensus against their nuclear activities, but she explains that, despite this, current U.S. nuclear disarmament policy must not be derailed. Finally, Jacqueline Shire closes this volume with an analysis of the "silent proliferators," with a focus on Myanmar and Syria. She explains that it is extremely difficult to acquire accurate information about the nuclear activities of this group of states, but that some of the suspicions of illicit nuclear procurement are well founded, and in any event the uncertainty and lack of transparency that feed international suspicions are detrimental to disarmament momentum.

As Howard argued in his 2008 *Survival* article, nuclear issues, once the chief preoccupation of strategic analysts at IISS and similar research institutes around the world, no longer hold the fascination they once did for many international security scholars. It is more fashionable to focus on what are legitimately seen as the most pressing twenty-first-century security issues: the threats posed by climate change, global terrorism, cyber security, and a range of topics associated with trying to make sense of our rapidly changing world. But nuclear weapons are as much a part of today's international security environment as they have been since the Second World War—what has changed are the perceptions of their utility among different groups of states and the associated cost/benefit analyses of the dangers that they pose. Recognition of the desirability of a nuclear-weapon-free future has grown in the most unexpected ways and in the most unexpected quarters. But as this volume shows, such recognition will not necessarily translate into sustained nuclear disarmament momentum unless the many obstacles to elimination are identified, understood, and eventually overcome—a process that demands intensive and rigorous scholarly attention, perhaps the same saturation treatment that nuclear deterrence debates garnered during the Cold War. This volume is just an early stepping-stone in what is likely to be a very long journey. Indeed, in the words of Tasker Bliss, a former chief of staff of the U.S. Army in the 1920s who wrote about the first truly multilateral disarmament project initiated after the First World War, "No one can realize its difficulties until he attempts to approach its solution in any really constructive way."[15] Clearly, this volume cannot claim to have found the solutions to the many problems faced by the current nuclear disarmament drive, but it does provide a comprehensive analysis of the state-level impetus and obstacles. In other words, it does not set out to slay the nuclear dragon but, instead, to inform future dragon slayers of the various opportunities and challenges that they are likely to face.

Notes

1. George Shultz, William Perry, Henry Kissinger, and Sam Nunn, "A World Free of Nuclear Weapons," *Wall Street Journal*, January 4, 2007, and "Toward a Nuclear-Free World," *Wall Street Journal*, January 15, 2008.

2. Discussions on the impact of nuclear weapons proliferation on international peace and stability are often referred to as "nuclear optimism/pessimism debates." Nuclear pessimists question the rational and unitary actor assumptions that underpin nuclear optimists' arguments, especially in the context of multipolarity and global terrorism. For an introduction to the debate, see Matthew Kroenig, "Beyond Optimism and Pessimism: The Differential Effects of Nuclear Proliferation," Managing the Atom Working Paper no. 2009-14, Harvard Kennedy School, Harvard University, November 2009.

3. Article VI of the Treaty on the Nonproliferation of Nuclear Weapons (NPT) requires all treaty members to pursue nuclear disarmament negotiations in good faith. The vast majority of states have come to regard nuclear-weapon state leadership on nuclear disarmament as a legal obligation and moral responsibility.

4. Michael Howard, "Are We at War?" *Survival* 50, no. 4 (August 2008): 248.

5. For a historical review of nuclear abolitionist waves, see Michael Krepon, "Ban the Bomb: Really," *American Interest* 3 (January/February 2008): 88–93.

6. Bernard Baruch, "Proposals for an International Atomic Development Authority

by the United States Representative to the Atomic Energy Commission," *Department of State Bulletin* 14 (June 23, 1946): 1057.

7. Paul Bracken, "The Second Nuclear Age," *Foreign Affairs* 79 (January/February 2000): 146–56.

8. Michael Quinlan, "Abolishing Nuclear Armouries: Policy or Pipedream," *Survival* 49 (Winter 2007–8): 8.

9. Lawrence Freedman, "A New Theory for Nuclear Disarmament," *Bulletin of the Atomic Scientists* 65 (July/August 2009): 14–30.

10. Quinlan, "Abolishing Nuclear Armouries," 10.

11. George Percovich and James M. Acton, "Abolishing Nuclear Weapons," Adelphi Paper no. 396, London, International Institute for Strategic Studies, 2008.

12. Other key contributions to this new body of literature include Scott Sagan and Steven E. Miller, eds., "The Global Nuclear Future, vol. 1," special issue, *Daedalus* 138, no. 4 (Fall 2009), and "The Global Nuclear Future, vol. 2," special issue, *Daedalus* 139, no. 1 (Winter 2010)—a two-volume special issue that takes a thematic approach to understanding the hurdles to disarmament. Significant studies have also been undertaken by the Stimson Center's "Unblocking the Road to Zero" Program, which has produced a number of descriptive country studies on disarmament. The latter can be found on the Stimson Center website, http://www.stimson.org/programs/unblocking-the-road-to-zero/.

13. Tanya Ogilvie-White and David Santoro, eds., "Special Section: The Dynamics of Nuclear Disarmament: New Momentum and the Future of the Nonproliferation Regime," *Nonproliferation Review* 17 (March 2010): 17–159.

14. For a review on the proliferation risks associated with peaceful nuclear cooperation agreements, see Matthew Fuhrmann, "Spreading Temptation: Proliferation and Peaceful Nuclear Cooperation Agreements," *International Security* 34 (Summer 2009): 7–41; and, more recently, Charles Ferguson, "Potential Strategic Consequences of the Nuclear Energy Revival," *Proliferation Papers* 35 (Summer 2010): 1–45.

15. Tasker H. Bliss, "What Is Disarmament?" *Foreign Affairs* 4 (April 1926): 367.

CHAPTER ONE

The Optimistic Nuclear Weapon States

The United States and the United Kingdom

David Santoro

THIS CHAPTER DISCUSSES THE ROLE played by the United States and the United Kingdom in driving current nuclear disarmament momentum. Both the United States and the United Kingdom are founding signatories and depositaries of the Nuclear Nonproliferation Treaty (NPT).[1] Along with France, Russia, and China, they are also de jure nuclear weapon states (NWS)—that is, the only nuclear-armed states recognized by the treaty and, therefore, those primarily responsible for moving forward the disarmament agenda. Although Article VI of the NPT requires *all* state parties to pursue disarmament "in good faith," its language clearly suggests that the NWS are meant to take the lead on the disarmament project. Moreover, over the years, the practice adopted by the vast majority of NPT state parties has been to consider leadership from the NWS not only as a legal obligation but also as a normative responsibility—that is, as their "expected and required" behavior, notably after the NWS strongly reaffirmed their commitments at the 1995 and 2000 Review Conferences (RevCon).[2]

Among the five NWS, however, only the United States and the United Kingdom have been truly active engines of current nuclear disarmament momentum. While both have demonstrated much enthusiasm to make progress toward that goal, France, Russia, and China have been more disheartened about the desirability and feasibility of a world without nuclear weapons. For the sake of brevity, in this volume we have labeled the United States and the United Kingdom the "optimistic nuclear weapon states," while we refer to France, Russia, and China as the "pessimistic nuclear weapon states." This chapter examines the former group of states, while chapter 4 looks at the latter. It goes without saying that the reality is much more complex than the division between "optimistic nuclear weapon states" and "pessimistic nuclear weapon states." This volume has chosen these labels for the sake of brevity.[3]

This chapter analyzes the following questions: What are the key features of U.S. and UK policies? How have they developed? How can they be explained, and what are the prospects for the future?

THE UNITED STATES

The United States developed nuclear weapons during the Second World War. It was the first nation to build these weapons and the only one to ever use them. After failed attempts to reach a nuclear disarmament agreement when the war ended, the onset of the Cold War with the Soviet Union led Washington to develop a huge nuclear arsenal that became central to its national security policy (and those of its allies, which it brought under its protection).

The end of the Cold War led to a major disarmament process in conjunction with Russia—in all weapon categories. In the nuclear field, to add to the Intermediate-Range Nuclear Forces Treaty, which Washington and Moscow had concluded in 1987 and which required them to eliminate their intermediate- and shorter-range nuclear missiles, the two parties concluded the 1991 Strategic Arms Reduction Treaty (START). This treaty gave them ten years to reduce their forces to 6,000 deployed strategic warheads each (and 1,600 delivery vehicles), slashing their arsenals by 25 to 35 percent. The U.S. and Russian presidents of the time also announced unilateral measures, known as the Presidential Nuclear Initiatives, to eliminate many of their tactical nuclear weapons (TNW).

In 1993, the Clinton administration decided that a review of U.S. nuclear policy was necessary in the changed (and changing) international security environment.[4] Although Secretary of Defense Les Aspin intended the review to make progress toward nuclear disarmament, he experienced opposition from the military, which led to a rather conservative document. While creating a role for nuclear weapons in the emerging doctrine of counterproliferation (destruction of nuclear, biological, and chemical [NBC] weapons and their production and storage facilities),[5] the 1994 Nuclear Posture Review (NPR) reaffirmed the centrality of strategic deterrence against Russia, which it still identified as the primary threat to U.S. national security. The document, therefore, confirmed the importance of the nuclear triad of land-based intercontinental ballistic missiles (ICBM), nuclear-powered ballistic missile submarines (SSBN), and strategic bombers. However, in addition to supporting an end to nuclear testing and promoting arms control (notably the NPT), the NPR committed the United States to deep reductions, while also calling for the creation of a warhead storage hedge force that could be reintegrated swiftly into the operational force if necessary.

The next NPR was released by the Bush administration in 2002.[6] It stressed that the main threat to U.S. national security had now shifted to the NBC capabilities of various states and explained that the United States would therefore need to develop a capabilities-based force to better respond to hard and deeply buried targets, mobile and re-locatable targets, and biological and chemical targets. This focus found full justification with the attacks of September 11, 2001 (9/11), and the subsequent anthrax attacks against the United States. Classified extracts of the document leaked to the *Los Angeles Times* and the *New York Times* also revealed that Washington had outlined contingencies where U.S. nuclear weapons could be used, and that it had listed seven countries as potential targets (China, Russia, Iraq, North Korea, Iran, Libya, and Syria).

Key to the new approach, the 2002 NPR explained, was a new triad of both non-nuclear and nuclear strike capabilities, active and passive defenses (including ballistic missile defense [BMD] systems), and a supporting infrastructure. The document also advocated the development of new nuclear weapons with low-yield and earth-penetrating capabilities. A year later, the Bush administration proposed the Robust Nuclear Earth Penetrator (RNEP) program, a type of nuclear weapon intended to penetrate into soil, rock, or concrete to deliver a nuclear warhead to a target.[7] After this program failed to get traction in the U.S. Congress, the administration proposed the Reliable Replacement Warhead (RRW) program, a program for the development of a new U.S. nuclear warhead design and bomb family, intended to be simple and reliable and provide a long-lasting and low maintenance future nuclear force for the United States. This program, however, also failed to receive funding from Congress.[8]

Another feature of the 2002 NPR was deep-seated suspicions about arms control. The administration subsequently rejected many arms control agreements, thinking that it would increase U.S. freedom of action. Shortly after rejecting the adoption of a verification protocol for the Biological and Toxin Weapons Convention (BTWC), the Bush administration withdrew from the 1972 Anti-Ballistic Missile (ABM) Treaty to allow for more ambitious BMD deployment. It also refused to seek ratification of the 1996 Comprehensive Nuclear-Test-Ban Treaty (CTBT), which had been rejected by the U.S. Senate in 1999, and abandoned traditional U.S. support for the conclusion of a verifiable fissile material cut-off treaty (FMCT) on the basis of the 1995 Shannon Mandate. More generally, nuclear disarmament was no longer considered a priority, and nuclear reductions with Russia, which had encountered difficulties since the mid-1990s over negotiations for a START II agreement, were pursued through a much looser arrangement, the 2002 Strategic Offensive Reductions Treaty (SORT). This treaty has obligated Washington and Moscow to reduce their deployed strategic nuclear warheads to 1,700–2,200 each by 2012, but unlike START, it is vague about what reductions should be made (and how), sets no limits on how many warheads can be kept in storage, and contains no verification measures. Finally, the Bush administration prioritized its strategic and commercial interests over arms control when it sought an exemption to well-established nonproliferation rules in order to allow India, a nuclear-armed NPT holdout, to engage in nuclear trade.[9]

Although the 2002 NPR technically reduced the role of nuclear weapons in U.S. national security, important concerns were raised throughout the world because the widely held perception was that it had weakened the firewall between nuclear and non-nuclear doctrine.[10] These concerns grew stronger when the Bush administration suggested in its 2002 National Security Strategy that the projection of U.S. military power, including unilaterally, preemptively, and if necessary for regime change (as was later done in Iraq), would bring more solutions than create problems.[11] This approach, however, receded quite quickly.

Halfway through the Bush administration's second term, Sam Nunn, Henry Kissinger, William Perry, and George Schultz called on Washington in two *Wall Street Journal* articles to refocus its efforts on nuclear disarmament.[12] While this call remained rather inconsequential for policy during the Bush administration, it generated a debate among experts, not so much because of what was said, but because of who said it: four former U.S. policy officials with experience at the highest level of government and absolutely no idealistic inclination for nuclear disarmament. Indeed, the "group of four," most commonly dubbed the "Four Horsemen," pleaded for a balance between the idealism of nuclear disarmament and the necessity for realistic steps to get there: "Without the bold vision, the actions will not be perceived as fair and urgent. Without the actions, the vision will not be perceived as realistic or possible."[13]

The force of these ideas became evident when in the 2008 U.S. presidential campaign, both candidates felt the need to position themselves on the desirability and feasibility of a world free of nuclear weapons. John McCain explained that "the United States should lead a global effort at nuclear disarmament consistent with our vital interests and the cause of peace."[14] Barack Obama went further, stressing that he would make "the goal of eliminating all nuclear weapons a central element of [U.S.] nuclear policy."[15]

Once Obama was elected, his endorsement of the Four Horsemen's logic was confirmed. On April 5, 2009, less than three months after taking office, he detailed his vision and outlined an ambitious arms control agenda in a landmark speech delivered in Prague, where he "state[d] clearly and with conviction America's commitment to seek the peace and security of a world without nuclear weapons." Yet, he remained cautious, stressing that "this goal will not be reached quickly—perhaps not in [his] lifetime" and that "as long as these weapons exist, the United States will maintain a safe, secure and effective arsenal."[16] At the same time, President Obama added that nonproliferation policy should be strengthened, a multilateral framework for civil nuclear cooperation should be developed, and all vulnerable fissile material should be secured within four years.

More specifically, President Obama announced that the United States would drive a process of nuclear reductions that would begin with the negotiation of a follow-on agreement to START with Russia, and that this treaty would set the stage for further reductions eventually including all the NWS. He also stated that the United States would reduce the role of nuclear weapons in its new NPR, seek CTBT ratification, and help conclude a verifiable FMCT.

Historically, these four grand steps have been central to any serious nuclear disarmament program. Although nuclear reductions have always been the focal point, the three other steps mentioned by the president have also been considered essential. As leading nuclear strategists George Bunn and Roland Timerbaev have shown, "The three [other] measures most mentioned in the negotiating history and in the parties' 1968 agreement on an agenda to implement [nuclear disarmament] were a ban on nuclear testing; a cut-off in the production of fissionable materials for nuclear weapons; and a prohibition on the use of nuclear weapons."[17]

On September 24, 2009, President Obama chaired a historic meeting of the UN Security Council. This meeting, which was attended by the heads of states or government of all but one (Libya) of the fifteen members, led to the unanimous adoption of Resolution 1887, which addressed nuclear security and enshrined the goal of a nuclear-weapon-free world at the multilateral level. Largely because of his good intentions and personal advocacy for nuclear disarmament, President Obama was subsequently awarded the Nobel Peace Prize. On hearing the news on October 9, 2009, he said that he would accept the award "as a call to action."[18] By then, the task of translating his vision into action was upon him. How has it proceeded? How far along the implementation of the Prague agenda has Washington progressed?

Nuclear Reductions

President Obama was quick to initiate negotiations with Russia for a follow-on agreement to START. The process took off rapidly because it was launched within the context of the notion of a "reset" of U.S.-Russian relations,[19] and because the Obama administration, unlike the Bush administration, wanted the treaty to follow the verifiable model of START, not SORT—a model that Moscow also preferred. On April 1, 2009, both parties agreed on the basic parameters of the future treaty, and three months later they issued a joint understanding on the planned reductions.[20] The subsequent U.S. decision to scrap the 2007 Bush plans to deploy BMD in Eastern Europe (and replace it with a system that is deemed more effective to provide for Europe's security and less provocative to Russia) removed further hurdles to progress.[21] After all, Russia had suggested that no progress on nuclear reductions would be possible if the original plan went ahead, as explained in more depth in chapter 4.

Mainly due to Russian concerns over verification issues and continuous worries over U.S. BMD plans in Europe, Washington and Moscow failed to conclude negotiations before START expired (December 5, 2009) and did not sign the new treaty, dubbed "New START," until April 8, 2010.[22] New START sets limits for each state at 1,550 deployed strategic warheads, a combined limit of 800 deployed and nondeployed strategic launchers, and a separate limit of 700 deployed strategic delivery vehicles.[23]

At present, Washington deploys approximately 500 warheads on 450 ICBM.[24] It will retain up to 420 ICBM, all with a single warhead (the W-62 warhead is being replaced by the modern W-87 warhead, and the LGM-30G Minuteman III ICBM, whose upgrade is nearing completion, will extend to 2030 until it is replaced). Washington also currently has 14 SSBN, 12 of which are continually operational and carry 288 Trident II D5 submarine-launched ballistic missiles (SLBM) (soon to be replaced by the D5LE version) for a total of approximately 1,150 warheads (the modern W-76-1/Mk-4A warhead is replacing the W-76/Mk-4). While the 14 SSBN will be retained, the Ohio-class SSBN, which will begin retiring in the late 2020s, will gradually be replaced by the new SSBN(X), which, for their part, will carry fewer missiles to permit more boats under future disarmament agreements and provide more operational flexibility. Moreover, Washington currently has 94 deployable nuclear-capable bombers, the B-2s and B-52s, some of which will be converted to a conventional-only role, and up to 60 will be retained. New START, however, will not affect the U.S. TNW stockpile, which consists of 500 active weapons, approximately 400 of which are air-delivered B-61 gravity bombs while 100 are W80-0 warheads for sea-launched, land-attack BGM-109 Tomahawk (TLAM/N) cruise missiles, although Washington has recently decided to retire the latter weapon (an additional 700–800 TNW are in storage).

New START's entry into force was delayed by an unexpected difficulty in the U.S. ratification process. The Obama administration submitted the treaty for Senate consent to ratification shortly after signature, but the Senate ratified it only months later, with time running out of the legislative clock during the lame-duck session. The Obama administration had to fight a fierce, uphill battle to get Senate approval of the treaty. The 71–26 vote reflected the difficulty; ratification of all previous arms control treaties were by overwhelmingly positive margins. The opposition to New START was unexpected because the nuclear reductions it mandates are not overly ambitious (down to 1,550 warheads from 2,200 in SORT) and, as analysts have noted, "are more modest than these figures suggest [because] current deployments are already less than the START I and SORT limits."[25] Moreover, New START leaves aside (and therefore unresolved) the most contentious issues on the U.S.-Russian arms control agenda: BMD, long-range conventional weapons, and TNW and nondeployed nuclear weapons. While New START's goals are laudable and undeniably represent progress toward nuclear disarmament, they are also relatively limited: the treaty is really only meant to provide a follow-on transparency and verification framework to the 1991 START agreement, lay the foundation to negotiate bolder disarmament treaties (the 2010 NPR states that the next round of negotiations should address TNW and nondeployed nuclear weapons),[26] and, more indirectly, provide a basis to strengthen U.S.-Russian cooperation in other areas, notably nuclear nonproliferation.

Therefore, despite skeptics in the Senate, New START received broad support from the U.S. national security establishment. Shortly after the Obama administration submitted the treaty to the Senate for ratification, Admiral Michael Mullen, chairman of the Joint Chiefs of Staff, opened up his statement to Congress stating that "this treaty has the full support of your uniformed military."[27] A few months later, the Senate Foreign Relations Committee voted 14–4 for ratification—with support from three Senate Republicans. Throughout the entire review process in the Senate, numerous Cabinet officials from administrations since Richard Nixon's also firmly expressed support for swift U.S. ratification.

Yet, skeptics in the Senate, led by influential Republican senator Jon Kyl, were able to considerably delay and almost derail U.S. ratification. In addition to uneasiness with New START itself (particularly the robustness of its verification system), their concerns revolved around four issues: BMD, long-range conventional weapons, TNW, and the modernization of the U.S. nuclear weapons complex. With the treaty's preamble indicating that there is an "interrelationship" between strategic offensive weapons and defensive systems (i.e., BMD) and Moscow issuing a unilateral statement on the day of signature warning that Russia could withdraw if there is a "qualitative or quantitative build-up in the missile defense system capabilities of the United States,"[28] several lawmakers sought to ensure that current and future U.S. BMD plans would not be limited. The administration insisted that New START does not affect current or planned U.S. BMD plans (or programs such as Prompt Global Strike [PGS]) and that U.S. BMD policy is solely guided by the principles developed in the 2010 BMD Review.[29] But several lawmakers remained unconvinced and even alleged that U.S. negotiators may have secretly agreed to concessions with Moscow on the matter.[30] Moreover, they criticized the fact that the Obama administration, as a concession to Russia, agreed to count any conventional systems it uses on ballistic missiles within the overall treaty limits.

The Republican opponents also attempted to force renegotiation of New START to include TNW, which Russia clearly opposed. Although the administration wants to focus on TNW in the next round of arms control talks, attempting to negotiate it in New START would have added years to the negotiations. Finally, some lawmakers sought to link New START ratification to commitments by the administration that nuclear reductions would be accompanied by the modernization of the U.S. nuclear weapons complex. The administration's decision to invest over $80 billion over the next decade in order to sustain and modernize U.S. nuclear forces (a figure subsequently raised again further by $4.1 billion in an effort to rally support for New START ratification) constitutes a massive increase and seems to honor President Obama's Prague commitment that "as long as [nuclear] weapons exist, the United States will maintain a safe, secure, and effective arsenal."[31] But it was not clear that anything would satisfy some of the Senate skeptics. Some of them oppose any form of arms control, and some did not want to give Obama any legislative victory.

In the end, however, the Obama administration was successful, and the U.S. Senate ratified New START, which subsequently led Moscow to follow suit, leading to the treaty's entry into force. But the New START ratification experience suggests that future disarmament treaties are likely to encounter major hurdles, notably in a Republican-dominated Senate. In fact, as Republicans picked up five Senate seats with the November 2010 midterm elections, more Republicans will now need to be persuaded to endorse future treaties, promising significant difficulties as the next items on the list of the U.S.-Russian arms control agenda (TNW and nondeployed nuclear weapons) are much more complex and controversial issues. Indeed, as nuclear policy analyst Steven Pifer concludes in a comprehensive analysis of the post–New START round, "Rather than taking eleven months, the time it took to finish New START, the next negotiating round will require several years and a fair amount of high-level intervention to break logjams in order to complete a new treaty."[32]

It is not clear how to make progress on TNW management. The New Strategic Concept of the North Atlantic Treaty Organization (NATO) suggests that negotiations over U.S. weapons stationed in Europe require Russia to become more transparent about its own TNW arsenal. Moscow, for its part, insists that it will not change its position until all U.S. weapons are removed from Europe (despite the fact that the Russian arsenal is much larger than that of the United States). Similarly, addressing nondeployed nuclear weapons is likely to be highly challenging because there is no prior experience in arms control history to deal with such weapons: to date, all treaties, including New START, have only limited *deployed* warheads, and they have done so through special accounting rules. Most importantly, controlling these weapons would require inspection of facilities considered extremely sensitive.

In short, U.S.-Russian negotiations on the TNW and nondeployed nuclear weapon fronts, which will be intertwined with BMD and conventional weapons issues, are likely to be long and intense. The work involved to convince Congress that the results truly enhance U.S. national security is likely to be immense, not to mention that the situation will be subsequently further complicated when China and other NWS are eventually involved in the process of nuclear reductions.[33]

Despite these difficulties, the Obama administration has already begun studying the possibility of undertaking additional nuclear reductions. In March 2011, the Associated Press reported that the U.S. Department of Defense had received a directive from the administration to study the possibility of further cuts, a move that unsurprisingly led forty-one Republican senators to issue a letter expressing skepticism and warning against ordering significant changes to the U.S. nuclear deterrent without first conferring with Congress.[34] It remains to be seen how the debate over future nuclear reductions will play out. In any case, as Gary Samore, White House coordinator for WMD security and arms control, put it in a recent interview with *Arms Control Today*, neither the United States nor Russia is "prepared [to launch formal arms control negotiations] because we haven't completed our internal reviews, so we wouldn't know what position to take. The Russians have indicated publicly that they're not prepared to consider additional reductions until their concerns about missile defense and weapons in space and a number of other things have been addressed. At this point, I don't anticipate we would begin formal arms control negotiations anytime soon."[35]

Reduction of the Role of Nuclear Weapons

The Obama administration spells out the reduction of the role of nuclear weapons in U.S. national security policy in the 2010 NPR. Here, the administration could have opted to remain at one end of the spectrum and continue the longstanding U.S. policy of "calculated ambiguity" (to the great displeasure of disarmament advocates), or go all the way to the other end and declare a "no-first-use" (NFU) policy—that is, a commitment that the United States would not be the first to use nuclear weapons in any circumstances (to the great displeasure of many Republicans and Democrats alike, and a step that would have worried some U.S. allies, notably Japan).[36]

The administration ended up opting for the middle way because, as Gary Samore explained, "as we crafted the [NPR] document, [we] very consciously intended to influence the perceptions of different foreign audiences. And of course, since different foreign audiences have different interests and perspectives, the document reflects a balance in terms of how we crafted the language and the substance of the review."[37] The NPR, therefore, states that "the *fundamental* role of U.S. nuclear weapons [. . .] is to deter nuclear attacks on the United States, [its] allies, and partners" and that the United States will continue to "reduce the role of nuclear weapons in deterring non-nuclear attacks, *with the objective of* making deterrence of nuclear attack on the United States or [its] allies and partners the sole purpose of U.S. nuclear weapons"[38] (emphases added). This way, the NPR reconciles ambitions (reduction of the role of nuclear weapons) with realities (concerns about a U.S. NFU pledge in various international and domestic constituencies).

Added to this was the clarification of U.S. negative security assurances (NSA), which explain that "the United States will not use or threaten to use nuclear weapons against non-nuclear weapons states that are party to the Nuclear Non-Proliferation Treaty (NPT) and in compliance with their nuclear nonproliferation obligations."[39] In the words of Morton Halperin, a member of the Congressional Commission on the Strategic Posture of the United States, "For the first time this is a promise to [proliferators such as North Korea, Iran, and others that if they] come back into full compliance with the Nonproliferation Treaty, [they] will have a commitment from the United States not to threaten or use nuclear weapons against them, period, full stop."[40] The NPR also for the first time stresses that the U.S. NSA will apply in case of biological and chemical weapon use (a provision that many Republicans criticized), but that Washington could adjust its position depending on the evolution and proliferation of biological weapons.

Although the NPR states that Washington will only consider using nuclear weapons "in extreme circumstances," it suggests that there remain contingencies in which nuclear weapons are useful to defend the United States or its allies (and that the current alert posture of U.S. strategic forces, in particular with many ICBM and a significant number of SLBM ready to be launched on short notice, should be maintained).[41] Precisely, the NPR stresses that extended deterrence will continue to protect U.S. allies against nuclear attacks or nuclear coercion. The NPR, however, explains that technological progress in the U.S. non-nuclear strategic force allows for it to "take on a greater share of the deterrence burden."[42]

The bottom line is that Washington continues to believe that its nuclear arsenal is relevant today. Hence the need, the NPR explains, for the United States to sustain "a safe, secure, and effective nuclear arsenal."[43] After stating that since the end of U.S. nuclear testing in 1992, warheads have been maintained and certified as safe and reliable by the Stockpile Stewardship Program, which has extended their lives through refurbishment (Life Extension Programs [LEP]), the NPR reveals that Washington will now implement the congressionally mandated Stockpile Management Program. This program ends authorization for RRW, which as mentioned earlier never received congressional funding, and neither endorses nor excludes the possibility of a new warhead, but simply provides for the "effective management" of the U.S. arsenal.[44] Thus, the NPR explains that the United States will refrain from nuclear testing, seek CTBT ratification, and steer clear of developing new warheads. Although the full range of LEP options will be considered (refurbishment of existing warheads, reuse of nuclear components from different warheads, and replacement of components), the NPR indicates that Washington will focus on the refurbishment and reuse options and that the replacement option would be considered only if deemed critical (and if so it would have to be authorized by the president and approved by Congress).

Consistent with these conclusions, the NPR recommends three warhead production projects (fund the W-76 and B-61 LEP and initiate a study of LEP options for the W-78) as well as important investments in the nuclear infrastructure and workforce. The presidential budget request for fiscal year (FY)2011, released in February 2010, was $7 billion, a 10 percent increase over FY2010.[45] In May 2010, the White House also indicated that the president had submitted a classified report to Congress (as required by Section 1251 of the FY2010 National Defense Authorization Act) that declares that the United States "will invest well over $100 billion in nuclear delivery systems to sustain existing capabilities and modernize some strategic systems," along with an intention "to invest $80 billion in the next decade to sustain and modernize the nuclear weapons complex."[46]

The long-term management of the U.S. nuclear arsenal has been very controversial (and, as mentioned earlier, intertwined with New START ratification). For starters, Secretary of Defense Robert Gates previously voiced his support for the RRW program.[47] Moreover, in December 2009, forty Republicans and one Independent wrote a letter to President Obama calling for increased modernization and the development of a new warhead. Even after the findings of JASON, an independent advisory panel that recently claimed that the U.S. arsenal could still be viable for decades using standard LEP approaches, many in the United States have remained unconvinced.[48] More recently, in September 2010, Air Force General Kevin Chilton, commander of the U.S. Strategic Command, praised the new NPR and the Obama administration's FY2011 budget, but he also expressed some important concerns about several aspects of U.S. nuclear capabilities.[49] The mid-November 2010 update to the Section 1251 report, which demonstrated an intention to increase the budget for the nuclear weapon complex by $4.1 billion (for a total of $85 billion), was very well received by the U.S. national security establishment. For instance, Thomas D'Agostino, head of the National Nuclear Security Administration, has indicated that the administration's approach is "the most robust, sustained commitment to modernizing our nuclear deterrent since the end of the cold war."[50] But although most agree that the FY2012 budget request seems to confirm that the administration follows through on its promise to modernize the U.S. nuclear weapon complex, many appear to remain unconvinced.[51] Indeed, at the beginning of May 2011, Republican senator Jon Kyl and representative Michael Turner began to spearhead legislation aimed not only at holding the Obama administration accountable for its nuclear modernization pledges but also at prohibiting unilateral U.S. warhead reductions or changes to U.S. missile defense plans.[52]

CTBT Ratification and FMCT Negotiations

In Prague, President Obama stated that his administration would "immediately and aggressively" pursue U.S. ratification of the CTBT.[53] This commitment was confirmed when he named no less than Vice President Joe Biden to lead the process, and when Secretary of State Hillary Clinton declared at the September 2009 Conference on Facilitating the Entry into Force of the CTBT that the CTBT was "an integral part of [the U.S.] nonproliferation and arms control agenda."[54] Washington had not sent a representative to the CTBT conference for a decade, and had never sent one of such a senior level.

Since then, however, no progress has been made. Despite growing support in the Senate, notably from Senators John McCain (R-Ariz.) and Joe Lieberman (I-Conn.), opposition has remained strong. Senator Jon Kyl (R-Ariz.), for instance, has always been categorical about his opposition to U.S. ratification of the CTBT, declaring in 2009 that "I will lead the charge against it and I will do everything in my power to see that it is defeated."[55] This is a statement that he reiterated more recently at the 2011 Carnegie International Nuclear Policy Conference, despite D'Agostino's insistence a few days earlier that "There's no need to conduct underground (nuclear) testing."[56] Moreover, now that Republicans have picked up five seats in the Senate with the November 2010 midterm elections, it is very uncertain whether Washington would win the required two-thirds majority for ratification of the CTBT, particularly in view of how difficult it was to obtain New START ratification. After all, unlike New START, U.S. ratification of the CTBT has always been extremely controversial: it was notably the only issue on which the 2009 bipartisan report of the Perry-Schlesinger Congressional Commission failed to reach consensus.[57]

At the October 2010 UN First Committee meeting, Assistant Secretary of State Rose Gottemoeller suggested that the administration would soon prepare for U.S. Senate reconsideration of the treaty.[58] Yet, the fact that Undersecretary of State Ellen Tauscher had previously made clear that there would be no attempt to seek ratification "unless we believe it can actually pass" seems to suggest that the administration is unlikely to press the issue any time soon.[59] Indeed, more recently she insisted on the need to "educate" the U.S. Senate and the public on the benefits on U.S. ratification of the CTBT.[60]

In the near future, an update of the 2002 National Academy of Sciences study on CTBT technical matters, which is currently undergoing classification review, will bring the issue back in the spotlights. The document is expected to highlight improvements in the treaty's International Monitoring System and help bolster U.S. ratification efforts.[61] In August 2010, a classified National Intelligence Estimate about the treaty's ability to detect secret nuclear tests was also sent to Capitol Hill, but it has reportedly not been seen by most lawmakers.[62] Whether this will impact on U.S. opposition to CTBT ratification is an open question. In any case, despite Indonesia's recent decision to ratify the treaty, entry into force will not happen even after the United States ratifies it because China, Egypt, India, Iran, Israel, North Korea, and Pakistan also need to follow suit. The road to CTBT entry into force, therefore, is still very long.

Similarly, in Prague, President Obama was adamant about his commitment to the conclusion of a verifiable FMCT on the basis of the 1995 Shannon Mandate, which the United States had consistently supported until the Bush administration. In May 2009, largely as a result of the new U.S. position, the Conference on Disarmament (CD) adopted for the first time in over a decade a program of work to initiate FMCT negotiations. Yet, progress has since been blocked by Pakistan, officially over concerns about possible asymmetries between its nuclear stockpile and India's, which have been exacerbated by the U.S.-India civilian nuclear cooperation agreement.[63]

Breakthrough on FMCT would require a wide-ranging U.S. diplomatic effort to which Washington has so far not been able to commit. True, in early 2011, U.S. officials began to suggest that Washington may push for negotiations to be conducted outside the CD if consensus cannot be reached there, a move discouraged by many.[64] But as Samore pointed out in a December 2010 interview, "Even if we succeed [in persuading Pakistan to allow discussion to begin], however, it will take years until the negotiations are completed."[65] Thereafter, the administration would also need to convince Congress that an FMCT can be verified and that it would enhance U.S. national security, which is likely to be difficult in view of trouble in convincing senators that even a treaty as straightforward as New START is verifiable.⁶⁶ In other words, if the road to CTBT is long, the one to FMCT appears even longer.

Other Steps

With the ambitious goal of securing all fissile materials within four years, the Obama administration hosted the Nuclear Security Summit on April 12–13, 2010, in Washington, D.C., the largest summit meeting hosted by the United States since the creation of the United Nations. Attended by forty-seven states and three international organizations (the United Nations, International Atomic Energy Agency [IAEA], and the European Union), the summit led to a communiqué affirming the participants' dedication to the goal of securing nuclear materials within four years and to a more specific (but voluntary) work plan to provide guidance for national and international actions to carry out these pledges.⁶⁷ In addition to signing on to the communiqué and work plan, many participants made unilateral national commitments—during the summit and thereafter—to enhance nuclear security. Examples of such commitments include, among others, the U.S.-Russia separate plutonium disposition agreement, the establishment of a nuclear security center of excellence in China, the removal of highly enriched uranium from Belarus and Ukraine, and, most recently, the agreement between the United States and China to establish a jointly financed nuclear security center in China. Although it is unclear whether the momentum will be sustained over the long term, the summit has undoubtedly raised the visibility of nuclear security at the international level and already enabled tangible and measurable progress in the field. Also significant is that world leaders have agreed to gather again in the Republic of Korea in 2012 to assess the post-Washington summit work and set new goals for nuclear security.

In the same vein, the Obama administration has continued to support U.S. policy in favor of the development of a multilateral framework for civil nuclear cooperation. This framework is intended to offer nations reactor fuel on an apolitical basis in hopes of deterring them from pursuing their own sensitive fuel-cycle technologies (i.e., uranium enrichment or spent fuel reprocessing technology), because these capabilities can also generate nuclear weapon fuel. After the Nuclear Threat Initiative and billionaire Warren Buffett made a $50 million commitment, in September 2006, to create an international low-enriched fuel bank contingent on the IAEA receiving an additional $100 million in funding to jump-start the reserve, the United States alone pledged no less than $50 million. At the September 2010 IAEA General Conference, U.S. energy secretary Steven Chu noted that the required funding had now been met for over a year (an additional $50 million had been gathered thanks to contributions from other countries), and he insisted that the IAEA Board of Governors should now approve the proposal swiftly, stressing that resources offered by the United States and others "will be at risk if we do not reach a decision soon."[68] On December 3, 2010, the IAEA Board approved the proposal, finally overcoming opposition by Non-Aligned Movement members that were suspicious that the initiative was intended to deny their right to enrichment. A week earlier, Russia had also announced the opening of a separate fuel bank facility at Angarsk, Siberia.

On the first day of the May 2010 NPT RevCon, Secretary of State Clinton disclosed the size of the U.S. nuclear arsenal, which sat at 5,113 warheads as of September 30, 2009.[69] She added that Washington would submit the South Pacific and African nuclear-weapon-free zone (NWFZ) protocols to the Senate for approval and stressed that the administration was prepared to consult with members of the Southeast Asian and Central Asian NWFZ to move toward signature.[70] (Subsequently, in May 2011, President Obama submitted the protocols of the South Pacific and African NWFZ to the U.S. Senate for its advice and consent to ratification; at the time of this writing, a vote is pending.)[71]

The Obama administration has been considerably credited for the deemed success of the 2010 RevCon, particularly on disarmament. Although no consensus could be found on a nuclear weapon convention, on restrictions on qualitative improvements in nuclear weapons, or on disarmament timelines, the negotiating time spent on these issues and the fact that they are mentioned in the Final Document have been considered important signs of progress.[72] Action 5 of the Final Document also establishes benchmarks for disarmament and calls on the five NWS to report on these undertakings before the next RevCon.[73] These achievements are generally believed to have been impossible without the new U.S. stance on the desirability of a world without nuclear weapons.

THE UNITED KINGDOM

The United Kingdom is a unique NWS because, unlike any other, its nuclear weapon program has been entwined so closely with that of the United States that it cannot be understood outside the UK-U.S. relationship.[74] Although cooperation on nuclear research between the two countries was strong during the Second World War, the United States halted joint research abruptly after the war ended because of fears that the new discoveries would proliferate to third parties. But because of concerns that it was falling behind in its arms race with the Soviet Union after the launch of Sputnik (1957), the United States reversed its policy when the U.S. Congress passed the 1958 Mutual Defense Agreement with the United Kingdom (MDA). Since then, London has been able to acquire U.S. weapon engineering expertise, delivery systems, and testing facilities, all of which have constituted the bedrock of its nuclear weapon program.

The UK arsenal, therefore, has been heavily dependent on U.S. technology. The United Kingdom has had to decide regularly whether it wishes to remain an NWS because the MDA requires regular renewal. The first occasion when London was faced with this decision came in 1962 when Washington canceled the expensive and unreliable GAM-87 Skybolt air-launched ballistic missile (ALBM), on which the UK program depended for its V-bomber force.[75] London opted to remain an NWS and received the support of Washington, which under the 1963 Polaris Sales Agreement committed to provide it with UGM-27 Polaris SLBM to equip its future SSBN fleet, to be built locally along with the associated warheads.[76] The question of replacement of the Polaris force arose again the late 1970s, and London announced that it would replace (not expand) its fleet of four Resolution-class SSBN, each of them carrying 16 Polaris (initially non-MIRVed) SLBM, by new Vanguard-class SSBN (to be built locally) and Trident II D5, the most modern U.S. MIRVed SLBM (to be purchased from Washington).[77]

Although London never came close to scrapping its arsenal during the Cold War, significant developments took place thereafter. Under the 1990 "Options for Change" document that sought to restructure UK armed forces, London removed and dismantled its WE-177 air-delivered nuclear weapons, leaving a force exclusively composed of SSBN.[78] The first of the four Vanguard-class SSBN equipped with U.S. Trident II D5 SLBM entered service in 1994, and four years later, in 1998, the newly elected Labour Party undertook the Strategic Defence Review (SDR).[79] The review did not reappraise the Trident Program but decided that each SSBN would carry a maximum of 48 warheads, down from 96. The number of operational warheads was also capped at 200 (half the 1980s number), and the deployed SLBM were de-targeted in an effort to lessen the danger of accidental launch. Moreover, London ratified the CTBT, expressed its strong support for the conclusion of an FMCT, and committed to security assurances to NNWS and NWFZ.[80] London, however, never changed its traditional opposition to an NFU policy and, in fact, arguably extended the role of nuclear weapons further after the 9/11 attacks to include deterring terrorist organizations. As stated in the SDR's 2002 "New Chapter," "The UK's nuclear weapons have a continuing use as a means of deterring major strategic military threats, and they have a continuing role in guaranteeing the ultimate security of the UK. But we also want to be clear, particularly to the leaders of states of concern and terrorist organisations, that *all our forces play a part in deterrence, and that we have a broad range of responses available.* We must influence leaderships by showing that we are prepared to take all necessary measures to defend ourselves" (emphasis added).[81]

In December 2006, Prime Minister Tony Blair issued a defense white paper that announced a further 20 percent cut in operational warheads (from 200 to 160). Simultaneously, he declared that because it was impossible to predict future threats, the United Kingdom would begin a £20 billion ($33 billion) process of replacing (not expanding) the Trident program, thereby remaining an NWS at least until the 2050s.[82] In March 2007, the House of Commons endorsed the government's decision. To ensure that the House of Commons would do so, the government promised members of Parliament (MPs) that they would have another chance to debate and vote before a final decision is taken by 2012–14.

Opposition, however, was important and has remained relatively strong. In addition to Blair's program being opposed by over a third of Labour MPs, a majority of MPs from all parties representing Scottish constituencies voted against the decision, which is significant because warheads are stored in Scotland. The Trident decision was also a key contributor to the Labour Party's victory in the May 2007 Scottish parliamentary elections. Not surprisingly, one month later, the Scottish Parliament passed a motion calling on London not to renew Trident. Yet, the Scottish government could not prevent this development because decisions on foreign and defense policy are made only in London. The Scottish government, however, appointed a Working Group on Scotland without Nuclear Weapons, which issued a report raising concerns about the development of new Trident forces in Scotland and stressing that the project would be costly and damaging to disarmament efforts.[83]

Several personalities, particularly former high-level military personnel, also voiced their opposition. In January 2009, General Jack Sheehan, former NATO Supreme Allied Commander Atlantic, called on London to take the lead on nuclear disarmament by giving up Trident.[84] This statement came shortly after Field Marshal Lord Edwin Bramall, General Lord David Ramsbotham, and General Sir Hugh Beach had declared that Trident renewal was expensive, pointless, and counterproductive.[85] A year later, in January 2010, former leader of the UK armed forces Lord Bramall reiterated these comments, urging London to postpone a final decision on Trident renewal "to give us more flexibility [in disarmament] negotiations."[86] In April 2010, Lord Bramall, Lord Ramsbotham, Sir Hugh, and Major-General Patrick Cordingley added that the Trident option would prevent highly needed investments in other areas of the military.[87]

Despite this opposition, however, Trident renewal continued to receive mainstream political support. Its future was only really discussed in the context of the financial crisis. In June 2009, the influential Institute for Public Policy Research published a report arguing that irrevocable financial decisions should not be taken until "a fundamental review of all options" is conducted in the 2010 SDR.[88] This was followed by a September 2009 ComRes poll that showed that most UK citizens believed that Trident should be abandoned given the state of public finances.[89] The Labour government stated its blunt opposition to examine Trident in the SDR (a position also shared by the opposition), but Prime Minister Gordon Brown considered options to reduce the bill. In late September 2009, he declared that London may opt to build three instead of four SSBN, a possibility also envisioned by the Conservatives.[90] The Royal Navy, however, quickly responded that the United Kingdom could not have its deterrent ready at all times with fewer than four SSBN.[91]

Debates continued until the May 2010 General Election, when the Labour Party was defeated after thirteen years in power. Although the Conservatives won the largest number of votes and seats, they fell twenty seats short of a majority and had to form a coalition government with the Liberal Democrats. This was significant for the Trident question because unlike the Conservatives, who had consistently supported renewal, the Liberal Democrats had pushed for its reexamination in the 2010 SDR. Before the election, they had even suggested that the need for "continuous [UK] deterrence at sea" no longer existed.[92]

However, once in power, the Liberal Democrats remained relatively quiet on the Trident decision. This was reflected in the statement issued by the new coalition government shortly after their election victory: "The Government will be committed to the maintenance of Britain's nuclear deterrent, and have agreed that the renewal of Trident should be scrutinized to ensure value for money." Although the statement stresses that "the Liberal Democrats will continue to make the case for alternatives," independent studies have shown that all other options would be more expensive and less reliable.[93] This explained why Defence Minister Liam Fox stated a month after the elections that "as part of the coalition agreement, we agreed that we would have a value-for-money study or examine the cost of the programme and see where we could achieve better value *within it*" (emphasis added). Fox, therefore, made it clear that while a reassessment would be conducted, the Trident decision was here to stay.[94]

Not surprisingly, five months later, the Trident Value for Money Review, an entire section of the new Strategic Defence and Security Review (SDSR), concluded that the United Kingdom "will maintain a continuous submarine-based deterrent and begin the work of replacing its existing submarines."[95] The SDSR stresses that the first investment decision ("Initial Gate") will soon be approved and that the next phase of the project will commence by the end of 2010. In order to drive value for money, however, the document explains that London will defer a decision on a replacement to the current warhead, reduce the cost of the replacement SSBN missile compartment, extend the life of the current Vanguard-class SSBN and re-profile the program to build replacement SSBN, and, as a consequence, take the second investment decision finalizing the detailed acquisition plans, design, and number of SSBN ("Main Gate") around 2016.[96] The SDSR also indicates that London will work with industry to improve efficiency and optimize to the expected demand its capacity to build and support SSBN.

As a result of this reassessment, the SDSR points out that the United Kingdom will reduce the maximum number of nuclear warheads onboard each Vanguard-class SSBN from 48 to 40 and reduce the number of operational missiles on each SSBN from 12 to 8.[97] It goes on to stress that these decisions will make it possible to reduce the requirement for operationally available warheads from fewer than 160 to no more than 120 and reduce the overall nuclear weapon stockpile from 225 to no more than 180 warheads. The review explains that these changes will reduce costs by £3.2 billion ($5.2 billion), saving approximately £1.2 billion ($2 billion) and deferring spending of up to £2 billion ($3.2 billion) from the next ten years. Shortly after the release of the SDSR, however, Defense Minister Fox pointed out that "there will be additional costs to maintaining the Vanguard class through to 2028." He also did not bluntly reject Labour claims that the delay would end up costing more overall, merely stating, "As no cost will actually be set out until after Main Gate, it is impossible to make that assumption."[98] This seems to have been confirmed by the Initial Gate Parliamentary Report, which was published in May 2011 and remains ambiguous about program costs.[99]

In a drive to further save costs, London has also strived to extend its cooperation with Paris on a range of military matters, notably including nuclear issues. Announced in a landmark summit in November 2010, future French-UK nuclear cooperation is expected to combine work on nuclear warhead testing conducted at the UK Atomic Weapons Establishment (AWE) at Aldermaston in Berkshire and at its French equivalent at Valduc in Brittany.[100] While Aldermaston will focus on developing technology, Valduc will do the computerized testing, thereby ensuring the long-term viability, security, and safety of UK and French nuclear warheads. In addition, the two countries also plan to jointly develop equipment and technology for the next generation of SSBN.

Therefore, it is mainly the state of public finances (and also possibly pressure, however discreet, from the Liberal Democrats) that has forced London to reassess the renewal of its deterrent. In the recent SDSR, the new government also decided to clarify its declaratory policy in a similar fashion as the United States did in its NPR, stating that "the UK will not use or threaten to use nuclear weapons against non-nuclear weapon states parties to the NPT." This was qualified by noting that this assurance would not apply to any state "in material breach" of their nonproliferation obligations.[101] Yet, at no point was the possibility of scrapping Trident altogether seriously on the table. Although a new independent commission was recently set up to examine the United Kingdom's nuclear weapon policy and the issue of Trident renewal, Prime Minister David Cameron insisted (on the day the new commission was launched) that he was "committed to full Trident replacement."[102] In other words, London does not seem prepared to eliminate its nuclear weapons in the near future.

In this context, how has it approached nuclear disarmament? Shortly after announcing its 2006 Trident plan, London unveiled an ambitious nuclear disarmament program in a landmark speech given by Secretary of State for Foreign and Commonwealth Affairs Margaret Beckett at the Carnegie International Nonproliferation Conference in June 2007.[103] Although the sincerity of the Beckett program was questioned because of its timing, it was more than an attempt to appease opposition to the Trident decision. In her speech, which began with a reference to the Four Horsemen's program, Secretary Beckett clearly recognized the interface of disarmament and nonproliferation as key to the NPT bargain and stressed that the NWS should intensify their efforts on nuclear disarmament as a means to solve proliferation issues. As she put it, "our efforts on nonproliferation will be dangerously undermined if others believe—however unfairly—that the terms of the grand bargain have changed, that the nuclear weapon states have abandoned any commitment to disarmament."[104]

Secretary Beckett also explained that there was an urgent need for a bold vision in favor of a world without nuclear weapons *and* significant actions to move toward that goal. She stressed that reaching this goal would take more than effective diplomacy because different international political conditions were needed. She made a case for incremental but steady progress. After referring to nuclear reductions undertaken by the United States, Russia, France, and the United Kingdom since the early 1990s, Secretary Beckett called for renewed efforts, the entry into force of the CTBT, and the conclusion of an FMCT. She explained that the greater share of the burden will have to be carried by the United States and Russia (because they have the largest arsenals), but she indicated that the United Kingdom would continue to be active, stressing that it would turn itself into a "disarmament laboratory." She noted UK support of an International Institute for Strategic Studies (IISS) study to help determine the requirements for nuclear disarmament (the study was published as an Adelphi Paper by George Perkovich and James Acton in September 2008)[105] and announced that the AWE would expand its disarmament verification research and collaborate with Norway and the nongovernmental organization Verification Research, Training, and Information Centre (or VERTIC) to bring together NWS and NNWS perspectives on the question.

Less than a year later, in a February 2008 statement at the CD, Secretary of State for Defence Des Browne reiterated the points developed by Secretary Beckett and elaborated on how the United Kingdom would become "a role model and testing ground for measures that we and others can take on key aspects of disarmament." He reported that AWE had now developed a technical cooperation initiative with Norwegian laboratories. Because "the international community needs a transparent, sustainable, and credible plan for multilateral nuclear disarmament," he stressed that in addition to NWS-NNWS research collaboration, NWS needed to build deeper technical relationships among themselves.[106] That is why he announced that to initiate that process, the United Kingdom would host a conference involving the five NWS. The conference subsequently took place behind closed doors in September 2009; it was reportedly not as productive as many had hoped because of lack of enthusiasm by some, particularly China, but this did not prevent the organization of a follow-on conference (by France) in June 2011.[107] According to a release from the UK Foreign and Commonwealth Office (FCO), "In a wide ranging discussion, the P5 considered the confidence-building, verification and compliance challenges associated with achieving further progress toward disarmament and non-proliferation, and steps to address those challenges. They looked at ways to increase mutual understanding by sharing definitions of nuclear terminology and information about their nuclear doctrines and capabilities. They made presentations on enhancing P5 strategic stability and building mutual confidence through voluntary transparency and other measures. They also considered the international challenges associated with responding to nuclear accidents and undertook to consider ways to co-operate to address these challenges."[108]

London elaborated further on how to establish the conditions for nuclear disarmament in *Lifting the Nuclear Shadow*, a policy paper issued by the FCO in February 2009. The paper opens by stressing that "establishing these conditions cannot be done unilaterally or in a single leap, but requires a series of incremental, mutually-reinforcing steps [that] requires the active participation of the entire international community."[109] The paper identifies three conditions: "watertight means" to prevent proliferation; minimum nuclear arsenals with an international legal framework that imposes tight and verifiable constraints on nuclear weapons and prevents redevelopment; and a road map to move from small arsenals to a nuclear-weapon-free world without jeopardizing security.

A month later, Prime Minister Brown explained that nuclear disarmament had to result from a multilateral effort involving all states because "No single nuclear weapons state can be expected to disarm unilaterally."[110] In July 2009, his cabinet released *The Road to 2010*, a document that details steps to be taken by the NWS and NNWS in order to reinvigorate the NPT bargain prior to the 2010 RevCon.[111]

In October 2009, London also launched the Top Level Group of UK Parliamentarians for Multilateral Disarmament and Nonproliferation.[112] Similarly to the U.S. Nuclear Security Project that was formed by the Four Horsemen after the publication of their famous opinion pieces, the formation of this group grew out of the publication in the *Times* in June 2008 of a letter by former foreign secretaries Lord Douglas Hurd, Sir Malcolm Rifkind, Lord David Owen, and Lord George Robertson, in which they all stressed the need to reach a world without nuclear weapons on a multilateral and incremental basis.[113] The goal of this cross-party group, which consists of numerous former UK foreign and defense secretaries, experts, and personalities, as well as three authors of the June 2008 letter, is to reach into the U.S. Congress and cooperate with European politicians in order to raise the level of debate on nuclear disarmament.

In a nutshell, although London is in the process of renewing its deterrent, it has been simultaneously extremely active in advancing toward a nuclear-weapon-free world. The change of power resulting from the May 2010 General Election is unlikely to fundamentally affect efforts on the nuclear disarmament front. Generally, the Conservatives have been more skeptical about nuclear disarmament, but they now seem to have endorsed their predecessors' policy direction. This was illustrated at the 2010 NPT RevCon, when, in addition to reporting the ongoing results of the UK-Norway Initiative, the new government officially disclosed for the first time the size of the UK nuclear stockpile, stating that the UK arsenal would not exceed 225 warheads, including the maximum 160 already declared as "operational available."[114]

EXPLAINING THE (CAUTIOUS) OPTIMISM OF THE UNITED STATES AND THE UNITED KINGDOM

While they remain determined to maintain their nuclear arsenals, both the United States and the United Kingdom have recently exhibited some important optimism toward nuclear disarmament. After eight years during which the topic was considered taboo in the United States, Washington has rekindled the idea of a nuclear-weapon-free world as a positive development. Although progress has been much slower than what the administration seemed to have initially envisioned, no key battles have been lost and current nuclear disarmament momentum has not dissipated. The United Kingdom's efforts seem to have been partly designed to make sure that the momentum does not fade away: of late, London has been essentially active in laying the technical foundations for the multilateral elimination of nuclear weapons. As King's College professor Lawrence Freedman explains, while the United States is without a doubt today's nuclear disarmament leader, the United Kingdom is the facilitator.[115] What are the drivers behind current U.S. and UK policies? What are the prospects for the foreseeable future?

The United States

Current U.S. interest in moving toward nuclear disarmament has to do with the belief that this quest will bring hope and help reinvigorate the nuclear nonproliferation and nuclear security regimes, strengthen them, and allow more vigorous actions against proliferators.[116] As President Obama put it in a speech he delivered in Moscow in July 2009, "while I know [that nuclear disarmament] won't be met soon, pursuing it provides the legal and moral foundation to prevent the proliferation and eventual use of nuclear weapons."[117] The new NPR makes this even clearer, stating that "we are pursuing arms control efforts [...] as a means of strengthening our ability to mobilize broad international support for the measures needed to reinforce the nonproliferation regime and secure nuclear materials worldwide."[118] The idea is that the letter and spirit of the NPT bargain, which, as mentioned earlier, have been confirmed and even reinforced over the years, remain sound: cooperation from the NNWS on nuclear nonproliferation (and nuclear security) is contingent upon progress from the NWS toward nuclear disarmament, and both the NWS and NNWS can freely access nuclear technology for peaceful purposes.[119]

The Obama administration believes that reaffirming this bargain is extremely urgent in order to repair some of the damages caused by the Bush administration. The latter tended to refuse to let arms control impose any substantial constraints on the United States and used it mainly to hold proliferators accountable and justify coercive actions against them, which has arguably sharpened differences between the NWS and NNWS and plagued nuclear nonproliferation and nuclear security efforts. The new administration has argued that it is high time to remedy the problem in view of growing concerns about nuclear terrorism and nuclear proliferation. After the 9/11 attacks, in particular, U.S. officials have come to consider that the most serious threat to U.S. national security lies "at the crossroads of radicalism and technology," that is, if terrorists get their hands on nuclear weapons or fissile material, which will be in greater circulation and thus potentially be more available as a result of the so-called nuclear renaissance.[120] Clearly, the prospect of terrorists igniting a nuclear device in Lower Manhattan, Washington, or any other U.S. city, which the 2010 NPR identifies as "today's most immediate and extreme danger," has over the past few years kept U.S. national security specialists awake.[121] They have also been deeply concerned by the possible emergence of new nuclear powers (North Korea and Iran in the lead), in particular for fear that this could lead to a domino effect of regional nuclear proliferation—"Today's other pressing threat" according to the new NPR. These concerns have been heightened by the generally widely held conviction that nuclear deterrence would likely be (1) largely ineffective against terrorists who have no territory to defend and may be prepared to die for their cause;[122] and (2) of much more limited effectiveness in a world with many more nuclear powers, particularly given that the new and want-to-be entrants to the nuclear club, unlike "the original members," are arguably fundamentally unsatisfied with the current international status quo.[123]

That is why the Obama administration has been anxious about re-establishing the leadership of the United States, in particular its responsibility, as the leading NWS, to drive efforts toward nuclear disarmament. The hope is that this will encourage greater cooperation from NNWS on the nuclear nonproliferation and nuclear security fronts. Nearly twenty years ago, Brad Roberts, now U.S. deputy assistant secretary of defense for nuclear and missile defense policy and lead drafter of the 2010 NPR, had already described the core tenets of this approach in one of his essays. As he put it, "This is a notion of leadership born of the idea that for one to lead, others must want to follow. The United States can only lead [. . .] if it is working from a position accorded it by others to safeguard shared interests [. . .]. The more simple-minded leadership that asserts narrowly defined U.S. interests aggressively and pursues them dogmatically is bound to prove counterproductive."[124]

This notion of leadership has been the very bedrock of the NPT bargain, which was, in fact, primarily developed by the United States. As UK nuclear analyst William Walker explains, "Throughout the nuclear age [. . .] most of the *ordering ideas* and most of the desire to realize those ideas, came from the United States."[125] Arguably, the NPT bargain is itself a by-product of U.S. post–Second World War diplomacy, which has been focused predominantly on forging cooperative relations among nations to help preserve peace and advance prosperity in the world. Today, Washington is seeking to reinvigorate, even strengthen, this bargain. As explained in the 2010 National Security Strategy, the United States is committed to "renewing American leadership so that we can more effectively advance our interests in the 21st century."[126]

What this suggests is that the rationale behind the Obama administration's stance on nuclear disarmament is fundamentally practical. Although the proposed approach is without a doubt ethical and perhaps even altruistic, it is certainly not naive or blindly idealistic. Rather, it proceeds from carefully calculated national interests. It is based on the belief that to better pursue its interests, the United States needs to also take the interests of others into account, meaning that in order to gather support to reinforce the nuclear nonproliferation and nuclear security regimes, the United States needs to lead on the nuclear disarmament front.

The practicality of the U.S. approach is best illustrated by the fact that Washington's nuclear disarmament policy has been exceedingly cautious. In Prague, immediately after stating that his administration is committed to seeking the peace and security of a world free of nuclear weapons, President Obama stressed that reaching this goal will probably not happen during his lifetime. He added that the United States would maintain a strong nuclear arsenal so long as nuclear weapons exist. Such cautiousness was confirmed by the conclusion of New START and the release of the 2010 NPR, which, respectively, reduce the numbers and roles of nuclear weapons in U.S. national security policy but do not do so dogmatically. As the NPR's drafters have explained, the agreed numbers and roles to be reduced are not arbitrary decisions: they are the result of a long and carefully thought-through analysis of what the many agencies involved in the NPR drafting process have concluded the United States could safely undertake in the current international security environment.[127] That is why, as detailed earlier, these reductions have sizeable limits and, in fact, for the problems for which numbers and roles remain uniquely relevant, the NPR makes clear that nuclear weapons should not only be maintained but also strengthened, hence the important investments allocated by the Obama administration in order to optimize the U.S. arsenal.

Of course, Washington also insists that the United States is committed to actively working to help create the conditions that will make it possible to further reduce, over time, the numbers and roles of its nuclear weapons (and those of others). Yet, the NPR explains that this process of incremental and multilateral progress will be extremely long and difficult: the document plainly states that the conditions for a world free of nuclear weapons do not currently exist, and, in fact, it suggests that these conditions are not even known. Simply put, never has the perspective of the United States disarming swiftly and unilaterally been on the table, which arguably should have been the case if Washington's approach had been motivated strictly by moral imperatives. Therefore, Frank Gaffney, founder and president of the Center for Security Policy and a columnist for the *Washington Times*, could not be more wrong when he predicted shortly after President Obama took office that his administration would "transform the 'world's only superpower' into a nuclear impotent," a claim also made by many other conservative critics.[128]

Why has the Obama administration been so cautious about moving toward nuclear disarmament? Although the utility of the U.S. nuclear arsenal has undeniably diminished in the post–Cold War world, Washington believes that its arsenal continues to have a key role to play, both to protect U.S. national security *and* to maintain international peace and security. As a result of U.S. superpower status, the purpose of the U.S. arsenal has gone beyond the "mere" protection of the U.S. homeland. For starters, the new NPR explains that "the

United States must continue to address the [...] challenge of ensuring strategic stability with existing nuclear powers—most notably Russia and China."[129] It stresses that the challenge for the U.S.-Russia-China triangle, identified as crucial for global strategic stability, will be to strengthen and, in fact, reinforce their relations as nuclear arsenals go down. The NPR, therefore, makes clear that the conditions are ripe for major powers to make progress toward nuclear disarmament, but it also suggests that this process will be gradual and that nuclear weapons will remain relevant for some time. To be sure, the choice of the concept of "strategic stability" over the traditional concept of "deterrence" is evidence that the United States emphasizes the potential for cooperation over the potential for conflict in major power relations. But that does not mean that effective nuclear deterrence is no longer relevant to manage these relations because the NPR clearly recognizes the potential for flashpoints.

Washington also argues that its nuclear arsenal remains paramount to deter minor powers (in situations for which nuclear weapons are uniquely relevant) and to reassure U.S. allies and partners and prevent regional instabilities, particularly because many of them remain strongly in favor of *nuclear* security guarantees. While stressing that extended deterrence will be conducted increasingly with non-nuclear elements, the new NPR stresses that the presence of U.S. forward-deployed TNW in Europe continues to be justified. Similarly, the document states that the United States still needs to offer nuclear security guarantees to its Asian and Middle Eastern allies and partners.[130] In the case of Europe, despite controversies among NATO member states over the future of U.S. TNW stationed there (Germany and four other northern states have explicitly called for withdrawal, while Baltic states fear that removing TNW would weaken the U.S. deterrent), the New Strategic Concept adopted in Lisbon in November 2010 clearly suggests that short of significant concessions on Russia's part, they are here to stay.[131] Moreover, the new NATO document recognizes the need to establish the conditions to move toward a nuclear-weapon-free world but also stresses that deterrence remains absolutely central to NATO's overall strategy. Although deterrence is no longer based only on nuclear elements but "on an appropriate mix of nuclear and conventional capabilities," the New Strategic Concept explains that "as long as nuclear weapons exist, NATO will remain a nuclear alliance," and that "the supreme guarantee of the security of the Allies is provided by the strategic nuclear forces of the Alliance, *particularly* those of the United States" (emphasis added).[132] In other words, the U.S. nuclear arsenal clearly remains a crucial element to the security of U.S. allies and partners.[133]

In a nutshell, the United States has had a cautious stance on nuclear disarmament because of perceived negative consequences not only for its own security, but also for international and regional stability.

There is an additional dimension that explains Washington's vigilance on nuclear disarmament: domestic politics. In the United States, the making of nuclear policy is much more partisan than in any other NWS. Leaving aside the pressure exerted by the powerful nuclear weapon complex that seeks to ensure that the United States maintains its nuclear arsenal, there are sharp differences among politicians, policymakers, and lawmakers about arms control and the desirability and feasibility of a world free of nuclear weapons. As UK political scientist Mark Smith explains, "it often seems that Washington goes through a cyclical process of disillusionment and revived interest in arms control and multilateral nonproliferation policy."[134] As explained earlier in the chapter, although power is now clearly in the hands of arms controllers, the concerns of many Republican senators have had to be tempered considerably to permit New START ratification. At least in the short term, further progress is uncertain on other Prague agenda items, perhaps particularly on CTBT ratification. Nuclear analysts Nikolai Sokov and Miles Pomper may well have a very good point arguing that "in agreeing to the modernization pledges as part of the New START ratification process, administration officials have already traded away what was seen as their potential trump card in any CTBT negotiation with Senate Republicans."[135] Put differently, because of domestic constraints, there is only so much that even a zealous administration like President Obama's can do on the nuclear disarmament front.

That being said, it is unlikely that a change of power in the United States would radically reverse the direction pursued by the Obama administration. With the exception of some (not all) aspects of the George W. Bush administration, there has been considerable continuity in U.S. nuclear policy over time. Indeed, since the end of the Cold War, with the threat changing, the United States has consistently moved toward nuclear disarmament. The return in power of a Republican administration would certainly change the U.S. approach to the question, but it would not reverse it, at least not radically. Today, more than ever, a nuclear-weapon-free world is on the U.S. policy agenda. It is certainly a goal far on the horizon, but it is a goal toward which future U.S. administrations will continue to march, however slow and indirect it may be, if only because it is fundamentally in U.S. interests. After all, in a nuclear-weapon-free world, U.S. military dominance and influence in the international system would be increased tenfold given the overwhelming superiority of its conventional forces—an argument, in fact, put forward by key U.S. national security figures, even the most conservative ones, since the 1990s to suggest that Washington should make every effort to move toward nuclear disarmament.[136] Of course, this dimension has not escaped the careful eyes of other states, notably Russia and China, which have begun to request that the United States exercise restraint on its non-nuclear strategic forces, particularly on BMD. Clearly, one can expect that as the nuclear disarmament process proceeds, such requests for restraint will evolve into demands for constraints.

The United Kingdom

Why does the United Kingdom wish to show a strong commitment to making progress toward a world free of nuclear weapons? Is it because it is driven by a strong moral imperative to get there? Or does its position proceed from carefully calculated national interests, like the United States? If London really wanted to play the moral imperative card, it would disarm swiftly and unilaterally. The fact that it does not do so suggests that national interests are clearly at play.

London, like Washington, believes that enhanced efforts to move toward nuclear disarmament are the best option to help reinvigorate the NPT bargain and allow more vigorous action against proliferators, which has always been a consistent UK concern. The key rationale behind London's nuclear disarmament diplomacy, therefore, proceeds from the same fundamentally practical perspective as Washington's: to reinforce nuclear nonproliferation policy (and bolster nuclear security efforts). Secretary Margaret Beckett made this clear in her June 2007 speech, stating that "any solution must be a dual one that sees movement on both proliferation and disarmament—a revitalisation, in other words, of the grand bargain struck in 1968, when the Nonproliferation Treaty was established."[137]

This explains why London has had the same cautious approach to nuclear disarmament as Washington. London began trimming its already small arsenal at the end of the Cold War because of the changed international security environment. The Conservatives launched the first reductions, which were pursued by the Labour Party after the 1997 General Election. These reductions have left the United Kingdom with a very small operationally active nuclear force that operates only one weapon system (SSBN). Because London does not contemplate disarming unilaterally but considers that nuclear disarmament is only possible on an incremental and multilateral basis, it has been left with very little, if any, numerical room to make additional reductions, particularly now that the new government has just recently announced further cuts. London, therefore, has had few options to show its commitment to actively move toward a world free of nuclear weapons. As a result, paving the way for abolition through the promotion of research studies and other collaborations has become the focus of its new nuclear disarmament diplomacy. This is likely to continue because little more can be achieved by London alone (as unilateral disarmament is not a politically acceptable option), not even with regard to transparency or at the doctrinal level now that the new government has disclosed the size of the UK nuclear stockpile and has clarified its declaratory policy.

At any rate, the United Kingdom will simultaneously continue to preserve (and optimize) its nuclear arsenal, for several reasons. For starters, it is linked to security concerns. The UK nuclear arsenal was first developed after the United Kingdom had been at war with a superior adversary (Germany) and as it was beginning to confront another one (the Soviet Union).[138] At the time, London thought that having nuclear weapons was crucial to its security. While it never really seriously associated the possession of nuclear weapons with the idea of national independence, London also argued that its nuclear deterrent contributed to NATO's deterrence strategy and that this enhanced its security.[139]

When the Cold War ended, UK nuclear strategy shifted from a deterrence doctrine targeting the Soviet Union to one "to whom it may concern."[140] In other words, London came to justify its nuclear status by pointing to open-ended issues: the possible resurgence of Russia, the rise of China, the outbreak of major regional conflicts, and, particularly after 9/11, the threat of terrorism and proliferation. When Prime Minister Tony Blair presented his December 2006 Defense White Paper, he justified Trident renewal as follows, "It is not possible accurately to predict the global security environment over the next 20 to 50 years. On our current analysis, we cannot rule out the risk either that a major direct nuclear threat to the UK's vital interests will re-emerge or that new states will emerge that possess a more limited nuclear capability, but one that could pose a grave threat to our vital interests. Equally there is a risk that some countries might in future seek to sponsor nuclear terrorism from their soil."[141]

The UK deterrent, therefore, is no longer needed to face a major nuclear threat, but London has argued that it remains necessary as an insurance policy against uncertainties. The Conservative opposition (now in power) echoed these ideas, with Liam Fox, then shadow minister for defense, stressing, "The nature of the threat that we face has changed quickly from the cold war to a range of other threats, and it could change quickly again. The onus is not on those of us who wish to retain a deterrent, but on those who want to scrap it to tell us why they believe that they can predict the risks that we will face in half a century's time."[142]

Naturally, the SDSR reiterates these claims, stressing that "we cannot dismiss the possibility that a major direct nuclear threat to the UK might re-emerge."[143] The security argument, however, does not appear compelling. Tony Blair admitted after the Trident decision that "starting from here," London would probably not choose to acquire a deterrent because nuclear weapons have a limited utility in today's world—an argument that the Conservatives had also previously made.[144] Rather, it seems that London wants to retain its deterrent because other NWS are not prepared to disarm (and because it fears the emergence of new nuclear-armed states that might hold the United Kingdom to ransom). As Tony Blair explained, "None of the present recognized nuclear weapons States intends to renounce nuclear weapons, in the absence of an agreement to disarm multilaterally, we cannot be sure that a major nuclear threat to our vital interests will not emerge over the longer term."[145]

Moreover, London continues to believe that its deterrent helps define its identity as a responsible world power, despite the fact that this role is not as pivotal as Washington's. As the late Sir Michael Quinlan, the United Kingdom's leading defense strategist, explained, "we are still among the countries which have both the capabilities and the will to take on difficult missions around the world; [...] nuclear weapons have a certain relevance to that."[146] London stresses that its nuclear arsenal not only provides a significant power projection capability completely interoperable with U.S. forces (because they use similar technology) but also serves a key role in sharing the nuclear defense burden of NATO. Indeed, the UK deterrent is fully assigned to NATO's Supreme Allied Commander Europe, although it remained independent due to the nature of NATO command and control systems, which allow UK commanders to communicate both with NATO and UK authorities.

London's attachment to its nuclear arsenal is also linked to regional and domestic dimensions. At the regional level, London must feel that it cannot leave France as the only NWS in Europe. Beyond historical reasons (France having been the United Kingdom's longtime rival for preeminence in Europe), London probably believes that Paris cannot be trusted to provide for European security, particularly as its nuclear arsenal was developed as a symbol of France's national power, strong leadership in Europe, and strict independence from Washington.

At the domestic level, some forces favor the retention of the UK deterrent.[147] The Ministry of Defence (MoD) has been the lead advocate, despite internal disagreements about how to proceed with Trident renewal in view of the poor state of the economy. AWE, the United Kingdom's nuclear weapons research, development, and manufacturing center acting on behalf of MoD, has also been a firm supporter and has therefore made sure to develop capabilities and maintain strong relationships with U.S. nuclear weapon laboratories so that the replacement of Trident goes ahead. Similarly, the nuclear submarine industry, British Aerospace Systems in particular, and its workforce have vested interests in the United Kingdom remaining an NWS that would prove very politically costly for any UK government to disappoint.

For the foreseeable future, therefore, the United Kingdom will remain an NWS *and* push the nuclear disarmament envelope at the same time, hoping that this will help on the nuclear nonproliferation and nuclear security fronts. Only the intensification of multilateral disarmament efforts will drive London to make further tangible commitments.

CONCLUSION

Both the United States and the United Kingdom have been key drivers of current nuclear disarmament momentum. After a few years of uncertainty, the United States has come back to the forefront and re-established itself as the indisputable leader of that process since Barack Obama arrived at the White House and laid out an ambitious agenda for the world in Prague. The United Kingdom, for its part, has been extremely active in facilitating that process and opening the march toward a nuclear-weapon-free world.

Behind U.S. and UK actions is the belief that progress on this front will help repair differences between the NWS and NNWS and reinvigorate, even strengthen, the nuclear nonproliferation and nuclear security regimes. The approach, therefore, is not naive or idealistic but fundamentally practical. It is born of the idea that leadership on nuclear disarmament will make it easier to rally international cooperation and better address other nuclear problems. The practicality of the U.S. and UK approach is best exemplified by the fact that both countries have been very cautious in moving toward a nuclear-weapon-free world: they consider it possible only on a step-by-step and multilateral basis (they have never seriously contemplated disarming unilaterally) and are in fact optimizing their nuclear forces because they intend to keep them so long as nuclear dangers exist in the world. The United States, in particular, has had to adopt a very cautious approach to nuclear disarmament because of its superpower responsibilities for maintaining strategic stability among major powers and for reassuring its allies and partners, processes in which nuclear weapons continue to play a crucial role; U.S. domestic politics has also considerably contributed to U.S. cautiousness.

However cautious they may be, both the United States and the United Kingdom seem determined to move the nuclear disarmament process forward. But it will take considerable time and efforts to get to a nuclear-weapon-free world. In particular, making steady progress and maintaining momentum is unlikely to succeed without strong cooperation of other states. In other words, the United States and the United Kingdom have firmly set the stage for the international community to advance toward nuclear disarmament. They now need all nations of the world to pick up the ball and work constructively with them to help reduce and ultimately eliminate nuclear dangers. While they—the United States in particular—can probably break the nuclear nonproliferation and nuclear security regimes all on their own, they do rely on the strong support and cooperation of others to build it.

Notes

1. Russia is also a founding signatory and depositary of the NPT.
2. Coral Bell explains that "[a]n international norm defines 'expected and required' behavior." See Bell, "Normative Shift," *National Interest* 70 (Winter 2002/2003): 44. The phrase was first used in the nuclear field by Brad Roberts in "Nonproliferation—Challenges Old and New," Counterproliferation Papers, Future Warfare Series 24 (Maxwell Air Force Base, Ala.: U.S. Air Force Counterproliferation Center, August 2004): 20.
3. It goes without saying that the reality is much more complex than the division between "optimistic nuclear weapon states" and "pessimistic nuclear weapon states." This volume has chosen these labels for the sake of brevity.
4. *Nuclear Posture Review Report* (Washington, D.C.: Department of Defense, 1994).
5. *Bottom-Up Review* (Washington, D.C.: Department of Defense, 1993) and Counterproliferation Initiative (Washington, D.C.: Department of Defense, 1993).
6. *Nuclear Posture Review Report* (Washington, D.C.: Department of Defense, 2002).

7. For a history of the RNEP program, see Jonathan Medalia, *"Bunker Busters": Robust Nuclear Earth Penetrator Issues, FY2005–FY2007* (Washington, D.C.: CRS Report for Congress Order Code RL32347, 2006).

8. For a history of the RRW program, see Jonathan Medalia, *The Reliable Replacement Warhead Program: Background and Current Developments* (Washington, D.C.: CRS Report for Congress Order Code RL32929, 2009).

9. For a background on the U.S.-India nuclear cooperation agreement, see Jayshree Bajoria, "The U.S.-India Nuclear Deal," Council on Foreign Relations, November 20, 2009.

10. Jean du Preez, "The Impact of the Nuclear Posture Review on the International Nuclear Nonproliferation Regime," *Nonproliferation Review* 9 (November 2002): 67–81. See also Lewis Dunn, Gregory Giles, Jeffrey Larsen, and Thomas Skypek, *Foreign Perspectives on the U.S. Nuclear Policy and Posture: Insights, Issues, and Implications* (SAIC for the Defense Threat Reduction Agency, DTRA01-03-D-0017, December 12, 2006).

11. *The National Security Strategy of the United States of America* (Washington, D.C.: White House, 2002).

12. George P. Schultz, William J. Perry, Henry A. Kissinger, and Sam Nunn, "A World Free of Nuclear Weapons," *Wall Street Journal*, January 4, 2007, and Schultz, Perry, Kissinger, and Nunn, "Toward a Nuclear-Free World," *Wall Street Journal*, January 15, 2008.

13. Shultz et al., "World Free of Nuclear Weapons."

14. "McCain Remarks on Foreign Policy," *Washington Post*, March 26, 2008.

15. "Speech by Barack Obama," Lafayette, Ind., July 16, 2008.

16. "Remarks by President Barack Obama," Prague, Czech Republic, April 5, 2009.

17. George Bunn and Roland Timerbaev, *Nuclear Disarmament—How Much Have the Five Nuclear Powers Promised in the Non-Proliferation Treaty?* (Washington, D.C.: Lawyers Alliance for World Security, 1994), 24. To be sure, reducing the role of nuclear weapons is much less ambitious than prohibiting their use, although it is undeniably moving in that direction.

18. "Remarks by the President on Winning the Nobel Peace Prize," White House, Washington, D.C., October 9, 2009.

19. U.S.-Russian relations had been strained since the 2008 Georgian War. The notion of "reset" was coined by Vice President Joe Biden. See "Remarks by Vice-President Biden at 45th Munich Conference on Security Policy," Munich, Germany, February 7, 2009.

20. "Joint Statement by President Dmitry Medvedev of the Russian Federation and President Barack Obama of the United States of America," April 1, 2009; "Joint Statement by President Barack Obama of the United States of America and President Dmitry Medvedev of the Russian Federation on Nuclear Cooperation," July 6, 2009.

21. "Remarks by the President on Strengthening Missile Defense in Europe," September 17, 2009; Mark Fitzpatrick, "A Prudent Decision on Missile Defence," *Survival* 51 (December 2009/January 2010): 5–12.

22. "Remarks by President Obama and President Medvedev of Russia at New START Treaty Signing Ceremony and Press Conference," Prague, Czech Republic, April 8, 2010.

23. For details, see "Key Facts about the New START Treaty," White House, Washington, D.C., March 26, 2010.

24. For an analysis of current U.S. nuclear forces, see Robert Norris and Hans Kristensen, "U.S. Nuclear Forces, 2010," *Bulletin of the Atomic Scientists*, May/June 2010, 57–71.

25. *Strategic Survey 2010: The Annual Review of World Affairs* (London: International Institute for Strategic Studies, 2010), 41.

26. *Nuclear Posture Review Report* (Washington, D.C.: Department of Defense, 2010), 19–30.

27. "Statement of Admiral Michael G. Mullen, USN Chairman of the Joint Chiefs of Staff before the 111th Congress Senate Armed Services Committee," Washington, D.C., June 17, 2010.

28. "Statement by the Russian Federation on Missile Defense," April 8, 2010.

29. Prompt Global Strike is a U.S. military initiative to develop a system capable of a precision conventional weapon strike anywhere in the world within an hour. For more details, see Amy Woolf, *Conventional Prompt Global Strike and Long-Range Ballistic Missiles: Background and Issues* (Washington, D.C.: CRS Report for Congress Order Code R41464, 2010). According to the BMD Review, the United States is committed to developing and deploying BMD systems to defend the U.S. homeland, U.S. forces, and its allies and partners (and to providing the latter with such systems) on condition that capabilities are operational, financially sustainable, and flexible enough to adapt as threats change. See *Ballistic Missile Defense Review Report* (Washington, D.C.: Department of Defense, 2010), iii–iv.

30. Bill Gertz, "Missile Defense Deal," *Washington Times*, June 16, 2010.

31. Elaine Grossman, "Offering Nuclear Plus-Ups, White House Awaits Kyl's Word on New START," *Global Security Newswire*, November 15, 2010. Hillary Clinton and Robert Gates, U.S. secretary of state and secretary of defense, respectively, also offered a strong pitch for ratification in an article, stressing that "time is running out for this Congress." See Hillary Rodham Clinton and Robert Gates, "We Can't Delay This Treaty," *Washington Post*, November 15, 2010; "Remarks by President Barack Obama," Prague, Czech Republic, April 5, 2009.

32. Steven Pifer, "The Next Round—The United States and Nuclear Arms Reductions after New START" (Washington, D.C.: Brookings Institution, 2010). For a summa-

rized version, see Steven Pifer, "After New START: What's Next?" *Arms Control Today* 40 (December 2010).

33. In a recent book, nonproliferation scholar James Acton lays out a multistep blueprint for cutting U.S. and Russian nuclear stockpiles to 500 weapons each and cutting other nuclear powers' arsenals by at least half and explains that achieving deep reductions will be extremely difficult, both for technical and political reasons. See James Acton, *Low Numbers—A Practical Path to Deep Nuclear Reductions* (Washington, D.C.: Carnegie Endowment for International Peace, 2011), and *Deterrence during Disarmament—Deep Nuclear Reductions and International Security* (London: Adelphi Books, 2011).

34. Desmond Butler, "U.S. Reviewing Nuclear Arsenal with Eye to New Cuts," Associated Press, March 23, 2011.

35. Gary Samore, interviewed by Peter Crail, Daniel Horner, and Daryl G. Kimball, "Pursuing the Prague Agenda: An Interview with White House Coordinator Gary Samore," *Arms Control Today* 41 (May 2011), http://www.armscontrol.org/act/2011_05/Samore.

36. Analysts Ralph Cossa and Brad Glosserman point out: "Few countries were as anxious to see the publication of the 2010 U.S. Nuclear Posture Review (NPR) Report as Japan." See "Extended Deterrence and Disarmament—Japan and the New U.S. Nuclear Posture," *Nonproliferation Review* 18 (March 2011): 125.

37. Gary Samore, remarks at "International Perspectives on the Nuclear Posture Review," Carnegie Endowment for International Peace, Washington, D.C., April 22, 2010.

38. *Nuclear Posture Review Report* (Washington, D.C.: Department of Defense, 2010), 15, 17.

39. Ibid., 15.

40. Morton Halperin, remarks at "Understanding New START and the Nuclear Posture Review," Arms Control Association, Washington, D.C., April 9, 2010, http://www.armscontrol.org/events/startandnprbriefing.

41. *Nuclear Posture Review Report*, 16, 25. The NPR, however, indicates that efforts to prevent accidental and unauthorized launches and to maximize the time available to the president to consider whether to authorize the use of nuclear weapons should continue.

42. *Nuclear Posture Review Report*, xiii. How much share of the deterrence burden the U.S. non-nuclear strategic force will take on remains so far an open question. For a discussion on this issue, see Brad Roberts, speech delivered at the conference on Conventional Deterrence in the Second Nuclear Age, Carnegie Endowment for International Peace, Washington, D.C., November 17, 2010, http://carnegieendowment.org/events/?fa=eventDetail&id=3070.

43. *Nuclear Posture Review Report*, 37–43.

44. For an overview, see Cole Harvey, "Nuclear Stockpile Modernization: Issues

and Background," James Martin Center for Nonproliferation Studies, February 15, 2010, http://www.nti.org/e_research/e3_nuclear_stockpile_modernization.html.

45. "U.S. Department of Defense Fiscal Year 2011 Budget Request," February 1, 2010, http://comptroller.defense.gov/budget.html; and Joe Biden, "The President's Nuclear Vision," *Wall Street Journal*, January 28, 2010.

46. "The New START Treaty—Maintaining a Strong Nuclear Deterrent," release from the White House, May 13, 2010, http://www.bits.de/NRANEU/docs/New%20START%20section%201251%20fact%20sheet.pdf.

47. "Gates: Nuclear Weapons and Deterrence in the 21st Century," transcript of remarks by Robert Gates, Carnegie Endowment for International Peace, Washington, D.C., October 28, 2008; and Gates, "A Balanced Strategy: Reprogramming the Pentagon for a New Age," *Foreign Affairs* 88 (January/February 2009): 28–40.

48. JASON Defense Advisory Panel, "Lifetime Extension Program (LEP) Executive Summary," JSR-09-334E, September 9, 2009; "Lab Directors Question Report on Warhead Reliability," *Global Security Newswire*, March 29, 2010.

49. "Nuclear Program Has Air Force Both Worried and Hopeful," *Global Security Newswire*, September 14, 2010.

50. Thomas D'Agostino, "Unprecedented Commitment to Modernize," *Washington Times*, December 13, 2010.

51. For an analysis of the FY2012 budget request, see Hans Kristensen, "The Nuclear Weapons Modernization Budget," *FAS Strategic Security Blog*, February 17, 2011.

52. See H.R. 1750, 112th Cong., 1st sess., May 5, 2011, http://www.gpo.gov/fdsys/pkg/BILLS-112hr1750ih/pdf/BILLS-112hr1750ih.pdf.

53. "Remarks by President Barack Obama," Prague.

54. Hillary Clinton, "Remarks at CTBT Article XIV Conference," UN Headquarters, New York, September 24, 2009.

55. Josh Rogin, "Push for Controversial Nuke Treaty Expected Next Spring at the Earliest," *Foreign Policy*, October 2, 2009.

56. "Keynote: Senator Jon Kyl," speech transcript, Carnegie International Nuclear Policy Conference, March 29, 2011. D'Agostino, reported in Daryl G. Kimball, "Reconsider the Nuclear Test Ban," *Arms Control Today* 41 (April 2011). In general, the arms control community is in favor of U.S. ratification. For counter-arguments to Kyl's, see Charles D. Ferguson and Stephen Herzog, "Kyl Should Reconsider Opposition to Nuclear Test Ban," *The Hill*, March 30, 2011.

57. William Perry and James Schlesinger, *America's Strategic Posture: The Final Report of the Congressional Commission on the Strategic Posture of the United States* (Washington, D.C.: U.S. Institute of Peace, 2009), xiii. Facilitated by the U.S. Institute of Peace in 2008–9, this commission was tasked by Congress to "examine and make recommendations with respect to the long-term strategic posture of the United States."

58. "Remarks by Rose E. Gottemoeller, Assistant Secretary of State for Arms Control, Verification, and Compliance, to the First (Disarmament and International Security) Committee of the United Nations General Assembly," UN Headquarters, New York, October 5, 2010.

59. "Pressing a Broad Agenda for Combating Nuclear Dangers: An Interview with Undersecretary of State for Arms Control and International Security Ellen Tauscher," interviewed by Daniel Horner and Tom Collina, *Arms Control Today* 39 (November 2009): 8–9.

60. Ellen Tauscher, "Remarks at the Third Nuclear Deterrence Summit," Arlington, Va., February 16, 2011.

61. For an update on CTBT's verification regime, see http://www.ctbto.org/verification-regime/.

62. Chris Schneidmiller, "Senate Decision Key to Future Test Ban Treaty," *Global Security Newswire*, July 18, 2011, http://gsn.nti.org/gsn/nw_20110714_9351.php.

63. Paul Meyer, "Breakthrough and Breakdown at the Conference on Disarmament: Assessing the Prospects for an FM(C)T," *Arms Control Today* 39 (September 2009).

64. Hillary Clinton, "Remarks at the Conference on Disarmament," Geneva, Switzerland, February 28, 2011; Ban Ki-moon, "Remarks to Advisory Board on Disarmament," Conference on Disarmament, Geneva, Switzerland, February 24, 2011.

65. "U.S. Plans Push for Nuclear Material Ban: Official," Reuters, December 28, 2010.

66. Experts generally agree that verifying an FMCT would not be impossible, but that it would be extremely challenging and costly. See *Banning the Production of Fissile Materials for Nuclear Weapons: Country Perspectives on the Challenges to a Fissile Material (Cutoff) Treaty* (Princeton, N.J.: International Panel on Fissile Materials, 2008), notably 64–69.

67. "Communiqué of the Washington Nuclear Security Summit," White House, Washington, D.C., April 13, 2010; "Work Plan of the Washington Nuclear Security Summit," White House, Washington, D.C., April 13, 2010.

68. "Statement by U.S. Energy Secretary Steven Chu at the IAEA General Conference," Vienna, September 21, 2010.

69. "Fact Sheet—Increasing Transparency in the U.S. Nuclear Weapons Stockpile," release from the Department of Defense, May 3, 2010, http://www.defense.gov/npr/docs/10-05-03_fact_sheet_us_nuclear_transparency__final_w_date.pdf.

70. Hillary Clinton, "Remarks at the Review Conference of the Nuclear Nonproliferation Treaty," United Nations, New York, May 3, 2010.

71. "Statement on Nuclear Free Zones in Asia and Africa," White House, Washington, D.C., May 2, 2011.

72. William Potter, Patricia Lewis, Gaukhar Mukhatzhanova, and Miles Pomper, *The*

2010 NPT Review Conference: Deconstructing Consensus (Monterey, Calif.: CNS Special Report, 2010), 8.

73. "Final Document," NPT/CONF.2010/50(Vol.I), 2010 NPT Review Conference, May 28, 2010, 21.

74. For a study on the origins of the UK nuclear deterrent, see Ian Clark and Nicholas Wheeler, *The British Origins of Nuclear Strategy—1945–1955* (New York: Oxford University Press, 1989).

75. For a history on the evolution of UK nuclear capabilities, see Lawrence Freedman, "British Perspectives on Nuclear Weapons and Nuclear Disarmament" in *National Perspectives on Nuclear Disarmament* (Washington, D.C.: Henry L. Stimson Center, 2010), 290–302.

76. Not surprisingly, because they have to fit U.S. missiles, UK warheads are based on U.S. designs: the current UK warhead for Trident is similar to the U.S. W-76 warhead. Note that the apparent planned incorporation of the U.S. upgraded W-76-1 warhead into the UK nuclear deterrent was revealed in a recent report by the Sandia National Laboratories. See *LABS Accomplishments* (Albuquerque, N.M.: Sandia National Laboratories, 2011).

77. A "MIRVed" warhead is the abbreviation for a "Multiple Independently Targetable Reentry Vehicle" warhead, i.e., a cluster of nuclear weapons carried on a single missile.

78. *Options for Change* (London: Ministry of Defence, 1990).

79. *Strategic Defense Review* (London: Ministry of Defence, 1998).

80. London has offered security assurances to the Latin American, South Pacific, and African NWFZ treaties, but not to the Southeast Asian and the Central Asian ones.

81. *Strategic Defense Review: A New Chapter* (London: Ministry of Defence, 2002), 12.

82. *The Future of the United Kingdom's Nuclear Deterrent* (London: Ministry of Defence, 2006).

83. *Working Group on Scotland without Nuclear Weapons* (Edinburgh: Scottish Government, 2009).

84. "General Calls for Trident Rethink," BBC News, January 29, 2009.

85. Field Marshal Lord Bramall, General Lord Ramsbotham, and General Sir Hugh Beach, "UK Does Not Need a Nuclear Deterrent," *Times* (London), January 16, 2009.

86. "UK Must Not Rush to Replace Nuclear Deterrent, Ex-Officials Says," *Global Security Newswire*, January 22, 2010.

87. Edwin Bramall, David Ramsbotham, Hugh Beach, and Patrick Cordingley, "Money Spent on Trident Can't Go on Troops," *Times*, April 21, 2010.

88. *Shared Responsibilities—A National Security Strategy for the UK* (London: Institute for Public Policy Research, 2009).

89. "Political Poll for the Independent 8 September 2009," http://www.comres.co.uk/page1901083022.aspx.

90. Richard Norton-Taylor, "Gordon Brown Considers Cut in Nuclear Warheads as Part of 'Global Bargain,'" *Guardian*, September 23, 2009; Norton-Taylor, "Arms Chiefs Question Need for Trident Nuclear Deterrent," *Guardian*, February 23, 2010.

91. Michael Evans, "Deterrence Cannot Be Guaranteed with Three Subs, Says Army Chief," *Times*, November 18, 2009.

92. Menzies Campbell, *Policy Options for the Future of the United Kingdom's Nuclear Weapons* (London: Policy Paper for the Liberal Democrats, 2010).

93. Quoted in Oliver Bloom, "The UK Elections and the Future of Trident," *CSIS Blog*, May 12, 2010.

94. Quoted in Oliver Bloom, "In Spite of British Austerity Measures, Trident Replacement Here to Stay," *CSIS Blog*, June 22, 2010.

95. *Securing Britain in an Age of Uncertainty: The Strategic Defense and Security Review* (London: Ministry of Defence, 2010), 38. See also "Fact Sheet 10: Trident Value for Money Review," release from the Cabinet Office, October 19, 2010, http://download.cabinetoffice.gov.uk/sdsr/factsheet10-trident-value-for-money-review.pdf.

96. The SDSR indicates that under the MDA, UK, and U.S. authorities have determined that a replacement warhead is not required until at least the late 2030s. The review concludes that with sufficient investment, the United Kingdom can safely operate the existing Vanguard-class SSBN into the late 2020s and early 2030s—a position that several high-ranking naval officers have contested, stressing that prolonging the operational lives of SSBN would jeopardize the nation's ability to keep at least one SSBN at sea at all times.

97. The SDSR stresses that together with Washington, London will proceed with a common design for the missile compartment that provides that capacity.

98. Alex Barker, "Fox Casts Doubts on Savings from Trident Delay," *Financial Times*, November 8, 2010.

99. "The United Kingdom's Future Nuclear Deterrent: The Submarine Initial Gate Parliamentary Report" (London: Ministry of Defence, May 2011).

100. "UK-France Summit 2010 Declaration on Defence and Security Cooperation," London, November 2, 2010.

101. *Securing Britain in an Age of Uncertainty*, 37–38. A "material breach" is generally defined as a breach of a provision that undermines the intent of the treaty. By employing this term, London's qualification of its NSA is more restrictive than the language of the U.S. NPR. Similar to the NPR, the SDSR adds that this assurance can be reviewed depending on the future threat, development, and proliferation of chemical and biological weapons.

102. The new commission was set up by the foreign policy think tank BASIC, the British American Security Information Council, on February 9, 2011. It is operating under the chairmanship of Lord Browne of Ladyton, former Labour secretary of state

for defense, Sir Malcolm Rifkind, former Conservative defense and foreign secretary, and Sir Menzie Campbell, former leader of the Liberal Democrats and shadow foreign secretary. The commission is scheduled to report in early 2012. For more details, see http://www.basicint.org/tridentcommission. "David Cameron 'Committed to Full Trident Replacement,'" BBC News, February 9, 2011.

103. "Remarks by Margaret Beckett, Secretary of State for Foreign and Commonwealth Affairs, United Kingdom," Carnegie International Nonproliferation Conference, Washington, D.C., June 25, 2007.

104. Ibid.

105. George Perkovich and James Acton, *Abolishing Nuclear Weapons* (London: Adelphi Paper no. 396, 2008).

106. Secretary Browne also drew from a speech given by Prime Minister Brown in New Delhi a month earlier. See Prime Minister Gordon Brown, "Speech at the Chamber of Commerce in Delhi," January 21, 2008. Secretary of State for Defence Des Browne, *Laying the Foundations for Multilateral Disarmament*, Conference on Disarmament, Geneva, February 5, 2008.

107. Rebecca Johnson, "United Kingdom," in *Reducing and Eliminating Nuclear Weapons: Country Perspectives on the Challenges to Nuclear Disarmament* (Princeton, N.J.: International Panel on Fissile Materials, 2010), 89.

108. "P5 Statement on Disarmament and Non-Proliferation Issues," release from the UK Foreign and Commonwealth Office, September 7, 2009, http://www.fco.gov.uk/en/news/latest-news/?view=News&id=20804873.

109. *Lifting the Nuclear Shadow: Creating the Conditions for Abolishing Nuclear Weapons* (London: Foreign and Commonwealth Office, 2009), 8.

110. Prime Minister Gordon Brown, "Speech on Nuclear Energy and Proliferation," Lancaster House, London, March 17, 2009.

111. *The Road to 2010—Addressing the Nuclear Question in the Twenty-First Century* (London: Office of Public Sector Information, 2009).

112. See Top Level Group, http://toplevelgroup.org/.

113. Nuclear Security Project, http://www.nuclearsecurityproject.org/; Douglas Hurd, Malcolm Rifkind, David Owen, and George Robertson, "Start Worrying and Learn to Ditch the Bomb," *Times*, June 30, 2008.

114. "Working Paper Submitted by Norway and the United Kingdom of Great Britain and Ireland," NPT/CONF.2010/WP, 41, *The United Kingdom-Norway Initiative: Research into the Verification of Nuclear Warhead Dismantlement*, 2010 NPT Review Conference, New York, April 26, 2010; "UK Minister Attends Review Conference Following UK Disclosure of Nuclear Stockpile," release from the Foreign and Commonwealth Office, May 26, 2010, http://www.fco.gov.uk/en/news/latest-news/?view=News&id=22285726.

115. Freedman, "British Perspectives on Nuclear Weapons," 320.

116. *Hope* is a word widely used by President Obama. See, for instance, Barack Obama, *The Audacity of Hope—Thoughts on Reclaiming the American Dream* (New York: Crown, 2008). To be fair, this is not new in American foreign (and domestic) policy, which has always had a strong idealist tradition.

117. Barack Obama, "Remarks by the President at the New Economic School Graduation," Moscow, July 7, 2009.

118. *Nuclear Posture Review Report*, 2010, vii.

119. Scott Sagan, a professor of political science at Stanford University, explains that although "these statements correctly highlight the important linkage between nuclear disarmament and nuclear nonproliferation [. . .] framing the linkage in this way—with NWS seen as responsible for disarmament and NNWS responsible for accepting nonproliferation safeguards on their nuclear power programs—is historically inaccurate and politically unfortunate" because both NWS and NNWS are—and always have been—responsible for disarmament and nonproliferation, and failing to acknowledge these shared responsibilities plague efforts to craft "a more comprehensive and more equitable implementation of the basic NPT bargains." See Scott Sagan, "Shared Responsibilities for Nuclear Disarmament," *Daedalus* 138, no. 4 (Fall 2009): 157–68.

120. "President Bush Delivers Graduation Speech at West Point," West Point, N.Y., June 1, 2002.

121. *Nuclear Posture Review Report*, 2010, iv.

122. See, for instance, James R. van De Velde, "The Impossible Challenge of Deterring 'Nuclear Terrorism' by Al Qaeda," *Studies in Conflict and Terrorism* 33 (August 2010): 682–99. There is, however, a school of thought that argues that deterring terrorists is possible. See, for instance, Gordon Drake, Warrick Paddon, and Daniel Ciechanowski, *Can We Deter Terrorists from Employing Weapons of Mass Destruction on the U.S. Homeland?* (Carlisle, Pa.: U.S. Army War College, 2003).

123. Thérèse Delpech, "Nuclear Weapons and the 'New World Order': Early Warning from Asia?" *Survival* 40 (January 1998): 57–76. In their most recent opinion piece, the Four Horsemen also stress that "the growing number of nations with nuclear arms and differing motives, aims, and ambitions poses very high and unpredictable risks and increased instability." See George Shultz, William Perry, Henry Kissinger, and Sam Nunn, "Deterrence in the Age of Nuclear Proliferation—The Doctrine of Mutual Assured Destruction Is Obsolete in the Post–Cold War Era," *Wall Street Journal*, March 7, 2011.

124. Brad Roberts, "1995 and the End of the Post–Cold War Era," in *Weapons Proliferation in the 1990s*, ed. Brad Roberts (Cambridge, Mass.: MIT Press, 1995), 469.

125. William Walker, "Nuclear Order and Disorder," *International Affairs* 76 (October 2000): 709.

126. *National Security Strategy* (Washington, D.C.: White House, 2010), 1.

127. For further explanations on this point, see "Nuclear Posture Review," tran-

script of the Department of Defense Bloggers Roundtable with Bradley H. Roberts and John E. Roberti, Washington, D.C., April 6, 2010, http://www.defense.gov/Blog_files/Blog_assets/20100406_NPR_transcript.pdf; and "Nuclear Posture Review," transcript of briefings with James Cartwright, Thomas D'Agostino, Robert J. Einhorn, and Bradley H. Roberts (presided by James M. Lindsay), Council on Foreign Relations, Washington, D.C., April 8, 2010, http://www.cfr.org/publication/21861/nuclear_posture_review.html.

128. Frank Gaffney, "Peace through Weakness," February 16, 2009, http://www.centerforsecuritypolicy.org/p17891.xml. For other critics see, for instance, John Kyl and Richard Perle, "Our Decaying Nuclear Deterrent—The Less Credible the U.S. Deterrent, the More Likely Other States Are to Seek Weapons," *Wall Street Journal*, June 30, 2009; or Melanie Kirkpatrick, "Why We Don't Want a Nuclear-Free World: The Former Defense Secretary on the U.S. Deterrent and the Terrorist Threat," *Wall Street Journal*, July 13, 2009.

129. *Nuclear Posture Review Report*, 2010, iv.

130. Note that U.S. allies and partners in Asia and the Middle East appear more wedded to *nuclear* security guarantees than U.S. allies and partners in Europe, where discussions about the removal U.S. forward-deployed nuclear weapons from Europe have intensified. See Lukasz Kulesa, "Roma Locuta, Causa Finita? The Nuclear Posture Review and the Future of U.S. Nuclear Weapons in Europe," *Proliferation Analysis*, April 27, 2010.

131. For a review, see Robert Norris and Hans Kristensen, "U.S. Tactical Nuclear Weapons in Europe, 2011," *Bulletin of the Atomic Scientists* 67 (January/February 2011), 64–73.

132. "Strategic Concept for the Defence and Security of the Members of the North Atlantic Treaty Organisation Adopted by the Heads of State and Government in Lisbon," *Active Engagement, Modern Defence*, Lisbon, November 19, 2010.

133. Note, however, that in the case of Europe and U.S. TNW, a recent comprehensive report concludes that there is sufficient political will within NATO to end deployment of such U.S. weapons on the European continent. The report indicates that Alliance cohesion, Russian reciprocity, and French resistance are the three main obstacles. See Susi Snyder and Wilbert van der Zeijden, *Withdrawal Issues—What NATO Countries Say about the Future of Tactical Nuclear Weapons in Europe* (Utrecht: IKV Pax Christi, 2011).

134. Mark Smith, "Disarmament in the Anglo-American Context," in *Nuclear Weapons after the 2010 NPT Review Conference* (Paris: European Union Institute for Security Studies, 2010), 83.

135. Nikolai Sokov and Miles Pomper, "New START Ratification: A Bittersweet Success," *CNS Feature Stories*, December 22, 2010.

136. See, notably, Paul Nitze, "Is It Time to Junk Our Nukes? The New World Dis-

order Makes Them Obsolete," *Washington Post*, January 16, 1994; Andrew Krepinevich and Steven Kosiak, "Smarter Bombs, Fewer Nukes," *Bulletin of the Atomic Scientists* 54 (November/December 1998): 26–32; and Paul Nitze, "A Threat Mostly to Ourselves," *New York Times*, October 28, 1999. In fact, the debate over the potential of advanced conventional weapons to allow a de-emphasis or replacement of nuclear weapons dates back from the mid-1970s, when the Pentagon-led Long-Range Research and Development Planning (LRRDP) program was launched. For a history, see Christopher Ford, "Conventional 'Replacement' of Nuclear Weapons?" Paper delivered at the conference on Conventional Deterrence in the Second Nuclear Age.

137. "Remarks by Margaret Beckett."

138. Mark Smith, "The United Kingdom and Nuclear Nonproliferation" in *U.S.-European Nonproliferation Perspectives* (Washington, D.C.: Center for Strategic and International Studies, 2009), 34.

139. Ibid., 38. Developing a rationale for an independent UK deterrent without repudiating the U.S. nuclear guarantee and NATO did not come without issues. It was solved when London shifted from an air-launched force to an arsenal mainly based on SSBN (because the latter made the premature outbreak of nuclear war less likely) and adopted the concept of multiple decision centers. London stressed its full confidence in the U.S. guarantee but explained that a second center of "nuclear decision" adds uncertainty to an adversary's calculations.

140. Michael Quinlan, "The Future of United Kingdom Nuclear Weapons: Shaping the Debate," *International Affairs* 82 (July 2006): 634.

141. *Future of the United Kingdom's Nuclear Deterrent*, 6.

142. Liam Fox, quoted in John Gittings, "After Trident: Proliferation or Peace?" *International Relations* 21 (2007): 391.

143. *Securing Britain in an Age of Uncertainty*, 37.

144. Freedman, "British Perspectives on Nuclear Weapons," 309.

145. *Future of the United Kingdom's Nuclear Deterrent*, 5.

146. Michael Quinlan, quoted in Nick Ritchie, "Relinquishing Nuclear Weapons: Identities, Networks, and the British Bomb," *International Affairs* 86 (March 2010): 471.

147. For an analysis, see ibid., 474–79.

CHAPTER TWO

Advocating the Elimination of Nuclear Weapons

The Role of Key Individual and Coalition States

Marianne Hanson

ALTHOUGH IT IS ARGUABLE THAT the high-profile opinion articles in the *Wall Street Journal* by George Shultz, William Perry, Henry Kissinger, and Sam Nunn in 2007 and 2008 galvanized the current debate on eliminating nuclear weapons and influenced the Obama administration to pursue such a policy actively, this disarmament agenda must be seen within the broader context of a long campaign by a particular group of states.[1] These articles, immensely important though they were, reflected what had been a series of arguments put forward by various state actors over the preceding dozen or so years. This chapter explores how the foundation for today's push toward "nuclear zero" was developed and kept alive by several key states that from the mid-1990s put forward a policy of seeking the elimination of nuclear weapons and that maintained this position even in the face of serious reversals in nuclear arms control (as was seen during the George W. Bush administration).[2] Without the many years of hard work and norm building conducted by what this chapter refers to as the "advocacy states," policies promoting nuclear elimination would almost certainly have had more difficulty gaining traction in the United States and on a global level. The major diplomatic and political activities aimed at eliminating nuclear weapons in the 1990s and 2000s were driven not by the United States but by these advocacy states, often small- or midsized nations, sometimes known as "middle powers." It is important to examine the role played by these actors, not just because this provides a more complete picture of causal factors and U.S. decisions, but also because these states, collectively and individually, continue to be important voices in the ongoing politics of nuclear weapons elimination.

Although it might seem surprising, given that a chief focus of their efforts was to persuade the United States to embrace disarmament, these states have been generally (and sometimes closely) aligned with the United States.[3] Unlike the calls for disarmament in earlier decades, which had come largely from the Non-Aligned Movement (NAM) states and the more strident critics of Western security policies, the prominent and activist voices are now largely Western states advocating, as necessary requirements for global security, a devaluing of the role of nuclear weapons in security doctrines, faster reductions, and the ultimate elimination of these weapons. The pressure they have placed on the nuclear weapon states (NWS), and especially on the United States, to move toward disarmament has been evident in multilateral diplomacy, as well as in the reports and analyses they have sponsored. The most prominent of these advocacy states have been Australia, Canada, Ireland, Japan, New Zealand, Norway, and Sweden.[4] And while the initiatives in which they participated often included other states—Brazil, Chile, Egypt, Indonesia, Mexico, and South Africa—the focus of this chapter is primarily on those drivers of disarmament norms notable for their Western orientation (if not outright alliance with the United States) and their prominent voice in multilateral and plurilateral forums.

This chapter, therefore, does not examine the activities of the 118-member NAM (or indeed other state groupings such as the Group of Eight—G8—states). Although there are some individual states within such groupings that have been active in seeking disarmament, the groupings have not been established specifically for the cause of nuclear disarmament. The NAM has, of course, been very vocal at forums such as the United Nations (UN) General Assembly's First Committee and the Conference on Disarmament (CD), at Nuclear Nonproliferation Treaty (NPT) Review Conferences (RevCons), and in the International Atomic Energy Agency (IAEA), and it is a very important force in disarmament debates. Nevertheless, it is composed of very diverse states, some of which have developed nuclear weapons. Moreover, in disarmament advocacy has invariably occurred when NAM members have acted in the disarmament-specific coalitions examined below. Other regional groupings have also been active,[5] but it is the issue-specific coalitions—which also happen to be Western led—that are examined here.

THE ADVOCACY STATES: ACTIVITIES FROM THE 1990S TO 2010

The advocacy states share a conviction that although nuclear weapons cannot be dis-invented, their possession and use, and their eventual elimination, can nevertheless be managed by strong norms and regulatory institutions, elements that the advocacy states have sought to uphold, strengthen, and publicize widely. This perception developed independently of U.S. policy preferences regarding nuclear weapons and indeed ran counter to these preferences.[6] It was a post–Cold War evaluation of what constituted a sound basis for global security, emanating primarily from states aligned with the West but differing significantly from the nuclear weapons beliefs and practices held by the United States, the main driver of Western security policy.

From the mid-1990s, the advocacy states—all non-nuclear weapon states (NNWS)—had engaged in various measures in pursuit of nuclear disarmament. Their call was not for unilateral U.S. disarmament, but rather for phased, balanced, and verifiable moves toward the eventual elimination of nuclear weapons—in other words, a cautious approach to a global project. Their various reports and representations have all accepted that the security concerns of the NWS would need to be effectively addressed during any moves to zero. Equally, however, they believed that the risks of use of nuclear weapons and of nuclear proliferation required that the NWS must fulfill their obligations under Article VI of the NPT to eliminate their nuclear arsenals.[7]

Promoting Investigations of the Role and Utility of Nuclear Weapons: State-Sponsored Reports

The earliest state-sponsored, formal, and studied attempt to address the issue of the dangers of nuclear weapons in the post–Cold War period was the Australian government-sponsored Canberra Commission on the Elimination of Nuclear Weapons.[8] Australia had demonstrated a general commitment to disarmament over the years and had been very active in seeking the Chemical Weapons Convention (CWC), but the Canberra Commission initiative took this commitment to a much higher level.[9] This was the first time a government had called explicitly for a serious, in-depth examination of the consequences of nuclear weapons and the options available to the international community for addressing their dangers. It was the first study to help reflect and generate a profound rethinking of the place of nuclear weapons in international security at a broad, "mainstream" level, weaving the main threads of the elimination debate together into a coherent set of proposals that subsequently gained acknowledgment and a degree of respect from both the NWS and NNWS.

Launched in 1995, the Canberra Commission was a reflection of the favorable political climate that followed the end of the Cold War, the NWS self-imposed moratorium on nuclear testing, the indefinite extension of the NPT that had taken place earlier in 1995, and the landmark agreement on the CWC two years earlier. Australia's Prime Minister Paul Keating and Foreign Minister Gareth Evans were also influenced by a series of studies on nuclear weapons elimination emanating from the Washington, D.C.–based Stimson Center and the U.S. National Academy of Sciences, as well as by later statements on nuclear weapons issued by international generals, admirals, and prominent civilian leaders. Their convening of the Canberra Commission, and an extensive range of background papers by various specialists, brought together seventeen independent commissioners with expertise on the political, legal, and strategic aspects of nuclear weapons. The commission issued its report in 1996 and called unequivocally for the phased, monitored, and verifiable reduction of the world's nuclear weapons down to zero. The report sought to address the fears of skeptics by producing a program of disarmament in which the security interests of the NWS and their allies would be taken into account and accommodated within a verifiable framework. Noting that because nuclear weapons are highly destructive and nondiscriminatory, they cannot realistically be used in war without incurring unacceptable loss of life, and that any use, accidental or deliberate, would be "catastrophic," the report's key message was that "nuclear weapons are held by a handful of states which insist that these weapons provide unique security benefits, and yet reserve uniquely to themselves the right to own them. This situation is highly discriminatory and thus unstable; it cannot be sustained." Moreover, "possession of nuclear weapons by any state is a constant stimulus to other states to acquire them."[10]

The timing of the report's release, however, coincided with the advent of a new, and more conservative, government in Australia, one that was not fond of any of its predecessor's "big-picture" global vision. As a result of this electoral change, the report's message was not promoted to the extent that the previous government wished. And when this conservative government fell more closely into line with the George W. Bush administration from 2000 onward, this was especially true.

Canada was also active in the mid- to late 1990s in promoting calls for eliminating nuclear weapons. Like Australia, Canada holds well-established credentials for supporting such a position.[11] Its ambassador to the 2000 NPT Review Conference noted that for more than half a century, "successive Canadian governments have sought the complete elimination of nuclear weapons through the steadfast implementation of unilateral, bilateral and multilateral measures."[12] In 1996, Foreign Minister Lloyd Axworthy had asked the Canadian government to review Canada's nuclear nonproliferation, arms control, and disarmament policies. Thus the Standing Committee on Foreign Affairs and International Trade (SCFAIT) was tasked with identifying policies to guide Canada's actions and to reflect its alliance commitments, in particular its North Atlantic Treaty Organization (NATO) membership.

The SCFAIT presented its report, "Canada and the Nuclear Challenge: Reducing the Political Value of Nuclear Weapons for the Twenty-First Century," in December 1998, after receiving hundreds of submissions and conducting numerous interviews and public hearings with expert witnesses, academics, politicians, nongovernmental organization (NGO) representatives, and other members of the public.[13] The report outlined fifteen steps that Canada could take to help reduce the political value of nuclear weapons. It should be noted that Axworthy requested the SCFAIT study on nuclear weapons elimination before his more famous initiative on banning landmines, the "Ottawa Process." It seems likely that, as with his political counterparts in Australia, the Canadian foreign minister was keenly attuned to the emerging body of literature and ideas that were challenging conventional thinking on the role of nuclear weapons in post–Cold War international society.

In one important respect, the Canadian study differed from the Canberra Commission report that preceded it; the SCFAIT report was produced by *national legislators*, assisted by expert testimony and public input.[14] The SCFAIT chairman noted that despite reports from the Stimson Center and the Canberra Commission and the legal opinion on nuclear weapons, there had been a lack of input from legislators. (This absence was subsequently addressed further in 2000 with the formation of Parliamentarians for Nuclear Non-Proliferation and Disarmament, a group with more than five hundred parliamentarians from seventy states and that acts as a forum for developing joint strategies to foster the elimination of nuclear weapons.)

While Canada prepared its 1998 study, the Japanese government launched its own examination of nuclear dangers and the need for disarmament, an initiative cosponsored by the Hiroshima Peace Institute and the Japan Institute of International Affairs. In many ways, the resulting report, "Facing Nuclear

Dangers: An Action Plan for the 21st Century" (or, simply, "The Tokyo Forum Report"[15]), was a direct response to the May 1998 nuclear tests conducted by India and Pakistan and to the possibility of an unraveling nonproliferation regime. Well before the South Asian tests, Ryuichi Imai, himself a former Canberra commissioner, had called on the Japanese government to establish a Japanese version of the Canberra Commission, especially given the new Australian government's reluctance to promote the commission's report.[16] The Indian and Pakistani tests added further impetus to this call. Although the Canberra Commission's report had established the foundations for a program of disarmament, it had not closely addressed the question of how to avoid further horizontal nuclear proliferation. Given that South Asia had just become the latest region of the world with nuclear weapons, Japan deliberately included in its forum representatives from India and Pakistan, as well as from other NWS and NNWS. Thus, the focus of the Tokyo Forum was very much one of balancing both nonproliferation *and* disarmament. Including twenty-three specialists and chaired by former UN undersecretary-general Yasushi Akashi, the forum was the most overt action by the Japanese government in support of the elimination of nuclear weapons. Japan had, of course, been instrumental over the years in the UN in sponsoring annual resolutions supporting nuclear disarmament, especially in the General Assembly's First Committee on Disarmament and International Security, but the forum was the first explicit Japan-sponsored examination of this important and, especially for Japan, poignant issue.

There was, however, another reason behind Japan's initiative. It had been asked to join the New Agenda Coalition (NAC), an eight-nation initiative formed in June 1998, but it had declined on the likely grounds that doing so would be problematic for its major ally, the United States. Yet Japan was caught in a difficult position. Because of its particularly close U.S. alliance, it was unwilling to support a high-profile initiative on nuclear disarmament such as that advocated by the NAC. At the same time, it wished to do something in line with domestic expectations and to differentiate itself from the NWS; its own unique place in nuclear history demanded at least some degree of moral leadership. The Tokyo Forum, therefore, was an alternative to the NAC, one that was less likely to cause concern in the United States but that also assuaged domestic opinion calling for a strong Japanese stance against nuclear weapons. In the end, however, the Japanese government distanced itself from and did not actively promote the report after its release, a likely indication of its uncertainty about such a stance and its potential domestic implications.[17]

Promoting Like-Minded Diplomatic Groupings: The Emergence of the NAC and the Seven Nation Initiative

In addition to the sponsored reports examined above, the advocacy states were active in promoting the formation of like-minded diplomatic groupings designed to place pressure on the NWS to move toward disarmament. After the indefinite extension of the NPT in 1995, and faced with the fact that the NNWS now lacked any real bargaining power to compel the NWS to disarm, a group of states formed the NAC to keep this idea prominent, lest it be relegated to the back burner by the NWS, which were now secure in the indefinite continuation of a treaty that accorded only them the "right" to possess nuclear weapons. The establishment of the NAC was thus an attempt to galvanize the elimination debate at a time when it was becoming apparent that, in contrast to the majority of states, which had yet again just forsworn possession of nuclear weapons, the NWS might be cooling to their promises of disarmament.[18]

Just after the South Asian nuclear tests, Irish foreign minister Darach MacFhionnbhairr led his counterparts from Brazil, Egypt, Mexico, New Zealand, Slovenia, South Africa, and Sweden in sending a Joint Declaration to the UN secretary-general calling for immediate action to halt proliferation and to move toward elimination. Decades earlier, in 1961, Ireland had sponsored a unanimously adopted UN General Assembly resolution calling for greater control of nuclear weapons and in June 1965 had led a UN Disarmament Commission resolution calling for all states to accord special attention to the problem of nuclear proliferation. These important early actions had presaged the basis, although not the structure, of the NPT.

Ireland's selection of its NAC partners was careful, representing a broad cross-section of like-minded states from the West, but also from the NAM. In particular, New Zealand had been an ardent advocate of non-nuclearism.[19] New Zealand had raised international headlines in the mid-1980s when it defied the United States by refusing to allow nuclear-powered or nuclear-armed vessels into its territory. Subsequently, on June 8, 1987, its conservative National government passed the New Zealand Nuclear Free Zone, Disarmament, and Arms Control Act, consolidating the country's rejection of U.S. nuclear weapon policies and leading to the suspension of New Zealand from the Australia, New Zealand, and United States Security Treaty.

New Zealand had also been instrumental in bringing the question of the legality of the use of nuclear weapons to the International Court of Justice (ICJ).

Following (and buoyed by) the 1987 nuclear-free legislation, a group of citizens was successful in mobilizing public opinion around the world, and their government pursued an anti-nuclear stance in international forums, activism that led eventually to the UN General Assembly in December 1994 seeking an advisory ruling from the ICJ.[20] New Zealand, together with Australia, had also been active in the 1970s in seeking an opinion from the ICJ on the legality of French atmospheric testing of nuclear weapons in the South Pacific. Thus while New Zealand did not produce any disarmament-specific reports for global consumption or initiate any particular grouping in the period under review here, its actions, driven clearly by ideational forces and supported in multilateral forums by its conservative and liberal governments, were important in creating a global political and legal context within which states could subsequently investigate and pursue the case for disarmament in a way that had not been possible earlier.[21]

New Zealand's involvement in the NAC followed a 1997 parliamentary inquiry into New Zealand's place in the world. A Foreign Affairs, Defence, and Trade Committee spokesperson had recommended an approach that should be "a large scale exercise, mobilizing world opinion, without any of our traditional friends being in the group of activists."[22] This presumably meant that New Zealand, while remaining within the broadly defined Western camp, was willing to (continue to) act independently of large Western powers such as the United States, Britain, and, one might add, Australia (which by 1998 had moved to a much closer political and strategic relationship with the United States).

The initial NAC statement was firm in its criticism of the NWS. Its members noted that they could "no longer remain complacent with the reluctance of the NWS and the three nuclear weapons-capable states to take that fundamental and requisite step, namely a clear commitment to the speedy, final, and total elimination of their nuclear weapons capability and we urge them to take that step now."[23] While the NAC reiterated much of what the Canberra Commission had stated, its tone was notably more pronounced. This was deliberate; the NAC sought to move beyond what it perceived as the relatively benign calls emanating from some Western states. Yet the coalition collectively did not wish to replicate the harsher statements that NAM members had employed in the past.[24] Indeed, the NAC can be seen as a carefully created attempt to bridge that gap. At the same time, it accommodated non-aligned state concerns more firmly than the Canberra Commission or the Tokyo Forum report had done.[25] Although it failed, predictably, to win support from the NWS, its UN First General Assembly resolution of 1998 (which set out a road map toward the creation of a nuclear-weapon-free world) passed overwhelmingly, with 114 states voting in favor and 18 against. There were also 38 abstentions, including Germany and Canada, which likely felt unable to vote in favor of the statement because of NATO alliance sensitivities, but which nevertheless did not wish to vote against such an initiative.[26]

The NAC's major achievement was the way in which, as a subgroup within the 2000 NPT RevCon, it negotiated a historic agreement that was put forward and eventually accepted by the NWS as part of the overall conference result. The agreement stipulated that nuclear disarmament should proceed independently of general disarmament, thus taking the language of nuclear disarmament significantly beyond that of Article VI in the NPT, which had always provided the NWS with a useful ambiguity.[27] The NAC's concerted activism at this time prompted the NWS to provide their now famous "unequivocal undertaking" to eliminate their nuclear arsenals. These states agreed clearly to adopt the detailed NAC-sponsored "Thirteen Practical Steps" for undertaking disarmament quickly, verifiably, and irreversibly.[28]

Two further NAC characteristics are worth noting here. First, in line with their desire for a more inclusive international order, NAC members were keen to emphasize the view that decisions about international security—and by extension, about nuclear weapons—were not the sole preserve of the NWS. Their position strongly evoked the need for broader processes of international negotiations and consultations, favoring plurilateral and multilateral initiatives, especially to help overcome what seemed to be ongoing impasses in the U.S.-Russian relationship. Second, the NAC was unusual in that it drew unto itself a very strong civil society following, which coalesced into the Middle Powers Initiative, and which came to be institutionalized as a supportive and important civil society body in its own right.

While the NAC was clearly not able to move disarmament further in the years following 2000, which saw the Bush administration reject most of the previous U.S. disarmament commitments, it was nevertheless revived as a promising instrument in the lead-up to the 2010 NPT Review Conference. The statement on behalf of the NAC at the 2008 NPT Preparatory Committee (PrepCom) by Don Mackay, New Zealand's permanent representative to the United Nations, reiterated a pointed need for action and at the same time offered assistance from the NAC states to the global community to achieve these goals. Mackay specified seven areas requiring urgent attention: "universality, nuclear doctrines, reductions in nuclear forces, security assurances, nuclear-weapon-free zones, negotiation of a treaty on fissile material, and a prohibition on the testing of nuclear weapons."[29]

Another prominent NAC member was Sweden. It, too, made an individual contribution to advancing disarmament norms, largely as a result of the wishes that had been expressed by its foreign minister, Anna Lindh, before her assassination in 2003. That year, Sweden had launched the Weapons of Mass Destruction (WMD) Commission, chaired by former IAEA head Hans Blix, which issued its final report in June 2006, titled *Weapons of Terror: Freeing the World of Nuclear, Biological, and Chemical Arms*.[30] Main funding for the commission's secretariat and work was provided by the Swedish government, supplemented by funding from other government and NGO sources.

In many ways, the Blix Commission (as it came to be known) reiterated the findings of the studies that preceded it. Its importance, however, lay in the timing of its work. As its members noted, while much of what the previous reports had said remained true, "the political context ha[d] changed dramatically since those Commissions reported."[31] The presence of failing states, threats from nonstate actors, and sophisticated terrorist networks now rendered a further study on the elimination of WMD essential. As former Australian foreign minister Gareth Evans, a member of the Blix Commission, noted, the preceding decade had seen a "serious, and dangerous, loss of momentum and direction in disarmament and non-proliferation efforts."[32] As such, the Blix Commission was another key example of how advocacy states—in this case Sweden—sought to keep alive a focus on nuclear weapons dangers when great powers were either not fulfilling their commitments to disarmament or were diverted by other issues. Such advocacy was necessary given that disarmament had become subordinated to a new, overarching imperative—the preoccupation with the war in Iraq, specifically, and the "war on terror," more generally.

The NAC had been created in 1998, a time when there was some impatience with the pace of nuclear arms control but nevertheless a degree of hope that some positive changes would continue to occur. By contrast, the Norwegian-led Seven-Nation Initiative to Strengthen Adherence to Nuclear Non-Proliferation and Disarmament Agreements (7NI) arose seven years later out of a sense of deep disappointment that not only was the disarmament agenda not prospering, but also that previous efforts at advancing this norm had been rolled back by the United States. This was evidenced most clearly at the 2005 NPT RevCon and the subsequent July 2005 UN World Summit. At both, the U.S. delegation refused even to allow discussion of the achievements made at previous Rev-Cons, notably, the Thirteen Practical Steps. Indeed, the 2005 statement issued by the 7NI states—Australia, Chile, Indonesia, Norway, Romania, South Africa, and the United Kingdom—noted their deep "regret that an opportunity to strengthen international resolve on nonproliferation and disarmament was missed at the 2005 Review Conference."[33] Norway nevertheless sought to salvage something from the failed Conference. Publicizing this initiative, its Foreign Minister noted that "Norway is working actively through the 7NI on nuclear disarmament and non-proliferation to build bridges over past differences, and to define the elements that could form a new international consensus."[34]

In some contrast, however, with the Blix, Canberra, Canadian, and Tokyo reports, the Norwegian government sought to support opportunities for member states and partnering organizations to engage in a range of activities designed to foster disarmament and nonproliferation, including education, technical cooperation and assistance, research, and advocacy. The initiative has fostered many projects, a large percentage of which receive support from the Royal Norwegian Ministry of Foreign Affairs. These include an examination of the critical role of developing countries in strengthening the nuclear nonproliferation regime; how it might be possible to reduce the role of nuclear weapons in national security policies (a study conducted by the Brookings Institution); how to manage a nuclear industry renaissance in ways that can prevent proliferation and augment nuclear disarmament; building a network of scientists in developing countries (a program conducted by the Carnegie Endowment for International Peace); the launching of a new regime for biotechnology safety (conducted by the Stanford University's Center for International Security and Cooperation); collating lessons learned from nuclear inspections (a project conducted by the Center on International Cooperation); promoting disarmament and nonproliferation education in developing countries; identifying core components of a possible "new package" of agreements, ahead of the 2010 NPT RevCon (conducted by the James Martin Center for Nonproliferation Studies); promoting nuclear transparency in Southeast Asia (conducted by the International Institute for Strategic Studies); promoting regional workshops on implementing UN Security Council Resolution 1540, and supporting a South Asian dialogue on bilateral fissile material control (conducted by the Verification Research, Training, and Information Centre, or VERTIC).

From these activities, it can be seen that the 7NI has been very much aimed at fostering on-the-ground practical activities and involving organizations, think tanks, academics, and others in building a close network of actors to further disarmament. Unlike earlier reports that argued strongly in favor of disarmament and nonproliferation and that created a broad normative vision, the Norwegian goal appears to be the establishment of bottom-up projects that could develop the political, educational, and especially technical building blocks necessary for confidence and trust building in the disarmament process. One of the most noteworthy of such activities between member states is the UK-Norway Initiative to verify the dismantlement of nuclear arms. Building expertise such as this—which will be essential in any move to a nuclear-weapon-free world—remains a key objective of the 7NI states, especially Norway. Indeed, these practical programs of devising small steps toward disarmament differentiate the 7NI from the NAC, which continues to act more as a diplomatic pressure group, one that places the argument for disarmament at its core. In addition to the sizable amount of funding Norway provides for these activities, it was also instrumental in hosting an international conference on disarmament and nonproliferation in February 2008 in Oslo, cosponsored by the Nuclear Threat Initiative, the Hoover Institution, and the Norwegian Radiation Protection Authority.[35]

A noteworthy and unique feature of the 7NI is its membership. Unlike previous like-minded gatherings and the sponsors of individual reports, this group includes an NWS, the United Kingdom. This was an important development, which, while reflecting British government statements about the need to eliminate nuclear weapons, brought into the grouping a country that some years earlier would have resisted incorporation into a group dedicated to fostering the elimination of nuclear weapons. Given that the 7NI is a relatively new endeavor, it remains to be seen how this novel interaction between an NWS and its non-nuclear partners might provide new insights or how the work program might affect future directions in the call for disarmament. It seems likely that the initiative's fostering of grassroots advocacy, research, and technical activities will grow rather than diminish, especially in light of the pro-disarmament atmosphere generated by the 2010 NPT RevCon.

Renewed Initiatives with New Leadership in Washington

Not surprisingly, the advocacy states have stepped up their activities since the election of U.S. president Barack Obama in 2008, sensing an opportunity for their views to receive a more favorable reception by the NWS, thanks to the new U.S. commitment to disarmament. Moreover, and in line with the earlier point that changes in government affected the extent to which certain states continued to advocate for disarmament, Australia's 2007 election generated new momentum for its disarmament activities. After eleven years in opposition, during which a conservative government had aligned itself more closely with the United States and its "war on terror," the new Australian Labor government, under Prime Minister Kevin Rudd, promised that it would revive the ideas of the 1996 Canberra Commission and resuscitate the philosophy of "good international citizenship." Tellingly, government members saw a new commitment to disarmament as "repairing" Australia's reputation in this field.[36]

In line with this decision, Rudd announced during a visit to Japan in 2008 that Australia would launch the International Commission on Nuclear Non-Proliferation and Disarmament (ICNND), to be cochaired by former Australian and Japanese foreign ministers Gareth Evans and Yoriko Kawaguchi, respectively.[37] The initiative was expressly designed to "reinvigorate international efforts in non-proliferation and disarmament in the context of both the 2010 Non-Proliferation Treaty Review Conference and beyond."[38] But because previous reports had already—and repeatedly—made the argument for disarmament, the new Commission was more empirically focused, addressing the opportunities, as well as potential obstacles, flagged by the commitment to disarmament made in Barack Obama's 2008 election campaign.

The commission has targeted its message primarily at politicians, making the case for nuclear disarmament in a way that is clear and unequivocal but that also addresses the risks and challenges that a process of disarmament will inevitably bring. Indicative of the wish to ensure as wide an audience for the commission's ideas as possible, and keen to project its studies as serious-minded and realistic examinations, one of the four *Wall Street Journal* op-ed writers, William Perry, is a commissioner, while the other three, George Schultz, Henry Kissinger, and Sam Nunn, have been appointed to the ICNND's Advisory Board. Like the 7NI, the ICNND has commissioned a range of studies. These address a plethora of political and strategic factors associated with nuclear reductions and the non-proliferation regime, including questions of verification, missile defense, the future of tactical nuclear weapons, the growing proliferation risks associated with the nuclear fuel cycle, regional security issues, and many more.[39] The commission has convened numerous meetings around the world, including in February 2009 in Washington, D.C., where commissioners expressed that what they heard from the U.S. administration was greatly encouraging.[40] This, together with meetings in China, Russia, and Japan and regional outreach meetings in Latin

America, the Middle East, South Asia, and Northeast Asia, enabled the commission to publish its first report in December 2009, in time for presentation at the 2010 NPT RevCon. The report was listed as "practical and action-oriented," incorporating short-, medium-, and long-term dimensions.[41] It is likely that the commission, in a reconvened form, will continue its work into the future, conscious of the fact that earlier reports that produced only one document and that were limited in time were at risk of being neglected by subsequent governments.[42] In sum, the ICNND has been designed as an ongoing and pragmatic initiative designed to foster a long-term goal of eventual disarmament.

The Australia-Japan initiative has been supplemented by a loose grouping, as announced in September 2010 in New York, in which the foreign ministers of both states (with former prime minister Rudd by now in a new role as Australian foreign minister) have sought to promote nuclear disarmament and nonproliferation. While not disengaging itself from the 7NI, which remains an informal grouping in its own right, albeit one driven largely by Norway, its initiator, Australia has continued to focus attention on nuclear weapons elimination at the highest diplomatic level. In this latest forum, Rudd and Japanese minister Maehara have led Canada, Chile, Germany, Mexico, the Netherlands, Poland, and Turkey in a disarmament initiative for a world with "a decreased nuclear risk," and with the hope of placing pressure on states such as North Korea and Iran to adhere to norms of nonproliferation.[43]

For its part, Norway, in addition to convening the 7NI, since the election of Obama has focused much of its attention on petitioning NATO to remove tactical nuclear weapons from Europe. Together with Germany, Belgium, the Netherlands, and Luxembourg, all states that have been keen to address the thorny question of the alliance's nuclear future, it succeeded in placing the issue on the agenda for discussion at the NATO meeting in Estonia in April 2010.[44] While it was unlikely that this advocacy would have resulted in any removal of NATO's tactical nuclear weapons from European soil in the short term (and particularly given the Baltic NATO members' continuing mistrust of Russia),[45] the debate gained significant momentum throughout 2010. It resulted in the new Strategic Doctrine unveiled in Lisbon in November 2010 downplaying somewhat the previously central role that had been assigned to nuclear weapons in the 1999 NATO document. Importantly, the new Strategic Doctrine stated in its preface that its members "will seek to create the conditions for further reductions in the future."[46] This advocacy has clearly placed expectations on NATO's leadership to reassess the role of nuclear weapons in current international security dynamics.

While it is thus unlikely that real change in NATO's nuclear deployment is imminent, the campaigning by states such as Norway has meant that the Alliance will inevitably have to reconsider the issue in line with what is bound to be an ongoing scrutiny of its nuclear policies.

Another issue that has engaged many of the advocacy states recently is whether nuclear weapons elimination can be enhanced by the imminent negotiation of a nuclear weapons convention (NWC). This question has emerged more clearly than ever after the 2010 NPT RevCon, given the debates there on whether a convention should be pursued as a means of accelerating disarmament. The advocacy states have shown varying opinions on this question, but all appear to be more receptive to the idea than they were some years ago. This shift is in large part due to the outcome of the 2010 RevCon, whose final document made mention, for the first time and despite resistance from the NWS, that many countries now wished to see negotiations commence for a legal document banning nuclear weapons.[47] There had been—especially among the civil society actors from the advocacy states—a long history of such calls, but these had not taken on the prominence and visibility that they were able to gain in the lead-up to, the negotiations during, and the aftermath of the 2010 Conference.

The positions shown by the advocacy states on this issue vary somewhat and are not necessarily reflective of the degree of support for nuclear disarmament otherwise shown by their governments. In fact, Austria and Switzerland (rather than the advocacy states examined here) called most loudly for the creation of an NWC at the 2010 Conference and continue to lobby for such an outcome, clearly advocating for this in the UN General Assembly and NPT forums. Nonetheless, Ireland, New Zealand, Norway, and Sweden have all indicated general support for it in their statements and votes at international gatherings. Ireland has claimed that while it is not opposed to the idea, it believes that "the pursuit of a convention now could distract from the more immediate challenge of implementing agreed measures related to the NPT."[48] Even so, Ireland "sees a nuclear weapons convention as a medium- to long-term goal" and votes in favor of the annual UN General Assembly resolution calling for the immediate commencement of negotiations leading to a convention.[49] New Zealand has been more clearly supportive: it called for negotiation of a convention and has voted unambiguously in favor of the relevant General Assembly resolutions. Indicative of the strong and bipartisan New Zealand support for the elimination of nuclear weapons, during the 2010 RevCon the New Zealand Parliament unanimously adopted a resolution calling on its government to work with other nations to give serious consideration to an NWC.⁵⁰ Norway's government, too, believes that eventually a legal instrument will be required,⁵¹ and it has cosponsored events with a key NGO, the International Campaign to Abolish Nuclear Weapons to explore the feasibility of an NWC. However, it voted against the 2009 UN General Assembly resolution calling for a convention.⁵² Norway had expressed concern, with some justification, that the 2009 UN General Assembly resolution was premised on the view that a convention would be negotiated in the CD, a forum whose "functionality and universality" remained in doubt.⁵³ Sweden, for its part, has voted in favor of UN General Assembly resolutions calling for a convention, but it has resisted calls by civil society to advocate for such a convention in international forums.⁵⁴

Australia, Japan, and Canada have been less receptive to calls for a convention, making any support for such a process conditional and suggesting that they would rather focus their attention on the unfinished business of existing treaties and agreements. Australia has agreed that a convention might be necessary in the longer term for the achievement of a nuclear-weapon-free world,⁵⁵ but it has decided not to advocate for its negotiation yet. Its position is that it will focus its diplomatic efforts on what it considers to be more immediate goals toward achieving a world free of nuclear weapons, namely, the conclusion of currently incomplete processes such as the Comprehensive Nuclear-Test-Ban Treaty (CTBT) and a fissile material cut-off treaty (FMCT).⁵⁶ The ICNND had noted that detailed work on a convention could commence now, with government support, and the Australian Joint Standing Committee on Treaties, a cross-party parliamentary committee, had recommended unanimously in September 2009 that Australia make clear in international forums its support for an NWC.⁵⁷ However, the Australian government has stated that it does not see this as something to be pursued in the short term. (The ICNND, although initiated by the Australian government in 2008, and cosponsored by Japan, remains an independent body, and its report and recommendations do not necessarily reflect the official policies of the Australian and Japanese governments.) Still, the Australian government has shown some movement on the question of a convention: under the conservative Howard government, it had voted against the annual UN resolutions; by 2009, it was abstaining from, rather than opposing, such a position.⁵⁸ Canada, too, has abstained on these UN General Assembly votes, but in an indication of a possible shift, the Canadian Senate in June 2010 adopted a motion endorsing the UN secretary-general's five-point plan on nuclear disarmament and encouraging the Canadian government to engage in negotiations for an NWC.⁵⁹

Much of the sentiment regarding an NWC seems to be based on the differing views of the timing of such a convention, uncertainty about what a convention would actually do, and how it might contribute to zero. For those who advocate that it is necessary now, an NWC is seen as something that can help to sustain the momentum by providing a missing legal (and moral) framework, a framework that would be supplementary to existing endeavors. For others, an NWC will be necessary only when we are actually at or close to zero; from this perspective, calls for negotiating a convention now are seen as unnecessary and distracting.

EXPLANATIONS AND MOTIVATIONS: SETTING A NORMATIVE CONTEXT FOR ADVOCACY STATE BEHAVIOR

From the above activities, it can be seen that the advocacy states have invested considerable political, diplomatic, and, in some cases, financial capital in promoting calls for the elimination of nuclear weapons. And, indeed, the shift in the way that nuclear weapons have come to be viewed can be attributed to a large extent to the activities of these states. At the heart of their activities is a set of motivations that have driven them to export the call for nuclear weapons elimination to a global level. This section of this chapter examines the ideas that pushed these states to sustain their advocacy campaigns, even when it was evident that little progress could be made for many years. The driving factors in their thinking include both material and ideational elements, reflecting both a pragmatic and a principled approach to the problem of nuclear weapons. Appearing in the various reports and statements put forward by these states, these factors can be broken down into five interrelated motivations.

The first of these motivations revolves around humanitarian factors. Ethical considerations against the use of nuclear weapons were not new in the 1990s and 2000s, but they came to take on an additional prominence at the turn of the century.[60] Thus Norway states that it seeks to pursue humanitarian policies, such as nuclear weapons elimination, as a matter of responsibility, and "unfettered by other political and strategic considerations."[61] In their various reports, the advocacy states argued that as nuclear weapons will inevitably cause massive loss of civilian life, the use—and, by implication, the threat of use—of these weapons violates international humanitarian law that seeks to regulate the conduct of warfare.[62] The two core principles of humanitarian law—which specify that parties to a conflict must distinguish between combatants and noncombatants, and that such parties are prohibited from causing superfluous injury or unnecessary suffering—would certainly be violated by resorting to nuclear warfare. The mention in the 2010 RevCon—for the first time in NPT debates—that nuclear weapons pose a threat to international humanitarian law was a keen reflection of how much this element of humanitarianism has now come to color views on this issue.[63]

A second factor concerns the strategic case against nuclear weapons. As practical instruments of warfare, nuclear weapons were perceived by these states to have no military utility or, at best, an extremely limited utility. As the various reports and studies implied, such weapons are unsuitable for achieving strategic goals; their use, advocacy states point out, would most likely negate any perceived military or political benefit. In any case, the advent of sophisticated conventional weapons rendered the more indiscriminate and unpredictable nature of a nuclear strike unlikely to be chosen as a preferred alternative. When examining the consequences attendant on nuclear use in war-fighting scenarios, states active in disarmament norms concluded that it was hard to mount an argument that nuclear weapons retained any strategic utility.

Third among the advocacy states' motivations was the need to create a climate in international security more conducive to reversing and halting nuclear proliferation. Given that nuclear nonproliferation is a fundamental goal shared by the vast majority of the international community, a strong case can be made for the complete elimination of nuclear weapons as vital to strengthening this goal.[64] Central to this issue is the inequality inherent in the NPT, which enables a select group of states to retain nuclear arsenals while denying them to other states. Reinforcing a strong taboo against the possession of nuclear weapons by *any* state was thus seen as a crucial factor in addressing the problem of proliferation.

The point not lost on the advocacy states was that the status quo, in which there is no effective global prohibition against the possession of nuclear weapons, does little to encourage global restraint. As many of their statements noted, if nuclear zero can be achieved, then any subsequent episode of nuclear proliferation, or "breakout," would be of far greater significance than it is today. (Moreover, advocacy states have noted that should breakout occur, a range of options exists that does not require a nuclear response; modern conventional weapons and various political factors would have a strong role to play. Indeed, increasingly sophisticated verification and monitoring methods and developing international capabilities for responding effectively to breakout are receiving attention in the research sponsored by the advocacy states.)[65] The argument is that international condemnation would carry far more weight in a climate of zero nuclear weapons than in the current two-tiered system. Therefore, while generally supporting nonproliferation and counterproliferation activities, the advocacy states believe that these can be strengthened if the NWS demonstrate a more equitable approach to the possession of nuclear weapons. Essentially, disarmament is seen as a necessary (if not sufficient) condition for dissuading proliferation.

A fourth motivation for those states placing pressure on the NWS to disarm is the continuing reliance on nuclear deterrence. Although the view that possession of nuclear weapons deters their use by others had some credibility during the Cold War, the reports of advocacy states note that this utility would no longer apply if nuclear weapons could be eliminated. The risks and dangers inherent in relying on postures of nuclear deterrence have long been evident. This is not a new reason for arguing against nuclear policies, but it is one the advocacy states believe worth restating. With its assumption of rational actors, deterrence is not seen as a reliable instrument for preventing a nuclear strike. Claims that nuclear weapons must be retained to deter attack or because of a vague, undefined necessity—what Michael MccGwire describes as a wish for an "all-purpose security blanket"—not only ignore the problems associated with nuclear use but also risk perpetuating a nuclear weapons culture that only increases the risks of proliferation and accidental use.[66] Related to the questioning of deterrence is the view that terrorist forces threatening international security are in any case not rational and thus not likely to be "deterrable." The added fear that substate groups might one day gain access to nuclear materials further complicates the existing, uneasy basis of deterrence. The dangers of this kind of proliferation have led the advocacy states to support tighter controls on fissile material and abolition of nuclear weapons in order to avoid a terrorist-conducted nuclear catastrophe.

A fifth motivation focuses strongly on the dangers of accidental use of nuclear weapons. It is salutary to remember that there were many documented instances during the Cold War that recorded a near-descent into a nuclear exchange because of miscalculation or misperception. For the advocacy states, there is no guarantee of the prevention of accidental nuclear war in the future.

What these motivations suggest is that for these states, it was essential to contribute actively to policies on international security. Taking a back seat in international debates was not an option.[67] While influencing Cold War decisions might have been beyond their ability, changes since the 1980s, together with new ideas about what constituted security, propelled these states to take up a more prominent position in global security politics. Indeed, the self-conscious positioning of some of these states in the post–Cold War period is notable; they have gone to some lengths to identify themselves as active states, keen to play a role that averts nuclear war, that might help to divert resources to the challenges of underdevelopment and other pressing problems, or that might bridge Western and non-Western security policies.

Thus for the advocacy states, there was often a clear thematic underpinning to their foreign policy initiatives. For Australia, the Canberra Commission report and subsequent ICNND process are key components of what the governments of the day have called "good international citizenship" and the wish to instill into foreign policy an explicitly declared sense of principle and morally informed action.[68] Canada, at the time of its SCFAIT report on nuclear weapons, prided itself as focused on human security, on the previously undervalued concept of securing human needs and rights. Norway's government has spoken of "commitment politics," of its obligation, as a rich and peaceful nation, to work at the international level to achieve peace and prosperity globally. Perhaps more than any of the states listed here, Norway has explicitly linked global action to eliminate nuclear weapons—part of an overall program to prevent conflicts and to reduce poverty—as one of the elements that makes up its national interests. It speaks of a "moral responsibility" and an "ethical duty" to work for such outcomes.[69]

In this sense, states such as Australia, Canada, and Norway can be considered prime examples of middle-power diplomacy and, more specifically, of active leadership in international relations.[70] The cooperative and "morally entrepreneurial" activities of these states have played an influential role in key areas of the post–Cold War international order, and nowhere more so than in nuclear arms control. Central to this positioning were reconsiderations of ideas about what "security" meant and how it might best be achieved and the evolution of state "identity politics." The post–Cold War period allowed states to pursue principles that were expressly linked to their positioning on the global stage as ethical or morally informed actors.[71] This is not to claim that their foreign policies always *were* ethically motivated, but rather to show that issues such as transnational justice, human rights, and interdependence were now filtering into decision-making processes in ways that had not occurred earlier.

Indeed, if nuclear military capabilities and self-interest dominated world politics for much of the twentieth century, these same elements have come to be substantially affected by growing norms that have focused on moral issues, on the problems of proliferation in a two-tiered nuclear world, and on the new strategic circumstances that render possession of nuclear weapons arguably more problematic than ever before. Articulating these arguments has enabled a basis for a review of self-interest that takes these norms into account and modifies previous perceptions that an abundance of nuclear military power could best serve a nation's (or, indeed, a global) interest. Thus the ideas put forward by advocacy states contested traditional realist perceptions of self-interest, and their articulation and reinforcement by these states has provided a vital context for the current disarmament position shown by Obama and, increasingly, others. Together with the growth over the past few decades of attention to human rights, international law, and ethics in world politics, this refocusing has allowed for an important questioning of traditional postures.

An important caveat is noted here: changes of government in some cases affected the consistency or degree to which some of these states continued to position themselves as advocates of disarmament. Australia and Canada are the clear examples—the degree of advocacy and zeal displayed depended heavily on which government was in power and on the particular individuals concerned with formulating foreign policy. Foreign Minister Axworthy's emphasis on "human security" as an underlying concept of Canadian foreign policy was downplayed by succeeding governments. As with the Canberra Commission initiative, which was part of a Keating-Evans stated campaign of "good international citizenship," there was a departure by the new Canadian government away from the human security-focused foreign policy that Axworthy had driven and a lessened desire to be seen as overtly challenging American sensitivities.[72] In the same way, the re-election of a Labor government in Australia in 2007 allowed for a resurrection of the Canberra Commission's arguments after a twelve-year hiatus, during which the Conservative government placed its foreign policy within an overtly traditional "national interest"—rather than "good international citizen" or morally driven national interest framework.[73]

CONCLUSION

Notwithstanding this element of governmental change, it is likely that state identity, and the self-conscious positioning of a state within an increasingly interdependent world—will remain an important factor in international relations negotiations in the future. Certainly states like Norway—wealthy, democratic, and positioned within Western alliances but nevertheless attuned to the need for sustainable security processes—are well placed to continue to push for changes to the status quo. All the advocacy states have been encouraged by the relative success of and goodwill generated by the 2010 NPT RevCon, and they remain active in sponsoring various resolutions in the UN urging, inter alia, full ratification of the CTBT, the need to de-alert existing nuclear weapons, further weapons reductions on the part of the United States and Russia, and the need for the moribund CD to play an effective role in the process of disarmament.[74]

The broad implications of these advocacy state activities are significant. They represented an important shift in agency and norm reinforcement in global politics, a novel move away from traditional great power negotiations on security issues.[75] At the systemic level, they reveal shifts in the way that we now think about global order and security, as well as a new convergence between governmental and nongovernmental processes. They have also been instrumental in stimulating a strong civil society sector, ranging from mass-appeal nongovernmental organizations to think tanks and academic institutions supportive of the elimination of nuclear weapons.

The nature of these initiatives indicated that their sponsoring states sought to avoid the sometimes belabored progression of bilateral and multilateral talks and formal negotiations (such as exist, for example, in the CD) and to produce reports and processes that might have a more pronounced impact than do normal diplomatic negotiations. The extent to which these activities could determine policy decisions or arms control efforts remained limited, but they undeniably helped to articulate and reinforce the idea of disarmament at a diplomatic level in a way that is still essentially new in the practice of international relations. This way of exerting influence over pressing global issues such as the role of nuclear weapons is likely to continue. At the least, these states will continue to hold the nuclear weapon states accountable at future RevCons and are likely to play an increasing role in bridging Western and non-Western views and to push for changes in the strategic doctrines of the NWS and the NATO alliance.

This is not to say that they will overcome easily the resistance to the elimination of nuclear weapons still found among some policymakers in the NWS. But this is not likely in any case to be their major achievement; arguably, their most effective contribution will be to reinforce the norm of disarmament at a global level and to provide the kind of contextual support that decision makers such as President Obama will need in their pursuit of a world without nuclear weapons.

Notes

1. George P. Shultz, William J. Perry, Henry A. Kissinger, and Sam Nunn, "A World Free of Nuclear Weapons," *Wall Street Journal*, January 4, 2007, A15; Shultz, Perry, Kissinger, and Nunn, "Toward a Nuclear-Free World," *Wall Street Journal*, January 15, 2008, A13.

2. This chapter recognizes the crucial role that civil society and nongovernmental organization (NGO) actors have also played in sustaining momentum toward the elimination of nuclear weapons, especially over the past ten years. It focuses, however, on the role of *sovereign states and state-sponsored activity*; therefore, the nature and impact of NGO activities are not considered here, other than as they explicitly relate to and interact with the initiatives of particular states.

3. Australia, Japan, Norway, and Canada are formal U.S. allies. Sweden, while not a member of NATO, is broadly Western in orientation. New Zealand formally ruptured its ties with the Australia–New Zealand–United States alliance in the 1980s as a result of U.S. nuclear policies. Nevertheless, New Zealand continues to consider itself as part of a broad Western grouping, despite its political distance on nuclear matters from Washington.

4. These states have been joined recently by Austria and Switzerland, which were both highly vocal in their support for the goal of "nuclear zero" at the 2010 NPT RevCon, and who are strongly in support of a Nuclear Weapons Convention. This chapter, however, confines itself to a primary focus on Australia, Canada, Ireland, New Zealand, Norway, and Sweden, because these states have demonstrated a longer pattern of activism extending back over a decade or more in support of the elimination of nuclear weapons. Although Japan has been important in showing support for nuclear disarmament, this state is not examined here in detail, as it is explored in other parts of this volume more fully.

5. See, for example, the Arab States' recent call for disarmament, Fareed Mahdy, "Dramatic Arab Appeal for Nuclear Free World," *Global Geopolitics and Political Economy*, April, 4 2010, http://globalgeopolitics.net/wordpress/2010/04/04/dramatic-arab-appeal-for-a-nuclear-free-world/.

6. One thing that becomes immediately evident is that for some of these states, their position within a U.S. extended nuclear deterrence umbrella (even if this is only an *assumed* guarantee, as in the case of Australia) sits oddly against their calls for disarmament. While this might seem a contradictory position, the relevant states have defended their alliance links as necessary while nuclear weapons exist, but they have argued that this does not preclude them from working actively to eliminate eventually the presence of nuclear weapons.

7. It is important to note here that while much of the advocacy states' actions were

aimed at the United States—because it was felt that a change of heart in Washington was the first step in persuading other NWS to commit to genuine reductions, and because Washington was deemed more likely to listen than were Moscow or Beijing—these reports were addressed to all the NWS.

8. *Report of the Canberra Commission on the Elimination of Nuclear Weapons* (Canberra: Australian Department of Foreign Affairs and Trade, 1996), http://www.dfat.gov.au/cc/index.html.

9. For an overview of Australian policy on nuclear weapons, see Richard Butler, *Australia and Disarmament* (Canberra: Peace Research Centre, Australian National University, 1989); and Trevor Findlay, *The Making of a Moral Ornament: Australian Disarmament and Arms Control Policy, 1921–1991* (Canberra: Peace Research Centre, Australian National University, 1991).

10. *Report of the Canberra Commission*.

11. See Albert Legault and Michel Fortmann, *A Diplomacy of Hope: Canada and Disarmament, 1945–1988* (Montreal: McGill-Queens University Press, 1992).

12. Christopher Westdal, "Statement to the Main Committee of the Sixth Review Conference of the States Parties to the Treaty on the Non-Proliferation of Nuclear Weapons," New York, United Nations, May 2, 2000.

13. "Canada and the Nuclear Challenge: Reducing the Political Value of Nuclear Weapons for the Twenty-First Century," Report of the Standing Committee on Foreign Affairs and International Trade, House of Commons, Ottawa, Canada, December 10, 1998, http://www.ccnr.org/scfait_recs.html.

14. Marianne Hanson, "Advancing Disarmament in the Face of Great Power Reluctance: The Canadian Contribution," Working Paper no. 37, Liu Institute of International Relations, University of British Columbia, Vancouver, 2001.

15. "Facing Nuclear Dangers: An Action Plan for the 21st Century," Report of the Tokyo Forum for Nuclear Non-Proliferation and Disarmament, Tokyo, Japan, July 25, 1999, http://www.nti.org/db/china/engdocs/tokyo799.htm.

16. Cited in Satsuo Sigesawa, "From Canberra to Tokyo," *Hiroshima Research News* 2 (1999): 2.

17. For further details of this initiative, see Marianne Hanson, "New Initiatives to Advance Arms Control: The Tokyo Forum Report," in *The Politics of Nuclear Non-Proliferation*, ed. Carl Ungerer and Marianne Hanson (Sydney: Allen and Unwin/ANU, 2001).

18. For detailed studies of the NAC, see Tad Daley, "The New Agenda Coalition for Nuclear Abolition," *Humanist* 61, no. 2 (March/April 2001); Jean E. Krasno, *The United Nations: Confronting the Challenges of a Global Society* (Boulder, Colo.: Lynne Reinner, 2004); Darach MacFhionnbhairr et al., "Constructing a New Agenda," in *Repairing the Regime: Preventing the Spread of Weapons of Mass Destruction*, ed. Joseph Cirincione

(New York: Routledge and the Carnegie Endowment for International Peace, 2000); and Carl Ungerer, "The Force of Ideas," in Ungerer and Hanson, *Politics of Nuclear Non-Proliferation*.

19. For a history of New Zealand's activism in this area, see Kate Dewes and Alyn Ware, "Aotearoa/New Zealand: From Nuclear Ally to Pacific Peacemaker," paper presented at the symposium "The Security of the Asia-Pacific Region in the Post–Cold War Era," Nihon University, Japan, November 19, 2004, http://www.disarmsecure.org/publications/papers/aotearoa_New_Zealand_From_Nuclear_Ally_to_Pacific_Peacemaker.php; Naoki Kamimura, "Nuclear Disarmament Policies of Australia and New Zealand," in *Nuclear Disarmament in the Twenty First Century*, ed. Wade L. Huntley, Mitsuru Kurosawa, and Kazumi Mizumoto (Japan: Hiroshima Peace Institute, 2005); Lawrence Wittner, "Nuclear Disarmament Activism in Asia and the Pacific, 1971–1996," *Asia-Pacific Journal* 25-5-09 (June 22, 2009); Andreas Reitzig, "In Defiance of Nuclear Deterrence: Anti-Nuclear New Zealand after Two Decades," *Medicine, Conflict and Survival* 22, no. 2 (2006): 132–44.

20. This group of citizens included, among others, prominent lawyers such as Harold Evans and activists such as Kate Dewes and Robert Green. See Harold Evans, "The World Court Project on Nuclear Weapons and International Law," *New Zealand Law Journal*, July 1993, 249–52; and Kate Dewes and Robert Green, "The World Court Project: History and Consequences," *Canadian Foreign Policy Journal* 7, no. 1 (Fall 1999).

21. Alyn Ware, "NGO and Government Cooperation in Setting the Disarmament Agenda: The Impact of the 1996 International Court of Justice Advisory Opinion," in *Reframing the Agenda: The Impact of NGO and Middle Power Cooperation in International Security*, ed. Kenneth Rutherford, Stefan Brem, and Richard Matthew (Westport, Conn.: Praeger 2003).

22. Matt Robson, cited in Kamimura, "Nuclear Disarmament Policies," 228.

23. New Agenda Coalition, "Joint Declaration by the Ministers for Foreign Affairs of Brazil, Egypt, Ireland, Mexico, New Zealand, Slovenia, South Africa, and Sweden," June 9, 1998.

24. Ungerer, "Force of Ideas."

25. Ultimately, however, the NAC resolution was voted against by India as not going far enough in condemning the established NWS and the unequal nature of the NPT. See Ungerer, "Force of Ideas."

26. Ibid.

27. Daley, "New Agenda Coalition."

28. Krasno, *United Nations*, 202.

29. H. E. Don Mackay, "New Zealand, on Behalf of the New Agenda Coalition," Prepatory Committee for the 2010 Review Conference of the Parties to the Treaty on the Non-Proliferation of Nuclear Weapons, Cluster 1, Geneva, April 30, 2008, http://

www.reachingcriticalwill.org/legal/npt/prepcom08/statements/Cluster1/April30New Zealand.pdf.

30. "Weapons of Terror: Freeing the World of Nuclear, Biological and Chemical Arms," Report of the Weapons of Mass Destruction Commission, Stockholm, Sweden, 2006, http://www.blixassociates.com/wp-content/uploads/2011/02/Weapons_of_Terror.pdf.

31. Ibid.

32. Gareth Evans, "The Blix Commission's Wake-Up Call: Meeting the Nuclear Challenge," presentation to International Conference on a Comprehensive Approach to Nuclear Disarmament, Brussels, April 19, 2007, http://www.crisisgroup.org/en/publication-type/speeches/2007/evans-the-blix-commissions-wake-up-call-meeting-the-nuclear-challenge.aspx.

33. "Declaration by the Foreign Ministers of Australia, Chile, Norway, Romania, South Africa, and the United Kingdom on Strengthening Adherence to International Non-Proliferation and Disarmament Efforts," Seven-Nation Initiative, July 26, 2005.

34. Jonas Gahr Støre, "Arms Control, Disarmament and Non-Proliferation: A Norwegian Perspective," in *Deutschland in der Globalisierung: Chancen und Herausforderungen* [Germany in Globalization: Opportunities and Challenges], ed. Peter Struck and Ditmar Staffelt (Berlin: Detlev Prinz, 2008).

35. This was the landmark Conference on Achieving the Vision of a World Free of Nuclear Weapons, February 26-27, 2008; its proceedings can be accessed at <http://disarmament.nrpa.no/?page_id=6>.

36. See, for instance, the speeches by Robert McClelland, "Time to Repair Our Reputation: The Rise and Fall of Australia as a Good International Citizen," speech to the Lowy Institute, Sydney, June 17, 2007; Kelvin Thomson, "Australia as a Good International Citizen: Security, Overseas Aid, and Nuclear Disarmament," speech given at VCE Foreign Affairs Forum, August 7, 2009; and Stephen Smith, "A New Era of Engagement with the World," speech given at the Sydney Institute, August 19, 2008.

37. Rudd's stop at Hiroshima on the same trip was the first time a Western head of government had visited that city while in office, itself an indication of Australia's new position.

38. International Commission on Nuclear Nonproliferation and Disarmament (ICNND), 2008/2009, http://www.icnnd.org/Pages/default.aspx.

39. These studies can be accessed at http://www.icnnd.org/Pages/Research.aspx.

40. International Commission on Nuclear Nonproliferation and Disarmament.

41. "Eliminating Nuclear Threats: A Practical Agenda for Global Policymakers," report of the International Commission on Nuclear Non-Proliferation and Disarmament; the report can be viewed at http://www.icnnd.org/Reference/reports/ent/default.htm.

42. The ICNND website notes that the original mandate for the commission expired in July 2010.

43. "Japan, Australia and 8 Others Form Group to Promote Nuke Disarmament," *Stock-Analyst*, September 22, 2010, http://www.istockanalyst.com/article/viewiStockNews/articleid/4526030.

44. "European Nations Seek NATO Nuclear Debate," *Global Security Newswire*, March 3, 2010, http://gsn.nti.org/gsn/nw_20100303_6094.php.

45. The United States had indicated a reluctance to remove these weapons until Russia demonstrated a similar interest in reducing its own tactical arsenal. Moreover, while Norway and its like-minded partners view these weapons as serving no useful purpose, the newer NATO member states seem determined to retain a nuclear arsenal, at least in the short to medium term.

46. "Active Engagement, Modern Defence: Strategic Concept for the Defence and Security of the Members of the North Atlantic Treaty Organisation adopted by Heads of State and Government in Lisbon," North Atlantic Treaty Organization, November 19, 2010, http://www.nato.int/cps/en/natolive/official_texts_68580.htm?.

47. The Final Document noted, "The Conference affirms that the final phase of the nuclear disarmament process and other related measures should be pursued within an agreed legal framework, which a majority of States parties believe should include specified time-lines." It also listed the UN secretary general's Five-Point proposal, which urges consideration of negotiations on a nuclear weapons convention. "Final Document of the 2010 Review Conference of the Parties to the Treaty on the Nonproliferation of Nuclear Weapons," New York, 2010, http://cns.miis.edu/treaty_npt/pdfs/2010_FD_Part_I.pdf.

48. Remarks made by Ireland to nongovernment organizations, Dublin, June 15, 2010, cited in *Government Positions on a Nuclear Weapons Convention*, ICAN, August 2010, http://www.icanw.org/files/NWC-positions-August2010.pdf.

49. See Ireland's vote on A/RES/64/55, December 2, 2009, in *Government Positions*.

50. Introduced by Phil Twyford MP and adopted on May 5, 2010, cited in *Government Positions*.

51. Statement by Norway at the NPT Review Conference, New York, May 12, 2010, cited in *Government Positions*.

52. Vote on A/RES/64/55, December 2, 2009, cited in *Government Positions*.

53. Cited in *Government Positions*.

54. Ibid.

55. "Statement by Australia to the NPT Preparatory Committee session," New York, May 6, 2009; statement by Australia to the NPT Preparatory Committee session, Geneva, April 30, 2008, cited in *Government Positions*.

56. Letter from Stephen Smith (foreign minister) to ICAN, July 9, 2010, cited in *Government Positions*.

57. Joint Standing Committee on Treaties, *Report 106: Nuclear Non-Proliferation and Disarmament*, Commonwealth Parliament of Australia, September 2009, 21.

58. Vote on A/RES/64/55, December 2, 2009, cited in *Government Positions*.

59. "Motion to Recognize the Danger Posed by the Proliferation of Nuclear Materials and Technology to Peace and Security," June 2, 2010; introduced by Senator Hugh Segal, cited in *Government Positions*.

60. For an overview of the development of the taboo against nuclear weapons, see Richard Price and Nina Tannenwald, "Norms and Deterrence: The Nuclear and Chemical Weapons Taboos," in *The Culture of National Security: Norms and Identity in World Politics*, ed. Peter Katzenstein (New York: Columbia University Press, 1996); and Nina Tannenwald, "Stigmatizing the Bomb," *International Security* 29 (Spring 2005): 5–49.

61. Ministry of Foreign Affairs, Reflex Project, *National Interest: Foreign Policy for a Globalised World: The Case of Norway* (Oslo: Departementenes servicecenter, December 2008).

62. The International Court of Justice's 1996 advisory opinion on the legality of nuclear weapons use, while not categorical, was important in concluding that the use of nuclear weapons would generally be contrary to the rules of international law.

63. The conference report noted its "deep concern at the catastrophic humanitarian consequences of any use of nuclear weapons and reaffirms the need for all States at all times to comply with applicable international law, including international humanitarian law." Final Document of the 2010 RevCon.

64. There is, for instance, little sympathy with the "more is better" argument advocated most famously by Kenneth Waltz in "The Spread of Nuclear Weapons: More May Be Better," Adelphi Paper no. 971 (London: International Institute for Strategic Studies, 1981). Further proliferation, whether by so-called rogue states or even by Western allies such as Japan, South Korea, or Germany, is likely to be viewed overwhelmingly as destabilizing to the international system.

65. See, for example, the papers accompanying the Canberra Commission, WMD and the ICNND reports on monitoring, verification and breakout, especially Andrew Mack, "Nuclear 'Breakout': Risks and Possible Responses," Working Paper 1997/1, ANU Department of International Relations, http://ips.cap.anu.edu.au/ir/pubs/work_papers/97-1.pdf.

66. See Michael MccGwire, "Is There a Future for Nuclear Weapons?" *International Affairs* 70, no. 2 (April 1994): 213.

67. Some of these states had sought such a voice during the Cold War: Sweden's Palme Report of 1982, and Norway's Brundtland Report of 1987, for example, indicate that for these Scandinavian countries, recent initiatives to address pressing issues and to further the broader interests of global society were not a wholly new endeavor.

68. Gareth Evans and Bruce Grant, *Australia's Foreign Relations in the World of the 1990s* (Melbourne: Melbourne University Press, 1995), 86–87.

69. Ministry of Foreign Affairs, *National Interest*, 197–99.

70. Andrew F. Cooper, Richard A. Higgott, and Kim Richard Nossal, *Relocating Middle Powers: Australian and Canada in a Changing World Order* (Vancouver: University of British Columbia Press, 1993); Ungerer, "Force of Ideas." On active leadership in international relations, see Malnes and Young, cited in Ungerer, "Force of Ideas."

71. On the reconceptualizing of security and the impact of state identity, see Bill McSweeney, *Security, Identity and Interests: A Sociology of International Relations* (New York: Cambridge University Press, 1999).

72. The recent stance of the Canadian government would tend to bear this out; in 2008, Canadian observers were disappointed by their government's unwillingness to be as zealous in its non-nuclear stance as Axworthy had been. A prominent conference on "Restoring Canada's Nuclear Disarmament Policies," sponsored by the Middle Powers Initiative, the Canadian Network to Abolish Nuclear Weapons, the Rideau Institute, the Canadian Pugwash Group, Physicians for Global Survival, and the Simons Foundation, noted in its key summary that "despite the government's claims to the contrary, Canada has been slowly shifting away from its traditionally strong support for nuclear disarmament at a time when the global propensity to use nuclear weapons has increased dramatically in the last several years." Rideau Institute, "Restoring Canada's Disarmament Policies," Expert Seminar, February 3–4, 2008, Cartier Place Hotel, Ottawa, http://www.rideauinstitute.ca/file-library/disarmament-seminar.pdf, April 9, 2008.

73. The very first white paper of this new government was self-consciously titled *In the National Interest*.

74. For details of the various state positions, see *Statements from First Committee 2010*, 4 October–1 November 2010, collated by the NGO Reaching Critical Will, http://www.reachingcriticalwill.org/political/1com/1com10/statements.html.

75. Marianne Hanson, "Regulating the Possession and Use of Nuclear Weapons: Ideas, Commissions, and Agency in International Security Politics—The Case of the Canberra Commission," in *International Commissions and the Power of Ideas*, ed. Ramesh Thakur, Andrew Cooper, and John English (Tokyo: UN University Press, 2005), 123–41.

CHAPTER THREE

The Rollback States
South Africa and Kazakhstan

Stephen F. Burgess and Togzhan Kassenova

THERE IS RENEWED OPTIMISM that nuclear-armed states might eventually walk the path from possessing nuclear weapons to renouncing them. South Africa and Kazakhstan, two rollback countries, walked that path.[1] Although their rollback decisions and circumstances were different, they both renounced nuclear weapons based on consideration that doing so would be in their national interest.

This chapter explores how these two countries' policies on nuclear nonproliferation and nuclear disarmament have evolved since then. South Africa and Kazakhstan are chosen as case studies for this chapter because their rollback decisions provide important insights that could potentially help shape effective policies to address contemporary nuclear disarmament challenges. Both countries play a significant role in current nuclear disarmament discussions and, albeit in different ways, have been trying to move the agenda forward.

The first part of this chapter is devoted to South Africa and presents an overview of the country's approach to nuclear nonproliferation and disarmament, with a specific focus on developments after the Prague speech. It argues that South Africa has moved away from the reformist New Agenda Coalition (NAC) and "middle powers" such as Ireland, Sweden, and New Zealand, which for the past two decades have tried to bring the nuclear weapon states (NWS) and non-nuclear weapon states (NNWS) together to strengthen nonproliferation and encourage eventual disarmament. South Africa now demonstrates more solidarity with the revisionist Non-Aligned Movement (NAM) and states such as Egypt on nuclear issues.[2]

The second half of the chapter is devoted to Kazakhstan, which at the end of the Cold War inherited nuclear weapons from the Soviet Union on its territory.

Kazakhstan's renunciation decision is important because any attempt to retain the Soviet arsenal or to develop an indigenous nuclear weapon program would have undermined the nuclear nonproliferation regime. Because of its rollback decisions and by virtue of its nuclear expertise and resources, Kazakhstan is in a position to make a practical and normative contribution to the nuclear nonproliferation regime and global nuclear disarmament.

The chapter concludes with an analysis of similarities and differences in South Africa's and Kazakhstan's nuclear nonproliferation and disarmament policies and assesses their potential impact on global disarmament momentum.

SOUTH AFRICA'S NUCLEAR WEAPONS PROGRAM AND ROLLBACK

South Africa's disarmament diplomacy needs to be understood in the context of the apartheid regime's development of nuclear weapons in the 1970s and 1980s, the opposition of the African National Congress (ANC) to the apartheid regime and its nuclear policies, the rollback decision of 1989, and the post-apartheid disarmament process.

In the 1970s, South Africa's apartheid regime decided to develop nuclear weapons in the face of perceived rising external threats.[3] Once the regime decided to use its nuclear energy program and a mixture of imported and home-grown technology to initiate the development of nuclear weapons, it began to devise strategies to use them and develop missiles and aircraft to deliver them. In 1975, South African leaders experienced a sudden threat escalation caused by Soviet-backed Cuban intervention and presence in Angola, as well as emerging guerrilla activity by the South West African Peoples Organization (SWAPO) and ANC. In response, the regime considered instituting a strategy of threatening to use or actually using tactical nuclear weapons in case the Soviets brought nuclear weapons or other weapons of mass destruction (WMD) to Angola to threaten South Africa. It also considered a strategy of threatening or even launching tactical nuclear attacks against SWAPO and ANC guerrilla bases and African states that actively supported the movements, especially if the states and guerrillas were found to possess WMD. At the same time, the apartheid regime began developing a strategy to manipulate the United States, in case regime survival was threatened by the Soviet Union, its regional allies, and the ANC: the regime developed a three-stage strategy, in which the threat of a nuclear test would cause the United States to side with South Africa.

In November 1989, however, a combination of pressures led President F. W. de Klerk to put an end to apartheid, terminate South Africa's nuclear weapons program, and bring the country back into line with the West. He wanted to end an expensive program that he believed would do little for the country's security in the context of a post–Cold War world and post-apartheid South Africa.[4] At the beginning of July 1990, the uranium enrichment plant at Pelindaba East was decommissioned, the six nuclear devices (and a seventh partially completed device) that had been developed in the 1980s were dismantled, the hardware and technical documents were destroyed, and the Advena production facility was decontaminated and converted for commercial use. As a precursor to signing the Nuclear Nonproliferation Treaty (NPT) in the summer of 1991, South Africa invited the International Atomic Energy Agency (IAEA) to make on-site inspections. By early September 1991—just ten days before South Africa signed a full-scope safeguards agreement with the IAEA—all its highly enriched uranium (HEU) had been recast and sent to the Atomic Energy Corporation for storage. Under the agreement, South Africa's nuclear plants and previously produced enriched uranium were placed under IAEA safeguards. In addition, South Africa renounced its missile and space-launch vehicle program and joined the Missile Technology Control Regime. Finally, on March 24, 1993, de Klerk acknowledged the existence of the nuclear weapon program in a speech to Parliament, describing in detail how the Botha regime had developed nuclear weapons, how the end of the Cold War and cessation of hostilities in Angola and Namibia had ended any rationale for the weapons, and how his government had dismantled the program.[5]

THE NEW SOUTH AFRICA'S COMMITMENT TO NUCLEAR DISARMAMENT

The ANC and global Anti-Apartheid Movement played a significant role in pressuring for an end to South Africa's nuclear weapons program. In the 1970s and 1980s, they worked in the United Nations Special Committee against Apartheid, where they denounced Western nuclear collaboration with South Africa and called for all forms of nuclear collaboration to be ended. Subsequently, the ANC-led South African government, which came to power in May 1994, placed nuclear disarmament high on its foreign policy agenda, using its unique status as the first state to unilaterally dismantle a fully fledged nuclear weapons program to push for progress in international nuclear disarmament forums. The energetic leadership provided by two key officials proved very significant in the government of President Nelson Mandela: Kader Asmal, an ANC and Anti-Apartheid Movement leader and strong advocate of the NPT and the nuclear taboo, who was appointed as the head of the Weapons of Mass Destruction Committee, and Abdul Minty, who was appointed to a top position in the Department of Foreign Affairs. Both men played a major role in shaping the new South Africa's proactive disarmament diplomacy, successfully leading regional and international disarmament negotiations in the mid-1990s.

The 1995 NPT Review and Extension Conference brought South Africa onto the world stage as an influential middle power committed to disarmament—a position it consolidated later in the 1990s when it joined the New Agenda Coalition.[6] During this time, South Africa played a lead role in building support among NNWS for the indefinite extension of the NPT. Its diplomats served as bridge builders, garnering support from NAM members for indefinite treaty extension—something many developing states initially opposed. The South African delegation argued that continued support for the existence of the NPT should not be jeopardized by an incipient struggle between the nuclear "haves" and "have-nots." In particular, South Africa's diplomats played an important role in reassuring Egypt, which had raised major objections to Israel's nuclear weapons program. South Africa joined with Egypt in gaining agreement to pursue efforts to establish a Middle East nuclear-weapons-free zone (MENWFZ).

At the same time, South African diplomats stressed that the NPT review process should be strengthened: during the 1995 Review and Extension Conference, they played an active role in the discussions that led to the adoption of the "Principles and Objectives for Nuclear Non-Proliferation and Disarmament." The latter was a political document comprising a set of proposals that focused on compliance with the provisions of the NPT, nuclear disarmament, the conclusion of the Comprehensive Nuclear-Test-Ban Treaty (CTBT), and the establishment of regional nuclear-weapons-free zones NWFZ. South Africa viewed the decision to adopt these proposals as initial steps toward the achievement of the goals of the NPT and total nuclear disarmament.[7]

In addition to South Africa taking a proactive role on the international stage, the 1990s were also a very active period for South Africa's regional disarmament diplomacy. Before taking power in May 1994, the ANC undertook initiatives in the Organization of African Unity to gain agreement among member states that Africa should establish an NWFZ. After taking power, the ANC-led government spearheaded diplomatic efforts to negotiate the zone.[8] The Department of Foreign Affairs negotiated the African Nuclear-Weapon-Free Zone

(ANWFZ) with more than fifty African states and the five NWS.[9] After extensive negotiations, the ANWFZ Treaty of Pelindaba was adopted on June 2, 1995, at the site of the Atomic Energy Commission (AEC) of South Africa. African states agreed that the headquarters of the African Commission on Nuclear Energy for the peaceful development of nuclear energy would be situated in South Africa. Later that month the Organization of African Unity (OAU) Assembly of Heads of State and Government meeting in Addis Ababa, Ethiopia, approved the Treaty of Pelindaba, which they subsequently endorsed at the fiftieth session of the UN General Assembly in the fall of 1995. The treaty was opened for signature on April 11, 1996, at a special summit in Cairo, where African states declared their intentions to undertake, through an international agreement to be concluded under UN auspices, not to manufacture or acquire control of nuclear weapons. All of the NWS signed the relevant protocols to the treaty, and Algeria, South Africa, Tanzania, Zimbabwe, and a number of other leading African states quickly ratified. The treaty was broad in scope, declaring Africa an NWFZ, strengthening the nonproliferation regime, and promoting cooperation in the peaceful uses of nuclear energy, disarmament, and regional peace and security. The NWS could not test nuclear weapons in Africa nor transport them through African territory or waters, and they had to provide negative security assurances that they would not use nuclear weapons against African states.

Ratification of the Treaty of Pelindaba by the fifty-three African states was slow between 1995 and 2009 because South African nuclear disarmament had taken the urgency out of the issue, and many African parliaments had more pressing business to manage.[10] South African diplomats took the lead in persuading African states to complete the ratification process. Eventually, South Africa persuaded twenty-eight states to ratify the treaty, which eventually came into effect on July 15, 2009.[11] However, the negative security assurance and nuclear testing protocols to the treaty remain an issue. Although all the NWS have signed the protocols, Russia has only recently ratified them, and the United States has not yet done so.[12] In May 2011, however, the Obama administration submitted the protocols of the treaty (along with those of the South Pacific NWFZ) to the U.S. Senate for its advice and consent to ratification; it remains to be seen whether or not ratification will happen.

In the late 1990s, South Africa became a key participant in the NAC, playing an important role in the coalition's bridge-building efforts in the lead-up to the 2000 NPT Review Conference (RevCon). But after the adoption of the Final Document at the end of that conference (a consensus document that included

"Thirteen Practical Steps" toward disarmament), South Africa began steadily moving away from NAC positions on NPT issues. At the same time, it began closing ranks with the more strident positions of NAM members and observers, including Egypt, Mexico, and Brazil.[13] This reflected the foreign policy priorities of President Thabo Mbeki (1999–2008) and the transition from the Interim Government under Nelson Mandela to ANC rule. The change of foreign policy direction was also reinforced after South Africa suffered strained relations with the United States following the Bush administration's decision to invade Iraq. This came to a head after a South African delegation visited Iraq to show how a nuclear weapon program could be ended.

At the 2005 NPT RevCon, which ended without a consensus document, the South African representative, Abdul Minty, delivered a statement expressing his concern over the lack of commitment by the NWS to move toward nuclear disarmament. He also criticized the United States and other states for what he believed to be their unfair treatment of states attempting to develop nuclear energy for peaceful purposes: "There is growing concern that while demands are being made for non-nuclear-weapon States to agree to new measures in the name of nonproliferation, concrete actions towards disarmament are neglected. South Africa wishes to reiterate that it cannot support unwarranted restrictions on the NPT's guaranteed access to such nuclear capabilities for peaceful purposes by States that are fully compliant with their obligations under the NPT."[14]

A significant decision that exposes one of the self-interested material drivers of South Africa's nonproliferation policy came from its vote in the September 2008 Nuclear Suppliers Group approval of the U.S.-India civilian nuclear cooperation agreement. South Africa supported India's efforts to win U.S. agreement to end NPT sanctions that had been imposed since the 1974 "peaceful nuclear test" and open the way to nuclear trade. However, South Africa did not use the same line of reasoning as the United States (i.e., that India was a good nuclear citizen and could be trusted with nuclear trade). Instead, South Africa supported India because it is a fellow NAM leader and because of the influence of South Africa's wealthy Indian community.[15]

SOUTH AFRICA'S BEHAVIOR IN THE WAKE OF OBAMA'S PRAGUE SPEECH

In the wake of Obama's Prague speech, South Africa welcomed the U.S. pledge to move steadily toward nuclear disarmament. However, South African nuclear weapon experts in the Department of International Affairs and Cooperation also expressed skepticism regarding U.S. willingness and ability to follow through on its commitment. South Africa also became concerned about the Obama administration's increased pressure on the NNWS to enhance safeguards against proliferation. The debate about Iran's HEU program was related to what South Africa saw as U.S. attempts to curtail the right that all nations have to nuclear technology.[16]

In March 2009, Ambassador Abdul Minty began a campaign to replace Mohamed ElBaradei as IAEA head, with the backing of NAM states. Judging Minty to be too sympathetic to Iran, the Obama administration supported Japanese diplomat Yukia Amano. After an initial round of voting proved inconclusive, Amano defeated Minty on July 3, 2009. However, U.S. opposition to Minty did not adversely affect U.S.-South African cooperation on nuclear issues. Instead, South Africa and the United States stepped up their nuclear cooperation. In September 2009, South Africa signed a bilateral agreement with the United States on cooperation regarding advanced nuclear energy systems and reactor technology, particularly with regard to improving the cost, safety, and proliferation-resistance of next-generation nuclear power systems.[17] Moreover, in the lead-up to the 2010 Fédération Internationale de Football Association (FIFA) World Cup, the United States and South Africa worked in partnership with the IAEA to enhance the physical protection of radiological sources—for example, at nuclear storage sites to prevent terrorist access to the material.[18] Also with cooperation from the United States, the conversion of South Africa's Safari research reactor from the use of HEU to low-enriched uranium (LEU) fuel was completed.

On November 27, 2009, South Africa joined with Afghanistan, Brazil, Egypt, Pakistan, and Turkey in abstaining from an IAEA resolution that called on Iran to stop work on a clandestine uranium-enrichment facility. The resolution, passed by a 25–3 vote, urged Iran to halt construction of the Fordow uranium-enrichment plant, located in a mountain bunker near the city of Qom. The IAEA also demanded that Iran should immediately freeze its uranium-enrichment project. The resolution asked Iran to clarify the original purpose of the Fordow facility and to confirm that it did not have any further hidden facilities. The resolution was supported by Russia and China (as well as NAM member India), which had sometimes shied away from censuring Iran in the past. The Russian and Chinese support for the IAEA resolution conveyed to Iran a clear message of international disappointment about the secrecy and defiance surrounding its controversial nuclear program. Meanwhile, the six countries that abstained from the vote were part of an effort to find a NAM solution to the Iranian nuclear impasse.[19]

On March 26, 2010, the New Strategic Arms Reduction Treaty (New START) between the United States and Russia was concluded, which promised further reduction in the nuclear arsenals of the two countries. The United States hoped that New START would signal to countries participating in the Nuclear Security Summit in Washington, D.C., the positive political intentions of the two nuclear powers. On one level, South Africa's nonproliferation and disarmament officials responded as the United States had hoped: in an appearance at the Council on Foreign Relations in New York, for example, Minty argued that the new U.S. disarmament leadership indicated that the Obama administration was taking its Article VI obligation more seriously, adding that "the development so far in the atmospherics is very good."[20] However, at the same time, South African opinion leaders questioned whether the new treaty was really significant and whether it signaled a genuine commitment to disarmament.[21]

In the lead-up to the Nuclear Security Summit in Washington, D.C., and the NPT Review Conference in New York, Minty expressed concerns about maintaining balance among the three pillars of the NPT, especially the obligation of NWS to disarm:

> In 2010, one finds a rather unique situation, where all three pillars face challenges. While the first pillar of disarmament has recently experienced some positive advocacy, there remains little notable action in this regard. In addition, proliferation—both horizontal and vertical—has been a cause for concern. This worry has impacted the third pillar—the inalienable right of states parties to pursue peaceful uses of nuclear technology—with some states seeking to limit access to such technology in order to offset their proliferation concerns. It is not necessarily negative that these challenges exist, as long as one takes the view that they present an opportunity for the 2010 Review Conference to reaffirm the commitment of all states parties to all three pillars of the NPT and to redress perceived past imbalances.[22]

Before the Nuclear Security Summit, a U.S.-South African energy dialogue built on a bilateral nuclear cooperation agreement that had been negotiated in Vienna in 2009. The United States and South Africa promised to work together to develop a nuclear security support center in South Africa, which would enable South Africa and members of the Southern African Development Community to develop the expertise and capacity building critical for the region's rising nuclear energy needs. The center would enhance the capacity provided by IAEA courses conducted in South Africa and other African countries.[23]

At the Nuclear Security Summit in April 2010, South Africa was singled out for praise by the United States thanks to its unilateral nuclear disarmament in the early 1990s and its efforts to reduce the threat of nuclear terrorism.[24] In her speech, Bonnie Jenkins, the U.S. coordinator for Threat Reduction Programs, highlighted South Africa's contributions: "South Africa is making its own unique contribution to the [nuclear security] effort. Through its active participation in the Nuclear Security Summit, as well as the U.S.–South Africa strategic partnership and ongoing bilateral dialogues, the two countries are working together to help prevent nuclear proliferation and terrorism, while expanding the peaceful uses of nuclear energy. We look to South Africa continuing in our partnership to serve in an even greater capacity on the African continent and beyond, to help make the world both safer and more prosperous."[25]

Soon after the Nuclear Security Summit, the 2010 NPT RevCon convened at the United Nations in New York. South Africa came determined to promote a balance among the three pillars of the NPT. Minty commented that "positive signals" such as the disclosure of long-classified details on the U.S. arsenal (especially the number of warheads) have "contributed to an atmosphere of cautious optimism."[26]

During the RevCon, Minty associated himself with statements delivered on behalf of the NAM and NAC.[27] He emphasized the NPT's "grand bargain" in which the NWS agreed to disarm in exchange for the NNWS forgoing nuclear weapons, and he saw moves by the United States, Russia, and other NWS toward arms reduction as a positive development. He urged the NWS to build upon their "unequivocal undertaking" made to accomplish the total elimination of their nuclear arsenals in "a concrete, transparent, irreversible and verifiable manner in accordance with Article VI of the NPT." While he acknowledged that full implementation of nonproliferation commitments was important, he stressed the equal importance of complete nuclear disarmament and the right of NPT members to peaceful uses of nuclear energy. He stressed that the IAEA was the only internationally recognized competent authority responsible for verifying and assuring compliance with safeguards agreements, calling for further funding for the IAEA and implying that parallel organizations would not enjoy legitimacy. He also cautioned that the Additional Protocol to safeguards agreements was a voluntary measure and claimed that it should be recognized merely as a confidence-building measure. His core argument, which reflected the concerns of many NAM states, was that the nonproliferation aspects of the treaty should not be used as a tool to deny access to developing countries to the peaceful use of nuclear energy.[28]

These concerns over equity and fairness in the nonproliferation regime have shaped South Africa's response to Iran's nuclear defiance. At the RevCon, the issue of Iran's nuclear program arose in advance of the June 2010 UN Security Council vote on whether to increase sanctions. On May 16, Turkey and Brazil announced that agreement had been reached with Iran to ship 1,200 kilograms of LEU from Iran to Turkey.[29] In discussions about the IAEA's role in the Brazil-Turkey-Iran agreement, Minty commented that the "IAEA cannot avoid being involved" as a verification body. In response to a question as to whether developing countries think that sanctions are an ineffective nonproliferation tool, he observed that sanctions are a "very blunt tool," adding "these sanctions are not making any real difference to the actual nuclear capacity of Iran."[30] These comments reflected South Africa's position that all countries that sign the NPT, including Iran, have the right to the entire nuclear fuel cycle under IAEA supervision.

The same concerns over equity and fairness influence South Africa's position on Israel's NPT holdout status. In his speech to the 2010 RevCon, Minty urged agreement on measures to implement the 1995 Resolution on the Middle East and joined with Egypt to promote acceptance of the MENWFZ, stating: "The 1995 Middle East resolution is a matter of paramount importance. To date, no progress has been achieved on the establishment of a weapons-free zone in that region."[31] He added: "The conference should renew its call to Israel as the only state of the region not yet a party to the treaty to accede to it" promptly and "without conditions."

EXPLAINING THE POST-MANDELA SHIFTS IN SOUTH AFRICA'S DISARMAMENT DIPLOMACY

On the one hand, the South African reaction to President Obama's Prague initiative was fundamentally a redoubling of efforts to seek the disarmament of the NWS and Israel and to defend the rights of Iran and other states to develop the whole nuclear fuel cycle and of India—a non-NPT signatory—to trade in nuclear materials. On the other hand, South Africa made efforts to work with the Obama administration in the areas of nuclear safety and security, especially against the threat of nuclear terrorism. The prospects for further U.S.-South African cooperation on nuclear issues remain largely positive.

South Africa's shift in position on nuclear issues is linked to the change in the country's foreign policy under the influence of Thabo Mbeki and—on arms control issues—Abdul Minty. From 1994 to 1999, Nelson Mandela and his interim government maintained a moderate foreign policy, which helped to explain why South Africa played a constructive role at the 1995 RevCon to indefinitely extend the NPT. In 1999, Thabo Mbeki became president and began to steer South African foreign policy to the left and in closer cooperation with the NAM. Thus, South Africa began to play less of a mediator role in the NAC and became a stronger proponent of NAM positions, notably with regard to the disarmament of Israel and the right of Iran and India to nuclear energy. The 2003 invasion of Iraq under the guise of stopping WMD helped move South African foreign policy even further to the left. The leftward movement was manifested in South African behavior at the 2005 NPT review conference, which was far less concerned with diplomatic bridge building than it had been at the 1995 and 2000 conferences and more focused on expressing NAM opposition to Western—especially U.S.—nonproliferation agendas.

In December 2007, Thabo Mbeki was forced to step down as head of the ANC, which led to his ouster as president in September 2008. He was succeeded by an interim president and in May 2009 by Jacob Zuma. Subsequently, South African foreign policy became more pragmatic. With the end of the Bush presidency and the election of Barack Obama, the South African government became more amenable to American positions. This helps to explain why South Africa has been willing to cooperate with U.S.-led efforts to boost nuclear security collaboration, as demonstrated by its constructive role in the April 2010 Nuclear Security Summit.

The ANC is likely to be the ruling party in South Africa for some time to come, and its foreign policy is likely to remain stable. Therefore, one can expect South Africa to continue to press the United States and other NWS to disarm.[32] However, South Africa under President Zuma is becoming less concerned with grand international issues and is focusing more on national interests. With Abdul Minty's retirement after his defeat in the IAEA leadership election, there is no one in a position of power to take over his role as a major player on the international arms control stage. South Africa may therefore adopt a lower-profile role at the 2015 RevCon, despite the enthusiasm for nuclear issues that still exists below the ministerial level.

KAZAKHSTAN'S NUCLEAR INHERITANCE AND ROLLBACK DECISION

Kazakhstan is striving to be a leading voice in the current debate on global nuclear disarmament and nuclear nonproliferation. A combination of factors makes it an ideal candidate for such a role.[33]

First, as a developing, non-nuclear-weapon state, it can relate to concerns shared by many countries around the world about the weaknesses and "double standards" of the main pillar of the nonproliferation regime—the NPT. It is sensitive to the frustration of many NNWS regarding the perceived lack of progress in disarmament, while the NWS continue to increase pressure on them to tighten domestic nonproliferation controls. Kazakhstan has its own concerns about the discriminatory nature of the global nonproliferation regime, such as division into nuclear "haves" and "have-nots," the lack of legally binding security assurances from the NWS to the NNWS, and the lack of universal support from the NWS for NWFZs. However, despite these concerns, the country is a staunch supporter of strengthening nonproliferation controls. In an important sense, Kazakhstan combines both disarmament and nonproliferation values.

Second, Kazakhstan has the nuclear expertise, resources, and technical capacity to play a role in a whole range of initiatives critical for the eventual disarmament process. It has already made a practical contribution to the Comprehensive Test Ban Treaty process by hosting monitoring stations critical for the CTBT's verification once the treaty enters into force. It has also hosted the Comprehensive Test Ban Treaty Organization's (CTBTO's) largest on-site inspection simulation exercise. Together with its Central Asian neighbors, Kazakhstan has established a NWFZ in Central Asia. Kazakhstan is especially well positioned to contribute to multilateral fuel cycle arrangements that are designed to discourage the spread of sensitive technologies. It has offered to host an IAEA fuel bank and already participates in an International Uranium Enrichment Center in Angarsk, Russia. Kazakhstan can also contribute to the development of technologies and protocols to verify the dismantlement of nuclear weapons around the world. Finally, it can contribute usefully to the Cooperative Threat Reduction process, a key initiative for tackling proliferation challenges in various parts of the world and integral to efforts aimed at the military denuclearization of countries such as North Korea, should this become possible. Kazakhstan's involvement in both verification and cooperative threat reduction projects would likely be free of political sensitivities in host countries due to its relatively neutral standing on the international scene.

The example of Kazakhstan is worth studying because it is a striking example of disarmament success as well as providing a guide to successful nonproliferation efforts in the future.

Kazakhstan's Renunciation of Nuclear Weapons

The fall of the Soviet Union in 1991 raised many serious concerns for the international community, including the fate of the Soviet nuclear arsenal, part of which was located in Kazakhstan.

Kazakhstan was at the heart of the Soviet nuclear weapons program. When the Soviet Union collapsed, Kazakhstan inherited the world's fourth-largest nuclear arsenal. In 1991, Kazakhstan had 1,410 strategic warheads, 104 "Satan" (SS-18) intercontinental ballistic missiles, and 40 TU-95MS "Bear H" heavy bombers on its territory.[34] Significant amounts of nuclear material were also present in Kazakhstan—both highly enriched uranium and weapons-grade plutonium.[35] It housed a plethora of military and nuclear research facilities, including six nuclear test sites, a fast breeder reactor BN-350, a uranium fuel pellet production facility, several nuclear research reactors, and a space launching facility, as well as facilities integral to the Soviet strategic defense system. Kazakhstan's rich uranium resources were crucial to the Soviet nuclear program, both for military and peaceful purposes.[36] Kazakhstan's nuclear "inheritance" was more than nuclear weapons, nuclear material, and numerous facilities. It also had critical expertise, notably in the fields of nuclear testing and nuclear material production.

From the very beginning, the debate on the fate of nuclear weapons in Kazakhstan indicated that decision makers perceived a whole range of negative consequences with the nuclear retention scenario. The immediate constraints were technical and operational: crucially, Kazakhstan's leaders did not have access to the command and control system of the nuclear weapons on their territory.[37] Attempts to gain control over the weapons or to prevent their removal to Russia would have ultimately led to confrontation with Russia. Strains in the Russia-Kazakhstan relationship would likely have jeopardized interethnic relations inside Kazakhstan, a crucial consideration given the ethnic Russian population in Kazakhstan just before the Soviet collapse was about 6 million people (roughly 37 percent of total population).[38] Even if Kazakhstan had gained control of the nuclear weapons, it would have faced serious and immensely costly technical challenges. The weapons required maintenance for which Kazakhstan had neither the infrastructure nor the capacity, at least not immediately. While there were specialists with critical weapons knowledge in Kazakhstan, there was no indigenous structure that could take over command and control of nuclear weapons, and the expertise available was not sufficient for an immediate jump-start of an independent weapons program.[39]

The perceptions of Kazakh decision makers regarding the role of nuclear weapons in the international system, and in the context of Kazakhstan's domestic politics and foreign policy interests, were possibly even more important than technical and operational issues. If Kazakhstan had decided to develop its own nuclear weapons program, the technical hurdles discussed above could have been overcome eventually.

For the purposes of the current study, it is important to understand why on balance Kazakhstan saw nuclear weapons as more detrimental than beneficial to its security, development, and position in the international arena. Indeed, the key factors that drove Kazakhstan's leadership to relinquish the Soviet nuclear weapons left on its territory have a direct relation to Kazakhstan's current nuclear disarmament and nonproliferation policies and to its potential role as a key NNWS leader in this field.

Kazakhstan's foreign policy experts and practitioners recognized that if the country attempted to force its way into the "nuclear club," it would have seriously undermined the global nonproliferation regime. Kazakhstan's scholars and government officials deserve credit for taking this into consideration. It was Kazakhstan's own experts who warned that an attempt by Kazakhstan to become a nuclear-armed state would create a precedent for nuclear threshold countries and could be used as an additional excuse for them to go nuclear.[40]

At a tactical level, Kazakhstan's leaders also saw no practical use for nuclear weapons as a military tool. On the contrary, the country's policy experts warned that possession of nuclear weapons would make Kazakhstan a potential enemy in the eyes of its neighbors and, more disturbingly, that it would make Kazakhstan a potential target for nuclear-armed states. Kazakhstan's policy experts were very clear that "if drawn into a nuclear conflict of any sort, Kazakhstan faces a greater risk of being turned into ashes, being a nuclear state, than if it remains a non-nuclear one."[41]

Perhaps most importantly, in the minds of the Kazakh leadership, the issue of nuclear weapons was directly tied to how the young country would position itself in the international system. Tulegen Zhukeev, who was President Nazarbayev's "right-hand man" in the early 1990s and the key negotiator dealing with the United States on nuclear issues, commented: "We did not want to be a Central Asian North Korea. We did not want to be a pariah state."[42]

In the mid-twentieth century, geopolitical factors and historic circumstances had resulted in a near-total isolation of all Central Asian republics from the outside world. Once the walls of Soviet separation started to crumble, Kazakh officials were eager to have their country accepted as a respected new member of the international community. The newly independent state could proceed with renouncing nuclear weapons and open numerous doors to the world, or it could insist on keeping the weapons and have all those doors shut. Kazakhstan's leaders decided that the country's future depended on having access to new technology, foreign investment, international institutions, and international markets. Blessed with many of the world's most valuable natural resources, Kazakhstan needed foreign investment and companies to start developing them. Nuclear weapons were an obstacle to all of this.

Domestic factors also weighed strongly toward getting rid of nuclear weapons. Kazakhstan's population had suffered tremendously from Soviet nuclear testing. Soviet authorities had made Kazakhstan the site of six nuclear testing grounds, including the world's largest underground testing facilities in Semipalatinsk. The Soviet military conducted 456 nuclear tests at Semipalatinsk, including 116 above ground.[43] Disregard for the health of the local population and environment by Soviet officials resulted in a tragedy: radiation-related diseases among many thousands of people and contamination of vast tracts of land. This exploitation of Kazakhstan for the sake of the Soviet nuclear program, without regard to the country's people, their health, or the environment, engendered in the majority of people in Kazakhstan a strong aversion to anything nuclear.

Besides the extremely strong feelings about nuclear testing, another key factor that helped bring about the Kazakh decision to relinquish nuclear weapons was the weakness of Kazakh social groupings that are traditionally strong supporters of nuclear weapons programs in other countries. Unlike in other countries, where various political interest groups, including the military-industrial complex, have a strong stake in nuclear policy and real potential to influence policymaking, Kazakhstan did not have much political diversity. The military establishment played only a supportive role to President Nazarbayev and his immediate advisers in the decision-making process on nuclear issues. The nuclear industry that played a crucial part in the Soviet nuclear weapons program was on the verge of bankruptcy when the Soviet Union dissolved. Some nationalist movements were vocal in their push for retention of Soviet nuclear weapons, but they were too marginalized and weak to a make a serious difference in the discourse.

Externally, the international community was able to address Kazakhstan's major concerns related to military denuclearization. Obtaining negative and positive security assurances from the NWS was of paramount importance to Kazakhstan. Kazakhstan's experts saw a lack of legally binding security assurances as one of the key weaknesses of the NPT and sought more substantive guarantees of its sovereignty and security from nuclear powers in exchange for giving up nuclear weapons. In a Memorandum on Security Assurances in Connection with Kazakhstan's Accession to the NPT, Russia, the United States, and the United Kingdom extended legally binding negative guarantees to Kazakhstan by reaffirming an "obligation to refrain from the threat or use of force" and a commitment "not to use nuclear weapons" against Kazakhstan. They also provided positive security assurances by pledging "to seek immediate United Nations Security Council action to provide assistance" if Kazakhstan "should become a victim of an act of aggression or an object of a threat of aggression in which nuclear weapons are used."[44]

Another major concern for Kazakhstan was how to deal with the dismantlement and removal of nuclear weapons. The assistance offered by the West, with the largest share of it provided by the United States, made denuclearization both feasible and safe. The Nunn-Lugar Cooperative Threat Reduction Program and other nonproliferation assistance programs paid for most of the operations associated with Kazakhstan's military denuclearization. It was also critical that the interaction between the United States and Kazakhstan in the early 1990s extended beyond just nuclear issues. Both U.S. and Kazakh actors involved in negotiations on the fate of nuclear weapons note that a broader dialogue on military and economic issues was key to successful cooperation on the dismantlement and removal of nuclear weapons from Kazakhstan.[45] Finally, it was U.S. support for Kazakhstan's sovereignty and independence that "sealed the deal." The first U.S. ambassador to Kazakhstan, William Courtney, recalls: "From the very outset the United States provided strong support for [Kazakhstan's] independence, sovereignty, and integrity."[46] Good relations with the West and U.S. support for Kazakhstan's statehood were critical to its leaders. Choosing an "obstructionist" path on the issue of nuclear weapons would have undermined a relationship important for a young country. Kazakhstan's Tulegen Zhukeyev notes: "The West's support and interest in our independence helped us tremendously in building our statehood."[47]

KAZAKHSTAN AND THE NEW NUCLEAR DISARMAMENT MOMENTUM

Kazakhstan is well placed both symbolically and practically to become a leading figure in the new nuclear disarmament movement. Kazakhstan had substantial nuclear weapon infrastructure, materials, and expertise, not to mention physical possession of the weapons themselves, which it decided to abandon;[48] in addition, it decided not to acquire an indigenous nuclear capability. This combination of factors makes Kazakhstan an important role model for the nonproliferation regime and for countries that may aspire to nuclear weapon acquisition. Kazakhstan has experienced a complete economic turn-around since renouncing nuclear weapons. Its non-nuclear choice has allowed the country to benefit from access to new markets, technologies, and foreign investment. It has paved the way for Kazakhstan to become an important and respected member of the international community. Attracting foreign investors to develop Kazakhstan's oil reserves was especially critical for Kazakhstan.[49] Chevron was the first Western oil company that entered Kazakhstan's market in 1993. Chevron-Kazakhstan Joint Venture JV Tengizchevroil is developing Tengiz oil field, which is among the world's top ten oil-producing fields.[50]

Another characteristic that lends Kazakhstan credibility as an effective actor in the nonproliferation regime is that its strong interest in global nuclear disarmament is coupled with a serious commitment to minimizing proliferation threats. This is especially important in the current international environment in which strong tensions exist between nonproliferation and disarmament agendas. Many countries, especially in the global South, express frustration with a lack of progress in nuclear disarmament, while an ever-growing push for nonproliferation is promoted mostly by the global North. Kazakhstan is attuned to both these perspectives.

Even before the renewed push for disarmament launched by the *Wall Street Journal* op-eds of the "four horsemen" (Henry Kissinger, Sam Nunn, William Perry, and George Shultz), and President Obama's 2009 speech in Prague, Kazakhstan's leadership persistently appealed to the international community with calls for a nuclear-weapon-free world. The momentum generated by developments in the United States and elsewhere gave Kazakhstan a much more conducive environment in which to make these appeals.

Kazakhstan's Nonproliferation and Disarmament Policy

Since gaining independence in 1991, Kazakhstan has become a state party to all major nonproliferation treaties and agreements. The first milestone was reached in 1993, when the Parliament of Kazakhstan voted 283–1 to ratify the country's adherence to the NPT as a NNWS.[51] In the following years, Kazakhstan became a state party to the CTBT, negotiated an IAEA Safeguards Agreement, and adopted the IAEA Additional Protocol.

Kazakhstan can make a difference in current nuclear discussions, and more importantly, it can contribute in practical terms toward disarmament. Nuclear disarmament and nonproliferation have become a "trump" card of Kazakhstan's foreign policy. Its record provides the country with a solid springboard from which to push for progress in nonproliferation and disarmament. The government of Kazakhstan has gone beyond simply joining existing international treaties and agreements. It has become a driving force behind several new initiatives.

Central Asian Nuclear-Weapon-Free Zone

In 2006, Kazakhstan and its Central Asian neighbors (Kyrgyzstan, Tajikistan, Turkmenistan, and Uzbekistan) established a nuclear-weapon-free zone covering all five countries.[52] In a symbolic move, the signing ceremony for the new treaty took place in Semipalatinsk, formerly the primary testing venue for the Soviet Union's nuclear weapons. The treaty entered into force in March of 2009 after all ratification procedures were completed.[53]

The Central Asian NWFZ represents a tangible contribution to global nuclear disarmament efforts. The treaty effectively bans any activities related to research, design, production, nuclear explosions, and acquisition of nuclear weapons in Central Asia. Central Asian states have an obligation not to seek nuclear weapons themselves and not to contribute to efforts of any other countries seeking to acquire nuclear weapons.[54]

The importance of the Central Asian NWFZ cannot be overstated. The region once hosted nuclear weapons and critical nuclear weapon infrastructure and was a site of extensive nuclear weapons testing. Central Asian countries border two nuclear powers (Russia and China), are in the vicinity of nuclear-armed India and Pakistan, and are not far from the nuclear-aspirant Iran. By creating an anti-nuclear weapon enclave in their neighborhood, Central Asian states seek to contribute to regional security by putting a cap on the proliferation of sensitive materials and technologies. In an important deviation from standard provisions of nuclear-weapon-free zones, the Central Asian states took up an obligation to sign the IAEA Additional Protocol that would make their nuclear facilities subject to stricter safeguards and to comply with the CTBT. The Central Asian treaty recognizes the environmental damage that the region suffered as a result of the Soviet nuclear weapon program and an undertaking to rehabilitate affected territories. The treaty also bans any import of foreign radioactive waste into the region, placing an additional emphasis on environmental security. By establishing a NWFZ, Central Asian countries are making a firm contribution toward the ambitious goal of a world free of nuclear weapons.

Support for New START, CTBT, FMCT, and CD

Kazakh officials voice strong support for treaties and agreements critical for eventual nuclear disarmament. President Nazarbayev in his statement in support for New START noted: "The world's two largest nuclear weapon states are showing [by this step] their firm political will to reduce their arsenals.... This instills hope that a nuclear weapons free future for mankind is both possible and achievable."[55]

During the 2010 NPT RevCon, Kazakhstan's permanent representative to the United Nations, Byrganym Aitimova, noted: "We highly value the step taken by Russia and the U.S. by signing the new START treaty. We now expect reciprocal measures from other nuclear weapons possessors."[56]

Kazakhstan has signed and ratified the CTBT and strongly supports the earliest possible entry into force of the treaty.[57] Kazakh officials repeatedly call for the signature and ratification of the CTBT by countries that have not yet done so.[58] At the 2010 NPT RevCon, Permanent Representative Aitimova noted that "ratification of CTBT by the United States will serve as a guiding example for other states and thus facilitate the Treaty's entry into force." She also added that Kazakhstan was "encouraged by the announcement of Indonesia that it will soon ratify the Treaty."[59]

In seeking the early entry into force of the CTBT, Kazakhstan extends full support for the CTBTO, contributes to CTBT verification capacity building, and participates actively in CTBTO exercises, making its nuclear expertise and facilities available for these.[60] In June 2010, the Kazakh government, with the help of the Norwegian Seismic Array, Norway's Ministry of Foreign Affairs, and the CTBTO, established an International Training Center for experts in seismic- and nuclear-monitoring activities in Almaty.[61] The center provides data analysis training not only to Kazakhstan's monitoring specialists but also to specialists from other Central Asian states. Kazakhstan's five seismic-monitoring stations are integrated into the CTBTO International Monitoring System and correctly detected a nuclear explosion carried out by North Korea in May 2009.[62] Kazakhstan also hosted the largest ever on-site inspection simulation exercise in 2008: "IFE08." The CTBTO called it "the largest and most ambitious project ever undertaken in the history of the CTBTO."[63] It involved forty inspectors and required the shipment of forty metric tons of equipment to the Kazakh steppes not far from a former nuclear testing site in Semipalatinsk.[64] On-site inspections will become an important component of CTBT's verification mechanism.

Kazakhstan's government proposed that August 29, the last day of Soviet nuclear testing at Semipalatinsk, be designated International Day against Nuclear Tests. The United Nations General Assembly unanimously adopted a resolution to that effect in December 2009.[65] Now there are activities all over the world to mark this day and to use it as a platform for public education and as a means of increasing pressure on all states to sign and ratify the CTBT.

In addition to its promotion of the entry into force of the CTBT, Kazakhstan actively promotes the adoption of a fissile material cut-off treaty. Kazakh diplomats call upon all states "not to delay the drafting" of such a treaty and attest that an FMCT is "an important step towards nuclear disarmament."[66]

Kazakhstan also promotes nuclear disarmament in regional forums. In 2010, as a chair of the Organization for Security Cooperation in Europe (OSCE), Kazakhstan proposed the establishment of an OSCE forum to discuss disarmament issues.[67] President Nazarbayev also called on the OSCE to adopt a declaration in support of a nuclear-weapon-free world at the OSCE summit held in Astana, Kazakhstan's capital, in December 2010.[68]

Kazakh diplomats have registered their support for the Conference on Disarmament (CD) as a forum for solving international security challenges, despite frustration with what Kazakhstan's then foreign minister Kanat has described as "the deadlock that [has] plagued the Conference for so many years."[69] In March 2011, UN secretary-general Ban Ki-moon appointed veteran Kazakh diplomat Kassym-Jomart Tokayev to the position of director-general of the UN Office in Geneva. In this capacity, Tokayev will serve as Ban Ki-moon's representative to the CD.[70]

Nuclear Security Summit and IAEA Nuclear Fuel Bank

Kazakhstan is both eager and well equipped to play a leading role in global nonproliferation efforts. In one of the most notable examples, Kazakhstan has offered to host the IAEA nuclear fuel bank on its territory. In 2006, the U.S.-based Nuclear Threat Initiative and U.S. billionaire Warren Buffett committed $50 million toward establishing a reserve of low-enriched uranium to be readily available to countries around the world. The thinking behind this proposal is that the availability of fuel on a commercial basis will reduce incentives for countries to pursue indigenous nuclear fuel cycles. This could minimize the spread of sensitive nuclear technologies (specifically, uranium enrichment and plutonium reprocessing) that can be utilized for weapons development. In 2009, the international community committed another $100 million to the IAEA for this purpose, and in 2010 the IAEA Board of Governors approved the establishment of the fuel bank.[71] It is worth noting that Kazakhstan's president formally announced his country's readiness to host a nuclear fuel bank on its territory during a joint press conference with Iranian president Mahmoud Ahmadinejad in Astana.[72] It remains to be seen whether Kazakhstan will be chosen as the site for the IAEA fuel bank. According to the Kazakh Foreign Ministry, U.S. support for Kazakhstan's initiative was confirmed by White House coordinator for arms control and WMD, proliferation, and terrorism Gary Samore in his meetings with Kazakhstan state secretary and foreign minister Kanat Saudabayev.[73]

Kazakhstan was among the forty-six countries invited to the Nuclear Security Summit in Washington, D.C., in April 2010. Kazakh president Nazarbayev had a one-on-one meeting with President Obama during his visit. In a show of goodwill and support for the objectives of the summit, President Nazarbayev promised to convert a HEU-fuelled research reactor and eliminate any remaining HEU; completely shut down a Soviet-era BN-350 fast breeder reactor and secure all spent fuel; host a Global Initiative to Combat Nuclear Terrorism (GICNT) event; and consider establishing a Nuclear Security Center of Excellence. Within one year, Kazakhstan completed work related to the BN-350 fast breeder reactor, moving all spent fuel to a secure location away from the reactor site. Kazakhstan also hosted a meeting of the GICNT on the topic of Countering the Financing of

Nuclear Terrorism. In September 2010, Kazakhstan hosted the first meeting of the GICNT Implementation and Assessment Group (IAG).[74] Work is also underway on the conversion of a research reactor at Alatau from HEU to LEU fuel.

Drivers behind Kazakhstan's Policies

Since giving up nuclear weapons, Kazakhstan has pursued a consistent policy in support of nuclear nonproliferation and global nuclear disarmament. Kazakhstan's history and its ambitions in the international arena are the main drivers of its current policy. The country's renunciation of nuclear weapons and closing of its nuclear testing site were to some extent its first important demonstrations of independence and sovereignty from Russia. Kazakhstan never chose to be a part of the Soviet nuclear weapon program: it was forced by Soviet authorities to be just that. Kazakhstan's people and its environment suffered tremendously as a result, especially from nuclear testing. The full extent of damage inflicted by testing at Semipalatinsk continues to be researched and might never be fully known. Testing operations at Semipalatinsk were shrouded in secrecy, and neither the local population nor the local government had access to information. Among a long list of health problems, people in the vicinity of the former Semipalatinsk testing site continue to suffer from high rates of cancer and mental deficiencies in children born to parents who were exposed to radioactive fallout.[75] In their collaborative studies, physicians from Kazakhstan and Japan showed that residents near the Semipalatinsk test site have similar lasting symptoms to those affecting the survivors of the nuclear attacks on Hiroshima and Nagasaki. Both groups suffer from lasting mental effects, including nightmares, depression, frustration, and other symptoms.[76]

In the aftermath of the Soviet collapse, Kazakhstan was confronted with a whole range of challenges related to dismantling and removing nuclear weapons, converting military facilities, rehabilitating the land, and dealing with health and environmental problems. Kazakhstan's experience, therefore, left the country deeply opposed to nuclear weapons.

Despite being a very young country, Kazakhstan has an ambitious foreign policy agenda. The government views nonproliferation and disarmament as key global issues that it can help to address. Kazakhstan's President Nazarbayev has placed these issues at the center of his personal international agenda. He has even written a book, entitled *Epicenter of Peace*.[77] He has proposed several related UN resolutions, including one adopted by the UN General Assembly in late 2009 declaring August 29 as the International Day against Nuclear Tests (Resolution 64/35).[78] The proposal from Kazakhstan's leadership to host the IAEA fuel bank was to a large extent motivated by an attempt to persuade Iran to accept an alternative to indigenous uranium enrichment.[79]

The factors that are driving Kazakhstan's approaches to nuclear nonproliferation and disarmament are directly related to the concerns it had when deciding the fate of its nuclear inheritance. For example, Kazakhstan has been pushing for the adoption of an international instrument that would provide legally binding negative security assurances to the NNWS and believes such assurances are critical for curbing what Kazakh secretary of state Kanat Saudabayev has referred to as the aspirations of "certain non-nuclear States to acquire nuclear weapons, which they regard as a guarantee of their own security."[80] The lack of a legally binding nuclear security assurance was a major source of concern for Kazakhstan when it debated joining the NPT as an NNWS. Kazakhstan also promotes establishment of NWFZs around the world, similar to the one it helped to create in Central Asia. Central Asian governments established CANWFZ in order to prevent the region from ever being used again for nuclear weapons–related activities. Kazakhstan's push to ban nuclear testing worldwide is also underpinned by its own experience.

PROSPECTS FOR KAZAKHSTAN'S FUTURE POLICY

Kazakhstan will likely continue its policy of supporting nuclear disarmament and seeking to strengthen the nuclear nonproliferation regime. The country's nonproliferation record to date is exemplary and suggests that its choices are driven by an ambition to emerge as an important actor in the global nuclear order.

Kazakhstan's nuclear energy policy is notable in this context because the country has a rich resource base and technological capacity for nuclear fuel production, and the choices the government makes in the future will have an impact on the nuclear nonproliferation environment.[81] First of all, from the nuclear nonproliferation point, it would be beneficial if the country continues not to seek sensitive nuclear fuel technology. Right now Kazakhstan relies on Russia for the enrichment needs of its nuclear fuel industry. Second, Kazakhstan's capacity to supply nuclear fuel (its potential role in the IAEA nuclear fuel bank, its participation in the International Uranium Enrichment Center at Angarsk established to supply enrichment services on a commercial basis) creates an opportunity to make a practical contribution to the global nonproliferation regime by virtue of creating additional incentives for third countries not to pursue indigenous sensitive technologies. Kazakhstan's desire to team up with Russia to supply enrichment services on a commercial basis and its offer to host the IAEA fuel bank are driven by economic and political incentives, and by the country's desire to utilize and further develop rich natural uranium resources and nuclear fuel-related infrastructure. Kazakhstan's ambitions to be an important player on the world nuclear fuel market and in the global nonproliferation regime mutually reinforce each other.

Kazakhstan is in a strong position to engage in specific initiatives integral to the disarmament process, such as the verification of the dismantlement of nuclear weapons and all aspects of cooperative threat reduction. For example, Kazakh specialists could be called upon to participate in verification exercises similar to the UK-Norway verification initiative completed in late 2010.[82] Similarly, Kazakhstan's experts have experience in carrying out CTR projects in their own country since 1991. These specialists would be good candidates to assist in the implementation of CTR-type projects in countries such as North Korea and Pakistan. Having them implement CTR projects might prove to be less politically challenging for some recipient governments.

Kazakhstan's continued support for an FMCT, the CTBT, the on-going Russia-U.S. nuclear arms reduction process, establishment of NWFZ worldwide, and global disarmament is critical for furthering the interdependent norms and processes of nonproliferation and disarmament. Kazakhstan's voice is important because it "leads by example" and has a high degree of legitimacy in promoting these issues.

CONCLUSION

South Africa and Kazakhstan share some similarities in their nuclear nonproliferation and nuclear disarmament policies. Their nuclear renunciation decisions came at the time of political transformation. South Africa's nuclear rollback was partly associated with the end of apartheid, and Kazakhstan's decision making on nuclear weapons took place when the country was transitioning from being a part of the Soviet Union to an independent state. Both countries are staunch supporters of nuclear disarmament, and both have already made a practical contribution to the cause by becoming members of nuclear-weapon-free zones in their respective regions.

What also unites these countries is a shared concern about a lack of progress in nuclear disarmament. In that respect, South Africa and Kazakhstan are in the company of numerous states around the world that have similar sentiments. Both South Africa and Kazakhstan have signed and ratified the CTBT, and both urge for the commencement of negotiations to ban fissile material production.

At the same time, there are some differences between the two countries. South Africa, while a strong actor in its own right, has had its policies closely associated with coalitions of states—the Non-Aligned Movement and the New Agenda Coalition. Kazakhstan's nuclear nonproliferation and nuclear disarmament policies are less contingent on factors outside of its own national interests, priorities, and values. The notable exception is a regional effort to create a Central Asian NWFZ. Moreover, while both countries express frustration with a lack of progress in nuclear disarmament, Kazakhstan differs from South Africa in that it is not pushing back against the international nonproliferation agenda.

South Africa and Kazakhstan have a significant political impact on the global nuclear nonproliferation regime by virtue of being important nuclear energy players. Both countries are members of the Nuclear Suppliers Group and influence its decision making. They are in a position to engage in nuclear trade (uranium, nuclear fuel, and technologies), and their choice of trading partners will be important for nonproliferation (e.g., decisions on trade with non-NPT members). In a notable example of divergence of views between two countries in the context of the Nuclear Suppliers Group, South Africa opposes having the IAEA Additional Protocol as a condition of supply of enrichment and reprocessing items.[83] Kazakhstan has made it clear that it wants to play a leading role in the multilateral fuel cycle arrangements: it offered to host the IAEA international nuclear fuel bank and teamed up with Russia to provide fuel enrichment services on a commercial basis. In early 2011, South Africa and Russia started negotiations on South Africa's potential shareholding in the International Uranium Enrichment Center founded by Russia and Kazakhstan.[84]

Rollback countries such as South Africa and Kazakhstan can play a distinct role in the global nuclear disarmament process for two key reasons. As countries that voluntarily gave up nuclear weapons, they serve as an example that a non-nuclear path is possible and feasible, and that it does not have to be detrimental to security. More importantly, these countries possess technical expertise that is valuable for various stages in the disarmament process: verification of dismantlement of nuclear weapons and, in the case of Kazakhstan, verification of the CTBT regime, once it comes into force.

Notes

1. Numerous states had active nuclear weapon programs that they chose to abandon. Cases of states that possessed actual nuclear weapons and chose to abandon them include Belarus, Kazakhstan, South Africa, and Ukraine.

2. Rian Leith and Joelien Pretorius, "Eroding the Middle Ground: The Shift in Foreign Policy Underpinning South African Nuclear Diplomacy," *Politikon: South African Journal of Political Studies* 36 (2009): 345–61; Noel Stott and Amelia Broodryk, "African States and the 2010 NPT Review Conference," Institute of Security Studies, occasional paper 211, 2010.

3. Helen E. Purkitt and Stephen F. Burgess, *South Africa's Weapons of Mass Destruction* (Bloomington: Indiana University Press, 2005); Helen E. Purkitt, "The Politics of Denuclearization," paper presented at the Defense Nuclear Agency's Fourth Annual International Conference on Controlling Arms, Philadelphia, June 21, 1995; David Albright, "South Africa and the Affordable Bomb," *Bulletin of Atomic Scientists*, July/August 1994, 37–47. David Albright, *South Africa's Secret Nuclear Weapons* (Washington, D.C.: Institute for Science and International Security (ISIS) Report, May 1994), 1–12; Renfrew Christie, "South Africa's Nuclear History," paper presented at the Nuclear History Program Fourth International Conference, Nice, France, June 23–27, 1992; Peter Liberman, "The Rise and Fall of the South African Bomb," *International Security* 26 (Fall 2001): 45–86; William J. Long and Suzette R. Grillot, "Ideas, Beliefs, and Nuclear Policies: The Cases of South Africa and Ukraine," *Nonproliferation Review* 7 (Spring 2000): 24–40; Leonard S. Spector with Jacqueline R. Smith, *Nuclear Ambitions: The Spread of Nuclear Weapons, 1989–1990* (Boulder, Colo.: Westview Press, 1990); Waldo Stumpf, "South Africa's Nuclear Weapons Program: From Deterrence to Dismantlement," *Arms Control Today* 25 (December 1995/January 1996): 4–7; Hannes Steyn, Richard van der Walt, and Jan van Loggerenberg, *Armament and Disarmament: South Africa's Nuclear Weapons Experience* (Pretoria, South Africa: Networks, 2003).

4. Liberman, "Rise and Fall," 45–86. Helen E. Purkitt and Stephen F. Burgess, "Correspondence: South Africa's Nuclear Decisions," *International Security* 27 (Summer 2002): 186–94. Steyn, van der Walt, and van Loggerenberg, *Armament and Disarmament*.

5. On August 14, 1994, the IAEA confirmed de Klerk's statement that one partial and six complete nuclear devices had been dismantled and announced the end of the South African nuclear weapons program. Stumpf, "South Africa's," 4–7. See Albright, *South Africa's Secret Nuclear Weapons*; Albright, "South Africa and the Affordable Bomb," 37–47; and Liberman, "Rise and Fall," 45–86.

6. The NAC consists of Brazil, Ireland, Egypt, Mexico, New Zealand, South Africa, and Sweden.

7. South Africa also played an active role in the successful 2000 NPT Review Conference, helping to bring together states as partners in the NAC for the elimination of all

nuclear weapons. The NAC lobbied the NWS for a commitment for the elimination of nuclear weapons. South Africa and the other members of the NAC also focused on reaching agreement on a series of steps for implementing the nuclear disarmament provisions under the NPT's Article VI. South Africa and the NAC were also active during the 2005 NPT Review Conference.

8. Nina Tannenwald, "Stigmatizing the Bomb: Origins of the Nuclear Taboo," *International Security* 29, no. 4 (2005): 5–49.

9. Thomas Markram, "An Assessment of the Development and Implementation of Policy on Disarmament, Non-Proliferation and Arms Control in South Africa, 1994–2004," *A Decade of Disarmament, Transformation, and Progress* (Pretoria, South Africa: Safer Africa, 2005).

10. Sola Ogunbanwo, "Accelerate the Ratification of the Pelindaba Treaty," *Nonproliferation Review*, Spring 2003, 132–36.

11. The ratifying countries are Algeria, Benin, Botswana, Burkina Faso, Burundi, Equatorial Guinea, Ethiopia, Gabon, Gambia, Guinea, Ivory Coast, Kenya, Libya, Lesotho, Madagascar, Malawi, Mali, Mauritania, Mauritius, Mozambique, Nigeria, Rwanda, Senegal, South Africa, Swaziland, Tanzania, Togo, and Zimbabwe. The countries that have not ratified the treaty are Angola, Cameroon, Central African Republic, Cape Verde, Chad, Comoros, Republic of the Congo, Democratic Republic of Congo, Djibouti, Egypt, Eritrea, Ghana, Guinea-Bissau, Liberia, Morocco, Namibia, Niger, Seychelles, Sierra Leone, Somalia, São Tomé and Príncipe, Sudan, Tunisia, Uganda, and Zambia.

12. Protocol I (negative security assurances) has been ratified by China, France, and the United Kingdom. Protocol II (ban on nuclear testing in the nuclear-weapon-free zone) has been ratified by China, France, and the United Kingdom. The United States hesitated in ratifying the Treaty of Pelindaba protocols, because it constricts U.S. freedom of action. For example, one protocol carries with it the prospect of new powers to regulate the flow of shipping and the exploitation of natural resources found in Antarctica. The treaty may also lead to new restrictions on the movement of nuclear materials though the Indian and Atlantic oceans. Some in the U.S. military initially wanted the U.S. government to oppose an NWFZ. The fact that the United States decided to support the treaty was an indication of how useful the United States felt the Mandela's government's nuclear nonproliferation policies and "nuclear trendsetter" activities were during the 1990s.

13. Leith and Pretorius, " 345–61; Stott and Broodryk, "African States."

14. Abdul Minty, "Statement by the Republic of South Africa during the General Debate of the 2005 Review Conference of the States Parties to the Treaty on the Non-Proliferation of Nuclear Weapons," May 3, 2005, http://www.un.org/events/npt2005/statements/npt03southafrica.pdf.

15. Leith and Pretorius, " 345–61; Stott and Broodryk, "African States."

16. Author's interview with Noel Stott, Institute of National Security Studies, Pre-

toria, South Africa, August 25, 2010. Stott observed that South Africa seeks to develop technologies across the fuel cycle, as Iran is doing.

17. "U.S. and South Africa Sign Agreement on Cooperation in Nuclear Energy Research and Development," *U.S. Federal News Service, Including U.S. State News*, September 20, 2009, General Interest Module, accessed through ProQuest, October 14, 2009.

18. Bonnie D. Jenkins, "Keeping Nukes in Check," *Mail and Guardian* (Johannesburg), April 16, 2010, 11.

19. "India votes against Iran nuclear program, Pakistan abstains," http://www.thaindian.com/newsportal/world-news/india-votes-against-iran-nuclear-program-pakistan-abstains_100281082.html#ixzz0uulTaTfJ.

20. Abdul S. Minty, deputy director-general, ambassador, and special representative for disarmament and the New Partnership for Africa's Development, Department of International Relations and Cooperation, Republic of South Africa, and governor, board of governors, International Atomic Energy Agency, "Remarks at Council on Foreign Relations Symposium: Rising Powers and Global Institutions," Second Annual Symposium of the International Institutions and Global Governance program, Washington, D.C., May 19, 2010, 6–7, http://www.cfr.org/content/thinktank/IIGG_SymposiumNote_May19.pdf.

21. Adam Habib, "South Africa: Nuclear Powers Need to Get Serious about Disarming," *Business Day*, April 13, 2010.

22. Abdul Samad Minty, "Perspectives on the 2010 NPT Review Conference," NGO Committee on Disarmament, Peace and Security, March 31, 2010, http://disarm.igc.org/index.php?view=article&catid=145%3Adisarmament-times-spring-2010&id=342%3Aperspectives-on-the-2010-npt-review-conference-ambassador-abdul-samad-minty-south-africa&option=com_content&Itemid=2.

23. Jenkins, "Keeping Nukes in Check," 11.

24. Ibid.

25. Ibid.

26. "Negotiations Begin at NPT Review Conference," *Global Security Newswire*, May 4, 2010, http://www.globalsecuritynewswire.org/gsn/nw_20100510_4085.php.

27. "Statement by Ambassador Abdul S. Minty to the NPT Review Conference," May 5, 2010, http://www.un.org/en/conf/npt/2010/statements/pdf/southafrica_en.pdf.

28. Ibid. Minty also called for efforts to build upon the 2000 NPT RevCon Final Document, in which it was agreed that legally binding security assurances would be given to states that had foregone the nuclear weapons option under the NPT; ratification of the CTBT and the commencement of negotiations on a verifiable universal ban on the production of fissile material for nuclear weapons and other nuclear explosive devices; and for the right of withdrawal from the NPT to be more clearly defined, particularly in relation to the continued application of safeguards on material, equipment and technology already transferred.

29. Joint Declaration by Iran, Turkey, and Brazil, May 17, 2010, http://www.guardian.co.uk/world/julian-borger-global-security-blog/2010/may/17/iran-brazil-turkey-nuclear.

30. Minty, "Remarks at Council on Foreign Relations Symposium," 6–7.

31. "Statement by Ambassador Abdul S. Minty to the NPT Review conference," May 5, 2010.

32. Stott, interview.

33. Togzhan Kassenova, author of the section on Kazakhstan, is grateful to Patrick Smith for research assistance and to Lyndon Burford, Dr. Rico Issacs, Dr. Nargis Kassenova, Kevin Mara, and Ward Wilson for comments on the earlier draft. A special word of gratitude goes to Lyndon Burford and Ward Wilson for numerous stimulating conversations on Kazakhstan's renunciation of nuclear weapons.

34. William C. Potter, with the assistance of Eve E. Cohen and Edward V. Kayukov, "Nuclear Profiles of the Soviet Successor States," Monterey Institute of International Studies, monograph no. 1, May 1993, 16; Steven Zaloga, "Strategic Forces of the CIS," *Jane's Intelligence Review*, February 1992, 79; "Kazakhstan Profile: Nuclear Overview," Nuclear Threat Initiative, updated February 2011, http://www.nti.org/e_research/profiles/Kazakhstan/Nuclear/index.html.

35. "Kazakhstan Profile," Nuclear Threat Initiative.

36. Potter, "Nuclear Profiles," 16; Zaloga, "Strategic Forces," 79; "Kazakhstan Profile"; William N. Szymanski, "The Uranium Industry of the Commonwealth of Independent States," *Uranium Industry Annual 1991*, October 1992, as cited by William C. Potter, "Nuclear Exports from the Former Soviet Union: What's New, What's True," *Arms Control Today*, January/February 1993, 4–5.

37. Author's interview with Alibek Kassymov, former defense minister of Kazakhstan, Almaty, September 2008; Alexander A. Pikayev, "Post–Soviet Russia and Ukraine: Who Can Push the Button?" *Nonproliferation Review*, Spring–Summer 1994, 35.

38. A. Smailov, ed., Census Results in the Republic of Kazakhstan, 1999 (in Russian), 11, http://www.unesco.kz/heritagenet/kz/content/information/mustafaev2.htm; Robert Greenall, "Russians Left Behind in Central Asia," November 23, 2005, http://news.bbc.co.uk/2/hi/asia-pacific/4420922.stm; I. O. Vendina, "Russians beyond Russia's Borders" (in Russian), http://geo.1september.ru/articlef.php?ID=200101108.

39. Unlike Ukraine, where ethnic Ukrainians were involved in weapons development, maintenance, and operation, hardly any ethnic Kazakhs served in the Soviet strategic nuclear forces.

40. Oumirserik Kassenov and Kairat Abuseitov, "The Future of Nuclear Weapons in the Kazakh Republic's National Security," Center for Strategic Studies, Kazakhstan Institute of Management, Economics, and Strategic Research, *The Potomac Papers*, Potomac Foundation, Vienna, Va., February 1993, 7.

41. Ibid., 8.

42. Author's interview with Tulegen Zhukeev, former state secretary of Kazakhstan, Almaty, 2009.

43. Robert S. Norris and William M. Arkin, "Soviet Nuclear Testing, August 29, 1949–October 24, 1990," *Bulletin of the Atomic Scientists* 54, no. 3 (May/June 1998): 70.

44. Memorandum on Security Assurances in connection with the Republic of Kazakhstan's accession to the Treaty on the Non-Proliferation of Nuclear Weapons. France and China were not members of the NPT in 1994 and therefore did not sign the memorandum.

45. Author's interviews with former U.S. and Kazakh officials, Almaty and Washington, D.C., 2008–9.

46. Author's interview with William Courtney, former U.S. ambassador to Kazakhstan, Washington, D.C., April 2008.

47. Zhukeev, interview.

48. The country is not a classic case of a nuclear rollback due to the fact that it inherited nuclear weapons rather than developed them.

49. In 1992–93, the World Bank estimated that Kazakhstan had 12 billion barrels of recoverable oil reserves. More recently *BP Statistical Review of World Energy 2010* estimated that Kazakhstan has 39.8 billion barrels of proven oil reserves. *Kazakhstan: The Transition to a Market Economy* (Washington, D.C.: World Bank, 1993), 8; *BP Statistical Review of World Energy 2010* (London: BP, 2010), 6, http://www.bp.com/liveassets/bp_internet/globalbp/globalbp_uk_english/reports_and_publications/statistical_energy_review_2008/STAGING/local_assets/2010_downloads/statistical_review_of_world_energy_full_report_2010.pdf.

50. "Major Expansion at Tengiz Field in Kazakhstan Completed," September 2008, Chevron, http://www.chevron.com/news/currentissues/tengiz/; *Success Stories: Foreign Investors in Kazakhstan* (Almaty, Kazakhstan: Foreign Investors' Council Association, 2010), 8, http://www.kazembassy.org.uk/img/Success%20story%20final.pdf.

51. R. Jeffrey Smith, "Kazakhstan Ratifies Nuclear Control Pact, Will Get U.S. Aid," *Washington Post*, December 13, 1993, Lexis Nexis.

52. Scott Parrish and William Porter, "Central Asian States Establish Nuclear-Weapon-Free-Zone despite U.S. Opposition," CNS Research Story, James Martin Center for Nonproliferation Studies, September 5, 2006, http://cns.miis.edu/stories/060905.htm.

53. William Potter, Togzhan Kassenova, and Anya Loukianova, "Central Asia Becomes a Nuclear-Weapon-Free-Zone," CNS Feature Story, James Martin Center for Nonproliferation Studies, December 11, 2008, http://cns.miis.edu/stories/081201_canwfz.htm.

54. "Central Asian Nuclear-Weapon-Free Zone," treaty text, CNS Inventory, James Martin Center for Nonproliferation Studies, http://cns.miis.edu/inventory/pdfs/aptcanwz.pdf.

55. "Kazakhstan's Nazarbayev Welcomes U.S.-Russia Upcoming Nuclear Pact, Says It Strengthens Hope for a Nuclear Weapons Free World," April 7, 2010, OSCE, http://www.amb-kazakhstan.fr/Documents/Kazakhstan%20Nazarbayev%20Nuclear%20Agreement.pdf.

56. "Statement by H.E. Ms. Byrganym Aitimova, permanent representative of the Republic of Kazakhstan to the United Nations at the General Debate of the 2010 Review Conference of the Parties to the Treaty on the Non-Proliferation of Nuclear Weapons," May 5, 2010, United Nations, New York, http://www.un.org/en/conf/npt/2010/statements/pdf/kazakhstan_en.pdf.

57. "Status of Signature and Ratification," CTBTO, http://www.ctbto.org/the-treaty/status-of-signature-and-ratification/.

58. "Kazakhstan Urges All UN Members to Endorse Treaty Banning Nuclear Tests," M2 Press Wire, September 27, 2010, Lexis Nexis.

59. "Statement by Aitimova."

60. "Kazakhstan Fully Supports Activity of Comprehensive Nuclear Test Ban Treaty Organization," *Times of Central Asia* (Bishkek, Kyrgyzstan), August 26, 2010, Lexis Nexis.

61. "Statement by H.E. Mr. Yerzhan Kazykhanov, Permanent Representative of the Republic of Kazakhstan to the International Organizations in Vienna, at the 34th Session of the Preparatory Commission for the Comprehensive Nuclear-Test-Ban Treaty Organization," June 28–29, 2010, Embassy of the Republic of Kazakhstan in Austria, http://www.kazakhstan.at/fileadmin/pdf/Kazakhstan_Statement_34th_PrepCom.pdf.

62. "Statement by H.E. Mr. Kanat Saudabayev, Secretary of State–Minister of Foreign Affairs of the Republic of Kazakhstan at the Conference on Facilitating the Entry into Force of the Comprehensive Nuclear-Test-Ban Treaty (Article XIV)," CTBTO, September 24, 2009, New York, http://www.ctbto.org/fileadmin/user_upload/Art_14_2009/240909_Morning_Session/240909_Kazakhstan.pdf.

63. "CTBTO to Test Its On-Site Inspection Regime in September 2008 in Kazakhstan," CTBTO, June 23, 2008, http://www.ctbto.org/specials/ctbto-to-test-its-on-site-inspection-regime-in-september-2008-in-kazakhstan/page-1-ife08/?Fsize=a.

64. Ibid.

65. Resolution A/64/391 International Day against Nuclear Tests, UN, January 12, 2010, http://daccess-dds-ny.un.org/doc/UNDOC/GEN/N09/463/93/PDF/N0946393.pdf?OpenElement.

66. Sean Kelly, "Report-Thursday, 2010-10-14 Afternoon Session," NGO Committee on Disarmament, Peace and Security, http://disarm.igc.org/index.php?view=article&id=412%3Areport—thursday-2010-10-14-afternoon-session&option=com_content&Itemid=81; "Statement by Saudabayev."

67. "Kazakhstan Proposes Creating OSCE Forums to Discuss Environmental and Disarmament Issues," Kazakhstan General Newswire, December 1, 2010, Lexis Nexis.

68. "Kazakhstan Calls on OSCE States to Adopt Declaration in Nuclear-Free World," Thai Press Reports, December 3, 2010, Lexis Nexis.

69. "Statement by H.E. Mr. Kanat Saudabayev Chairman-in-Office of the Organization for Security and Cooperation in Europe, Secretary of State–Minister of Foreign Affairs of the Republic of Kazakhstan at the Conference on Disarmament," United Nations Office in Geneva (UNOG), March 5, 2010, Geneva, available on the website of the Ministry of Foreign Affairs of Kazakhstan, http://portal.mfa.kz/portal/page/portal/mfa/en/content/ministry/minister/speeches/2010/The%20Conference%20on%20Disarmament%20(March%205%202010%20Geneva).

70. "Vice-President Tokayev Tapped for UN Geneva Post," OSCE Parliamentary Assembly, March 16, 2011, http://www.oscepa.org/index.php?view=article&id=1014%3Avice-president-tokayev-tapped-for-un-geneva-post&option=com_content&Itemid=73>.

71. "IAEA Board Agrees to Create International Fuel Bank, a 'Breakthrough' in Global Cooperation to Reduce Nuclear Dangers: Warren Buffet/NTI $50 Million Pledge Conditions Fulfilled," NTI press release, December 3, 2010, http://www.nti.org/c_press/release_fuel_bank_120310.pdf.

72. "Kazakhstan in Nuclear Bank Offer," April 6, 2009, BBC News, http://news.bbc.co.uk/2/hi/7986785.stm.

73. "USA Backs Kazakhstan's Nuclear Bank Initiative—Foreign Ministry," Interfax-Kazakhstan, January 27, 2011, BBC Monitoring Central Asia Unit, Lexis Nexis.

74. The GICNT Implementation and Assessment Group coordinates GICNT activities. IAG is an informal advisory body open to participation from all GICNT partner nations and official observers. It creates working groups to address priority and focus areas identified by the Plenary. "The Global Initiative to Combat Nuclear Terrorism," U.S. State Department, http://www.state.gov/t/isn/c37072.htm; Greg Delaney, "Kazakhstan Hosts Conference on Countering Nuclear Terrorism," KazakhstanLive.com, September 28, 2010, http://www.kazakhstanlive.com/2.aspx?ProdID=aff58bd5-42c4-460b-952d-1315c767b5cc&CatID=9f9f8034-6dd6-4f7e-adcf-0f6a7c0406d9&sr=100&page=1.

75. A. Akanov, S. Yamashita, S. Merimanov, A. Indershyiev, and A. Musakhanova, *Nuclear Explosions and Public Health Development* (Nagasaki-Almaty, Kazakhstan, 2008), 115–116 (in Russian).

76. Noriyuki Kawano, Kyoko Hirabayashi, Masatsugu Matsuo, Yasuyuki Taooka, Takashi Hiraoka, Kazbek Apsalikov, Talgat Moldagaliev, and Masaharu Hoshi, "Human Suffering Effects of Nuclear Tests at Semipalatinsk, Kazakhstan: Established on the Basis of Questionnaire Surveys," *Journal of Radiation Research* 47 (2006): A209–17.

77. "New Book: 'Epicenter of Peace' by President Nazarbayev," press release, Belfer Center for Science and International Affairs, April 12, 2002, http://belfercenter.ksg.harvard.edu/publication/3332/new_book.html?breadcrumb=%2Ftopic%2F47%2Fenvironmental_economics%3Fgroupby%3D0%26%3D%26filter%3D2002%26page%3D6.

78. Letter from the President of the UN General Assembly, Ali Abdussalam Treki, to All Permanent Representatives and Permanent Observers to the UN, July 29, 2010, http://www.un.org/ga/president/64/letters/ntbt290710.pdf.

79. Joanna Lillis, "Kazakhstan: Is Astana Aiming to Broker U.S.-Iran Nuclear Deal?" Center for Strategic Research and Analysis, http://cesran.org/index.php?option=com_content&view=article&id=291%3Akazakhstan-is-astana-aiming-to-broker-us-iran-nuclear-deal-&catid=57%3Amakale-ve-raporlar&Itemid=63&lang=en.

80. "Remarks by H.E. Kanat Saudabayev, Secretary of State and Minister of Foreign Affairs of the Republic of Kazakhstan at the International Conference, World Free of Nuclear Weapons: Nuclear Disarmament, Non-Proliferation and Export Control, October 12, 2010, Oslo, Norway," http://portal.mfa.kz/portal/page/portal/mfa/en/content/news/nws2010/2010-10-12; "Kazakhstan Urges All UN Members to Endorse Treaty Banning Nuclear Tests," M2 PressWIRE, September 27, 2010, Lexis Nexis.

81. For more information on Kazakhstan's nuclear energy policy, refer to Togzhan Kassenova, "Kazakhstan's 'Nuclear Renaissance,'" *St. Antony's International Review* 4, no. 2 (2009): 51–74.

82. Hassan Elbahtimy, "UK-Norway Initiative: Mapping Progress," VERTIC, http://www.vertic.org/media/assets/Events/UK-Norway%20Initiative-FINAL.pdf.

83. "Nuclear Suppliers Group (NSG)," CNS Inventory, http://www.nti.org/e_research/official_docs/inventory/pdfs/nsg.pdf.

84. Keith Campbell, "SA Offered Shareholding in International Uranium Enrichment Venture," *Engineering News*, January 14, 2011, http://www.engineeringnews.co.za/article/south-africa-invited-to-become-shareholder-in-international-uranium-enrichment-operation-2011-01-14.

CHAPTER FOUR

The Pessimistic Nuclear Weapon States
France, Russia, and China

David Santoro

THIS CHAPTER EXAMINES THE IMPACT of current nuclear disarmament momentum on France, Russia, and China. Like the United States and the United Kingdom, these three states are de jure nuclear weapon states (NWS) under the Nuclear Nonproliferation Treaty (NPT) and, therefore, have special responsibilities to lead the disarmament project (for more details, see chapter 1). Yet, they have not been drivers of the current momentum, unlike the United States and the United Kingdom. France, Russia, and China have been pessimistic about the prospects for a nuclear-weapon-free world and have expressed—through declarations or actions—strong skepticism about it, if not complete disinterest.

Paris has exhibited a laudable nuclear disarmament record but has remained deeply opposed to expressing its support for a world without nuclear weapons. Moscow has not been as categorical as Paris in its opposition but has remained mostly silent (and has preferred to prioritize sequential nuclear reductions) because it believes that a world free of nuclear weapons can be achieved only in the very, very distant future. For its part, Beijing has declared its strong support for nuclear disarmament, but the sincerity of this support has been seriously questioned in view of the limited tangible commitments it has made to advance the goal and, most importantly, in view of its force modernization program.

What are the ins and outs of the French, Russian, and Chinese nuclear weapon policies, and what are the specifics of their positions on nuclear disarmament? How have these policies developed and evolved, notably since Barack Obama arrived at the White House and laid out his Prague agenda? Most importantly, what are the rationales behind these policies, and how are they likely to develop in the foreseeable future? This chapter addresses this set of questions.

FRANCE

French nuclear doctrine has hardly changed since Paris first developed its nuclear weapons in the late 1950s. The French *force de frappe* (strike force) follows the principle of *stricte suffisance* ("minimum deterrent" in French) and is thus limited, although it is considered crucial to preserve France's "vital interests."[1] While these interests are deliberately left undefined, Paris is clear that nuclear weapons are solely meant to deter war.

The formulation of French nuclear doctrine has always been intimately linked to French presidents, so much so that France has been called a "nuclear monarchy."[2] Unlike any other NWS, French nuclear doctrine has been traditionally laid out in presidential speeches. Although known as a modernizer keen on championing a clean break with prior French practices, President Nicolas Sarkozy followed the nuclear tradition and detailed France's doctrine in a landmark speech delivered in Cherbourg (where French nuclear submarines are built) on March 21, 2008.[3] The main principles he developed were subsequently reiterated and expanded in a defense white paper published in June 2008, France's first since 1994.[4]

According to these latest documents, French nuclear weapons will cause "unacceptable damage" to adversaries, but France will use them only "in extreme circumstances of legitimate defense."[5] In 2006, former president Jacques Chirac suggested that France could now use nuclear weapons in the context of mass-casualty terrorism (presumably nuclear, biological, and chemical [NBC] terrorism).[6] Nicolas Sarkozy, however, did not reiterate the reference, stressing that the French deterrent protects the country "from any aggression against our vital interests emanating from a state—wherever it may come from and whatever form it may take."[7] France also maintains the option of a limited nuclear strike or warning against adversaries who have misjudged or miscalculated French vital interests—to "reestablish deterrence."[8] France, therefore, has constantly rejected the adoption of a no-first-use (NFU) policy, considering that nuclear retaliation is consistent with the right of self-defense defined in Article 51 of the United Nations (UN) Charter. Hence the reservations Paris has attached to the negative security assurances (NSA) it has offered to non-nuclear weapon states (NNWS) and nuclear-weapon-free zones (NWFZ) protocols it has ratified.

France has a traditional approach to the concept of deterrence, which it strictly interprets as *nuclear* deterrence. The French have been skeptical about ballistic missile defense (BMD) systems supplementing deterrence, let alone replacing it. Paris defended the Anti-Ballistic Missile Treaty until its demise in 2001 (when the Bush administration withdrew from it), explaining that BMD systems would be expensive and that they would trigger an arms race. Since then, however, the French position has evolved. Paris has agreed to the common North Atlantic Treaty Organization (NATO) decision to conduct a feasibility study on BMD systems to protect the European territory, and President Sarkozy has stressed that "missile defense capabilities against a limited strike could be a useful complement to nuclear deterrence, without being a substitute for it," suggesting that France would participate in the future NATO BMD system.[9] Yet, in the lead-up to the 2010 Summit Meeting of NATO Heads of State and Government, French defense minister Hervé Morin indicated that the proposed concept of expanded BMD would be endorsed, but he compared it to the Maginot Line of fixed defenses that failed to prevent the German invasion of France during the Second World War, adding, "The best way to guard against an apocalypse is to be in a position to gain respect from having credible military capabilities [read: nuclear weapons]."[10]

In this context, how has Paris approached nuclear disarmament? Until 1991, the French nuclear arsenal was consistently growing in size and capacity, although arguably always in line with the principle of *stricte suffisance*. Paris began to downsize its forces only after the Cold War, in the context of its accession to the NPT in 1992. From then on, as the following analysis shows, the French undertook important nuclear reductions as well as a range of very innovative initiatives. Yet, unlike their U.S. and UK counterparts, they have constantly shied away from declaring an ambition for a world free of nuclear weapons.

Between 1991 and 2008, Paris retired its thirty Mirage IV-P medium-range nuclear bombers, dismantled all eighteen S-3D intermediate-range ballistic missiles (IRBM) on the Plateau d'Albion, eliminated all thirty Hadès short-range nuclear-armed missiles (SRBM), and reduced the number of its nuclear-powered ballistic missile submarines (SSBN) from six to four, with only enough submarine-launched ballistic missiles (SLBM) for three of the four SSBN.

Today, France's nuclear arsenal is composed of just sea- and air-based forces, but these forces are being modernized. The sea-based deterrent consists of four Le Triomphant-class SSBN (with the fourth and final vessel of this class, *Le Terrible*, soon set to enter operational service) and forty-eight M45 SLBM that can carry up to six TN-75 warheads. *Le Terrible* will be able to carry the new, more accurate (and longer-range) M51 SLBM, which will gradually replace the M45 and be initially loaded with the same TN-75 warheads in its M51.1 version, until the M51.2 version enters service in 2015 to carry the new TNO warheads. France's air-based deterrent consists of sixty land-based Mirage 2000N aircraft and twenty-four sea-based Super Etendard aircraft (assigned to the *Charles de Gaulle* aircraft carrier), all of which carry Air-Sol Moyenne Portée (ASMP, medium-range air to surface missile) strategic missiles equipped with a single TN-81 warhead. The Mirage 2000N and Super Etendard aircraft are gradually being replaced by the new Rafale F3, and an improved version of the ASMP missile (the ASMP Amélioré) equipped with the new TNA warhead has recently entered service.

In addition to undertaking nuclear reductions (while continuing the modernization of its remaining forces), Paris abandoned its traditional opposition to nuclear test limitations after a 1995–96 campaign of nuclear tests, and it signed and ratified the Comprehensive Nuclear-Test-Ban Treaty (CTBT) shortly after its conclusion in September 1996. Paris also dismantled its test site in the South Pacific, becoming along with the United Kingdom the only NWS without a national test site. Since 1997, Paris has also supported the conclusion of a fissile material "cut-off" treaty (FMCT), which is consistent with its moratorium policy on the production of fissile material for weapon purposes and its decision to dismantle its production facilities at Pierrelatte (highly enriched uranium [HEU] production) and Marcoule (plutonium production). Moreover, in 1997, Paris announced the de-targeting of its nuclear forces and declared that it had taken steps to reduce the response times of its weapons and to prevent their use without presidential authorization.[11] Finally, Paris clarified and expanded its security assurances to the NNWS in an April 6, 1995, letter to the UN secretary-general and in a statement at the Conference on Disarmament (CD) delivered the same day, and it has also provided security assurances through NWFZ.[12]

In his Cherbourg speech, President Sarkozy proposed a fresh plan for disarmament. The plan does not shift the main post–Cold War direction taken by France but suggests that Paris may be willing to be more engaged in the newly revived international disarmament diplomacy.

The Sarkozy plan promises a review of how low French nuclear forces can go, a one-third reduction of France's airborne nuclear forces, a promise that France will possess no more than three hundred nuclear warheads, and increased transparency in French nuclear activities, notably through the invitation of international experts to observe the dismantlement of the former fissile material production facilities at Pierrelatte and Marcoule.[13] Moreover, the plan, which was endorsed by the European Union during the French presidency (in the second half of 2008),[14] calls for swift CTBT ratification, the conclusion of an FMCT, increased transparency among NWS on their nuclear forces, the universal accession and implementation of the Hague Code of Conduct against Ballistic Missile Proliferation, and the opening of negotiations on a treaty banning short- and intermediate-range surface-to-surface missiles.

The French contend that their disarmament policy is consistent with France's legal obligations defined in Article VI of the NPT. This is illustrated, they argue, by France's policy of nuclear restraint and its significant nuclear reductions.[15] However, Paris has a very strict interpretation of Article VI, emphasizing its multidimensional character, which also includes the goals of the cessation of the arms race (now achieved) and general and complete disarmament. According to Paris, nuclear disarmament cannot—and should not—be addressed separately from disarmament in other areas. At the 2010 NPT RevCon, for instance, French representative Eric Danon stressed, "In keeping with its obligations under Article VI of the NPT, France is also working in all areas that contribute to general and complete disarmament."[16] Thus, at the 2000 NPT Review Conference (RevCon), Paris resisted the adoption of the so-called Thirteen Practical Steps on nuclear disarmament and has continuously stressed its preference for the less "unequivocal" disarmament commitments made by the NWS in 1995. As French representative François Rivasseau stressed at the 2005 NPT RevCon, "France emphasizes *in particular* its commitment to the program adopted in 1995" (emphasis added).[17]

Not surprisingly, Paris has been categorically opposed to declaring its support for a nuclear-weapon-free world. From a French perspective, what really matters is security, which France believes simply cannot be achieved by eliminating nuclear weapons. Paris does not believe that abolition is currently possible or, even if it were, that abolition would solve today's security problems. To be fair, this analysis is shared by Washington and London, the difference being that the latter two trust that a strong commitment to moving toward a nuclear-weapon-free world is a positive development. In French eyes, this commitment is not considered helpful. As Danon explained at the 2009 NPT Preparatory Committee (PrepCom), "it is not by eliminating more nuclear weapons that we will convince countries in breach of their commitments to abide by them."[18] Similarly, at the September 2009 UN Security Council Summit, where

President Barack Obama advocated the vision of a nuclear-weapon-free world that he had developed in Prague five months earlier, President Sarkozy stressed that ambitious disarmament plans are laudable, but that the international community should first address the pressing Iranian and North Korean nuclear crises. As he explained, "the present comes before the future, and the present includes two major nuclear crises."[19]

In other words, the French do not believe that disarmament and nonproliferation are intrinsically linked, unlike their U.S. and UK counterparts. Paris considers that nonproliferation is—and should be—the main goal and that solving the Iranian crisis is the top priority. After voicing concerns about proliferation, President Sarkozy stressed in his Cherbourg speech that he is "thinking in particular of Iran."[20]

The current nuclear disarmament momentum, however, has had some impact on Paris's disarmament diplomacy. In July 2009, for instance, France subscribed to the common language on nuclear abolition hatched by the G8 heads of state and governments that reads, "We are all committed to seeking a safer world for all and to creating the conditions for a world without nuclear weapons, in accordance with the goals of the NPT."[21]

Yet, the French generally stop short of endorsing the nuclear abolition aspiration and prefer to promote their "practical commitment" to disarmament, congratulating themselves for their "concrete actions" in this area. Extensively used in French official documents and statements, these words clearly suggest that Paris considers a world without nuclear weapons impractical or mere abstract rhetoric.[22] Sometimes, it even appears as if the French believe that the current nuclear disarmament momentum is not only useless but also actually counterproductive because it diverts attention from today's proliferation problems. A recent report from the French Senate, for instance, labels it a "demagogue" discourse from which France should steer clear.[23] Similarly, in one of his essays, Tiphaine de Champchesnel explains that French philosopher Paul Ricoeur's description of a utopia as a dream that helps a society escape from hard realities may well be applicable to the current nuclear abolition debate.[24]

RUSSIA

Russia first developed nuclear weapons in the context of the Cold War against the United States. During that time, it built a massive arsenal and relied on the threat of nuclear devastation for its national security policy, although it made an NFU pledge (largely because of the superiority of its conventional forces).

The collapse of the Russian empire and the end of the Cold War brought about significant changes, not least of which was the initiation of a major disarmament process in coordination with the United States. In the nuclear area, this process, which built upon the Intermediate-Range Nuclear Forces (INF) Treaty that the two parties had concluded a few years earlier (1987), led to the 1991 Strategic Arms Reduction Treaty (START) and the announcement of the Presidential Nuclear Initiatives (for more details, see chapter 1).

Yet, Moscow continued to rely on its nuclear arsenal thereafter. In 1993, it revised its doctrine and reversed the traditional NFU policy, leading many to believe that it had elevated the role of nuclear weapons. In reality, their mission remained the same: strategic deterrence.[25] Some scholars even argued that their role had decreased because the threat from the West had receded. In the mid-1990s, Moscow did explore a possible greater reliance on tactical nuclear weapons (TNW) but ended up abandoning the idea after the 1997 NATO-Russia Founding Act.[26] Real change took place in the late 1990s and was formalized in the January 2000 National Security Concept, the April 2000 Military Doctrine, and the October 2003 Defense White Paper. In those documents, Moscow explained that it could now also use nuclear weapons in limited strikes for the purpose of regional (non-nuclear) war de-escalation.[27]

Beginning in 2007, Moscow initiated a further review of its doctrine. As it was being wrapped up, Nikolai Patrushev, secretary of the Russian Security Council, indicated in an October 2009 interview with *Izvestia* that Russia could decide to no longer exclude a preemptive nuclear strike on an aggressor. He added that nuclear weapons could be assigned not only to large-scale and regional wars but also to local wars, which would have further increased Russian reliance on its nuclear arsenal.[28]

Patrushev's statement, however, spurred so much criticism inside Russia that instead of further expanding the role of nuclear weapons, the new doctrine ended up slightly circumscribing it.[29] Released in February 2010, the new document continues to assign nuclear weapons both to large-scale and regional wars. Yet, it tightens the criterion of nuclear weapon use. Whereas the previous doctrine considered it possible "in situations critical to the national security of the Russian Federation," the 2010 document "only" considers weapon use in situations when "the very existence of [Russia] is under threat." Added to this is a new provision stipulating that the decision to use nuclear weapons is reserved to the Russian president.

Moreover, while reiterating that the main mission of nuclear weapons is the "prevention of nuclear military conflict and likewise any other military conflict" by inflicting "pre-determined damage," the new doctrine really focuses on *strategic* deterrence. This has led some to deduce that Russia's TNW may have a more limited role than generally thought. The 2010 doctrine also assigns high-precision conventional weapons to the mission of strategic deterrence, thereby continuing a process initiated in the mid-2000s that consists of equipping a growing number of Russia's strategic delivery vehicles with conventional warheads.[30]

In any event, Moscow clearly considers that its nuclear forces remain crucial to ensure Russia's security. This is illustrated by the fact that Russia maintains many of its nuclear weapons on a high-alert status. In early 2009, Colonel General Nikolai Solovtsov, the commander of Russia's intercontinental ballistic missiles (ICBM) force, indicated that "at least 96 percent of all Russian missile systems are ready for deployment within several dozen seconds."[31] This is also clearly illustrated by its arsenal management strategy. Although Moscow is disposed to undertake major reductions because many of its forces date back from the Soviet era and are decaying, it is also developing new weapons and modernizing some of its existing systems as part of a doctrinal shift from a "substantially redundant" to a "minimally sufficient" posture aimed at maintaining its traditional nuclear triad.[32]

According to the latest estimates, Russia has 4,600 operational nuclear warheads (2,600 strategic and 2,000 tactical) and 7,300 in reserve or awaiting dismantlement.[33] It deploys approximately 1,100 warheads on over 300 ICBM of six types, and although it is retiring many older ICBM, it is extending the life cycles of some, slowly deploying the new single-warhead RS-12M1/2 Topol-M ICBM and has begun deploying the new road-mobile RS-24 ICBM equipped with multiple independently targetable reentry vehicles (MIRVs). Russia also has 10 active SSBNs equipped with 160 SLBMs that can carry approximately 600 warheads, and it is upgrading six of them with the new Sineva SLBM, while the four others will be replaced by the Borey-class SSBN and its accompanying MIRVed RSM-56 Bulava SLBM, whose development has incidentally encountered numerous difficulties. Moreover, Russia deploys 75 nuclear-capable bombers of three types that can carry approximately 900 warheads (the targeting and navigation systems of some have been modernized). Finally, although many of Russia's TNW, on which Moscow releases little information, are old and will be retired soon, they continue to play a key role at present, and the life cycles of some are being extended.

In this context, how has Moscow approached nuclear disarmament? Clearly, long gone is the time when former Soviet president Mikhail Gorbachev described his vision of a nuclear-weapon-free world. Today, to Russia, this is a goal worth pursuing, but a very distant one. In diplomatic circles, Moscow often notes its laudable nuclear reductions and its support for the CTBT (which it has ratified) and an FMCT, but it tends to refrain from overtly endorsing the abolition debate, although it is not as intransigent as Paris. This is because Moscow does consider it possible and desirable, but only as a long process to be conducted on a step-by-step basis. As President Dmitry Medvedev recently put it, "In the near future, total disarmament is impossible; we need to exercise special efforts for that."[34] The Russian position, therefore, is more closely aligned with the U.S. and UK position than the French one, but is still much more pessimistic.

In recent years, Moscow has argued that the first step to make progress on this front is for Russia and the United States to agree on a follow-on treaty to the 1991 START agreement, whose expiration date was December 5, 2009.[35] Moscow first proposed follow-on START negotiations to Washington in 2006, but they were stillborn because of disagreements over the format of the future treaty. Unlike Washington, Moscow wanted a verifiable and irreversible treaty. Indeed, Moscow had been frustrated by the conclusion of the 2002 Strategic Offensive Reductions Treaty (SORT), which is loose, imprecise, and nonverifiable (see chapter 1 for more details). At issue were also Moscow's links to its concerns about the 2007 Bush plan to deploy BMD systems in Eastern Europe. As Foreign Minister Sergey Lavrov stressed in a February 2008 speech at the CD, "We cannot but feel concerned over the situation where, with the looming prospect of expiration of the treaty of limitations on strategic offensive arms, there are increasing efforts by the United States to deploy its global [BMD] system."[36]

The arrival of Barack Obama at the White House in early 2009 and his intention to resume the traditional disarmament process changed the situation. On April 1, 2009, the two parties agreed on the basic parameters of the future treaty and, three months later, issued a joint understanding about the reductions to be sought (see chapter 1 for more details).[37] The subsequent U.S. decision to scrap the Bush BMD plan (and replace it by a system that is deemed more effective to provide for Europe's security and less provocative to Russia) also tempered Moscow's concerns.[38] Indeed, as nuclear policy analyst Pavel Podvig explains, "by cancelling the parts of the plan that were the most objectionable to Moscow and by confirming its commitment to cooperation on missile defense, Washington created a new context for the domestic debate in Russia, eroding the positions of those who insisted on a confrontational response to the U.S. program [...] the Russian diplomatic corps was able to exercise much stronger control over the agenda, moving it toward joint threat assessment and cooperation."[39]

Although these new circumstances enabled negotiations to begin, Moscow quickly raised concerns over a U.S. plan that allowed inspectors to continue overseeing Russia's ICBM at its Votkinsk Plant. The issue was that because Washington is not producing new-design strategic missiles, there would be nothing for Moscow to monitor.[40] After Washington agreed to replace verification at Votkinsk by audits and close scrutiny of Russia's missile exercises, Moscow deemed the exchange of telemetry data from missile tests problematic because of the absence of such tests in the United States (it probably also feared that this data could be used to develop missile interceptors against Russian missiles).[41]

In the end, Moscow and Washington agreed on an exchange of a limited (but voluntarily chosen) amount of telemetry, which enabled negotiations to move forward. Hitting these roadblocks, however, meant that the completion deadline (START's expiration date) could not be met. The two parties ultimately signed the new treaty, dubbed "New START," on April 8, 2010.[42] Because Moscow remained concerned about U.S. BMD plans, notably following U.S. talks about possible deployments in other Eastern European countries, it attached to its signature of the treaty a unilateral statement warning that Russia could withdraw if there was a "qualitative or quantitative build-up in the missile defense system capabilities of the United States."[43]

Moscow was quick to push the treaty in its legislative system for ratification. Yet, although the original plan was to "synchronize" its vote with the U.S. Senate, the Duma ended up deciding to consider New START in three separate readings, blaming the long time it took for the Senate to ratify and the fact that a resolution was attached to U.S. ratification. Eventually, the Duma ratified the treaty on January 28, 2011, just over a month after the Senate. Quite noteworthy is that Russian lawmakers also attached a resolution to New START ratification that highlights in particular the issue of BMD systems (clearly the most divisive one on the U.S.-Russian arms control agenda) and also highlights the question of "build-up capacity," be it nuclear or conventional.[44] Indeed, while Russia has a clear advantage with TNW over the United States (it has a much larger arsenal), this is offset by the U.S. advantage in "build-up capacity"—that is, the U.S. ability to proceed with nuclear reductions by cutting the number of warheads on each delivery vehicle and putting them in storage. Russia has to eliminate delivery vehicles because most of them are old, and Moscow cannot afford to sustain large forces. Thus, if the United States decided to return warheads from storage (or use new conventional warheads) and add them to its missiles, it would acquire superiority—Russia would not be able to compensate with new missiles because they are introduced too slowly.[45] The Russian resolution, therefore, takes note of these aspects.

Since the conclusion of New START, Moscow has called on other NWS to participate in future multilateral disarmament efforts and has continued to push, as it has done since 2007, for the multilateralization of the INF Treaty.[46] It is unclear what the next stage will be, although the U.S. Nuclear Posture Review calls for the next round of U.S.-Russian arms control negotiations to include TNW and nondeployed nuclear weapons. So far, however, Russian military officers have expressed doubts that TNW could be subject to any curbs.[47] Most recently, Lavrov has echoed these concerns and explained, "We are convinced that before talking about any further steps in the sphere of nuclear disarmament, limitation, and reduction of nuclear weapons, it's necessary to fulfill the New START agreement. It will become clear then what further steps must be taken to strengthen global security and strategic stability."[48]

CHINA

Three core principles guide Chinese nuclear doctrine: counterdeterrence, sufficiency, and effectiveness. Since it demonstrated its nuclear weapons capability in 1964, China's forces have been intended to prevent nuclear attacks against its territory and prevent nuclear coercion by other powers. Although one could think that this relates to the traditional understanding of deterrence, the Chinese make a strong difference between "deterrence effects" and "deterrence strategy." They claim that their nuclear arsenal has the *effect* of deterring nuclear attacks against China, but they insist that Beijing does not pursue a deterrence *strategy* whereby nuclear weapons constitute a legitimate part of military capabilities that can be used to achieve security or political goals.[49] That is why they argue that China's nuclear strategy is best described as purely defensive and retaliatory or, in the recent words of Xu Guangyu, a retired major-general from the People's Liberation Army (PLA), "a deterrent [that] presents no threat" (the counterdeterrence principle).[50]

Beijing contends that the best evidence of the defensive character of its nuclear arsenal is its NFU policy. In its 2009 defense white paper, China explains that its nuclear missiles are not targeted in peacetime, will go into a state of alert and prepare for counter-attack only if China is threatened, and will be launched only in response to a nuclear attack.[51] This policy was reaffirmed in China's latest defense white paper, published in March 2011.[52] Based on comments made by some high-level Chinese military officers (notably that Beijing could use nuclear weapons if the United States attacked China with conventional forces),[53] some scholars have nevertheless questioned the validity of China's position. According to Mark Schneider, for instance, "A careful look at the Chinese wording of 'no first use' reveals that it commits them to nothing."[54] Similarly, although in a more measured manner, a 2008 U.S. Department of Defense report argues that Chinese "doctrinal materials suggest additional missions for China's nuclear forces including deterring conventional attacks against [Chinese] nuclear assets or conventional attacks with WMD-like effects."[55] In its 2010 issue, however, the same report concludes that although there is "some ambiguity over the conditions under which China's [nuclear declaratory] policy would or would not apply [...] there has been no indication that national leaders are willing to attach such nuances and caveats to China's 'no first use' doctrine."[56] In January 2011, Kyodo News reported that the PLA had recently produced a planning document entitled "Lowering the Threshold of Nuclear Threats" indicating that China "must carefully consider" the first-use of nuclear weapons "if a nuclear missile-possessing country carries out a series of airstrikes against key strategic targets in our country with absolutely superior conventional weapons."[57] But Beijing swiftly denied the existence of the report; incidentally informed analysts in the United States claimed the document in question was in fact neither new nor does it suggest that the Chinese are eyeing a preemptive nuclear attack in a crisis.[58]

The Chinese, however, acknowledge (grudgingly) the existence of a recent debate in Chinese policymaking circles about China's commitment to its NFU policy. Yet, they highlight that this debate is now settled, and that China continues to adhere to its traditional policy.[59] Moreover, they insist that China's NFU pledge can be discerned easily by looking not only at the nature and mission of China's nuclear arsenal but also at its size, configuration, readiness, war-planning exercises, and pace of development, and by considering other aspects of Chinese policy such as its unconditional NSA to NNWS (to extend its support for NWFZ).[60] Beijing stresses that the validity of its NFU pledge is best illustrated by the small size of its nuclear arsenal, which is solely intended to ensure that China has what nonproliferation expert Jeffrey Lewis has called "the minimum means of reprisal" (the sufficiency principle).[61]

Yet, heated debates have continued because China is the only NWS that is currently both enhancing and expanding its nuclear arsenal, although only at very moderate speed, notably in view of the substantial increase in financial resources allocated to Chinese armed forces over the past two decades, and because Beijing releases little information about what it does and why. The official line is that current efforts aim to develop "a lean and effective nuclear force capable of meeting national security needs,"[62] that is, a reliable, survivable, and penetrable nuclear second-strike retaliatory capability (the effectiveness principle).

The latest information available in the literature suggests that China's modernization program focuses on missile rather than warhead development.[63] Beijing seeks to enhance the reliability and survivability of its strategic nuclear force through the deployment of long-range, solid-fuel, road-mobile ICBM and a new generation of SLBM that are faster, more powerful, and more accurate than their liquid-fueled predecessors. It currently deploys approximately 130 land-based, nuclear-capable ballistic missiles: the old liquid-fueled medium-range DF-3A, which is being replaced by the solid-fueled DF-21 (China's primary regional nuclear missile, which has been produced in important numbers in recent years); the (also old) liquid-fueled long-range DF-4, which is also being replaced by the DF-21—and the DF-31; the liquid-fueled DF-5A, an ICBM that can deliver a multimegaton warhead; and the DF-31A, a solid-fueled road-mobile ICBM. Beijing's plans for its SSBN are unclear because it has only a single Xia-class SSBN and is building at least three (possibly more) Jin-class SSBN, but none of them has ever sailed on deterrent patrol, and their 12 SLBM (the JL-2) are not operational. Moreover, besides researching warhead and delivery system technologies to increase accuracy and penetration against (U.S.) BMD systems, Beijing is developing cruise missiles (the DH-10) and deploying anti-satellite (ASAT) and BMD programs, as exemplified by its ASAT and BMD tests of January 2007 and January 2010, respectively. Although details of its current force size and configuration are also shrouded in secrecy, the latest estimates indicate that China has approximately 175 active nuclear warheads (240 in total) and that, excluding TNW, its arsenal includes approximately 130 land-based missiles, 12 SLBM, and 40 strategic bombers (the H-6).

According to Beijing, it is more important to show transparency in doctrine than in force posture. Beijing believes that ambiguity about its forces helps strengthen its deterrence capabilities because China is a weaker nuclear power. In the words of one Chinese colonel, "it is not for the weak to reveal to the strong."[64] That is why Beijing has repeatedly turned down U.S. calls for a bilateral dialogue on strategic issues and, more recently, why it has been keen to dial down the 2010 NPT RevCon Final Document's language on nuclear arsenal transparency.[65]

Given its nuclear weapon policy, what is China's position on nuclear disarmament? As the following analysis shows, the Chinese stance may appear disingenuous because, despite its force modernization program, Beijing is a strong advocate of reaching a world free of nuclear weapons, even though it has taken few tangible steps in that direction.

On the same day that it conducted its first nuclear test (October 16, 1964), Beijing proposed that a global summit be held to discuss the complete prohibition and thorough destruction of all nuclear weapons.[66] Since then, the Chinese position has not changed. Today, Beijing is reiterating its traditional stance. At the UN General Assembly summit in September 2009, for instance, President Hu Jintao stated, "China has consistently stood for the complete prohibition and thorough destruction of nuclear weapons and a world without nuclear weapons."[67]

Similarly, Beijing's agenda to achieve this goal is largely identical to its 1964 plan. Then, China proposed "as a first step, [. . .] that there should be] an agreement to the effect that the nuclear powers [. . .] undertake not to use nuclear weapons either against non-nuclear countries and nuclear-free zones or against each other."[68] Today, Beijing continues to call for a substantial diminution of the role of nuclear weapons in national security policy. More specifically, it encourages all NWS to adopt NFU policies, ban policies that lower the threshold of using nuclear weapons, halt the development of new types of nuclear weapons, end the listing of countries as potential targets for a nuclear strike, remove all nuclear weapons deployed outside the territory of their possessors, and abandon the policy and practice of extended deterrence and nuclear sharing.[69]

As in the 1960s, China continues to support (verifiable and irreversible) nuclear reductions. Given that the United States and Russia have by far the largest and most destructive nuclear arsenals of all NWS, Beijing has always considered that both countries bear the responsibility for taking the lead on nuclear disarmament, stressing that such progress will help "create the necessary conditions for the participation of other nuclear weapon states [in the process]."[70] At the same time, however, Beijing has never said at what point it will join in.

Finally, Beijing has come to support the two treaties that restrict the quantitative and qualitative development of nuclear weapons (the CTBT and FMCT), although its position is a cautious one. Shortly after its conclusion in 1996, China signed the CTBT but has not yet ratified the treaty, arguably because the U.S. Senate rejected it in 1999. Since then, Beijing has continuously voiced its support for the treaty (and honored its moratorium on nuclear testing) and has reinforced that support by establishing a national agency to prepare for its implementation.[71] However, although Beijing's ratification seems poised to follow Washington's, China has never explicitly made that commitment.

Similarly, Beijing has officially supported the conclusion of an FMCT and has since 2003 dropped its insistence to engage in FMCT negotiations only if negotiations for a treaty on the prevention of an arms race in outer space (PAROS) were held simultaneously.[72] Yet, Beijing has refused to affirm a moratorium on the production of fissile materials for weapon purposes,[73] and it is the only NWS never to have admitted to have ceased such production, although it is believed to have done so since the late 1980s or the early 1990s. Recently, Beijing has also tacitly supported Pakistan in preventing progress on FMCT negotiations after a short-lived breakthrough on the issue at the CD.[74]

EXPLAINING THE PESSIMISM OF FRANCE, RUSSIA, AND CHINA

France, Russia, and China are deeply attached to their nuclear arsenals. All three also exhibit pessimism about nuclear disarmament, although in different ways. Paris displays an admirable nuclear disarmament record, but a staunch opposition to the idea of the elimination of nuclear weapons altogether. For its part, Moscow is open to important sequential nuclear reductions (if they promote strategic stability) and not opposed to a nuclear-weapon-free world per se, although it is very skeptical about its near-term feasibility. To Beijing, the elimination of nuclear weapons is welcome in principle, but its involvement in the process is merely declaratory and contains few tangible commitments, which has been a concern to many, particularly in view of its force modernization program, however slowly it may proceed. How can the French, Russian, and Chinese positions be explained? What are the prospects for the foreseeable future?

France

During the Cold War, Paris considered that it could not move forward on the nuclear disarmament front before the two superpowers had reduced their nuclear forces, the imbalance of conventional weapons in Europe had been resolved (and biological and chemical weapons had been eliminated), and the arms race had ceased. The end of the Cold War and its positive impact on the international security environment (along with budgetary considerations) led Paris to open up, albeit cautiously, to the idea of nuclear disarmament. According to Bruno Tertrais, the new nuclear reductions and initiatives proposed by President Sarkozy are the result of a further reassessment of the country's deterrence needs in the new environment. This reassessment, he stresses, has taken into account the ongoing modernization program, which provides greater flexibility and, therefore, makes more reductions possible.[75]

Paris, therefore, is continuing the reduction of its nuclear arsenal but is not prepared to eliminate the arsenal altogether—and it has always made this extremely clear. As President Sarkozy put it following a recent meeting with Russian president Dmitry Medvedev and German chancellor Angela Merkel, "France is not going to give up on its nuclear deterrent, whether or not this will disappoint you."[76] Although the French are known for their passion for good food and wine, they have also had a parallel love story with their nuclear weapons that is longstanding and driven by security concerns and international and regional ambitions.

France's attachment to its nuclear arsenal has deep historical roots based on security concerns.[77] Paris first launched its nuclear weapons program in the 1950s to protect itself from the Soviet Union, which had stationed forces at its doorstep (East Germany). With the 1940 invasion and subsequent humiliating defeat fresh in its mind, Paris saw a pressing need for a security guarantee to preserve France's independence. Because France did not trust the U.S. nuclear umbrella offered to NATO's West European members, it chose to develop its own nuclear arsenal.

Today, although Cold War threats have disappeared, Paris continues to believe that France should maintain (and modernize) its nuclear arsenal as an insurance policy against future uncertainties. It considers that the world is—and will remain—volatile for the foreseeable future, as exemplified by the rise of nationalism and the resumption of major power competition, not to mention the growth of some nuclear arsenals and the proliferation of WMD technology, which President Sarkozy describes at length in his Cherbourg speech. Paris also believes that its arsenal guarantees that no regional power could blackmail France with nuclear weapons or other WMD. Over the years, Paris, just like London, has come to dread the prospect that a WMD-armed regional competitor (today, Iran) could pressure France and limit its options. Therefore, in addition to bolstering its nonproliferation efforts (which were quite inconsistent during the Cold War), France continues to consider that "nuclear deterrence remains one of the foundations of France's strategy [and . . .] the ultimate guarantee of national security and independence."[78] The development of the French nuclear arsenal also resulted from France's quest for international status. In the 1950s, preserving great power status was essential to Paris because French officials were battling with the breakup of their empire and their country's loss of influence on the world stage. In French eyes, therefore, nuclear weapons would give them access to the highest negotiating table.[79]

Today, this quest for status has disappeared. In his Cherbourg speech, President Sarkozy stressed, "It is neither a matter of prestige nor a question of rank, it is quite simply the nation's life insurance policy."[80] Yet, although Paris does not link its country's possession of nuclear weapons to its status as a permanent member of the UN Security Council, nuclear weapons do underwrite some of France's foreign policy, particularly its European policy. Without explicitly declaring that the French nuclear arsenal covers its European partners, France has since the mid-1990s claimed that its nuclear forces are key to Europe's security, and it has called for a dialogue (reiterated in the Cherbourg speech) on the benefits of nuclear deterrence for European security.[81] Due to strong anti-nuclear traditions in the European Union (and France's refusal to share decision making over its weapons), these calls have so far been in vain. Time will tell whether France's rapprochement to NATO military structures (which so far has excluded French participation to NATO's Nuclear Planning Group) and the resurgence of Russia will change the equation. In the meantime, Paris has most recently worked hard to develop cooperation with London on a range of military and nuclear issues in an attempt to preserve and enhance their global player and NWS status in the face of economic hardship and massive budget cuts (see chapter 1 for more details).[82]

Because the idea that nuclear weapons have been the best solution for France's security concerns and international ambitions is deeply anchored in the French national mindset, France's nuclear weapons policy has always been overwhelmingly supported by the major political parties and the general public.[83] The future of French nuclear weapons is not even a subject of policy debate in France because these weapons are believed to be a French national institution. That is why the abolition debate has not caught on in France. This is best exemplified by the absence of debate following the publication in *Le Monde* on October 14, 2009, of an opinion piece by former prime ministers Alain Juppé and Michel Rocard (the latter being a [rare] long-term opponent of nuclear weapons), former defense minister Alain Richard, and retired general Bernard Norlain, who highlight the declining role of nuclear deterrence and insisted on the need for bold disarmament initiatives to help bolster the nuclear nonproliferation regime.[84] And another similar opinion piece published the following year by Rocard and nuclear policy analyst George Le Guelte in the same newspaper raised as little interest as the first one.[85]

What are the prospects for change? Clearly, Paris will not start contemplating the elimination of its nuclear weapons unless the security environment changes considerably. This would require a substantial improvement in major power relations involving major domestic changes in both Russia (particularly important for France in the European context) and China, as well as a durable political stabilization of most regional conflicts, particularly in the Middle East and South Asia. Other imperative conditions would include the successful resolution of the Iranian nuclear crisis, the (verifiably proven) disappearance of all proliferation threats, and significant progress toward non-nuclear stability. Only such a radically different environment could drive France toward nuclear abolition. Again, the French position is not completely at odds with that of the United States and the United Kingdom; the important difference is that the latter two believe that actively moving toward a nuclear-weapon-free world and overtly claiming their support for it is helpful. France does not.

Would Paris defy a U.S.-driven multilateral nuclear disarmament process and, as Bruno Tertrais wonders, be "the last to disarm?"[86] Paris insists that the size and capacity of its nuclear arsenal is not dependent on any other and that reductions proceed from a purely independent decision. However, it seems unlikely that France would resist such pressure if all key actors are involved, notably because smooth relations with Washington are important to Paris.

Russia

Although much more self-confident as a great power than immediately after the Cold War, Russia continues to regard its nuclear weapons as paramount to face its important security concerns and support its regional and global ambitions. Since the collapse of its empire, in addition to being faced with serious internal security issues (ethnic and religious conflicts, transnational crime, terrorism, proliferation), Russia has felt that its fantastic loss of power has exposed itself to external aggression. Thus Moscow has come to think that brandishing its nuclear arsenal—the only element of power left from the Soviet era—would help deter aggression, particularly from the United States and, increasingly, from China.

The expansion of the role of Russian nuclear weapons has its origins in the 1999 U.S.-led NATO military intervention against Serbia over Kosovo.[87] Because the war was waged without authorization from the UN Security Council and because it exhibited overwhelming U.S. conventional superiority, Moscow came to believe that although large-scale conflicts with the United States, NATO, or other powers were now unlikely, the use of force on a smaller scale by the United States against Russia was a real possibility that Russian forces could not deter conventionally. That is why the 2000 Military Doctrine stated that Russian nuclear weapons could now be used in limited strikes for the purpose of war (non-nuclear) de-escalation in addition to its traditional role of strategic deterrence.

Although the new military doctrine slightly circumscribes the criterion for nuclear weapon use, the fact that it does not change the main role of the weapons (and came close to expanding it further) suggests that Moscow remains deeply concerned with the strong growth of American military power. Indeed, to Russia, the United States is on a quest for global supremacy. The 2003 U.S.-led intervention against Iraq, conducted without a clear-cut UN mandate, is in Russian eyes a clear illustration of U.S. attempts to dominate the world. More specifically, Moscow has been profoundly distraught by the eastward expansion of NATO, now at its doorstep with country members in Central Europe, the Baltic region, and the Balkans, some of which will host U.S. BMD systems that the Russians believe are directed against them.[88] Moscow has also been troubled by U.S. support for leaders in Georgia, Ukraine, and Kyrgyzstan, which it believes is deliberately meant to weaken Russia. The U.S. handling of Russia's 2008 war with Georgia, in particular, was very disturbing to Moscow.

In addition to responding to a perceived threat from the United States, Russia's greater reliance on its nuclear arsenal has also increasingly been justified to address concerns over a possible future threat of China. As Russian nuclear strategist Dmitri Trenin explains, "Although Moscow signed an agreement with

Beijing on a set of confidence building measures along the Russo-China border in 1996, it is fully aware of its weaknesses and vulnerabilities. Should the Sino-Russian relationship turn sour, Moscow's only logical answer would be nuclear threats, both to deter war and, if necessary, to fight it, both at the strategic and tactical levels."[89]

Beyond security concerns, Moscow has relied on its nuclear arsenal to support its regional and global ambitions. Moscow believes that the maintenance of nuclear weapons and its stated intention to use them even for tactical purposes of war de-escalation provides the best guarantee of Russia's primacy over its "near abroad." A symbol of its glorious past, this regional primacy is considered to be an integral part of its core national interests, and Moscow is convinced that it could not exert that primacy without a nuclear deterrent, particularly in view of the difficulties it is already grappling with at present. Increasingly, Moscow has also looked beyond its region and sought to reemerge as a global actor, which has led it to believe that in addition to its permanent membership on the UN Security Council, having a strong nuclear arsenal is essential if Russia is to be taken seriously by the United States and other major powers. That is in part why it is modernizing its forces and has since 2007 resumed global air and naval patrols after an interruption of nearly two decades.[90]

Similarly, it is true that Moscow's interest in phased and coordinated nuclear reductions is motivated by the old age and expenses associated with many systems and components of the large nuclear arsenal it inherited from the Soviet era, which Moscow has no choice but to dismantle. Yet, this enthusiasm also comes from an assessment that participating in arms control negotiations helps enhance global status. Moreover, and perhaps most importantly, Moscow has been interested in negotiations in order to optimize its security relations with major powers. So far, Russia has put the onus on using such negotiations to regulate its relations with the United States, and the BMD issue has been—and will continue to be—the main flash point in negotiations. Yet, Moscow's recent calls for the NWS to participate in future multilateral nuclear disarmament efforts and its proposal to multilateralize the INF Treaty suggests that it may be increasingly anxious to have China, its other main competitor, join the process so that it can start optimizing its relations with Beijing as well.

Finally, one could be led to assume that Moscow supports the ultimate goal of nuclear disarmament only because, like the United States, it is gradually developing more modern and accurate conventional weapons, which means that it could at least in theory be considering that the day will eventually come when it can do away with nuclear weapons altogether. This process of weapons substitution, however, is both time and resource consuming, and most scholars stress that it will probably not be completed by 2020, as scheduled.[91] Moreover, even when—or if—it is eventually completed successfully, the likelihood of Russian capabilities matching those of the United States and even China is close to zero. It is fair to assume that Russia's reliance on its nuclear arsenal, therefore, will be more than a brief temporary fix and that the road to Russian nuclear disarmament will be long and difficult. This may well be why Moscow supports the goal of a world without nuclear weapons only as a very, very distant goal.

China

China has always been officially in favor of nuclear disarmament, but it has simultaneously been deeply attached to its nuclear weapons. This attachment runs deep: it has its roots in the origins of China's nuclear weapon program.

Beijing's decision to develop a nuclear arsenal was influenced by its experience in the Korean War, during which the United States made explicit nuclear threats against China.[92] At the time, the Chinese concluded that the only option to ensure their country's security and prevent further nuclear coercion or attack was to develop nuclear weapons. Despite former president Mao Zedong's well-known denigration of nuclear weapons as "paper tigers," the Great Helmsman clearly considered that having such weapons would benefit China, explaining, "If we are not to be bullied in the present-day world, we cannot do without the bomb."[93] The belief that nuclear weapons are essential to preserve China's security, whose territorial integrity had incidentally been threatened on various occasions in prior decades, quickly crystallized in the Chinese psyche and has remained deeply entrenched ever since. That is why Beijing has been protective of its arsenal and so sturdily committed to proceeding with its modernization, although it has done so at a relatively slow pace, arguably just to maintain an effective second-strike capability.

Moreover, developing nuclear weapons also helped demonstrate China's status as a major power in the world. To quote Mao again, "I hear that with such a big thing, if you don't have it, then others will say you don't count; fine, we should build a few."[94] Today, this dimension continues to be important for the Chinese. With the passage of time, China's nuclear arsenal has also become a strong symbol of the nation's excellence in mastering the most advanced scientific and technological processes of the modern world, particularly as the country was not long ago—and in some ways may still be considered—a backward economy. Subsequently echoed by succeeding Chinese leaders, former president Deng Xiaoping first expressed the sentiment of national pride produced by China's nuclear arsenal as follows: "It has always been, and will always be, necessary for China to develop its own high technology so that it can take its place in this field. If it were not for the atomic bomb, the hydrogen bomb and the satellites we have launched since the 1960s, China would not have its present international standing as a great, influential country. These achievements demonstrate a nation's abilities and are a sign of its level of prosperity and development."[95]

China's attachment to its nuclear arsenal and modernization plans, therefore, is strongly established in the Chinese national character and society. Although it is not solely motivated by security concerns, the nature of China's involvement in nuclear disarmament will depend on the future of the international security environment.

During the Cold War, China's benchmarks for its threat assessments and force modernization were U.S. and Soviet policies. At the beginning of the 1990s, the emphasis shifted almost exclusively to U.S. policies, notably to those on BMD, long-range conventional strikes, and advanced command, control, communications, computers, intelligence, surveillance, and reconnaissance capabilities, which Beijing considers threatening to China's nuclear forces. True, increasingly, Beijing's threat perceptions and contingency plans have also been complicated by the emergence of new regional nuclear powers located on China's periphery (India, Pakistan, and North Korea). Most scholars, however, stress that Beijing may simply address these new developments as a proliferation issue more than as a strategic problem, and that they have not changed Beijing's focus on the United States, which has been China's main concern for the past two decades.[96]

What are the sources of China's concerns about U.S. policies?[97] Shortly after the end of the Cold War, Beijing became concerned with the growing unmatched superiority of U.S. conventional weapons and the apparent U.S. determination to develop new, more usable nuclear weapons. Beijing also became worried that U.S. seemingly unbridled development and deployment of BMD systems, which it does not believe are purely defensive and solely aimed at "rogue" states, would neutralize China's small nuclear forces and subject the country to blackmail, particularly in a conflict over Taiwan.

These worries intensified following the U.S.-led military intervention in Kosovo, which was waged without a UN mandate (and during which the Chinese embassy was bombed). They then peaked with the release of the 2002 U.S. NPR and National Security Strategy, in which Beijing saw the confirmation of all its fears: the important role given to BMD systems and other advanced conventional weaponry, stated intentions to develop new, more usable nuclear weapons, and apparent advocacy of regime change and preemptive war. Beijing was also alarmed when it found out that the 2002 NPR contained contingency plans to use nuclear weapons against seven countries (including China), and when a year later the United States decided to lead yet another military intervention without a clear-cut UN mandate against Iraq, one of the seven countries listed as potential targets for U.S. nuclear weapons.

Moreover, Beijing was troubled by the unraveling of the traditional arms control agenda. In the early 2000s, the Chinese leadership watched with concern when the Bush administration replaced the U.S.-Russian START process with SORT. Beijing was also unsettled when the administration pulled out of the ABM treaty and bluntly refused to initiate any negotiations for a PAROS treaty. The administration's complete disinterest in seeking CTBT ratification and its opposition to negotiations for the conclusion of a verifiable FMCT were equally disturbing for Beijing.

Barack Obama arrived at the White House with the intention of making a clean break with the previous administration, holding the multilateralism banner high again and actively moving the world toward a nuclear-weapon-free world. Officially, the steps taken by the new administration are considered promising. Yet, to China, they are just that: steps in the right direction. Beijing has welcomed the new U.S. NPR, which reduces the role of U.S. nuclear weapons, but it deplores that U.S. NSA to NNWS are not unconditional and, most importantly, that "There is still some distance from the 'sole purpose policy,' and even more from the no-first-use policy as adopted and suggested by China."[98] Beijing also remains concerned about U.S. modernization plans, despite the NPR promise that the United States would not develop new nuclear warheads, and about the stated U.S. greater reliance on conventional military capabilities (and BMD systems). As nuclear policy analyst Lora Saalman shows in a comprehensive study of China's reaction to the new NPR: "Traditional concerns—such as hegemony, absolute advantage, BMD, and NFU—continue to make a significant showing, similar to textual research results. Yet they are surpassed by discussions of how conventional weapons advances and their replacement role for nuclear weapons could affect China."[99]

Similarly, Beijing has welcomed the resumption of U.S.-Russian verifiable arms control embodied in the conclusion of New START but believes that the levels of the new treaty are still much too high for China to rapidly jump on the nuclear disarmament bandwagon. As Chinese nuclear strategist Hui Zhang has stated about the Chinese view: "The question is not 'When will China join the United States and Russia in helping to achieve a world free of nuclear weapons?' It is rather, 'When will the United States and Russia join China on the way to that goal?'"[100]

That being said, Chinese scholars generally agree that Beijing will probably hop on after the United States and Russia reduce their stockpiles to approximately 1,000 warheads each (understood as the total number of warheads, not just that of strategic deployed warheads).[101] Realistically, however, the United States and Russia will not reach these levels in the near future. Does this mean that Beijing expects not to make any moves until then? Moreover, it is unclear what action Beijing would take when Washington and Moscow do reach the 1,000-warhead mark because no formal commitment has been made. Would China increase transparency over its nuclear forces to increase confidence and allow further U.S. and Russian reductions to proceed? Although it may be unfeasible, even at those levels, to expect China to start reducing its arsenal, would Beijing pledge a specific lower ceiling on its forces, thereby alleviating U.S. and Russian concerns about a possible Chinese "sprint to parity" as their arsenals continue to go down? These questions remain unanswered. In any case, it is unlikely that nuclear reductions will be the only decisive trigger to China's involvement in the nuclear disarmament process given its concerns about U.S. non-nuclear military superiority, notably BMD.

At present, Beijing doubts that the United States (and Russia) will be able to overcome the domestic and international resistance to get down to 1,000 warheads and, in the U.S. case, that it will be able to successfully push the CTBT (and an FMCT) through its bureaucratic system, as the Obama administration has promised.[102] To China, the New START ratification experience has clearly illustrated the limits of what the United States can achieve, and the Chinese doubt momentum will be sustained after Obama.[103] Some Chinese officials and analysts go even further and suspect that the current abolition debate and the U.S. call for a strategic dialogue with China conceal an agenda designed to constrain China's nuclear forces and modernization program. That is why Beijing is hedging its bets and has remained noncommittal on nuclear disarmament, except on its doctrine.

The Chinese are patient. So far, they have adopted a wait-and-see position to the direction proposed by the Obama administration. This is unlikely to change until and unless they see, as they would say, how "China's concerns can be harmoniously addressed." As a PLA colonel recently put it, "China's concern over [BMD systems and other issues] needs more than just dialogues and talks if it is to be relieved."[104] As Saalman explains,

> Although the 2010 NPR may in some ways represent an embryonic "new vision," until the NPR is issued in a form that contains concrete definitions and proposals, the perception within China that certain core elements of U.S. nuclear doctrine have ossified is likely to persist. Given that China itself is a country often given to using "slogans" (*kouhao*) and "principles" (*yuanze*) to guide its strategic relations, this demand for more concrete definitions, proposals, and confidence-building measures is significant. In fact, these trends indicate that the United States is facing a reversal of traditional roles in Sino-U.S. arms control relations. China is now the nation looking for precise definitions, combined with concrete measures and steps, while the United States has become the nation speaking in grandiose terms and slogans. Under such conditions, the United States has an opportunity to make specific proposals to change the trajectory of the Sino-U.S. quest for strategic stability. This current situation is also an opportunity for the Chinese side [...] to make a more significant impact on defining the issues for Sino-U.S. strategic relations.[105]

Until then, China's modernization program will continue, and the prospects for nuclear disarmament will remain uncertain.

CONCLUSION

To France, Russia, and China, nuclear disarmament is not a priority—quite the contrary. None of these three NWS is optimistic about the prospect of a nuclear-weapon-free world. They are all deeply attached to their nuclear arsenals, which they originally developed to respond to security challenges and to achieve international and regional ambitions or status. Today, they continue to believe that nuclear weapons are absolutely central to their national security policy (and standing in the world), and therefore they do not contemplate eliminating them, or at least not any time soon. In fact, France and Russia are modernizing their nuclear forces, and China is in the process of both enhancing *and* expanding its nuclear arsenal.

What is the way forward? How can progress, even slow progress toward nuclear disarmament, be achieved? Although France is monolithically opposed to a nuclear-weapon-free world, it has undertaken laudable nuclear reductions, increased transparency about its forces, and subscribed to important nuclear disarmament initiatives, such as the CTBT. Paris, therefore, has argued that France supports nuclear disarmament. Yet, the question that the French will have to ask themselves is how long they will be able to make that argument. Sooner or later, they will reach a point when they will no longer be able to take any more "concrete" steps toward nuclear disarmament. After all, Paris has already been categorical about not further reducing the role of nuclear weapons in its national security policy (such as declaring an NFU) and has suggested that it cannot follow the UK example and retain only SSBN forces because its M45 and newer M51 SLBM are no way near as accurate as the UK Trident II D5 SLBM (and because France's forces, unlike the United Kingdom's, are not integrated into NATO's military command).[106] So the "what's next?" question will soon be critical for the French to answer, particularly given that Paris has consistently explained that France, along with its European partners, is encouraging a balanced approach to progress on the three NPT pillars.[107]

For its part, Russia is not opposed to a world free of nuclear weapons, presumably because it may imagine a day when nuclear weapons are no longer relevant as more modern and accurate conventional weapons become operational. This process, however, will not happen overnight, hence Russia supports the goal of a world free of nuclear weapons only as a very long-term prospect. In the meantime, Moscow will pursue the downsizing of its nuclear forces while seeking to optimize its relations with the United States, and more and more with China. As nuclear reductions continue, however, Moscow will be increasingly at pains to reconcile that process with its nuclear doctrine, which stipulates that nuclear use is possible at the tactical level, notably to protect Russia's primacy over its "near abroad." Indeed, TNW and nondeployed nuclear weapons are expected to be part of the next round of disarmament negotiations.

China has declared itself in favor of a nuclear-weapon-free world, but this support has been largely declaratory: Beijing has made very few tangible commitments to reaching that goal. As the nuclear disarmament process progresses (particularly between the United States and Russia), Beijing will come under increased pressure to go beyond its traditional stance and reciprocate in some more concrete way. This will happen much more quickly than the Chinese seem to believe, in part because China's modernization program (and the fact that it remains for the most part shrouded in secrecy) is raising significant concerns—rightly or wrongly.[108]

Notes

1. For a study on French nuclear doctrine, see Bruno Tertrais, *La France et la dissuasion nucléaire: Concept, Moyens, Avenir* (Paris: La documentation française, 2007).

2. Samy Cohen, *La monarchie nucléaire: Les coulisses de la politique étrangère sous la Vème République* (Paris: Hachette, 1986).

3. Nicolas Sarkozy, "Presentation of *Le Terrible* in Cherbourg," Cherbourg, March 21, 2008.

4. *The French White Paper on Defense and National Security* (Paris: Odile Jacob, 2008).

5. Ibid., 61.

6. Jacques Chirac, "Speech by Jacques Chirac, President of the French Republic, during his Visit to the Strategic Air and Maritime Forces at Landivisiau/L'Ile Longue," Ile Longue, Brest, January 19, 2006.

7. Sarkozy, "Presentation of *Le Terrible*."

8. Ibid.

9. Prague Summit Declaration Issued by the Heads of State and Government Participating in the Meeting of the North Atlantic Council in Prague, November 21, 2002; Sarkozy, "Presentation of *Le Terrible*.

10. Quoted in Tom Collina, "NATO Set to Back Expanded Missile Defense," *Arms Control Today* 40 (November 2010), 32.

11. "Adapting Operational Features of French Forces," France TNP: Turning Commitments into Actions, http://www.francetnp2010.fr/spip.php?article91.

12. Paris has offered security assurances to the Latin American, South Pacific, and African NWFZ treaties, but not to the Southeast Asian and the Central Asian treaties.

13. This goal of three hundred warheads was achieved in September 2008. Robert Norris and Hans Kristensen, "French Nuclear Forces, 2008," *Bulletin of Atomic Scientists*, September/October 2008, 52–57. Visits to observe dismantling took place on September 16, 2008, with representatives from over forty CD member states and, six months later, on March 16, 2009, with nongovernmental experts. See "Working Paper Submitted by France," NPT/CONF.2010/PC.III/WP.37, *Nuclear Disarmament: A Concrete Step by France*, Third Preparatory Committee Meeting for the 2010 NPT Review Conference, New York, May 13, 2009 and the speech delivered by Captain Antoine Beaussant, "Visit of French Former Military Production Facilities at Pierrelatte and Marcoule," July 3, 2009.

14. "Statement by H.E. Eric Danon, Ambassador, Permanent Representative of France to the Conference on Disarmament on Behalf of the European Union," New

York, October 6, 2009. See also "Letter from Nicolas Sarkozy, President of the French Republic, to M. Ban Ki-Moon, UN Secretary General of the United Nations," Paris, December 5, 2008, http://www.francetnp2010.fr/IMG/pdf/Letter_from_Nicolas_Sarkozy_to_Ban_Ki-Moon.pdf.

15. Eric Danon, head of the French Delegation, 2010 NPT Review Conference, New York, May 4, 2010.

16. Danon, May 7, 2010.

17. "Statement by H.E. François Rivasseau, Ambassador, Permanent Representative of France to the Conference on Disarmament," 2005 NPT Review Conference, New York, May 5, 2005.

18. Danon, 2009 NPT Preparatory Committee, May 6, 2009.

19. Nicolas Sarkozy, remarks during the 6191st meeting of the Security Council, New York, September 24, 2009.

20. Sarkozy, "Presentation of *Le Terrible*."

21. "G8 L'Aquila Statement on Non-Proliferation," July 8, 2009.

22. "Working Paper Submitted by France," NPT/CONF.2010/WP.33, *Nuclear Disarmament: France's Practical Commitment*, 2010 NPT Review Conference, New York, April 14, 2010; Danon, 2010 NPT Review Conference, May 4 and May 7, 2010.

23. "Rapport d'information du Sénat no. 332 fait au nom de la commission des affaires étrangères, de la défense et des forces armées (1) sur le désarmement, la non-prolifération nucléaires et la sécurité de la France par M. Jean-Pierre Chevènement, Sénateur," February 24, 2010, 157.

24. Tiphaine de Champchesnel, "Un 'monde sans armes nucléaires' ou l'utopie du zéro" [A "world without nuclear weapons" or the utopia of zero], in *Annuaire Français de Relations Internationales* [French international relations yearbook] (Brussels : Bruylant, 2010).

25. *The Basic Provisions of the Military Doctrine of the Russian Federation* (Moscow: Russian Federation Security Council, 1993).

26. "Founding Act on Mutual Relations, Cooperation and Security between NATO and the Russian Federation," Paris, May 27, 1997.

27. For an analysis, see Nikolai Sokov, "Russia's Nuclear Doctrine," James Martin Center for Nonproliferation Studies/Nuclear Threat Initiative, August 2004.

28. "Russia Reserves Pre-emptive Nuclear Strike Right," Reuters, October 13, 2009.

29. For a study of the 2010 Military Doctrine, see Nikolai Sokov, "The New, 2010 Russian Military Doctrine: The Nuclear Angle," February 5, 2010; Volha Charnysh, "Russian Nuclear Threshold Not Lowered," *Arms Control Today* 40 (March 2010).

30. Denis Dyomkin, "Putin Pledges Russian Conventional Weapons Funds," Reuters, June 10, 2008.

31. Robert S. Norris and Hans M. Kristensen, "Nuclear Notebook: Russian Nuclear Forces, 2009," *Bulletin of the Atomic Scientists* 65 (May/June 2009): 56.

32. Shannon Kile, Vitaly Fedchenko, Bharath Gopalaswamy, and Hans Kristensen, "World Nuclear Forces," *SIPRI Yearbook 2009: Armaments, Disarmament, and International Security* (Oxford: Oxford University Press, 2009), 353.

33. Robert S. Norris and Hans M. Kristensen, "Russian Nuclear Forces, 2010," *Bulletin of the Atomic Scientists* 66 (January/February 2010), 74–81.

34. "Total Disarmament a Distant Dream: Dmitry Medvedev," *Daily News and Analysis*, December 22, 2010.

35. "Interview with Sergey Kislyak, Russian Ambassador to the United States," *Arms Control Today* 38 (December 2008).

36. "Statement by H.E. Mr. Sergey Lavrov, Minister of Foreign Affairs of the Russian Federation," Geneva, Conference on Disarmament, February 12, 2008.

37. "Joint Statement by President Dmitry Medvedev of the Russian Federation and President Barack Obama of the United States of America," April 1, 2009; "Joint Statement by President Barack Obama of the United States of America and President Dmitry Medvedev of the Russian Federation on Nuclear Cooperation," July 6, 2009.

38. "Remarks by the President on Strengthening Missile Defense in Europe," September 17, 2009; Mark Fitzpatrick, "A Prudent Decision on Missile Defence," *Survival* 51 (December 2009/January 2010): 5–12.

39. Pavel Podvig, "Instrumental Influences—Russia and the 2010 Nuclear Posture Review," *Nonproliferation Review* 18 (March 2011): 44–45.

40. Jeffrey Lewis, "Lugar on START Verification," Arms Control Wonk, November 5, 2009, http://lewis.armscontrolwonk.com/archive/2529/start-verification.

41. Alexander Pikayev, "New START: Preliminary Thoughts in Moscow," James Martin Center for Nonproliferation Studies, April 7, 2010.

42. "Remarks by President Obama and President Medvedev of Russia at New START Treaty Signing Ceremony and Press Conference," Prague, Czech Republic, April 8, 2010.

43. "Statement by the Russian Federation on Missile Defense," April 8, 2010.

44. For an analysis, see Nikolai Sokov, "New START Ratification in Russia: Apparent Smooth Sailing Obscures Submerged Drama and Revelations," CNS Feature Stories, James Martin Center for Nonproliferation Studies, January 25, 2011.

45. Alexei Arbatov, "The New START—A View from Moscow," Carnegie Endowment for International Peace, April 6, 2010.

46. "Russia Demands Broader Participation in Future Nuclear Cuts," Global Security Newswire, August 3, 2010. For details about the INF Treaty and Russia's proposal, see "Treaty between the United States of America and the Union of Soviet Socialist Republics on the Elimination of Their Intermediate-Range and Shorter-Range Missiles (INF Treaty)," http://www.nti.org/e_research/official_docs/inventory/pdfs/inf.pdf.

47. "Near-Term Curbs Unlikely for Nonstrategic Nukes, Analysts Assert," Global Security Newswire, August 6, 2010.

48. Lavrov, quoted by Vladimir Isachenkov, "Russia Lukewarm about Future Nuclear Arms Cuts," *Washington Post*, January 13, 2011.

49. Pan Zhenqiang, "China's Nuclear Strategy in a Changing World Strategic Situation," in *National Perspectives on Nuclear Disarmament*, ed. Barry Blechman (Washington, D.C.: Henry L. Stimson Center, 2010), 13–14. Scholars have argued that Chinese strategists have viewed nuclear deterrence as negative because of the Chinese translation of the term *deterrence* (*weishe*), which refers to the use of overwhelming force to intimidate an adversary into submission. See M. Taylor Fravel and Evans Medeiros, "China's Search for Assured Retaliation," *International Security* 35 (Fall 2010): 71.

50. Xu Guangyu, quoted in Chris Buckley, "China Military Paper Spells Out Nuclear Arms Stance," Reuters, April 22, 2010.

51. *China's National Defense in 2008* (Beijing: Information Office of the State Council of the People's Republic of China, 2009), 29.

52. *China's National Defense in 2010* (Beijing: Information Office of the State Council of the People's Republic of China, 2011). For an analysis, see "Lost in Translation: China's Opaque Defence White Paper," *IISS Strategic Comments* 17 (April 2011).

53. In July 2005, for instance, Major General Zhu Chenghu of China's PLA National Defense University indicated to journalists that "if the Americans draw their missiles and position-guided ammunition on to the target zone on China's territory, I think we will have to respond with nuclear weapons." Joseph Kahn, "Chinese General Sees U.S. as Nuclear Target," *New York Times*, July 16, 2005.

54. Mark Schneider, "The Nuclear Doctrine and Forces of the People's Republic of China," *Comparative Strategy* 28 (July 2009), 244. For a similar thesis, see Larry Wortzel, *China's Nuclear Forces: Operations, Training, Doctrine, Command, Control, and Campaign Planning* (Carlisle, Pa.: Strategic Studies Institute, U.S. Army War College, May 2007).

55. *Annual Report to Congress: Military Power of the People's Republic of China 2008* (Washington, D.C.: Defense Department, 2008), 26.

56. *Annual Report to Congress: Military and Security Developments Involving the People's Republic of China 2010* (Washington, D.C.: Department of Defense, 2010), 35.

57. "China Military Eyes Preemptive Nuclear Attack in Event of Crisis," Kyodo News, January 5, 2011.

58. Jeffrey Lewis, "China and No First Use," Arms Control Wonk, January 14, 2011, http://lewis.armscontrolwonk.com/archive/3446/china-and-no-first-use-3.

59. Fravel and Medeiros, "China's Search for Assured Retaliation," 80.

60. Zhenqiang, "China's Nuclear Strategy," 14–15.

61. Jeffrey Lewis, *The Minimum Means of Reprisal: China's Search for Security in the Nuclear Age* (Cambridge, Mass.: MIT Press, 2007). Note that Fravel and Medeiros highlight that China's nuclear strategy is not one of minimum deterrence, which would sug-

gest that China adheres to a package of ideas that prescribes the size, composition, and operations of nuclear forces—a claim that is unclear; rather, to them, China's nuclear capability is best described as a search for "assured destruction." See Fravel and Medeiros, "China's Search for Assured Retaliation," 79.

62. *China's National Defense in 2006* (Beijing: Information Office of the State Council of the People's Republic of China, 2006). See also Fravel and Medeiros, "China's Search for Assured Retaliation," 48–87.

63. For the latest data, see Norris and Kristensen, "Chinese Nuclear Forces, 2010," *Bulletin of the Atomic Scientists* 66 (November/December 2010): 134–41, *Annual Report to Congress: China 2010*; and Kile, Fedchenko, Gopalaswamy, and Kristensen, "World Nuclear Forces," 364–67.

64. Quoted by Dean Cheng on panel no. 5, "21st Century Security Environment and Implications for Deterrence," U.S. Strategic Command Deterrence Symposium—Exploring the Many Facets of Deterrence, Qwest Center, Omaha, Neb., August 11, 2010.

65. William Potter, Patricia Lewis, Gaukhar Mukhatzhanova, and Miles Pomper, "The 2010 NPT Review Conference: Deconstructing Consensus," CNS Special Report, James Martin Center for Nonproliferation Studies, June 17, 2010, 5.

66. "Statement of the Government of the People's Republic of China," October 16, 1964.

67. "Statement by H.E. Hu Jintao, President of the People's Republic of China at the General Debate of the 64th Session of the UN General Assembly," New York, September 23, 2009.

68. "Statement of the Government of the People's Republic of China."

69. *China's National Defense in 2008*, 51.

70. Ibid.

71. Chinese Ministry of Foreign Affairs, "Comprehensive Nuclear-Test-Ban Treaty (CTBT)," May 27, 2010, http://www.fmprc.gov.cn/eng/wjb/zzjg/jks/kjlc/hwt/t410740.htm.

72. "Statement by H.E. Li Baodong, Ambassador, Head of the Chinese Delegation at the 2010 NPT Review Conference," New York, May 4, 2010.

73. Potter et al., *2010 NPT Review Conference*, 8.

74. "Statement by Ambassador Wang Qun of China," Conference on Disarmament, Geneva, June 26, 2009.

75. For an analysis of French current nuclear forces and modernization plans, see Tertrais, "French Perspectives on Nuclear Weapons and Nuclear Disarmament" in Blechman, *National Perspectives on Nuclear Disarmament*, 45–47; and Norris and Kristensen, "French Nuclear Forces, 2008."

76. "Sarkozy: France to Hold onto Nukes," Global Security Newswire, October 20, 2010.

77. For a study on the origins of the French nuclear weapon program, see Camille Grand, *A French Nuclear Exception?* (Washington, D.C.: Henry L. Stimson Center, 1998).

78. *French White Paper*, 64.

79. Dominique Mongin, *La bombe atomique française, 1945–1958* (Brussels: Bruylant, 1997), 333.

80. Sarkozy, "Presentation of *Le Terrible*."

81. Ibid.

82. "UK-France Summit 2010 Declaration on Defence and Security Cooperation," London, November 2, 2010.

83. Only the Green Party, whose power has grown since the late 1990s, is officially in favor of nuclear disarmament and of a significantly downsized French nuclear arsenal. For general public support, see Tertrais, "French Perspectives," 50.

84. Alain Juppé, Bernard Norlain, Alain Richard, and Michel Rocard, "Pour un désarmement nucléaire mondial, seule réponse à la prolifération anarchique," *Le Monde*, October 14, 2009.

85. Michel Rocard and George Le Guelte, "Le rêve du Docteur Folamour: Il faut mettre un terme la prolifération nucléaire en éliminant les arsenaux," *Le Monde*, May 4, 2010.

86. Tertrais, "The Last to Disarm? The Future of France's Nuclear Weapons," *Nonproliferation Review* 14 (July 2007): 251–73.

87. See Nikolai Sokov, "The Origins of and Prospects for Russian Nuclear Doctrine," *Nonproliferation Review* 14 (July 2007): 212–18.

88. Although Article 19 of the new military doctrine stresses Russia's readiness to cooperate with NATO (and the European Union), NATO—and its eastward expansion—are also identified as the main threat.

89. Dmitri Trenin, "Russian Perspectives on the Global Elimination of Nuclear Weapons," in *National Perspectives on Nuclear Disarmament*, 254.

90. Norris and Kristensen, "Russian Nuclear Forces, 2010."

91. See, for instance, Nikolai Sokov, "The Evolving Role of Nuclear Weapons in Russia's Security Policy," in *Engaging China and Russia on Nuclear Disarmament*, ed. Cristina Hansell and William C. Potter, James Martin Center for Nonproliferation Studies Occasional Paper no. 15 (Monterey, Calif.: Monterey Institute of International Studies, 2009), 76.

92. For a study on the origins of the Chinese nuclear weapon program, see Alice Langley Hsieh, *Communist China's Strategy in the Nuclear Age* (Englewood Cliffs, N.J.: Prentice-Hall, 1963): John Wilson Lewis and Xue Litai, *China Builds the Bomb* (Stanford, Calif.: Stanford University Press, 1988): John Wilson and Xue Litai, *China's Strategic Seapower: The Politics of Force Modernization in the Nuclear Age* (Stanford, Calif.: Stanford

University Press, 1994); and Avery Goldstein, *Deterrence and Security in the 21st Century: China, Britain, France, and the Enduring Legacy of the Nuclear Revolution* (Stanford, Calif.: Stanford University Press, 2000), 62–110.

93. Mao Tse-tung, "On the Ten Major Relationships" (speech given on April 25, 1956), Mao Tse-tung, *Selected Works of Mao Tse-tung*, vol. 5, 1977.

94. Mao Zedong, quoted in Fravel and Medeiros, "China's Search," 61.

95. Deng Xiaoping, "China Must Take Its Place in the Field of High Technology," October 24, 1988.

96. See, for instance, Zhenqiang, "China's Nuclear Strategy," 26.

97. For a study, see Jing-dong Yuan, "Effective, Reliable, and Credible: China's Nuclear Modernization," *Nonproliferation Review* 14 (July 2007): 277–78.

98. Yunzhu Yao, "A Chinese Perspective on the Nuclear Posture Review," *Proliferation Analysis*, May 6, 2010.

99. Lora Saalman, *China and the U.S. Nuclear Posture Review* (Tsinghua, China: Carnegie Papers, 2010), 8–9.

100. Hui Zhang, "China's Perspective on a Nuclear-Free World," *Washington Quarterly* 33 (April 2010): 143.

101. See, for instance, Jing-dong Yuan, "Chinese Perceptions of the Utility of Nuclear Weapons—Prospects and Potential Problems in Disarmament," *Proliferation Papers* 34 (Spring 2010): 32.

102. Zhang, "China's Perspective," 142–45.

103. Saalman, *China and the U.S.*, 13–14.

104. Yao, "Chinese Perspective."

105. Saalman, *China and the U.S.*, 27.

106. Tertrais, "French Perspectives," 46–47.

107. See, for instance, "Working Paper on Forward-Looking Proposals of the European Union on All Three Pillars of the Treaty on the Nonproliferation of Nuclear Weapons to Be Part of an Action Plan Adopted by the 2010 Review Conference," NPT/CONF.2010/PC.III/WP.26, Third Preparatory Committee Meeting for the 2010 NPT Review Conference, New York, May 6, 2009.

108. Chinese professor Li Bin of Tsinghua University has recently argued that China's "reluctance to get involved in multilateral nuclear disarmament comes mainly from its inexperience in disarmament diplomacy rather than deliberate calculation" and further argues that its potential contribution to the process would therefore be enhanced if the five NWS were to successfully create a multilateral negotiating forum on nuclear disarmament, where they would be able to better understand one another's nuclear philosophies. See Lin Bin, "China's Potential to Contribute to Multilateral Nuclear Disarmament," *Arms Control Today* 41 (March 2011): 17–21.

CHAPTER FIVE

The Threshold States
Japan and Brazil

Maria Rost Rublee

THE GLOBAL DRIVE FOR DISARMAMENT, reinvigorated by President Barack Obama's Prague speech, now seems more hopeful than at any time over the past several decades. This chapter seeks to analyze the disarmament diplomacy of two significant nuclear threshold states, Japan and Brazil, by examining both the opportunities and challenges they pose to the drive for nuclear disarmament. Because they have chosen to remain non-nuclear despite having significant nuclear capability, threshold states are critical to future negotiations for a stable and secure nuclear-weapons-free world.

On the one hand, having made the political decision to stay non-nuclear, threshold states may embrace the disarmament initiative as a way to ensure the continued viability of their choice (which may not be possible in a proliferating world). Supporting disarmament efforts could be seen as an affirmation of their restraint, both self-congratulating and self-fulfilling. Additionally, the commitment to their non-nuclear status springs at least in part from a moral stance against nuclear weapons, which would lend itself to energetic support of global disarmament. On the other hand, disarmament initiatives could be seen as stripping the threshold states of their virtual nuclear capability, constraining their future choices. In addition, many of these states have large investments in the nuclear fuel cycle. Because global disarmament efforts may eventually seek to lock down even the civilian fuel cycle, they could be seen as a direct economic and energy threat by the threshold states.[1]

Who are the nuclear threshold states? Nuclear threshold states are defined as those states with significant material and scientific capability, but which have made the political decision to refrain from acquiring nuclear weapons.[2] This definition includes countries that previously had a military nuclear capability but gave it up. Using this definition, today's nuclear threshold states include Brazil, Japan, Egypt, South Africa, Canada, Germany, Taiwan, South Korea, and Argentina.[3] This chapter focuses on Japan and Brazil for a number of reasons. First, inherent in the concept of a nuclear threshold state is that if a political decision was made to acquire nuclear weapons, the state would be able to implement that decision reasonably quickly. Of all the threshold states, Japan has the technological capability to create nuclear weapons quickly, leading some to argue it has a "virtual" nuclear weapons capacity.[4] In addition, because of its security environment (including having three nuclear-armed neighbors), analysts often raise the question of whether Japan will "go nuclear." Examining the case of Japan will shed light on how threshold states manage to stay on the nonnuclear side of the divide. Brazil is an important case because while it remains a member in good standing of the Nuclear Nonproliferation Treaty (NPT), it has tested the boundaries of what is defined as "appropriate" behavior perhaps more than any other threshold state. In particular, its insistence on shielding at its uranium enrichment plant serves as a possible looking glass into the future as the possibility of additional states claiming their sovereign right to enrich uranium. The issues of sovereignty and rights are critical ones for threshold states, ones that Brazil illustrates well. In addition, the case of Brazil underscores the potential for disarmament diplomacy of threshold states—both the possibilities and the pitfalls.

BRAZIL'S HISTORICAL DISARMAMENT DIPLOMACY

Brazil's support of global nuclear disarmament began early as a member of both the Eighteen-Nation Committee on Disarmament and the Conference of the Committee on Disarmament.[5] It was the first country to promote a nuclear-weapon-free-zone in Latin America, beginning its active support in 1961. In 1962, Brazil presented a draft resolution to the UN General Assembly calling on Latin American states to reject nuclear weapons.[6] A year later, Brazilian president João Goulart announced the Five Presidents' Declaration, an agreement among the presidents of Brazil, Mexico, Chile, Ecuador, and Bolivia to create a multilateral pact "whereby their countries would undertake not to manufacture, receive, store, or test nuclear weapons or nuclear launching devices."[7] But the Brazilian leadership role in advocating for a nuclear-free Latin America was a casualty of the military coup of 1964. The military regime did not oppose multilateral action for disarmament but also did not advocate for it.[8] In negotiations for the Treaty of Tlatelolco, the military government advocated for very strict conditions for entry into force. Once the treaty was finalized, Brazil signed it but did not waive the condition of universal ratification before adhering to it, as most other signatories did.[9] This stance foreshadowed the interest in nuclear weapons that was soon to become apparent. The military government began a nuclear weapon program in the late 1970s and succeeded in developing centrifuges for uranium enrichment. Motivations for nuclear weapons included a drive to match Argentina's nuclear program, as well as a desire for both regional and international prestige.[10] The program was ended in the early 1990s under the democratically elected civilian government. Since terminating the program and signing the NPT in 1998, Brazil has become an energetic supporter of nuclear disarmament.

Brazil's engagement with nuclear disarmament up until 2009 can be best understood through understanding how it has presented both opportunities and challenges for disarmament.

Brazil: Opportunities for Disarmament

Although Brazil was a relative latecomer to the NPT and has been involved in a significant dispute with the International Atomic Energy Agency (IAEA), it has offered a number of opportunities to further the drive for global nuclear disarmament: in particular, through its active leadership and a model constitution.

Leadership. Since the late 1990s, Brasilia provided both regional and international leadership in the push for global nuclear disarmament. As an active member of the New Agenda Coalition (NAC), it joined with other like-minded states to forcefully call on the nuclear weapon states (NWS) to move more quickly toward disarmament. The NAC was formed in 1998 and is widely credited with fostering the success of the 2000 NPT Review Conference (RevCon), which produced the "Thirteen Practical Steps" toward nuclear disarmament. The country takes leadership roles in a number of international forums focused on nuclear disarmament, including the Conference on Disarmament (which it chaired in 2000), the 2005 NPT RevCon (which it chaired), and the International Panel on Fissile Materials (which top Brazilian nuclear expert José Goldemberg co-chaired until 2007).[11] Brazil is also a member of the Nuclear Suppliers Group (NSG) and the Missile Technology Control Regime.

The main focus of Brazil's disarmament efforts has been to push the NWS to fulfill their end of the NPT bargain. Policymakers have been critical of the discriminatory nature of the NPT, which is part of the reason why Brasilia took so long to sign and ratify it. In fact, the Brazilian Congress ratified the NPT based on the understanding that "effective measures will be taken with a view to the cessation of the nuclear arms race at an early date and the total elimination of nuclear weapons."[12] The country's diplomats make continued, explicit references to the grand bargain of nonproliferation for disarmament in their calls for greater action. For example, an official statement by the Brazilian ambassador to the 2005 NPT Review Conference warned, "The decision made by 182 state parties to the NPT to forgo the option of nuclear weapons as instruments of security cannot live with the continued possession of nuclear weapons by the five nuclear weapons states."[13]

Model constitution. Another opportunity that Brazil offers the disarmament movement is the example provided by its constitution. Adopted in 1988 under the civilian government, Brazil's constitution is among the most stringent in the world on the issue of nuclear weapons. Brazilian diplomat Achilles Zaluar notes that the Brazilian constitution "forbids the manufacture or possession of nuclear weapons. Budget funds cannot be allocated to such activities, and a president who secretly orders a nuclear weapon program could even be impeached."[14] The constitution also places all nuclear activities under the authority of the national Congress. Analysts George Perkovich and James Acton note that these constitutional constraints on military nuclear capability could be a model for other states and would provide an additional "societal barrier against cheating."[15]

Brazil: Challenges for Disarmament

Despite its vocal support for nuclear disarmament, as a threshold state, Brazil has posed a number of potential challenges to global nuclear disarmament. The three most important are its atypical stance on safeguards, its uranium enrichment program, and its plan for nuclear-powered submarines.

Safeguards. Brazil and Argentina enjoy a unique safeguards arrangement for their nuclear facilities. The two countries agreed in 1991 to use nuclear energy for nonmilitary purposes and established the Brazilian-Argentine Agency for Accounting and Control of Nuclear Materials (ABACC) for verification purposes.[16] The relationship of the IAEA to ABACC was established shortly afterward: "Argentina, Brazil, ABACC and the IAEA signed a comprehensive safeguards agreement (Quadripartite Agreement), which entered into force in March 1994 and that allows the IAEA to apply its safeguards regime in both countries taking into account the findings of the SCCC [ABACC's Common System of Accounting and Control]."[17] However, even ABACC personnel have noted the difficulty in ensuring that both organizations can reach independent conclusions while avoiding overlap of inspections: "In spite of good cooperation between both agencies [IAEA and ABACC], an important challenge that faces both organizations is to implement fully the provisions of the Quadripartite Agreement. The need to reach an independent conclusion and to avoid unnecessary duplication of ABACC safeguards is still a provision to be fully accomplished. [Despite] the good will of all parties, an institutional framework that [allows] the IAEA to verify the SCCC findings is not yet envisaged and should be considered seriously."[18]

Complicating the imprecise relationship with the IAEA is Brazil's rejection of the Additional Protocol (AP), which gives expanded right of access to the IAEA for both nuclear sites (declared and undeclared) and information related to the country's nuclear program. Brasilia has given a number of reasons for its refusal to support or sign the AP. Diplomats argue not only that the AP could hamper commercial nuclear development, but also that it creates unnecessary financial burdens on developing countries by creating more regulations to which they must adhere. Given that Brazil considers itself a leader in safeguarding practices, Brasilia argues the AP is unnecessary.[19] In addition, Brazil asserts that adding to the original inspection requirements on non-nuclear weapon states (NNWS) while the NWS fail to adhere to their original promise to seriously pursue disarmament is unacceptable—a position held by other NNWS, including South Africa. As Brazilian ambassador Celina Assumpção do Valle Pereira said, "The strengthening of the safeguards system and the maintenance of a robust nonproliferation regime for all weapons of mass destruction is not sustainable without parallel positive development in the fields of arms control and disarmament."[20] Finally, the intrusive nature of the AP is an affront to Brazilian national pride: Brazil does not want its autonomy curtailed even further.[21]

Why has the Brazilian position on the AP been a challenge for disarmament diplomacy? As the case of Iraq in the early 1990s shows, the inspection requirements of the standard IAEA safeguards agreement are not robust enough to ensure civilian nuclear technology is not misused for military purposes.[22] Verification that civilian nuclear programs are for peaceful purposes only is critical to disarmament—in the short run to provide confidence for NWS to move toward disarmament, and in the long run to ensure that all states remain nuclear-free. Brazil's opposition to the AP also complicates NSG efforts to ensure enrichment and reprocessing technologies are exported only to responsible countries. One of the proposed criteria for blocking such transfers would be that the importing country had not signed the AP, but Brazil opposed it.[23] In the context of pursuing credible universal disarmament, national enrichment facilities will need to be subject to safeguards beyond the standard IAEA safeguards agreement. Therefore, Brazil's hesitancy on the AP is in tension with its desire for disarmament.

Uranium enrichment. Brazil is one of only thirteen countries in the world capable of enriching uranium.[24] Its uranium enrichment facility, Resende, is a small commercial plant designed to enrich uranium to 3.5–4.0 percent. The goal is to create low-enriched uranium (LEU) to fuel its nuclear power plants and eventually sell LEU in the commercial market. In addition to making use of the substantial investment in the nuclear program made during the military years, the civilian power program is intended to help diversify Brazil's energy supply. Currently hydroelectric dams provide 95 percent of Brazil's energy, but low rainfalls in past seasons have led to severe energy rationing and blackouts.[25] Brazil's need for reliable energy is unquestioned, and no serious doubts exist about Brazil's intent to use Resende only for LEU.

The particular disarmament challenge related to Brazil's uranium enrichment revolves around safeguards at the Resende facility. In early 2004, while the facility was still under construction, Brazil denied IAEA inspectors full visual access to the equipment.[26] During the initial visits, Brazilian authorities shrouded the centrifuges with panels, hiding both the rotors and casings of the centrifuges. Brazilian authorities insisted that full visual access of the centrifuges was not necessary to determine whether diversion was taking place. They cited the need to protect proprietary technology as justification for shrouding the centrifuges.[27] The claim is that Brazilian centrifuges are innovative, with rotors that "levitate, spinning frictionlessly, thanks to actively controlled electromagnetic bearings," which make them 25 percent more efficient than typical centrifuges.[28] Brazilian scientists argue that the technology is completely indigenous, developed by the navy. However, others argue that Brazil wants to hide the centrifuges because they are based on a design by the European enrichment consortium URENCO, which would be evident without the shrouding.[29] If this were the case, it would undermine Brazil's claim to indigenous development of the centrifuges, as well as raise questions about how the design was acquired. Brazilian officials emphatically deny the charge, but others remain puzzled about why Brazil insists on shrouding the centrifuges. As Thomas L. Neff, a physicist from the Massachusetts Institute of Technology, noted: "The Brazilians say they have proprietary technology. Well, others have proprietary technology, and they don't seem to think that is a problem. No one else conceals their centrifuges from the IAEA."[30] Even Brazilian scientists have noted that the shielding that the IAEA permitted on the navy's small-scale enrichment facility may not be appropriate at a commercial plant because of "a substantial increase of the installed capacity and, consequently, a significant reduction of the time required for the production of a relevant amount of highly enriched uranium."[31] In other words, shielding on a larger facility that can produce enriched uranium more quickly may undermine trust in safeguards, since illicit activity may not be detected in a timely fashion.

Although Brazil and the IAEA worked out an agreement later in 2004 (which allowed for a reduction in size of the shrouding panels), Resende has remained a challenge for global nuclear disarmament. First, although few expect Brazil to secretly manufacture nuclear weapons, the lack of full access to the plant means that the potential remains. For example, panels could hide a hidden supply of uranium, allowing Brazil to secretly stockpile LEU, which would give the country a "breakout capacity" because producing highly enriched uranium (HEU) from LEU takes less time than enrichment to LEU.[32] More important, however, is the precedent created by Brazil's rejection of full visual inspections. Other countries may demand similar concessions on inspections—countries that *are* interested in building a secret breakout capacity. In a larger sense, if the IAEA faces serious challenges to its inspection authority, the future for disarmament becomes bleaker. Disarmament will require intrusive inspections that go to the heart of state national security; if some countries do not trust the IAEA to conduct basic visual inspections in small commercial enrichment facilities, other states may wonder why they should allow the same agency into their nuclear weapons stockpiles.

Nuclear submarines. Brazil's plan for nuclear submarines has been another potential challenge to global nuclear disarmament. While nuclear submarines no longer have to be fueled with HEU, the "fuel would be near the 20 percent enrichment HEU/LEU threshold, and so relatively simple to convert."[33] Not only is the actual fuel a concern in terms of acquiring a breakout capability, but the question of inspections further complicates the issue. Since Resende would have to produce 20 percent enriched uranium, this "would require significantly more intrusive inspections, containment, and surveillance."[34] Given the Brazilian authorities' reluctance to provide even basic visual access, such negotiations could be very challenging. In addition, "the question of how nuclear material could be withdrawn from safeguards for military, non-explosive purposes would be difficult to resolve."[35]

Perkovich and Acton argue that nuclear submarines complicate the goal of disarmament: "Would these states, or any other non-nuclear-weapons states that might be inclined to consider the use of naval reactors in the future, be prepared to renounce them permanently in order to help bring about a nuclear-weapons-free world as part of a non-discriminatory agreement? Or would they be willing to give international inspectors unprecedented access to some of their most sensitive technologies in order to assuage international concerns?"[36]

Brazil is committed to its investment—both monetary and national prestige—in nuclear submarines. The formal program began in 1979 but languished due to lack of funds. However, in 2008, Brazil committed $160 million to the program, with more promised.[37] President Luiz Inácio Lula da Silva announced that the country would "soon" have a nuclear submarine, but experts place a realistic completion date at 2020 or later.[38] Nevertheless, the armed forces are heavily invested in the program: a top Brazilian general said, "Brazil's number one military priority is the development of a nuclear submarine."[39] Given the extended time frame, this particular challenge is less urgent than the questions over safeguards at Resende. However, the tension between nuclear submarines and disarmament has remained.

The combination of secrecy at Resende and plans for nuclear submarines has led to speculation that Brazil may be actively retaining a military nuclear option. If Brazil uses the shielding to secretly enrich greater quantities of uranium than declared, they could create a breakout capability. Or Brazil could declare facilities related to its nuclear submarines as restricted military areas and seek to keep IAEA inspectors out. In either case, detecting cheating would be more difficult. Adding fuel to the fire are pro-nuclear statements by senior officials. In October 2007, General José Benedito de Barros Moreira, a senior four-star army officer, argued: "We must have in Brazil the future possibility, if the State agrees, of developing a nuclear device. We cannot be oblivious to the world's reality." He also said that Brazil's treaty commitments could be ignored if necessary.[40] Then, in September 2009, Brazil's vice president and former defense minister Jose Alencar argued that Brazil needed nuclear weapons, both for deterrence and international respect.[41] In both cases, government officials played down the remarks and said that the comments were personal opinion and did not represent the official views of Brazil. (Vice President Alencar was a member of a different political party than President Lula.) Nonetheless, the combination of technical capacity, secrecy, and comments by senior officials has raised concerns about Brazil's long-term commitment to nuclear disarmament. However, because Brazil faces no serious military threats in its region, it is hard to see a compelling security rationale for nuclear weapons. The most likely scenario in which Brazil seeks nuclear weapons is one in which the nuclear nonproliferation regime breaks down, leading Brasilia to want to keep pace for status reasons. In his argument for acquisition of nuclear weapons, Alencar "cited the case of other emerging regional powers, such as Pakistan, which he said has won international relevance 'precisely because it has a nuclear bomb.'"[42] Along the same lines, a former high-level U.S. bureaucrat cautioned that should India ever be given a permanent seat on the UN Security Council without Brazil also receiving one, "Brazil will light fire to the NPT and they will test."[43]

JAPAN'S HISTORICAL DISARMAMENT DIPLOMACY

Japanese views on nuclear disarmament were shaped indelibly by the U.S. atomic bombings of Hiroshima and Nagasaki.[44] The "nuclear allergy" that developed as a result has created an inhospitable political environment for Japanese acquisition of nuclear weapons, as well as a strong grassroots demand for Japanese leadership on nuclear disarmament.[45] Despite the negative sentiment toward nuclear capability, the country has developed an impressive civilian nuclear industry that provides more than 30 percent of Japan's energy. Japan's approach to disarmament has been starkly different from Brazil's: in contrast to unaligned Brasilia's boldness and insistence on immediate progress on nuclear disarmament, U.S.-allied Tokyo has taken a much lower-key, cooperative approach with an emphasis on incremental movement toward disarmament. Nevertheless, as with Brazil, Japan has offered both opportunities and challenges to the drive for global nuclear disarmament.

Japan: Opportunities for Disarmament

The three most important Japanese contributions to the disarmament movement have been leadership, financial and technical support, and keeping alive the memory of Hiroshima and Nagasaki.

Leadership. Japan has engaged in active nuclear disarmament diplomacy, but in a different way than Brazil's bold manner. Instead, Japan's efforts have been called timid and passive.[46] Japanese diplomats respond that while Japan's approach is not flashy or confrontational, it focuses on results: "Compared to a high profile 'confrontational performance,' Japan may have appeared to be playing a less spectacular role, yet such efforts by Japan certainly deserve to be commended. Indeed, what the Japanese public wants to see its government to be doing is not just a stage performance but 'honest efforts' for real progress in nuclear disarmament."[47] Japan's reliance on U.S. nuclear deterrence limits Japan's scope for assertiveness on the issue. Nevertheless, the country has devoted considerable resources to the effort, with a long list of products.

Japan *has* exerted leadership in the disarmament movement, not in confrontational stances designed to push negotiations forward, but rather in the creation of spaces for discussions and negotiations so that common understandings can result in greater progress. Tokyo has an impressive list of financial and intellectual sponsorship of such open spaces for dialogue. Since 1983, Japan has sponsored study visits to Hiroshima and Nagasaki though the UN Programme of Fellowships on Disarmament, which has trained more than 650 diplomats from 150 different countries in disarmament issues.[48] Every year since 1989, Japan has sponsored an annual UN Conference on Disarmament Issues in a different Japanese city, "providing a valuable opportunity for distinguished disarmament experts from around the world to engage in useful discussions."[49] Tokyo has hosted the annual Asian Export Control Seminar since 1993.[50] After the Indian and Pakistani nuclear tests in 1998, the government cosponsored the Tokyo Forum meetings with nongovernmental organizations (NGOs), an important contribution to the dialogue on ways to promote disarmament and nonproliferation.[51] Japan hosted the annual Asian Senior-Level Talks on Non-Proliferation for six years; it also cosponsored two international conferences with the IAEA on nuclear security in Asian countries during the same time period.[52] In February 2007, Tokyo arranged a seminar, "NPT on Trial: How Should We Respond to the Challenge of Maintaining and Strengthening the Treaty Regime?," in Vienna "to provide an opportunity for an informal exchange of views on key issues among participants and to prepare the ground for a smooth start to the First Session of Preparatory Committee of the 2010 NPT Review Conference."[53] The cost—in both financial and human capital—of consistently and enthusiastically calling parties together to wrestle with the complex issues of disarmament is not insignificant and displays a commitment that few other states have been willing to make.

Financial and technical support. In addition to financially supporting the creation of venues to discuss disarmament, the Japanese government has provided monetary and technical aid to a wide array of important disarmament initiatives. In the 1990s, Tokyo committed $1 billion to the Korean Peninsula Energy Development Organization to provide light water nuclear power reactors to North Korea in exchange for it giving up its plutonium production program. In the mid-1990s, Japan also spent approximately $100 million helping Russia and other former Soviet republics to "disassemble nuclear warheads and safely dispose of nuclear waste material."[54] Almost a decade later, Tokyo provided an additional $200 million to help dispose of excess Russian weapons-grade plutonium and to dismantle decommissioned Russian nuclear submarines.[55] To emphasize the importance of the CTBT, Japan has given technical assistance to several developing countries in the field of earthquake monitoring so that they can fulfill their CTBT responsibilities.[56] The country also financed a large portion of the costs of the CTBT negotiations.[57] Tokyo provided "generous financial support" to negotiations for the Central Asian Nuclear-Weapon-Free Zone.[58] Such committed monetary aid underscores Japan's dedication to disarmament; given the fact that disarmament measures cost money, the Japanese commitment is invaluable to the movement.

Remembrance of nuclear horror. The world's only experience with the wartime use of nuclear weapons was sixty-five years ago. The horror of Hiroshima and Nagasaki precipitated a global grassroots movement against nuclear weapons, but as the experience recedes deeper into history, memories of it fade. For this reason, the Japanese ability to keep alive the memory of Hiroshima and Nagasaki is an important contribution to the disarmament movement. Indeed, this is one of the central goals of Japanese nuclear diplomacy. As Foreign Minister Hirofumi Nakasone said, "It is Japan's mission to convey to all people around the world the facts of the calamity of nuclear bombings that happened in August

1945 in Hiroshima and Nagasaki, across the boundaries of various political viewpoints and ideologies."[59]

Japan carries out this mission in numerous ways. In its sponsorship of diplomatic study visits to Hiroshima and Nagasaki (through the UN Programme of Fellowships on Disarmament), Tokyo arranges visits for the fellows at the memorial museums at the atomic bomb hypocenters, meetings with survivors, and lectures on the social and medical legacies. According to a Ministry of Foreign Affairs report, the visits are sponsored so that young diplomats have an "opportunity to witness the horrendous and long-lasting consequences caused by atomic bombs."[60] The government has supported universities, NGOs, and local governments in arranging exhibitions around the world related to the atomic bombings, including the Hiroshima-Nagasaki A-bomb exhibitions in La Paz, Bolivia, in August 2006 and a joint exhibition, "Against Nuclear Arms," with Kazakhstan at UN Headquarters in 2009.[61] Local governments assist as well: "The city of Hiroshima spends approximately 2 billion yen each year (approximately U.S. $18.4 million) on outreach and education efforts through its Peace Cultural Foundation, including a number of international initiatives: a new multidisciplinary set of courses on the effects of nuclear war held at universities around the world, special travelling museum exhibitions, and non-nuclear lobbying through the Conference of Mayors."[62]

Japan: Challenges to Disarmament

Despite its unique history and consistent commitment to supporting disarmament, as a threshold state Japan has posed a number of challenges to global nuclear disarmament. The three most important are its plutonium program, reliance on U.S. nuclear deterrence, and potential for nuclear acquisition.

Plutonium program. Japan is energy poor and can only supply 4 percent of its energy needs through domestic sources (nuclear power is not considered indigenous since the country currently imports LEU for nuclear power plants).[63] As a result, the country has created one of the most advanced civilian nuclear power programs in the world, with a focus on reprocessing plutonium for use in power plants, as well as planned fast breeder reactors (which create more plutonium than they consume).[64] As a Japanese nuclear industry official has argued, "Nuclear energy and the recovery and reuse of plutonium as a nuclear fuel will significantly enhance energy security and reduce reliance on foreign fossil-fuel sources."⁶⁵ The focus of Japan's reprocessing program is the Rokkasho Reprocessing Plant, originally expected to begin operations in 2005, but as of 2011 it was still not fully functional. Once operational, Rokkasho will be able to process eight hundred tons of spent fuel each year, approximately 80 percent of the spent fuel Japan produces annually but almost as much as the total spent fuel reprocessed in the past three decades.⁶⁶ Rokkasho was built with concerns about proliferation in mind: the facility separates the plutonium and combines it with uranium so that mixed oxide (MOX) fuel is "created under a single roof."⁶⁷ (This is more proliferation resistant than a program in which plutonium is separated in one plant and then combined with uranium in another, because the plutonium could be diverted between plants.) The MOX will then be used to fuel a portion of Japan's nuclear power plants; the goal is to have fifteen to eighteen reactors (out of the country's fifty-three) using MOX by 2015.⁶⁸

Rokkasho, as with all of Japan's nuclear facilities, is under IAEA inspections. In contrast with Brasilia, Tokyo strongly supports the AP and was the first nonnuclear weapons state with a nuclear power program to sign it. As Foreign Minister Nakasone said: "Japan believes that it is important to enhance transparency over the nuclear activities of individual countries by ensuring that all countries promoting peaceful uses of nuclear energy implement the highest level of the IAEA safeguards, specifically, the NPT Comprehensive Safeguards Agreements and the Model Additional Protocol, and Japan has been actively working towards their universalization. On various occasions, including the IAEA seminars and the Asian Senior-Level Talks on Non-Proliferation, Japan has shared its knowledge and experiences concerning the implementation of the IAEA safeguards with other countries. Japan will continue such efforts."⁶⁹

The challenge to disarmament posed by Japan's plutonium program is not concern about safeguards, as with Brazil; rather, the concern is the inherent proliferation risk of reprocessing plutonium. If Tokyo decided to pursue nuclear weapons, Rokkasho would make it very easy to do so. It is not difficult to separate out plutonium from MOX, so the plant is less proliferation resistant than assumed.⁷⁰ This would be difficult to do secretly, but conceivably Japan could withdraw from the NPT after it establishes its own nuclear fuel supply without worries about energy security. As is discussed below, Japan joining the nuclear weapons club would likely end movement toward disarmament, at least for the short term. In addition, because reprocessing can create fissile material for weapons as well as power plants, the Japanese insistence on reprocessing keeps the door open for other countries, as Shinichi Ogawa and Michael

Schiffer point out: "Despite all evidence of good intentions, Japan's policy may be setting a poor precedent. Its pursuit of the nuclear fuel cycle may legitimize the actions of other countries to pursue similar technologies and ultimately attain "breakout" capability. They too may seek to build up similarly robust civilian energy programs that, at the flip of the switch, could be militarized."[71]

In fact, Iran has already used Japan as an example several times in its justification of its own nuclear program, as well as to deflect criticism of its own nuclear program. In response to a critical IAEA report on Tehran, Iran's ambassador to the IAEA called for an inspection of Japan's stockpiles of plutonium and low- and highly enriched uranium.[72] In addition, both South Korea and Taiwan have raised the issue of following Japan's lead in developing enrichment and reprocessing capabilities; both states had nuclear weapons programs that were stopped only through U.S. pressure.[73] Additionally, some argue that Japan plays a pivotal role in plutonium commerce; if Japan were to discontinue its plutonium program, scholar Paul L. Leventhal argues "it might then be possible to build an international consensus to eliminate commerce in plutonium as well as bomb-grade uranium."[74] By emphasizing the importance of plutonium, it is argued, the Japanese set a risky example for the rest of the world—and thus undermine disarmament.

Reliance on U.S. extended deterrence. Despite its committed actions on behalf of disarmament, for decades Tokyo remained just as committed to the U.S. security guarantee, which is backed by nuclear weapons. Impassioned calls from domestic peace groups to reduce or eliminate reliance on the U.S. nuclear umbrella are diametrically at odds with Japan's dependence on the U.S. alliance for security in a region where Japan now faces three nuclear-armed potential adversaries. In fact, the North Korean nuclear test of October 2006 led a number of Japanese experts to consider asking the United States to station nuclear weapons on Japanese soil (which would require, among other things, modification of Japan's Three Non-nuclear Principles).[75] Later, in 2009, Japanese embassy officials in Washington lobbied the U.S. Strategic Posture Commission for the retention of nuclear-armed Tomahawk submarine-launched cruise missiles.

Japanese reliance on U.S. extended deterrence might be considered to be corrosive to global disarmament for a number of reasons. First, Japan's moral weight on disarmament has been weakened by its reliance on U.S. nuclear weapons. For example, after Japan levied sanctions against India after its 1998 nuclear tests, Indian defense experts accused Japan of hypocrisy, given Japan's reliance on nuclear weapons for security.[76] As one expert noted, "the voice of Japan calling for reduction and elimination of U.S. nuclear weapons is diminished because Japan is depending on the U.S. nuclear umbrella."[77] More important, Japan's dependence on U.S. nuclear deterrence has led it to dilute its own stand on disarmament. Sociologist Anthony DiFilippo notes the contradiction in Japan's disarmament policy: "[Tokyo is] seeking the abolition of nuclear weapons while refusing to relinquish Japan's perceived security under the U.S. nuclear umbrella, and opposing a nuclear free zone for northeast Asia. The continued existence of this contradiction in Japanese policy has caused Tokyo to accept a gradualist path to nuclear disarmament, much preferred by the United States and the other nuclear weapons countries than the more expeditious course advocated by NAC. The gradualist position is fully consistent with virtually all politicians' views that nuclear weapons should be abolished—someday."[78]

Japanese experts note that the Disarmament section of Japan's Ministry of Foreign Affairs is fearful of pushing too hard on disarmament because of concerns over U.S. displeasure.[79] Thus, to the extent that more forceful Japanese leadership could advance regional or global disarmament, the hesitancy created by their dependence on the U.S. nuclear umbrella is an obstacle to disarmament. Indeed, it could be argued that reliance on the United States not only keeps Japan from taking more robust positions but also leads them to oppose measures that could move disarmament forward. For example, Tokyo has historically opposed a nuclear-free zone in Northeast Asia, as well as requiring a no-first-use declaration by nuclear weapons states, and adopts a more minimalist position on a fissile material cut-off treaty.[80] Thus, dependence on U.S. extended deterrence both softens Japan's position on disarmament and weakens its credibility on the stands that Tokyo does take.

Threat of nuclear acquisition. Concerns over a nuclear-armed Japan arise occasionally, and after two rounds of North Korean nuclear tests, unease has grown. However, North Korea is not Japan's main security concern, and short of a nuclear attack by North Korea, the country is unlikely to push Tokyo into a nuclear option.[81] Rather, possible U.S. abandonment of Japan and anxiety over China's rise are far more likely to trigger a Japanese nuclear response, although even these are unlikely to do so.[82] A combination of abandonment and anxiety might be the most lethal threat to Japan's nuclear restraint. While highly unlikely in the foreseeable future, if Washington were ever to make a strategic decision to align with Beijing over Tokyo, Japanese elites may rethink how best to ensure their country's security. As one Japanese nuclear expert noted, if the United States wants to keep Japan non-nuclear, "Don't abandon us for China."[83]

The threat of nuclear acquisition has been compounded by Japan's other challenges to disarmament. Many experts question why Japan insists on having a plutonium reprocessing and fast breeder program when it is inordinately expensive and unpopular both domestically and internationally; the implication is that Tokyo may want a nuclear breakout capacity. Occasional unscripted statements made by Japanese politicians that link Japan's plutonium stockpile with a nuclear weapons capability amplify this concern. For example, in 2002, Ozawa Ichiro, leader of the Democratic Party of Japan (DPJ) from 2006 to 2009, publicly stated that he had told a member of the Chinese Communist Party that Japan could use its civilian plutonium stockpiles for nuclear weapons: "It would be easy for us to produce nuclear warheads. We can produce thousands of nuclear warheads overnight. We may have enough plutonium at nuclear power plants for 3,000 or 4,000 rounds."[84] While analysts around the world understand Ozawa was exaggerating, they are concerned that some Japanese politicians might see Japan's plutonium stockpile as a virtual nuclear weapons capability.

Thus, threat of nuclear acquisition by Japan hinders global disarmament. If there is a serious global perception that Japan may soon acquire nuclear weapons, it may plunge both nonproliferation and disarmament into disarray. If Japan—the only country to be attacked with nuclear weapons, the only country to argue for nonproliferation and disarmament from a tragic historical experience, one of the main financial supporters of the regime—were to be seen as potentially withdrawing from the NPT, many other threshold states may wonder if the ship is sinking and whether it is time for them to abandon ship as well. While we would probably not see a race to nuclearization, at the very least, most countries would wonder whether tackling the many difficult issues related to disarmament was worth it, given the Japanese defection.

CURRENT ACTIVITIES

Since U.S. president Obama's groundbreaking disarmament initiative, we have seen dramatic activity in both Brazil and Japan. While not all of the changes are attributable to Obama's push for disarmament, some are—and those that aren't are supported by the generally positive international environment created by Obama's prioritization of disarmament.

BRAZIL'S CURRENT DISARMAMENT DIPLOMACY

Brazil remains active in the NAC, which most recently submitted a working paper to the 2010 NPT RevCon. However, its most dramatic change in disarmament policy has resulted in an additional opportunity for disarmament: outreach to problem states.

While Brazil's willingness to directly confront the NWS may not endear it to these states, it is precisely this boldness that presents opportunities for advances in disarmament. One of the many challenges in getting to zero is to convince states outside the regime to join it as non-nuclear states; another is to coax NPT members thought to be flirting with military capabilities (such as Iran) to forgo such an option. These countries are unlikely to be persuaded to give up their suspected nuclear weapons ambitions by the NWS, who are seen as hypocritical and slow-moving in relinquishing their own arsenals. Indeed, social psychology research indicates that conflict polarizes actors and leads them to reject normative influence from those with whom they clash.[85] Therefore, Brazil's credentials as an independent state—one that is clearly not a mouthpiece of Washington—make it an excellent candidate for outreach to these tough cases. This is particularly true given that Brazil is not a U.S. ally (unlike North Atlantic Treaty Organization [NATO] members France and Germany). In addition, Brazil can speak from experience about the economic benefits of giving up a nuclear weapons program, as well as the ability to pursue regional and global status without a military nuclear capability. Actors are more likely to accept and act on normative messages from those they like or with whom they believe they share similarities.[86]

Brazil already has nurtured diplomatic relationships with North Korea. Brazil established diplomatic relations with Pyongyang in 2001, and in 2005 North Korea opened an embassy in Brasilia and a business office in São Paulo. The North Korean foreign trade minister visited Brazil in late 2005, when the two countries signed a trade agreement. The relations were characterized as "enthusiastic" until the North Korean nuclear test in October 2006; Brazil condemned the test and called on Pyongyang to sign the Comprehensive Nuclear-Test-Ban Treaty (CTBT) and return to the Six-Party talks.[87] Relations gradually thawed, with Brasilia opening an embassy in Pyongyang in July 2009. (North Korea's second nuclear test only delayed the embassy's opening by several weeks.) The countries plan to continue expansion of economic ties; trade between Brazil and North Korea in 2008 alone totaled $381 million, and by 2009 Brazil had become North Korea's third most important trading partner.[88]

Brazil has also strengthened ties with another state that presents obstacles to nuclear disarmament: Iran. Indeed, Brazil's most prominent disarmament diplomacy centers on a uranium-swap agreement with Iran, brokered by Brasilia and Ankara, in an effort to break through the nuclear impasse with Tehran. Obama promoted Brazil's outreach to Iran, twice asking President Luiz Inácio da Silva (known as President Lula) to encourage Iranian president Mahmoud Ahmadinejad to accept a fuel swap deal being offered by the IAEA and supported by Western countries.[89] Washington approached Brasilia because of the country's strengthened ties with Iran, not only economic but also "scientific, industrial, technological, and cultural cooperation."[90] Indeed, between 2003 and 2008, trade between Brazil and Iran quadrupled to $2 billion.[91] Iran has responded warmly to the Brazilian overtures: the Iranian foreign minister noted that "Brazil has a special place in Iran's foreign policy," and Ahmadinejad stated that he is "determined to develop comprehensive cooperation with Brazil."[92]

However, Iran rejected the proposed Western fuel swap in late 2009 and in January 2010 started uranium enrichment to 19.75%, for fuel for the Tehran Research Reactor so it could be used to produce medical isotopes.[93] In May 2010, Lula brokered a deal, working with Turkey, to create a similar nuclear fuel swap with Iran. Obama personally wrote to Lula about the negotiations, encouraging Lula to modify the swap so that the LEU would be "escrowed" in Turkey while the nuclear fuel for Iran's medical reactor was being enriched.[94] The resulting nuclear fuel exchange, outlined in the Joint Declaration by Iran, Turkey, and Brazil in May 2010, did indeed contain this provision. However, the declaration did not require Iran to export the bulk of its LEU, which was one of the key features of the original U.S.-proposed fuel exchange. While the Joint Declaration arranged for 1,200 kilograms of LEU to be shipped to Turkey, it left another 1,200 kilograms or more LEU remaining in the country. Nor did the May agreement require Iran to stop enriching uranium to 20 percent. Indeed, shortly after the Joint Declaration, Iran announced that it would not stop this enrichment, much to the surprise of Lula.[95] For these reasons, the United States pursued further sanctions against Iran, which were accepted by the UN Security Council in June 2010 (twelve countries voted for the sanctions, Lebanon abstained, while Brazil and Turkey voted against the sanctions). While Lula agreed to implement the sanctions, he has repeatedly criticized the Western approach, arguing "there are a lot of sanctions and not enough conversations with Iran. It will get harder and harder to reach an agreement."[96]

Brazil's new disarmament diplomacy—attempting to serve as a bridge between the West and problem states—did not succeed. Why not? Some criticize Obama, given the agreement was similar to that originally proposed by the IAEA and agreed to by Obama.[97] Others note that the march for sanctions had already begun, and the Joint Declaration was too little, too late.[98] It has been argued that Washington may have been resentful of Brasilia's newfound diplomatic endeavors. This is not particularly likely, however, given that Obama had been encouraging Lula to work with Iran to reach an acceptable agreement. The most likely reason for the failed effort was that while the differences between the Joint Agreement and the original IAEA proposal were small, they were also significant. The point of the initial agreement was to move Iran's LEU out of the country and keep them from enriching more while negotiations progressed. The Joint Declaration accomplished neither of these two tasks (when originally proposed, moving the 1,200 kilograms of LEU from Iran would have taken almost all of Iran's LEU, but by the time of the Joint Declaration, this amount was less than half). However, as is discussed in a later section, we are likely to see more attempts at similar disarmament diplomacy by Brasilia.

JAPAN'S CURRENT DISARMAMENT DIPLOMACY

As with Brazil, Japan's disarmament diplomacy has increased in both frequency and intensity. The core change is due to domestic politics, but the U.S. initiative to promote disarmament has made the change easier to justify to domestic critics. The change began under the more conservative party, the Liberal Democratic Party (LDP), in April 2009. Minister of Foreign Affairs Hirofumi Nakasone moved the government beyond its comfort zone and announced a bold plan for advancing disarmament, "11 Benchmarks for Global Nuclear Disarmament." The plan was well received globally, with some calling it an improved update to the Thirteen Practical Steps.[99] With the sweeping defeat of the LDP in August 2009 elections, however, additional changes have taken place to create more opportunities for disarmament, particularly around a "no-first-use" policy and the willingness to lead new disarmament initiatives.

No First Use

The winning party in the August 2009 elections, the Democratic Party of Japan (DPJ), has promised less reliance on the United States and a greater emphasis on global nuclear disarmament.[100] In fact, in October 2009, 61 percent of Lower House DPJ members surveyed wanted to end reliance on the U.S. nuclear protection, while fewer than 30 percent surveyed wanted to remain under the U.S. nuclear umbrella.[101]

The DPJ's first foreign minister, Katsuya Okada, was a strong proponent of the United States declaring a no-first-use policy with regard to its nuclear weapons. However, conservative Japanese bureaucrats have resisted the change and, in fact, have implied that a no-first-use policy could erode Japanese confidence in the U.S. security guarantee.[102] This was illustrated by the rift in the International Commission on Nuclear Non-Proliferation and Disarmament (ICNND), sponsored by Canberra and Tokyo. Most experts on the commission wanted to call on NWS to adopt a no-first-use policy, but the Japanese cochair, former foreign minister Yoriko Kawaguchi, "refused to back the proposal, reflecting common official fears in Japan that the change would diminish the protection offered by the U.S. nuclear umbrella from large armies in countries such as North Korea."[103]

However, the Japanese position on no first use has continued to evolve. For example, the ICNND report (published in late 2009) did issue a call for the NWS to adopt no first use "as soon as possible." The report adds that if states were not prepared to do so, they "should at the very least accept the principle that the 'sole purpose' of possessing nuclear weapons is to deter others from using such weapons against that state or its allies."[104] Then, in February 2010, more than two hundred Diet members signed a letter to Obama calling "on the U.S. to adopt as a first step a 'sole purpose' policy (i.e. that the U.S. nuclear weapons are only for deterrence against others from using nuclear weapons against the United States or its allies), and assert[ing] that Japan will not seek the road toward possession of nuclear weapons if the U.S. adopts such a policy."[105] In addition, the new Japanese foreign minister Seiji Maehara has asked for global discussion on no first use and sole use policies.[106]

Leadership in Global Disarmament Initiatives

Most of Japanese leadership for disarmament has been focused on unilateral efforts, as described earlier in the chapter. Even with the sponsorship of the Tokyo Forum (to promote dialogue on advancing nonproliferation and disarmament after the 1998 Indian and Pakistan nuclear tests), the Japanese government distanced itself from the body's conclusions. Recently, however, Tokyo has begun to embrace a leadership role in global disarmament initiatives. On the heels of the ICNND, Canberra and Tokyo have led the formation of a new initiative of foreign ministers, the Cross-Regional Group on Non-Proliferation and Disarmament. The group's mission statement is "The only guarantee against the use and threat of nuclear weapons is their total elimination."[107] Maehara argued that the group would not only help implement agreements of the 2010 NPT Review Conference commitments but would also focus on creative solutions to disarmament challenges. In addition, he proposed that the group "pursue 'a world of decreased nuclear risks' as transition strategy on the path to a 'world without nuclear weapons.'"[108] The next meeting of the group is planned for early 2011, where the foreign ministers will create an action plan. In addition to this new initiative, Japan has been working with Germany to place further pressure on states to pursue disarmament. In May 2010, the foreign ministers of Japan and Germany coauthored opinion pieces in the *Asahi Shimbun* and the *Wall Street Journal* to argue for "the moral challenge of a nuclear-free world."[109] Finally, Japan has been using its diplomatic leverage in international nuclear negotiations regarding both the CTBT and an FMCT; in fact, Maehara proposed that "Japan is ready to offer a new venue for negotiations" if the deadlock over an FMCT cannot be broken in the Conference on Disarmament.[110]

EXPLANATIONS

Why have we seen shifts in disarmament diplomacy from both Brazil and Japan? What motivates such changes? For Brazil, the individual level of analysis explains a great deal, given President Lula's drive to expand his country's global stature and his own status. For Japan, the state level of analysis explains more; discontent with the long-ruling LDP brought the DPJ to power and, along with it, more progressive disarmament policies. However, for both countries, the systemic effect of the U.S.-led push for disarmament engaged and enhanced these other drivers, resulting in striking differences in disarmament diplomacy.

BRAZIL AND THE INDIVIDUAL LEVEL

Brazil's foray into mediating international nuclear disputes should not been seen in isolation, but rather as part of President Lula's larger campaign to expand his country's global reach. Lula took office in 2003 under the theme of change, and he has pursued change vigorously. In contrast to former President Cardoso, Lula has emphasized Brazilian autonomy, South-South relations, and creating a global leadership role for Brasilia (driven in part by a desire to gain a permanent seat in the UN Security Council).[111] In particular, creating linkages with other developing countries has been Lula's route to generating more leverage with developed countries. As Latin American experts Tullo Vigevani and Gabriel Cepaluni argue, "Lula seeks strategic partners in the South in order to gain more bargaining power in international negotiations."[112] For example, Lula spearheaded the IBSA Dialogue Forum (representing India, Brazil, and South Africa) shortly after being elected; one of the main goals of this South-South coalition is UN Security Council reform.[113] Lula's foreign minister, Celso Amorim, argued that IBSA illustrates the "willingness and a commitment from emerging powers to redefine world governance."[114] Just as Lula has pursued social justice at home, he has made it a priority to reduce inequality politically on the global stage. As Soares de Lima and Hirst indicate, "Brazil has come to lay much greater emphasis on the need for both the conceptual revision and the practical reform of major multilateral institutions, especially the UN, and has expressed particular concern over the unequal distribution of power and wealth within such institutions and the distortions that the existing framework imposes."[115] Economic growth at home has added to both Lula's domestic and international legitimacy and likely served to encourage him to continue pursuing his policies. Under Lula, "Brazil has emerged as a beacon of prosperity and growth in the Americas, and a powerful new player on the global stage."[116]

Within this context, the Brazil-Turkey deal with Iran makes sense. Negotiating the joint declaration met all of Lula's objectives for foreign policy: a South-South coalition that stressed both peaceful development and autonomy from the North, all the while fixing a problem important to the West, but yet one that the West wasn't able to fix itself. If the Joint Declaration had been successful, it would have been a bright feather in Lula's cap. The failure of the UN Security Council to recognize the deal, and to proceed with sanctions, stung bitterly for the Brazilians. Amorim noted that the negotiations "followed precisely the script that had been on the table for some months and whose validity had been recently reaffirmed at the highest level," and that the West's failure to recognize the Joint Declaration "confirmed the opinions of many analysts who claimed that the traditional centers of power will not share gladly their privileged status."[117]

JAPAN AND THE STATE LEVEL

In Japan, changes in disarmament diplomacy can be traced directly back to domestic politics. In August 2009, the DPJ came to power in a landslide election, winning over 300 seats in the 480-seat lower house. Voters elected the DPJ not because of the party's policies on nuclear disarmament but rather because of "frustration with years of stagnation and mismanagement under the LDP."[118] Nevertheless, with the ringing endorsement of the populace, the DPJ became free to pursue a much more progressive disarmament program. The DPJ's nuclear policy, issued in 2000, outlines the intention to seek a type of no-first-use declaration from the United States.[119] Since coming into power, the DPJ has promoted a model NWFZ treaty for Northeast Asia.[120] Almost 90 percent of Lower House DPJ members surveyed want a no-first-use policy, and in October 2009, Foreign Minister Katsuya Okada raised the issue of the U.S. adopting a no-first-use posture.[121] The DPJ's election likely has something to do with Japan's reversal on the ICNND regarding demands for no-first-use pledges from NWS. It is hard to imagine the LDP undertaking the kind of changes that the DPJ have made in Japan's disarmament diplomacy.

BRAZIL, JAPAN, AND THE SYSTEM LEVEL

The new activity and intensity in disarmament diplomacy are hard to imagine in Brazil without Lula, and in Japan without the DPJ's rise to power. Nevertheless, in both countries, Obama's disarmament drive encouraged and enhanced their efforts. Lula was elected in 2003, but his engagement in the Iranian nuclear issue did not begin until late 2009. At the G8 summit in Italy in July 2009, Obama asked Lula to talk with Ahmadinejad regarding Iran's nuclear program.[122] As Lula prepared to receive Ahmadinejad for a state visit to Brazil in November 2009, Obama wrote Lula a letter, again asking him to help persuade Tehran to cooperate with the IAEA.[123] After Iran rejected the Washington-backed IAEA fuel swap deal, Lula decided to work with Turkey to negotiate directly with Iran. Obama's personal requests to Lula to help with Iran likely played a significant role in this decision. As analysts have noted, Obama's compliments to Lula at the 2009 G20 meeting—remarking "That's my man right here. I love this guy. The most popular politician on earth"—fueled Lula's popularity at home, and some would say his own ego.[124]

While the "Obama effect" has been less personal in Japan, without compliments and direct requests for assistance, the U.S. president's drive for disarmament has clearly added to the DPJ's desire to move forward. As one analyst noted, "President Obama's April 2009 speech in Prague on a nuclear-free world was seen by the DPJ as a rallying call for Japan to take a leading role in strengthening the NPT."[125] The DPJ faces an uphill battle against conservative bureaucrats in pursuing a no-first-use pledge from the United States, as well as other actions that could be seen as too bold for disarmament. However, the momentum created by the Obama agenda lends international weight to their domestic plans.

PROSPECTS

For both Brazil and Japan, opportunities and challenges to disarmament await. The scales are tipped toward the challenges for several reasons. First, in both countries the new disarmament diplomacy was fueled by domestic political changes that may erode. Second, Obama's vocal commitment to disarmament spurred on activities in both countries, but it is unclear if Obama will win a second term as U.S. president. Third, even if both domestic and international forces continue to support efforts toward disarmament, Brazil and Japan are unlikely to surrender their sensitive fuel cycle technologies—constituting one of the most serious challenges to disarmament globally.

With Lula's presidential term having ended in November 2010 (the Brazilian constitution does not permit a president to run for more than two consecutive terms), Brazil's dynamic diplomacy may lose some of its fire. A politician with an independent streak, Lula was fueled by a personal drive to raise Brazil's international profile and wanted to be seen as a peacemaker in the Middle East (he was the first Brazilian president to visit Israel).[126] His hand-picked successor, Dilna Rouseff, who easily won election to succeed Lula, has little political experience. While she has signaled that she will continue Lula's policies, analysts argue that unlike Lula, she is a "disciplined intellectual" who is "unlikely to invest so much of her persona in high-stakes foreign policy initiatives."[127] This by itself would not rule out Brazil's continuing outreach to nuclear problem states; in fact, such outreach might be done in a more considered fashion. However, others point to Rouseff's lack of personal charisma and international flair: "Rouseff, while in alignment with most of Lula's foreign and domestic priorities, does not enjoy nearly the international respect of her former boss. Under her leadership, Brazil could easily slide back into its comfortable position of South America's regional leader and mediator—to stand between Colombia and Venezuela—despite Lula's attempts to pull Brazil out of this traditional geopolitical rut."[128]

However, Lula's own record shows that it is risky to predict a leader's performance. Before his election in 2003, some worried that he would turn Brazil into a "Marxist banana republic"—and instead Lula has presided over a major period of both economic expansion and poverty reduction.[129] Indeed, Rouseff has already met with Obama several times as part of Lula's governing team, and there may be the possibility for a closer working relationship on disarmament. While Rouseff will probably not engage in the high-risk, high-reward disarmament diplomacy of the Lula era, there is the potential for Brazil to continue its outreach to problem states.

In Japan, weakening and fracturing of the DPJ may erode its ability to continue to forcefully promote disarmament. The party lost its majority in the Upper House in July 2010 elections, and they lack a supermajority in the Lower House to be able to override any Upper House vetoes of bills. In addition, the DPJ's leadership has been in crisis, with their first prime minister, Yukio Hatoyama, resigning over the U.S. military base controversy in Okinawa, and their second prime minister, Naoto Kan, had to overcome a leadership challenge from party heavyweight Ichiro Ozawa. Indeed, Ozawa may end up splitting the party. Although he was acquitted by one court of political funding irregularities, he may still face trial, as well as Diet questioning, and the DPJ cannot decide whether to force him out of the party. In addition, the DPJ has found working with Ministry of Foreign Affairs bureaucrats more difficult than expected; their conservatism has slowed down the progress of their disarmament agenda.

So far, Kan has managed to stave off the challenges from Ozawa. In addition, in a bid to wrest power from bureaucrats (not just in the Ministry of Foreign Affairs but throughout the government), the DPJ has forced ministries to publicly defend their budgets in hearings streamed live online.[130] With key members of the DPJ interested in disarmament, it is likely that Japanese diplomacy on the issue will continue. However, should the party weaken further, Japan's disarmament diplomacy will likely feel the effects.

While Brazil and Japan's opportunities for disarmament face threats, both countries' main challenge to disarmament is likely to continue unabated: insistence on fissile material production and the right to the complete fuel cycle. The NPT guarantees the right of all members to civilian nuclear technology. However, this right has the potential effect of undermining nonproliferation and disarmament. Perkovich states: "The most sensitive issue in the short term is the development of indigenous abilities to produce nuclear fuel, which even when legal in NPT terms, would potentially allow a state to master the technically most difficult part of a nuclear weapons program." This is especially the case considering the increased interest in nuclear power. As Perkovich further notes: "If the number of nuclear power reactors and states that host them grows dramatically, so too will the number of facilities for enriching uranium and, perhaps, for separating plutonium from spent reactor fuel. The same technologies and people that produce fissile material for civilian purposes can be employed to produce weapons. More broadly, as nuclear know-how, equipment, and material spread around the world, so too does the wherewithal to develop nuclear weapons. The difficulty of detecting weapons proliferation rises as the overall density of nuclear commerce, training and cooperation increases."[131]

Do national enrichment and reprocessing facilities represent a threat to global nuclear disarmament? Certainly more immediate challenges to nuclear elimination exist, from entry into force of the CTBT, willingness of states outside the NPT to join, and deep reductions in U.S. and Russian nuclear arsenals. But in terms of challenges posed by threshold states, the ability to create fissile material may be the gravest danger to achieving zero. Not only do enrichment and reprocessing give the countries the capability to take the nuclear option, but they also announce to the world that nationally owned enrichment and reprocessing are acceptable and perhaps necessary for a large-scale civilian nuclear program. If these types of facilities spread, it will undermine confidence in nonproliferation (as fear over breakout capabilities increases) and disarmament (as NWS hesitate to permanently renounce nuclear arms when numerous other states can create them easily).

Threshold states are unlikely to give up their right to the fuel cycle: Perkovich counts ten states unwilling to limit their access to fuel-cycle capacity.[132] Both Brazil and Japan have articulated their intention to continue to exercise their right as responsible members of the NPT to engage in all aspects of civilian nuclear power. For Tokyo, its transparent and responsible adherence to the regime provides the solution to the puzzle: Japan has proposed a behavioral-based set of rules on enrichment and reprocessing. For states with transparent nuclear programs with "verification, safeguards, the physical protection of fissile material, and effective measures to prevent illicit trafficking," creation of fissile material is permissible.[133] Given Brazil's shielding of its enrichment equipment and refusal to accept the AP, one could surmise that Brazil would not qualify under the Japanese proposal. Brazil, on the other hand, argues that civilian nuclear technology is a basic right in the NPT that cannot be curtailed. As the Brazilian ambassador argued at the 2008 NPT PrepCom, "The inalienable right of sovereign states to develop and use nuclear energy for peaceful purposes, as recognized by Article IV of the Treaty, is imperative for the implementation of the NPT."[134]

Nuclear experts, however, increasingly argue that unfettered access to the complete fuel cycle is not necessarily guaranteed by the NPT. Deutch et al. argue that "a better interpretation—indeed, the only one that invests each NPT article with independent meaning as part of a coherent whole—is that Article IV promotes sharing nuclear technology only to the extent consistent with the nonproliferation aims codified in Articles I and II of the Treaty."[135] Perkovich and Acton propose: "If disarmament is viewed not as an end in itself but as a means to enhance global security, then non-proliferation is essential for nuclear weapons to be safely prohibited. Developing safeguards that build confidence in the peaceful use of declared facilities and in the absence of clandestine activities is an integral part of the disarmament and nonproliferation challenges."[136] Scott Sagan suggests that international management of the fuel cycle could be seen as a prerequisite for nuclear disarmament, and that "non-nuclear-weapon states also need to recognize that entering into negotiations about international control of the nuclear fuel cycle is actually part of *their* Article VI commitment."[137]

Numerous proposals for international control of the fuel cycle have been circulated.[138] However, if the impasse between the threshold states and the NWS over fuel cycle access is to be broken, attention must be paid to threshold state concerns about the lopsided nature of NPT implementation. Without substantial progress on disarmament, international management of the fuel cycle simply increases NNWS responsibilities while stripping away their rights. Therefore, it is critical that considerable advancements are made in more basic disarmament commitments, from further reductions in stockpiles to entry into force of the CTBT, *before* threshold states are asked to compromise their right to create nuclear fuel. Even Brazil may be willing to consider strengthening of the safeguards system and the nonproliferation regime, so long as it is accompanied by "parallel positive development in disarmament, as Brazil argued in 2002."[139]

CONCLUSION

As nuclear threshold states, Brazil and Japan share a number of commonalities. Both have exercised leadership in the disarmament movement, and both offer inspiration for a world without nuclear weapons. Both possess advanced nuclear facilities with the ability to create fissile material, including for weapons if they so choose. Yet both states have remained part of the nuclear nonproliferation regime as NNWS. However, the countries are also quite dissimilar in a number of ways—a lesson in itself that threshold states cannot all be expected to act and react the same way to disarmament challenges. On the positive side, Brazil speaks boldly and can credibly serve as a bridge to potential problem states. In contrast, Japan speaks softly but consistently initiates open space for serious discussion of disarmament. On the challenges side, Brazil opposes the universalization of the AP (which Japan strongly supports), and Brazil refuses to give full visual access to IAEA inspectors (whereas Japan offers complete access to the IAEA). On the other hand, Japan continues a fast breeder program despite a massive plutonium stockpile (while Brazil has no fissile material stockpile), and for decades Japan dragged its feet on a nuclear-weapon-free zone in its region (whereas Brazil was the first to propose such a zone in its region).

In both countries, disarmament diplomacy has been invigorated since Obama began his campaign for getting to zero. For both Brazil and Japan, their domestic circumstances combined with the international push provided by the United States to lead to vigorous activities supporting nonproliferation and disarmament. While the future remains uncertain, and certainly challenges related to fuel cycle technology linger, there is potential for long-lasting, sustained disarmament diplomacy from both of these critical nuclear threshold states.

Notes

1. Any future restrictions on national enrichment and reprocessing capabilities would likely take place in conjunction with multilateral fuel banks or other regional or global institutions to ensure countries retained access to nuclear fuel (as noted later in this chapter). Nonetheless, concerns about energy independence have made threshold states nervous about such proposals.

2. For an in-depth discussion of the concept of nuclear threshold states, see George H. Quester, "Conceptions of Nuclear Threshold States," in *Security without Nuclear Weapons?*, ed. Regina Cowen Karp (Oxford: Oxford University Press, 1991).

3. As discussed by Quester, some use "nuclear threshold" to describe states that are suspected of desiring nuclear weapons. In that case, creating a list of nuclear threshold states would be far more controversial, because it implies intent as well as capability. In addition, some may question whether Egypt should be considered a nuclear threshold

state, given its technical and material capacity is not as substantial as other states on the list. However, despite its lack of enrichment or reprocessing capability, Egypt has retained significant expertise in other nuclear technologies and is currently planning several nuclear power plants. For more details, see Maria Rost Rublee, *Nonproliferation Norms: Why States Choose Nuclear Restraint* (Athens: University of Georgia Press, 2009), 126–28. Other possible additions to the list include Syria and Burma, whose motivations are questionable, but their technical and material capability is not substantial enough to warrant inclusion.

4. Jing-Dong Yuan, "Beijing Keenly Watching Japan's Nuclear Debate," *WMD Insights*, October 2006, http://www.wmdinsights.com/I10/I10_EA1_BeijingKeenly.htm.

5. "Statement by Ambassador Luiz Filipe de Macedo Soares, Conference on Disarmament," Geneva, May 20, 2008, http://www.reachingcriticalwill.org/political/cd/speeches08/2session/May20Brazil.pdf.

6. Hugh B. Stinson and James D. Cochrane, "The Movement for Regional Arms Control in Latin America," *Journal of Interamerican Studies and World Affairs* 13 (1971): 7.

7. Ibid., 6.

8. Ibid., 7–9. Mexico ended up taking the leadership role for the nuclear-weapon-free zone.

9. Ibid., 11.

10. For analyses of motivations behind both the nuclear weapons program and its renunciation, see Michael Barletta, "The Military Nuclear Program in Brazil," Center for International Security and Arms Control, Stanford University, August 2007; T. V. Paul, *Power versus Prudence: Why Nations Forgo Nuclear Weapons* (Montreal: McGill-Queen's University Press, 2000); Mitchell Reiss, *Bridled Ambition: Why Countries Constrain Their Nuclear Capabilities* (Washington, D.C.: Woodrow Wilson Center Press, 1995); Etel Solingen, "Macropolitical Consensus and Lateral Autonomy in Industrial Policy: Nuclear Industries in Brazil and Argentina," *International Organization* 47 (Spring 1993); and Jean Krasno, "Non-Proliferation: Brazil's Secret Nuclear Program," *Orbis* 38 (Summer 1994). For a norm-centered analysis of Brazil's decision to forgo nuclear weapons, see Thiago Grijó Dal-Toé, "Constructivist Explanations for Brazil's Nuclear Posture," unpublished master's thesis, University of Kent, Brussels, Belgium, 2007.

11. Sharon Squassoni and David Fite, "Brazil as Litmus Test: Resende and Restrictions on Uranium Enrichment," *Arms Control Today*, October 2005, http://www.armscontrol.org/act/2005_10/Oct-Brazil.

12. "Statement by H.E. Ambassador Celina Assumpção do Valle Pereira, Deputy Permanent Representative of Brazil to the United Nations," First Session of the 2005 NPT PrepCom, New York, April 8, 2002.

13. Ibid.

14. Achilles Zaluar, "A Realistic Approach to Nuclear Disarmament," in *Abolishing*

Nuclear Weapons: A Debate, ed. George Perkovich and James M. Acton (Washington, D.C.: Carnegie Endowment for International Peace, 2009), 195.

15. George Perkovich and James M. Acton, "What's Next?" in Perkovich and Acton, *Abolishing Nuclear Weapons*, 324.

16. Jessica Lasky-Fink, "Brazil, Argentina to Pursue Nuclear Cooperation," *Arms Control Today*, April 2008, http://www.armscontrol.org/act/2008_04/BrazilArgentina.

17. Marco A. Marzo and Hugo E. Vicens, "Safeguards Challenges from the ABACC View," Brazilian-Argentine Agency for Accounting and Control of Nuclear Materials (ABACC), 2003.

18. Ibid.

19. Dal-Toé, "Constructivist Explanations," 25.

20. "Statement by Assumpção do Valle Pereira."

21. Frank Braun, "Analysis: Brazil and Additional Protocol," UPI International Intelligence, July 1, 2005.

22. Ibid.

23. Daryl Kimball, "Unfinished Business for the NSG," *Arms Control Today*, October 1, 2008.

24. The thirteen states capable of uranium enrichment are the United States, Russia, the United Kingdom, France, China, Germany, Japan, Pakistan, India, Israel, the Netherlands, Brazil, and Argentina.

25. Denise Lavoie, "Specialists Seeking to Restart Brazil Nuclear Plant," *America's Intelligence Wire*, January 26, 2005. See also Matthew Flynn, "Brazil: Nuclear to the Rescue?" *Bulletin of the Atomic Scientists*, September/October 2001, 15–17.

26. Daphne Morrison, "Brazil's Nuclear Ambitions, Past and Present," Center for Nonproliferation Studies/Nuclear Threat Initiative, September 2006, http://www.nti.org/e_research/e3_79.html; see also Squassoni and Fite, "Brazil as Litmus Test."

27. Morrison, "Brazil's Nuclear Ambitions."

28. Erico Guizzo, "How Brazil Spun the Atom," *IEEE Spectrum*, March 2006, http://spectrum.ieee.org/energy/nuclear/how-brazil-spun-the-atom.

29. Liz Palmer and Gary Milhollin, "Brazil's Nuclear Puzzle," *Science* 306 (October 22, 2004): 617.

30. Thomas L. Neff, quoted in Guizzo, "How Brazil Spun the Atom."

31. Elias Palacios, "Preserving Technological Secrets vs. Proliferation Risk," *ABACC News*, no. 3 (June–October 2004): 5.

32. Palmer and Milhollin, "Brazil's Nuclear Puzzle."

33. George Perkovich and James Acton, "Managing the Nuclear Industry in a World without Nuclear Weapons," in Perkovich and Acton, *Abolishing Nuclear Weapons*, 94.

34. Squassoni and Fite, "Brazil as Litmus Test."

35. Ibid.

36. Perkovich and Acton, "Managing the Nuclear Industry," 95.

37. Bradley Brooks, "Brazil Spending $160M on Nuclear Propelled Sub," *America's Intelligence Wire*, August 30, 2008.

38. "President Says Brazil Soon to Have Nuclear Submarine," *BBC Monitoring International Reports*, December 12, 2008.

39. Lasky-Fink, "Brazil, Argentina Pursue Nuclear Cooperation."

40. Sarah Diehl and Eduardo Fujii, "Brazil's Pursuit of a Nuclear Submarine Raises Proliferation Concerns," *WMD Insights* (October 2008).

41. "Brazil VP: Country Needs Atom Bomb," *Al-Jazeera*, September 28, 2009, http://english.aljazeera.net/news/americas/2009/09/200992682936702272.html.

42. Andres Oppenheimer, "A Nuclear Brazil? Not Likely," *Miami Herald*, October 21, 2009 http://www.mcclatchydc.com/2009/10/21/v-print/77411/commentary-a-nuclear-brazil-not.html.

43. Interview, former senior U.S. Department of State official, Washington, D.C., January 2003.

44. Demands for disarmament did not seriously begin in Japan until 1954, after a Japanese tuna boat was contaminated by fallout from a U.S. nuclear test in the Pacific (the *Daigo Fukuryu-Maru*, or *Lucky Dragon*, incident). Within a few months, more than half of Japan's registered voters had signed petitions calling for immediate disarmament, and the Japanese Diet passed a resolution calling for the prohibition of nuclear weapons. It was the *Lucky Dragon* incident that reactivated the horror from the atomic bombings, giving them political significance. For further discussion, see Nobumasa Akiyama, "The Socio-political Roots of Japan's Non-nuclear Posture," in *Japan's Nuclear Option: Security, Politics and Policy in the 21st Century*, ed. Benjamin Self and Jeffrey Thompson (Washington, D.C.: Henry L. Stimson Center, 2003), 64–91.

45. For an overview of Japanese nuclear weapons decision making, see Paul, *Power versus Prudence*; Kurt Campbell and Tsuyoshi Sunohara, "Japan: Thinking the Unthinkable," in *The Nuclear Tipping Point: Why States Reconsider Their Nuclear Choices*, ed. Kurt Campbell, Robert Einhorn, and Mitchell Reiss (Washington, D.C.: Brookings Institution Press, 2004); Rublee, "Taking Stock"; Rublee, *Nonproliferation Norms*; Mike M. Mochizuki, "Japan Tests the Nuclear Taboo," *Nonproliferation Review* 14 (July 2007): 303–28; Llewelyn Hughes, "Why Japan Won't Go Nuclear (Yet)—an Examination of the Domestic and International Constraints on the Nuclearization of Japan," *International Security* 26 (Spring 2007): 67–96; and Etel Solingen, *Nuclear Logics: Contrasting Paths in East Asia and the Middle East* (Princeton, N.J.: Princeton University Press, 2008).

46. See, for example, the criticisms reported by Marianne Hanson, "New Initiatives to Advance Arms Control: The Tokyo Forum Report," in *The Politics of Nuclear Non-Proliferation*, ed. Carl Ungerer and Marianne Hanson (St. Leonards, NSW: Allen & Unwin, 2001), 180.

47. "Japan's Proactive Peace and Security Strategies—Including the Question of 'Nuclear Umbrella,'" National Institute for Research Advancement (NIRA), Research Report no. 20000005 (Tokyo: NIRA, March 2001), 21.

48. Hirofumi Nakasone, "Conditions toward Zero: 11 Benchmarks for Global Nuclear Disarmament," Japanese Ministry of Foreign Affairs, April 27, 2009.

49. "Japan's Efforts in Disarmament and Nonproliferation Education," working paper of the delegation of Japan to the Conference on Disarmament, April–May 2007, http://www.disarm.emb-japan.go.jp/statements/Statement/0704-05-1NPT.htm.

50. Ibid.

51. Despite being a sponsor, the Japanese government distanced itself from the negotiations and written reports. For an excellent discussion of the Tokyo Forum initiative, see Hanson, "New Initiatives."

52. Nakasone, "Conditions toward Zero."

53. "Implementation of Article VI of the Treaty on the Non-Proliferation of Nuclear Weapons and Paragraph 4(c) of the 1995 Decision on 'Principles and Objectives for Nuclear Non-Proliferation and Disarmament,'" Japanese Ministry of Foreign Affairs, April–May 2007, http://www.mofa.go.jp/policy/un/disarmament/npt/review2010/report0704.html.

54. Anthony DiFilippo, "Can Japan Craft an International Nuclear Disarmament Policy?" *Asian Survey* 40 (July–August 2000): 592.

55. "Implementation of Article VI."

56. Peace Depot 2005 Report Card, "Evaluating Implementation of the NPT (13+2) Steps: Japan's Report Card on Nuclear Disarmament, 2002–5," http://www.peacedepot.org/e-news/nd/engfinalreport2005.pdf.

57. Rublee, *Nonproliferation Norms*, 82.

58. Scott Parish, "Prospects for a Central Asian Nuclear-Weapons-Free Zone," *Nonproliferation Review* 8 (Spring 2001): 147.

59. Nakasone, "Conditions toward Zero."

60. "Implementation of Article VI."

61. "Japan, Kazakhstan Share Fate as Nuclear Victims," *Japan Times*, August 12, 2009; "Japan's Efforts in Disarmament."

62. Rublee, *Nonproliferation Norms*, 79.

63. Hiroyuki Koshoji, "Japan Pursues Plutonium-Based Fuel," UPI Asia, April 6, 2009.

64. For an in-depth discussion of Japan's plutonium program, see Selig S. Harrison, ed., *Japan's Nuclear Future: The Plutonium Debate and East Asian Security* (Washington, D.C.: Carnegie Endowment for International Peace, 1996).

65. Koji Kosugi, "Letters: Still Powering up in Japan," *Bulletin of the Atomic Scientists*, September/October 2001, 4–5, 19–20.

66. On the amount of spent fuel Japan produces annually, see "Reprocessing," Japan Nuclear Fuel Limited, undated, http://www.jnfl.co.jp/english/operation/reprocessing.html. On the comparison to the total amount of spent fuel reprocessed in the past thirty years, see Shinichi Ogawa and Michael Schiffer, "Japan's Plutonium Reprocessing Dilemma," *Arms Control Today*, October 2005, http://www.armscontrol.org/act/2005_10/Oct-Japan. For additional analysis, see Masafumi Takubo, "Wake Up, Stop Dreaming: Reassessing Japan's Reprocessing Program," Nonproliferation Review 15, no. 1 (March 2008): 71–94.

67. Ogawa and Schiffer, "Japan's Plutonium Reprocessing Dilemma."

68. "Japan Delays MOX Nuclear Fuel Goal by 5 Years," Reuters, June 12, 2009.

69. Nakasone, "Conditions toward Zero."

70. Ogawa and Schiffer, "Japan's Plutonium Reprocessing Dilemma."

71. Ibid.

72. Mark Hibbs, "Iran, the NAM, and Amano," *Arms Control Wonk*, September 22, 2010, http://hibbs.armscontrolwonk.com/archive/71/iran-the-nam-and-amano.

73. For details on the seriousness of the South Korean and Taiwanese nuclear weapons programs, and the forceful U.S. pressure required to stop the programs, see Rebecca K. C. Hersman and Robert Peters, "Nuclear U-Turns: Learning from South Korean and Taiwanese Rollback," *Nonproliferation Review* 13 (November 2006): 539–53.

74. Paul L. Leventhal, "Introduction: Nuclear Power without Proliferation?" in *Nuclear Power and the Spread of Nuclear Weapons*, ed. Paul Leventhal, Sharon Tanzer, and Steven Dolley (Dulles, Va.: Brassey's, 2002), 8.

75. Rublee, "Taking Stock," 437.

76. "Japan's Proactive Peace," 18. See also Shinichi Ogawa, "How Japanese View Nuclear Proliferation?" *South Asian Journal*, January–March 2004.

77. Kazumi Mizumoto, "Non-nuclear and Nuclear Disarmament Policies of Japan," in *Nuclear Disarmament in the Twenty-First Century*, ed. Wade L. Huntley, Kazumi Mizumoto, and Mitsuru Kurosawa (Hiroshima: Hiroshima Peace Institute, 2004), 259.

78. Anthony DiFilippo, "Breaking the NPT (Nuclear Nonproliferation Treaty) Stalemate: Japan Could Help," *Foreign Policy in Focus*, June 21, 2005.

79. Rublee, "Taking Stock," 443.

80. One of the main controversies over an FMCT is whether it merely stops all future production of fissile material for weapons purposes (Japan's view, along with the United States, India, and Russia), or if it should be called the Fissile Material Treaty, incorporating all fissile material for weapons purposes, not just future production (the view of many NNWS, including Brazil and South Africa).

81. See, for example, Hajime Izumi and Katsuhisa Furukawa, "Not Going Nuclear: Japan's Response to North Korea's Nuclear Test," *Arms Control Today*, June 2007, http://www.armscontrol.org/act/2007_06/CoverStory. On the likely impact of a North Korean

nuclear attack against Japan, see Maria Rost Rublee, "The Future of Japanese Nuclear Policy," *Strategic Insights* 8 (April 2009), http://www.nps.edu/Academics/centers/ccc/publications/OnlineJournal/2009/Apr/rubleeApr09.html.

82. See, for example, Mochizuki, "Japan Tests the Nuclear Taboo"; and Hughes, "Why Japan Won't Go Nuclear (Yet)."

83. Interview, Japanese defense expert, Tokyo, March 2007.

84. "Tokyo Politician Warns Beijing It Can Go Nuclear 'Overnight,'" *AFP*, April 8, 2002. For additional discussion, see Rublee, *Nonproliferation Norms*, 74–76.

85. Rublee, "Taking Stock," 430–31.

86. See, for example, Richard E. Petty and Duane T. Wegener, "Attitude Change: Multiple Roles for Persuasion Variables," in *The Handbook of Social Psychology*, vol. 2, ed. D. T. Gilbert and S. T. Fiske (New York: McGraw Hill, 1998). For a discussion of the application of this principle to nuclear decision making, see Rublee, *Nonproliferation Norms*, 49–52.

87. "North Korean Nuclear Test Upsets Efforts toward Closer Ties with Brazil," *BBC Monitoring International Reports*, October 13, 2006.

88. "Brazil Opens Embassy in North Korea," PressTV, July 9, 2009, http://www.presstv.com/detail.aspx?id=100195&sectionid=351020405. On Brazil's trading partner status with North Korea, see Bertil Lintner, "Brazil, North Korea: Brothers in Trade," *Asia Times*, June 3, 2010.

89. Alexei Barrionuevo, "Obama Writes to Brazil's Leader about Iran," *New York Times*, November 24, 2009.

90. "Amorim Says Brazil-Iran Ties Can Move beyond Trade Exchanges," *Tehran Times*, November 3, 2008.

91. "Brazil Reaches Out to Iran, Suggests Presidential Visit," Associated Press, November 2, 2008. On the expanding trade between the two countries, see Joshua Goodman and Ladane Nasseri, "Iran's Ahmadinejad Cancels Brazil Trip Indefinitely," Bloomberg News, May 4, 2009, http://www.bloomberg.com/apps/news?pid=20601086&sid=apRIS8bKWwPw.

92. "Amorim Says Brazil-Iran Ties."

93. For a comprehensive analysis of the Western proposal and Iran's rejection, see Mark Fitzpatrick, "Iran: The Fragile Promise of the Fuel-Swap Plan," *Survival* 52, no. 3 (June–July 2010): 67–94.

94. U.S. President Barack Obama, Letter to Brazilian President Lula regarding Iranian nuclear fuel swap, April 20, 2010, http://www.politicaexterna.com/11023/brazil-iran-turkey-nuclear-negotiations-obamas-letter-to-lula.

95. Eduardo Fujii and Sarah Diehl, "Brazil Challenges International Order by Backing Iran Fuel Swap," *NTI Issue Brief*, James Martin Center for Nonproliferation Studies, July 15, 2010, http://www.nti.org/e_research/e3_brazil_iran_diplomacy.html.

96. "Brazil's Lula Rejects Iran Sanctions, Urges Talks," Reuters, September 6, 2010.

97. Jill Dougherty and Charley Keyes, "Obama Administration Tries to Dampen Dispute with Allies over Iran," CNN, May 29, 2010, http://edition.cnn.com/2010/POLITICS/05/28/us.allies.iran/index.html.

98. Andrew Parasiliti, "Let's Make Iran Sanctions a Prelude to Engagement," *Houston Chronicle*, June 9, 2010, http://www.chron.com/disp/story.mpl/editorial/outlook/7045017.html.

99. Sharon Squassoni, "Grading Progress on 13 Steps toward Nuclear Disarmament," Carnegie Endowment Policy Outlook no. 45, May 2009.

100. For example, at the August 2009 commemoration activities in Hiroshima, Prime Minister Taro Aso emphasized the importance of the U.S. nuclear umbrella and argued that nuclear disarmament was "unimaginable." The DPJ leader Yukio Hatoyama (now prime minister) said that Japan would strongly support Obama's drive for disarmament and argued that Japan must play a leading role. See "U.S. Nuclear Umbrella Crucial: Aso," *Japan Times*, August 7, 2009.

101. "Many in DPJ Want Japan to Cut Link to U.S. Nukes," Kyodo News, *Japan Times*, October 11, 2009.

102. Masa Takubo, "The Role of Nuclear Weapons: Japan, the U.S., and 'Sole Purpose,'" *Arms Control Today*, November 2009.

103. Daniel Flitton, "Australia, Japan in Nuclear Rift," *Age*, September 4, 2009.

104. International Commission on Nuclear Non-Proliferation and Disarmament, *Eliminating Nuclear Threats: A Practical Agenda for Global Policymakers* (Canberra: ICNND, 2009), xx.

105. "204 Japanese Legislators Call on President Obama to Adopt 'Sole Purpose' Doctrine," Parliamentarians for Nuclear Nonproliferation and Disarmament, February 19, 2010, http://www.gsinstitute.org/pnnd/archives/Diet_Obama.html.

106. "Nuclear Disarmament," *Asahi Shimbun*, September 28, 2010, http://www.asahi.com/english/TKY201009270235.html.

107. "Germany Joins New International Initiative for Nuclear Disarmament," *Deutsche Welle*, September 23, 2010, http://www.dw-world.de/dw/article/0,,6035871,00.html.

108. "Statement by H.E. Mr. Seiji Maehara, Minister for Foreign Affairs of Japan, First Foreign Ministers Meeting on Disarmament and Non-Proliferation," New York, September 22, 2010.

109. See Katsuya Okada and Guido Westerwelle, "The Moral Challenge of a Nuclear-Free World," *Wall Street Journal*, September 4, 2010, A15; and Katsuya Okada and Guido Westerwelle, "Japan, Germany Seek Consensus on Nuke Cuts," *Asahi Shimbun*, May 5, 2010.

110. "Nuclear Disarmament," *Asahi Shimbun*; on CTBT diplomacy, see "Statement

by Mr. Seiji Maehara, Minister for Foreign Affairs of Japan," The Fifth CTBT Ministerial Meeting," New York, September 23, 2010.

111. Tullo Vigevani and Gabriel Cepaluni, "Lula's Foreign Policy and the Quest for Autonomy through Diversification," *Third World Quarterly* 28, no. 7 (2007): 1309–26.

112. Ibid., 1323.

113. Maria Regina Soares de Lima and Mônica Hirst, "Brazil as an Intermediate State and Regional Power: Action, Choice and Responsibilities," *International Affairs* 82, no. 1 (2006): 36.

114. Celso Amorim, "Let's Hear from the New Kids on the Block," *International Herald Tribune*, June 14, 2010, http://www.nytimes.com/2010/06/15/opinion/15iht-edamorim.html.

115. Soares de Lima and Hirst, "Brazil as an Intermediate State," 21.

116. "In Brazil, There's Life after Lula," *Globe and Mail* (Toronto), October 11, 2011, http://www.theglobeandmail.com/news/opinions/editorials/in-brazil-theres-life-after-lula/article1750538/.

117. Amorim, "Let's Hear."

118. "In Landslide, DPJ Wins over 300 Seats," *Japan Times*, August 31, 2009, http://search.japantimes.co.jp/cgi-bin/nn20090831a1.html.

119. Akira Kurosaki, *Japan, U.S. "Nuclear Umbrella" and Trans-alliance Cooperation for Nuclear Disarmament* (Melbourne: Nautilus Institute for Security and Sustainability, September 2009), 8.

120. "Joint Parliamentary Statement on North Korean Nuclear Tests," Parliamentarians for Nuclear Non-Proliferation and Disarmament, *PNND Update* 24 (June 2009), http://www.gsinstitute.org/pnnd/updates/24.html.

121. On the poll of Lower House DPJ members, see "Many Want Japan to Cut Link." On Foreign Minister Okada's remarks, see Atsuko Tannai and Hiroyuki Maegawa, "International Commission Weighs No-First Use of Nukes," *Asahi Shimbun*, October 19, 2009, http://www.asahi.com/english/Herald-asahi/TKY200910190053.html.

122. "Obama pede que Lula ajude a convencer Irã a abandonar programa nuclear," BBC Brazil, July 9, 2009, http://noticias.uol.com.br/bbc/2009/07/09/ult5022u2650.jhtm.

123. Alexei Barrionuevo, "Obama Writes to Brazil's Leader about Iran," *New York Times*, November 24, 2009, http://www.nytimes.com/2009/11/25/world/americas/25brazil.html?_r=1&ref=todayspaper.

124. Alexandre Marinis, "Obama's 'Man' Goes Nuclear as Global Fixer," Bloomberg, February 24, 2010, http://www.bloomberg.com/news/2010-02-23/obama-s-man-goes-nuclear-as-global-fixer-alexandre-marinis.html.

125. Weston S. Konishi, *The Democratic Party of Japan: Its Foreign Policy Position and Implications for U.S. Interests*, Congressional Research Service Report for Congress, Washington, D.C., August 12, 2009.

126. Eraldo Peres, "Lula's Surprising Legacy," *Macleans*, August 25, 2010, http://www.2.macleans.ca/2010/08/25/lulas-surprising-legacy.

127. Vinod Sreeharsha, "Brazil's Embrace of U.S. Adversaries Likely to Continue," *Miami Herald*, October 2, 2010.

128. Samuel Logan, "Limits of Brazil-Iran Relationship Revealed," *ISN Security Watch*, August 17, 2010.

129. Peres, "Lula's Surprising Legacy."

130. Hiroko Tabuchi, "Japan Forces Bureaucrats to Defend Spending," *New York Times*, April 28, 2010, http://www.nytimes.com/2010/04/29/business/global/29debt.html.

131. George Perkovich, *Abolishing Nuclear Weapons: Why the United States Should Lead*, Carnegie Endowment for International Peace Policy Brief, October 2008, 2, http://carnegieendowment.org/files/abolishing_nuclear_weapons.pdf.

132. Ibid., 4.

133. Ogawa and Schiffer, "Japan's Plutonium Reprocessing Dilemma."

134. "Statement by the Head of the Delegation of Brazil, Ambassador Luiz Filipe de Macedo Soares," Second Session of the NPT PrepCom," Geneva, April 28, 2008.

135. John Deutch et al., "Making the World Safe for Nuclear Energy," *Survival* 46 (Winter 2004/2005): 67.

136. Perkovich and Acton, "What's Next?" 325.

137. Scott Sagan, "Good Faith and Nuclear Disarmament Negotiations," in Perkovich and Acton, *Abolishing Nuclear Weapons*, 209.

138. For an excellent review of the most recent proposals, see Fiona Simpson, "Reforming the Nuclear Fuel Cycle: Time Is Running Out," *Arms Control Today*, September 2008, http://www.armscontrol.org/act/2008_09/Simpson.

139. "Statement by H.E. Ambassador Celina Assumpção do Valle Pereira, Deputy Permanent Representative of Brazil to the United Nations," New York, April 8, 2002. Before the 2005 NPT Review Conference, the Brazilians also stated they would consider adopting the Additional Protocol, based on progress made on disarmament in conference. Their position on this has since hardened, however.

CHAPTER SIX

The Nuclear Energy Aspirants
Egypt and Vietnam

Tanya Ogilvie-White and Maria Rost Rublee

THE DESIRE FOR CLEANER, more reliable energy sources has spawned a new generation of nuclear energy aspirants, almost half of which are located in the Middle East and Southeast Asia. Many scholars and practitioners believe this development has the potential to stall disarmament momentum, particularly once nuclear reductions among the nuclear weapon states (NWS) reach a certain threshold.[1] These concerns are understandable because history has shown that nuclear weapons programs have often developed under the guise of peaceful nuclear programs.[2] Moreover, despite the introduction of stronger nuclear nonproliferation measures to address this and other nuclear dangers (such as access to nuclear materials by terrorist groups), there has been resistance among some nuclear energy aspirants to what are often regarded as burdensome and discriminatory new obligations.[3] The potential for a new tranche of nuclear threshold states to emerge in the future, all with latent nuclear capabilities and breakout options, is impossible to rule out while this resistance continues. This is a major driver of renewed U.S. and UK disarmament leadership, on the basis that efforts to demonstrate concrete progress on disarmament could reinvigorate commitment to nuclear nonproliferation, including (perhaps especially) among new nuclear energy aspirants.[4]

This chapter examines the nuclear energy programs and nonproliferation and disarmament diplomacy of two key nuclear energy aspirants: Egypt and Vietnam. Of the many nuclear energy aspirants that could have been chosen as individual case studies, these two states were selected for three reasons: (1) both states have the potential to develop indigenous enrichment and reprocessing capabilities at some point in the foreseeable future if they choose to do so; (2) both states are located in regions where nuclear energy aspirations are now widespread and well established, but which differ significantly in terms of their security dynamics; and (3) both states have significant potential to influence regional and global nonproliferation and disarmament momentum because they are key regional players and are likely to remain so. A goal of the analysis is to explore the attitudes of Egypt and Vietnam to existing nonproliferation measures, such as the safeguards Additional Protocol (AP) (a voluntary measure that increases the transparency of nuclear programs) and to new and proposed initiatives, such as internationalized fuel cycle arrangements (the goal of which is to prevent the further spread of indigenous enrichment and reprocessing capabilities—the sensitive parts of the nuclear fuel cycle that can provide a latent nuclear weapons capability). First, how are Egypt and Vietnam responding to efforts to strengthen the nuclear nonproliferation regime, and what factors are influencing their policies? Second, is there any evidence to suggest that new disarmament momentum is influencing (or could influence) the willingness of Egypt or Vietnam to jump on board and introduce new nonproliferation measures? Lastly, are there any indications that the nuclear intentions of either state might be anything other than the peaceful ones they declare, and can any credible scenarios be foreseen that might encourage them to develop nuclear weapons? These are all important questions, the answers to which will help us assess the prospects for sustaining disarmament momentum in the years ahead.

THE NUCLEAR ENERGY PLANS OF ASPIRANT STATES

Nuclear power is either under consideration or being actively pursued by more than forty-five countries that do not currently have it, a development that is sure to generate nonproliferation challenges. In the Middle East (defined to include the Maghreb, Levant, and Persian Gulf) the contenders include Algeria, Egypt, Jordan, Kuwait, Libya, Morocco, Qatar, Saudi Arabia, Syria, Tunisia, the United Arab Emirates (UAE), and Yemen; in Southeast Asia, they include Indonesia, Malaysia, Philippines, Singapore, Thailand, and Vietnam.[5] Of these nuclear energy aspirants, Egypt's current nuclear energy plan is among the most credible and the most likely to be followed through (given its already well-developed nuclear infrastructure), and Vietnam's is among the most ambitious and advanced—to the extent that the latter is considered a front runner in the current global nuclear energy expansion.

Egypt's Nuclear Energy Plans

Plans to restart Egypt's mothballed nuclear energy program were first announced in September 2006 by Gamal Mubarak, the eldest son of President Hosni Mubarak at the annual National Democratic Party conference.[6] President Mubarak publicly supported those plans, a reversal of his long-standing caution on nuclear issues, and one month later, the Egyptian Parliament approved the proposal.[7] Initially, Cairo announced a goal of building ten nuclear power plants, providing up to 20 percent of Egypt's energy needs, but more recently the plans have been scaled back to a more realistic four plants, to provide capacity of four thousand megawatts.[8] To move forward, Cairo signed a ten-year, $200 million contract with the Australian-owned company Worley-Parsons in 2009. According to the Australian news media, WorleyParsons will be involved in many aspects of Egypt's nuclear program, from choosing reactor technology to training personnel.[9]

The program faced an early challenge: business interests argued that the most likely site for the first nuclear power plant (Al-Dabaa, on the Mediterranean Coast), would be better used for tourism than nuclear facilities. One businessman proposed that "the land around Al-Dabaa on the Northern Coast could be sold for as much as LE40 billion. That would build nine nuclear power stations without costing the state a penny." Nuclear advocates appealed to President Mubarak to ensure the plans for Al-Dabaa continued, since it had been deemed the most probable and suitable site for anywhere from one to four power plants.[10] In August 2010, Mubarak sided against the tourism business interests and said that construction in Al-Dabaa would begin in 2011.[11] Mubarak's decision was not surprising, given that the country has "spent over LE500 million since the 1980s on feasibility studies that confirm it is among the most suitable locations for a nuclear power plant."[12] The first reactor is expected to come online in 2019, with hopes that the additional three will be ready by 2025.

Egypt's need for greater energy resources is clear. While the country does not yet have to import to meet energy demands, consumption is rising quickly. Egypt has among the highest rates of electrification in Africa, with 100 percent in urban areas and 99.1 percent in rural areas.[13] As a result, demand surges during the hot summers, leading to electricity brown-outs. Large parts of Egypt's cities and towns—including Cairo—still have to bear constant and sometimes daily power outages during June, July, and August. The government responded by dimming street lights on the main roads by 50 percent, as well as tripling electricity prices during peak hours and imposing laws forcing citizens to reduce their daily consumption.[14]

Rising domestic energy consumption has led to a decline in Egypt's natural gas exports, as well as delays in export expansion plans.[15] Cairo estimates that oil and gas reserves in Egypt will be dangerously close to depletion within a few decades; currently, 90 percent of the country's energy is derived from these sources. (Approximately 9 percent comes from hydraulic and less than 1 percent from solar and wind power.)[16] Former International Atomic Energy Agency (IAEA) inspector and head of the nuclear program at the Alexandria University, Yousry Abushady concluded that while Egypt should also look to develop renewable sources of energy, nuclear power is critical to the country's long-term energy needs. "There is no other solution for Egypt—and the world—but to further develop nuclear energy capacity," he said. "To block its expansion would be a crime."[17]

The planned nuclear power plants will add to Egypt's already well-developed civilian nuclear program. Egypt operates two research reactors, has explored uranium deposits, runs a fuel fabrication facility and hot cells at its Hot Laboratory and Waste Management Center, and has established a heavy water facility. "It also has medical facilities, accelerators, and other laboratories that enable Egypt to produce isotopes and perform various experiments."[18] In addition, Egypt is engaged in a technical cooperation project with the IAEA on managing nuclear power plant programs and has also requested training from South Korea for Egyptian nuclear energy technicians through a program conducted in cooperation with the IAEA.[19] The Korea International Cooperation Agency has confirmed it will issue invitations for Egyptian nuclear engineers to enroll in its courses, which run three to five years.[20]

Vietnam's Nuclear Energy Plans

Vietnam's nuclear energy strategy calls for the development of commercial nuclear power by the year 2020 to reduce the country's dependence on hydro and fossil fuel resources.[21] The decision to introduce nuclear power was embodied in the "Strategy for Peaceful Uses of Atomic Energy up to 2020" signed by the prime minister in January 2006.[22] This document sets out guidelines to diversify Vietnam's energy sources by developing nuclear energy, initially with a target of bringing a 2,000-megawatt nuclear power plant online by 2020 and gradually raising the ratio of nuclear power in the national electricity mix to

25–30 percent by 2040–50. Total nuclear power capacity is planned to reach 20,000 megawatts by 2040. The strategy calls for a complete exploration of uranium reserves, as well as the development of both the technical and personnel infrastructure in nuclear science and technology. The goal is to train five hundred nuclear scientists by 2020. In addition, the strategy calls for the nationwide use of other nuclear applications, including the construction of a National Centre for Radioactive Medical Treatment and a network of ten regional centers.

In 2007, Prime Minister Nguyen Tan Dung approved an ambitious "Strategy Implementation Master Plan," which sets out Vietnam's nuclear energy plan in detail, including milestones.[23] The first stage of the plan includes the construction of two 1,000-megawatt reactors in Phuoc Dinh, southern Ninh Thuan province, scheduled to begin in 2015, with an expectation that they will come into operation in 2020. Following this, another 2,000-megawatt nuclear power plant (with two reactors) is planned for Vinh Hai, a picturesque seaside community forty kilometers from Phuoc Vinh, to come online in 2021 with a further 6,000 megawatts by 2030. The plan was approved by the National Assembly in June 2008 in a "Law on Atomic Energy" that provides a comprehensive legal framework for the development of nuclear energy.

Although Vietnam currently has limited physical infrastructure and immense funding challenges (each nuclear reactor is estimated to cost $2 billion or more), the government does appear to be seriously committed to developing nuclear energy. Recent developments show rapid progress in implementation of the master plan, with numerous milestones achieved in 2010. These include the development of a legal framework for the development of nuclear energy; official approval for the establishment of a national council on nuclear safety and for the development of national centers for public affairs and nuclear science; the launch of an ambitious nuclear training program that aims to train 2,400 nuclear engineers (mostly overseas) by 2020; and the announcement by the prime minister of a longer-term plan to develop seven nuclear power plants with fourteen reactors in eight possible locations.[24] In 2010, Vietnam also signed an agreement with Russia's Rosatom Corporation to build its first power plant, concluded a nuclear technology supply arrangement with France, and reached the final stages of negotiations with the United States over a comprehensive civilian nuclear cooperation agreement.[25]

There is no doubt that economic growth and associated mounting energy demands are driving Vietnam's nuclear development. The Ministry of Industry, which submitted the energy master plan, has forecast that the country's electricity demand will double in just over four years, continuing to rise 17–22 percent annually over the 2010–15 period.[26] Driving this surging energy demand is Vietnam's rapid economic expansion, which aims to integrate Vietnam into the world economy. In the six months between joining the World Trade Organization in January 2007 and the release of midyear economic development figures in June 2007, Vietnam's growth accelerated by 7.9 percent and investment by 14 percent.[27] Although growth subsequently slowed following a series of antiinflationary measures that were taken in response to global macroeconomic turbulence, it picked up again in 2009–10.[28] At the same time, however, concerns over current and future energy shortages have been undermining confidence that this growth can be sustained, with the government particularly troubled by the country's dependence on unreliable hydropower plants (which currently generate approximately 40 percent of Vietnam's electricity output), and the potential for outages to disrupt the economy and deter future direct foreign investment.[29] To prevent this, Vietnamese officials are determined to diversify their country's power industry and to develop more reliable sources of energy.

Vietnam depends heavily on forging bilateral nuclear cooperation agreements with advanced nuclear states and on technical assistance from the IAEA to implement its nuclear program. Russia has been Vietnam's partner in developing its nuclear research capabilities. This relationship dates back to the 1970s, when the Soviet Union supplied the Da Lat nuclear research reactor. Since that time, nuclear cooperation between the two states has continued, and all signs suggest that Russia will play a significant part in Vietnam's commercial nuclear energy program.[30] Additionally, Vietnam has signed bilateral nuclear cooperation agreements with Argentina, China, France, India, Japan, South Korea, and—most recently—the United States, following four years of intensive energy diplomacy.[31] Hanoi has also received help from the IAEA Technical Assistance Program, with $1 million in equipment, technical support, and training provided annually since 2001, and nine new nuclear projects valued at $2.5 million approved in the period 2009–11.

NONPROLIFERATION AND DISARMAMENT DIPLOMACY

Neither Egypt nor Vietnam would expect to be the subject of suspicions in terms of their long-term nuclear intentions: both regularly state their strong opposition to nuclear weapons, consider themselves to be in good standing with the nonproliferation regime, and are actively engaged in disarmament diplomacy.

But there are nevertheless some important differences in their approaches to nuclear issues, which could have implications for the nuclear nonproliferation regime and its capacity to manage the challenges posed by nuclear energy expansion. Despite its role in the New Agenda Coalition (NAC), Egypt has tended to focus its diplomatic efforts on disarmament advocacy, increasingly associating itself with the strident disarmament rhetoric of the Non-Alignment Movement (NAM), and has been reluctant to demonstrate equivalent nonproliferation leadership. On the other hand, Vietnam (which is not a NAC member but is part of the NAM) has adopted a more balanced approach to disarmament and nonproliferation and has demonstrated a greater willingness to prove its nonproliferation credentials. These differences—and the reasons for them—are explored in the following section, which analyzes the nonproliferation and disarmament diplomacy of both states.

Egypt's Nonproliferation and Disarmament Diplomacy

Disarmament diplomacy has been a central part of Egyptian foreign policy for decades, both to pressure Israel to end its nuclear weapons program and to promote nuclear disarmament generally. Much of the focus has been on blunting Israel's nuclear advantage through the use of the United Nations and other international forums. Since 1974, Egypt has sponsored a resolution in the General Assembly of the United Nations calling for a nuclear-weapon-free zone in the Middle East. In 1990, President Mubarak proposed a zone free of weapons of mass destruction (WMD) in the Middle East. Egypt brought the Working Group on Arms Control and Regional Security (a multilateral peace process, established in the early 1990s to encourage Middle East security cooperation) to a halt in 1995 by insisting that any progress must be linked to Israel's nuclear disarmament. With the 1995 Nuclear Nonproliferation Treaty (NPT) Review and Extension Conference, "Egypt hit the high pitch on nuclear non-proliferation," according to a former U.S. diplomat. Egypt helped convince Arab countries to sign the NPT, in exchange for supporting the Middle East resolution. With the lack of implementation of the 1995 Middle East resolution, Egypt played the role of spoiler in the 2005 NPT Review Conference (RevCon), contributing in part to the conference's lack of a concluding consensus document. In the most recent NPT RevCon (2010), Egypt played the leading role in pressuring the United States to accept the commitment to a conference in 2012 on the establishment of a Middle Eastern WMD-free zone, with a specific reference to Israel.[32]

Cairo has also been active in promoting general nuclear disarmament. As a member of the NAC, Egypt helped to promote far-reaching proposals for nuclear disarmament at the 2000 NPT RevCon. As a result, the conference agreed on thirteen practical steps toward disarmament, a dramatic advance in commitments from NWS. Cairo has continued its involvement in the NAC, with Ambassador Hisham Badr delivering the official NAC statement at the 2010 RevCon. However, Egypt is a powerful player outside of its NAC involvement; some argue that Egyptian diplomats were critical to the conference's success. For example, Egypt was able to convince members of the NAM to accept weaker language on disarmament measures in return for an explicit reference to Israel in the call for the 2012 Middle East WMD-free conference.[33] As Potter et al. note, "Egypt was very well served by its strong cadre of diplomats led by Ambassador Maged Abdelazis, and needed all of that fire power as it simultaneously chaired the NAM and the NAC, while leading the charge for the Arab states on the 1995 Middle East Resolution. The Egyptian delegation was particularly adept at managing the large and diverse body of NAM members, and bringing them on board once the Middle East language was agreed."[34]

However, some of Egypt's diplomatic measures could serve to undermine nuclear disarmament. Cairo refuses to sign the AP; at the 2010 RevCon, Egypt, along with Brazil and South Africa, "led the charge at the Conference to recognize the AP only as a voluntary, albeit valuable, measure."[35] Cairo also refuses to become party to the Chemical Weapons Convention and the Biological and Toxin Weapons Convention.[36] Likewise, while Egypt has signed the Comprehensive Test Ban Treaty (CTBT) and the Treaty of Pelindaba (for an African nuclear-weapon-free zone [NWFZ]), it refuses to ratify either.[37] Cairo's refusals are motivated by Israel's nuclear weapons; the country is unlikely to make any additional treaty commitments until Israel takes serious steps toward disarmament, in part because unilateral action could be embarrassing regionally and costly domestically.[38] Egypt has also been a vocal critic of fuel bank proposals, arguing that they are intended to pressure states into giving up their right to enrich uranium, which Egypt considers an unfair restriction on developing states' rights to develop nuclear technology for peaceful uses.[39]

Vietnam's Nonproliferation and Disarmament Diplomacy

As a member of the NAM, Vietnam votes in favor of NAM-sponsored disarmament resolutions in international forums. However, this is not necessarily indicative of an unfaltering commitment to NAM positions, given the diplomatic pressure on NAM members not to break ranks with the caucus. More significant are the independent statements occasionally issued by Vietnam's foreign affairs officials, who stress the importance of a balanced approach to nonproliferation and disarmament and the right of the non-nuclear weapons states (NNWS) to develop nuclear energy for peaceful purposes.[40] Vietnam's disarmament officials have been increasingly outspoken on these issues, pushing states that have not done so to sign and ratify the CTBT and to live up to the commitments made at the 2000 and 2010 NPT RevCons.[41] Vietnam is also taking a strong stand on the issue of security assurances, arguing that the NNWS have a "legitimate right" to receive unconditional security assurances from the NWS. Such assurances are essential to promote the confidence of the NNWS and to strengthen the NPT and regional nuclear-weapons-free zones. Perhaps most significant of all, Vietnam has criticized its Association of Southeast Asian Nations (ASEAN) partners for not going far enough to tackle proliferation threats, commenting on the complacency of some Southeast Asian states, which mistakenly believe their commitment to the Bangkok Treaty excuses them from pursuing a more proactive nonproliferation agenda.[42]

Over the past five years, the Vietnamese government has also been taking steps to boost international confidence in its ability to function responsibly in the realm of nonproliferation and counter-terrorism. These actions were partly motivated by Vietnam's successful quest for a nonpermanent seat on the UN Security Council in 2008–9 and its desire to maximize support for its candidacy, but this needs to be viewed in the context of Vietnam's long-term progression toward greater international engagement and cooperation. The most relevant of the progressive steps referred to above was the announcement, in November 2006, that Vietnam would sign the AP, increasing the transparency of its embryonic nuclear program and committing itself to a relatively intrusive monitoring regime.[43] This decision was approved by the IAEA Board of Governors at its meeting on March 6, 2007, and finally carried out the following August. Vietnam subsequently hosted a safeguards seminar (with support from the IAEA, Japan, and Australia) to familiarize its officials with the goals of the AP and with global nonproliferation objectives more generally.[44] These steps offer an encouraging indication that Hanoi intends to abide by the word and spirit of the NPT and avoid the path taken by Iran. The fact that as of November 2010, more than three years after Ambassador Nguyen Truong Giang signed the AP, the agreement had not yet been ratified appears to be due to a major legislative backlog (Vietnam's parliament meets only twice a year) rather than a lack of commitment.[45] Delays have also affected the implementation of Vietnam's 2008 Atomic Energy Law, Article 12 of which prohibits Vietnam from "researching, developing, manufacturing, trading in, transporting, transferring, storing, using, or threatening to use nuclear or radiation weapons."[46] The fact the Law includes this provision is an encouraging sign, as it fulfills an important obligation set out in Security Council Resolution 1540 and is another indication that Hanoi takes its nonproliferation obligations seriously. But as of January 2011, documents associated with the 2008 law are still being drawn up "to make it more transparent and consistent with IAEA guidelines."[47]

Alongside its decision to sign the AP and approve its Atomic Energy Law, Vietnam has taken an increasingly proactive stance in formal and informal (Track I and Track II) discussions on counter-terrorism initiatives. With the United States, Vietnam cochairs the Council on Security Cooperation in the Asia Pacific Study Group on WMD Proliferation and has regularly attended meetings of the subgroup on WMD export controls. It has also submitted relatively detailed reports (known as counter-terrorism action plans) to the Asia-Pacific Economic Cooperation Counter-Terrorism Task Force and the 1540 Committee, outlining the actions that it is taking to prevent WMD proliferation within and across its borders, and it is cooperating when asked to provide additional information.[48] Despite longstanding resistance to joining ad hoc groups outside the purview of the United Nations, and despite its continuing reservations over its legal status, in March 2007 the Vietnam Ministry of Foreign Affairs spokesman, Le Dung, announced that Vietnam "welcomes the spirit of [the Proliferation Security Initiative (PSI)]" and has agreed to consider joining. Vietnam subsequently participated in the Asia-Pacific forum of the PSI in Auckland, New Zealand, on March 29, 2007.[49]

RESPONSES TO DISARMAMENT MOMENTUM

As noted above, part of the rationale driving the reinvigorated disarmament leadership of the United States and United Kingdom is the belief that if the NWS are seen to be taking their disarmament responsibilities seriously—and acting on them—NNWS will approach nonproliferation and nuclear security goals with equal vigor, and that these joint efforts will improve the prospects for disarmament momentum to be sustained over the longer term. Scott Sagan made this point very forcefully in his article "Shared Responsibilities for Nuclear Disarmament," which called for rethinking on the balance of responsibilities in the nuclear nonproliferation regime and urged more discussion of what the NWS and NNWS can do to help the disarmament process move forward.[50] Responses to Sagan's article from influential scholars from around the world suggest that there is support for this line of reasoning within the academic and think tank communities, but at this stage it is not easy to gauge how nuclear decision makers are responding.[51] The following section explores this important question, analyzing how Egypt and Vietnam have reacted to the Obama administration's disarmament leadership.

Egypt's Response

Obama's disarmament initiative has been met with a mix of cautious enthusiasm and suspicion in Egypt. Certainly Egyptian diplomats were pleased that Obama made nuclear disarmament a priority, and response to the U.S.-Russian New START treaty has been positive. Obama's diplomatic outreach to the Muslim world in his June 2009 speech at Cairo University also generated goodwill.[52] However, Cairo is concerned that Obama will not be able to live up to his promises; one Egyptian commentator noted that after bruising battles with Republicans, Obama has acted "more like a man concerned about his second term in office than like a leader concerned about his role in history."[53] Egypt is also concerned that Washington will try to leverage its disarmament rhetoric to pursue initiatives that Egypt does not support, such as making the AP mandatory and raising barriers to NPT withdrawal. This apprehension was evident in Foreign Minister Ahmed Aboul-Gheit's address to the 2010 NPT RevCon; the bulk of the speech was aimed at criticizing the NWS for weak efforts toward disarmament or for their proposals, "under the pretext of proliferation prevention," that Egypt saw as limiting the rights of NNWS.[54] Finally, Cairo is a vocal critic of what it sees as U.S. pandering to Israel on nuclear issues, raising the question of whether Washington is serious about disarmament at all. One commentator noted, "The absence of any mention of Israel in U.S. rhetoric has also called its credibility into question."[55]

As noted in the previous section, Egypt is willing to work with the United States on disarmament, but only on its own terms. In the 2010 RevCon, Egyptian diplomats refused to budge on universality of the AP, proposals to limit enrichment or encourage fuel banks, and negotiations over raising the barriers to NPT withdrawal. Indeed, Cairo drove a hard bargain, insisting on specific language about Israel in exchange for persuading NAM members to accept softer language on global nuclear disarmament.

Vietnam's Response

The Obama administration's strong push on disarmament and nonproliferation coincided with Vietnam's chairmanship of ASEAN and a year of sustained nonproliferation and disarmament leadership by the Vietnam Communist Party (VCP) in 2010. It is difficult to assess how much of Vietnam's proactive leadership during this period has been influenced by U.S. efforts to stimulate disarmament momentum and the more cooperative atmosphere this has fostered in international disarmament forums. Most of the evidence suggests that Vietnam's disarmament diplomacy has been gradually stepping up over a period of several years, partly in response to UN disarmament initiatives, such as the UN secretary general's "five point action plan," proposed in September 2008. But even in the context of Vietnam's long-standing disarmament advocacy, Hanoi's most recent leadership on disarmament and nonproliferation within ASEAN has been noteworthy. Of particular significance are Vietnam's comments on the role of the Bangkok Treaty, made at the NPT RevCon in May 2010; its national statement on nuclear energy, delivered at the IAEA General Conference in September 2010; and its statements on disarmament, nonproliferation, and nuclear security, delivered at the UN First Committee meetings in October 2009 and 2010 and at the Nuclear Security Summit in April 2010. While passionate speeches delivered in diplomatic forums do not necessarily equate to genuine commitment to nonproliferation and disarmament, in Vietnam's case proactive diplomacy has been backed up with a series of concrete actions. It is worth exploring some of the detail of Vietnam's recent regional leadership in this area, as it paints a picture of a state that is taking every opportunity to demonstrate strong national nonproliferation and disarmament credentials and to encourage its neighbors to follow the same path.

Vietnam's statement in the First Committee of the UN General Assembly in October 2010 made a powerful plea to the international community to break the deadlock in the Conference on Disarmament (CD) and the stalemate in the UN Disarmament Commission and to take radical action to accelerate the elimination of nuclear weapons.[56] In its references to the "exceptionally catastrophic consequences of these horrific weapons for mankind," it was one of the most powerful speeches delivered during the general debate, but it was also balanced, in that it assessed both the positive and the negative recent developments in global arms control and disarmament, set out the steps Vietnam has been taking to abide by its nonproliferation and disarmament obligations, and contained a pledge to "work harder" to "achieve the noble cause for sustainable peace and security of the world." The speech echoed similar sentiments that were expressed by Vietnamese diplomats at the April 2010 Nuclear Security Summit, the May 2010 NPT RevCon, the September 2010 General Conference of the IAEA, and the September 2009 Security Council Summit: a declaration that the NWS, as the possessors of the largest nuclear arsenals, have an obligation to lead the way on multilateral nuclear disarmament; an acknowledgment of the constructive steps the NWS have taken to fulfill that obligation, and recognition that all states have an important part to play in creating the benign international conditions that would be conducive to global nuclear disarmament—especially those that already possess nuclear energy programs and those that aspire to them.[57] This last point is key, as the leadership of Vietnam clearly recognizes the potential for the renaissance of nuclear energy to increase proliferation and terrorism fears and undermine disarmament momentum.[58]

Vietnam regards the Bangkok Treaty as an important instrument for promoting regional and international confidence in the nuclear-weapons-free future of Southeast Asia, particularly in the context of the development of nuclear energy by key states in the region. But rather than viewing the treaty primarily as a symbolic commitment to nonproliferation (as it was in the past), Vietnam—in concert with its ASEAN partners—has recently been taking steps to strengthen the treaty framework and to ensure that it becomes deeply embedded in ASEAN and the nonproliferation regime. Three recent developments have been significant in this regard: (1) at the 2010 ASEAN Summit in Hanoi, implementation of the Bangkok Treaty was highlighted as a priority and an important part of the road map for creating an ASEAN Security Community by 2015; (2) at the 2010 NPT RevCon, Vietnam issued a memorandum on activities relating to the NWFZ in order to raise the treaty's international profile and encourage the NWS to accede to the Treaty Protocol; and (3) in numerous regional and multilateral forums throughout 2010, Vietnam's diplomats stressed that the "wind of change" generated by new international disarmament momentum has created opportunities for ASEAN to strengthen the Bangkok Treaty so that it can become part of a permanent structure of a nuclear-weapons-free world.[59]

Although Vietnam's most recent nonproliferation and disarmament diplomacy has been proactive and supportive of new U.S.-led momentum, there are limits within which the VCP is operating. Multilateral fuel cycle proposals, for example, which are seen by many experts as the key to preventing further proliferation (and an important step in the creation of a nuclear-weapon-free world), have not attracted the support of Vietnam's leaders, who appear to share the concerns of their NAM partners over the risks of technology denial and the potential consequences of long-term energy dependency.[60] Unlike the UAE, which has been willing to forgo its rights to indigenous enrichment and reprocessing, Vietnam has retained the option to develop the sensitive parts of the fuel cycle in the future, if it chooses to do so.[61] The civilian nuclear cooperation deal being negotiated between Washington and Hanoi lacks a provision prohibiting Vietnam from engaging in enrichment and reprocessing, provoking criticism from some nonproliferation commentators, who have criticized the double standards in U.S. nonproliferation policy.[62] But the deal does not contravene NPT provisions, and furthermore, it is difficult to see how a UAE-style deal would have been acceptable to Vietnam, given its ambitious nuclear plans and sensitivity over technology denial issues. Stimulating informed debate among Southeast Asia's nuclear energy aspirants on the benefits of a regional approach to fuel supply and spent fuel take-back arrangements could help overcome some of these sensitivities, but at the moment ASEAN leaders consider such discussions to be premature and are more interested in finding regional solutions to nuclear safety and waste management initiatives.[63]

EXPLAINING NONPROLIFERATION AND DISARMAMENT DIPLOMACY

It is important to try to identify the different factors that are driving the nonproliferation and disarmament diplomacy of the nuclear energy aspirants, as this analysis can help inform assessments of how these states are likely to respond to new initiatives going forward, and the extent to which their actions are likely to stall or feed global disarmament momentum. The scholarly literature on this subject is thin, as efforts to date have tended to focus on explaining proliferation rather than disarmament dynamics.[64] This next section offers a preliminary analysis of the motivations driving the nonproliferation and disarmament diplomacy of Egypt and Vietnam.

Egypt

Egypt's nonproliferation and disarmament diplomacy is motivated by several factors, including status, regional security concerns, and domestic politics. But exploring this mix of motivations first requires an understanding of how Egypt came to give up its nuclear weapons program in the late 1960s. After the military purposes of the Israeli nuclear reactor Dimona became public in 1960, Egyptian leader Gamal Nasser directed his Atomic Energy Establishment to begin work on nuclear weapons. However, a series of obstacles—from export controls to Israeli sabotage to domestic political clashes—led to only halting progress, and Nasser was not committed enough to nuclear weapons to apply the personal political capital that would have been necessary to move forward.[65] After a humbling defeat against Israel in the 1967 war, Nasser approached both the Soviet Union and China for nuclear weapons. Both countries declined, and the Soviets suggested to Nasser that he sign the NPT to use it as a diplomatic tool against Israel. Abandoning nuclear weapons and adhering to the NPT would allow Egypt to claim moral and diplomatic superiority, shaming Israel and gaining status in the Arab world. Nasser did just that, and Sadat followed course by ratifying the NPT in 1981. Thus, from the beginning, Egypt's promise to forgo nuclear weapons was intimately tied to its desire to embarrass Israel and pressure Tel Aviv to give up its military nuclear capability.

Indeed, Israel's nuclear weapons program is the most important motivator for Egypt's disarmament diplomacy. As noted in the previous section, much of Egypt's disarmament diplomacy is specifically directed toward Israel or a WMD-free zone in the Middle East. Egypt prioritizes the issue of Israel's nuclear weapons so highly that it overtakes most other diplomatic initiatives. For example, although the Middle East arms control and regional security initiative, ACRS, was initially successful, producing agreements on confidence-building measures and confidence-and-security-building measures, in the end it was brought to a halt by the Egyptian insistence on linking "the entirety of the ACRS agenda to the nuclear issue."[66] Cairo injects its agenda against Israeli nuclear weapons in other international forums as well. For example, Egyptian diplomats have insisted on including Israeli nuclear waste in environmental negotiations, illustrating "the intensity with which Egypt has pursued its NPT-related objectives."[67] Egyptian diplomats approach the issue with enthusiasm; one senior official in the Foreign Ministry noted, "We use diplomatic initiatives in many arenas: disarmament conferences, the review conferences, preparatory sessions for the next review conference. We are hammering on the importance of getting Israel to adhere to the NPT, or the Middle East NWFZ, or the Middle East WMDFZ, or to accept mutual inspections between Israel and Egypt. We are trying to use diplomacy to push Israel to accept the NPT, in all fora that we are involved in."[68]

While the Israeli nuclear program is the most pressing motivation behind Egyptian disarmament diplomacy, it is by no means the only driver. By taking the lead on the Israeli nuclear program, Egypt also gains regional status and domestic legitimacy. Jentleson and Kaye argue that the nuclear issue provides Egypt with "a bona fide for Arab leadership," and that regional normalization of relations with Israel could simultaneously increase Israel's regional status while decreasing Egypt's influence.[69] The international status that Egypt gains from its disarmament diplomacy also translates into domestic credibility. A former Egyptian military officer stated: "Egypt's leadership role in the Middle East is of real interest, even to the public. It's as important to them as economic development."[70] Some believe that Egypt's activist stance on nuclear disarmament is part of a calculated attempt to improve Mubarak's standing both regionally and domestically: "Leading the charge on the nuclear issue may have been an attempt to restore Egypt's leadership in the Arab world by making it appear as the guardian of the Arab states' security interests. Egypt's tough position also made Cairo a central address for appeals for indefinite extension of the NPT. Thus, Egypt's militant position may have been intended to compensate for its domestic troubles and diminished standing in regional affairs. This became increasingly apparent as the NPT campaign evolved; Egypt's position evoked strong nationalist sentiments, increasing domestic support for the Mubarak government."[71]

Both the regional and domestic status gained by disarmament diplomacy may help explain Egypt's prioritization of disarmament over nonproliferation. Nonproliferation initiatives are unlikely to accrue any accolades among the peer groups from which Egypt seeks approval. Of course, Egypt's stance on the Israeli nuclear program also helps to explain why Cairo tends to reject proposals that could strengthen nonproliferation; they refuse to give anything additional until they see movement on the Israeli program. Finally, like other technically advanced NNWS (such as South Africa and Brazil), Egypt believes the NPT already benefits the NWS disproportionately and fights any additional nonproliferation responsibilities being placed on NNWS.[72]

Vietnam

Vietnam's proactive nonproliferation and disarmament diplomacy is driven by a combination of cultural, political, economic, and strategic imperatives. Its long-standing opposition to nuclear weapons and support for disarmament has been underpinned by a genuine belief on the part of the government and VCP leadership that these weapons pose unacceptable dangers and that their possession or use by any state or group cannot be justified on any grounds. The country's disarmament advocacy is often expressed in the context of its own traumatic experience of toxic chemicals, its fear of nuclear annihilation by the U.S. during the Vietnam War, and its empathy for those in other countries who have suffered WMD attacks. These sentiments were expressed very clearly by Do Thanh Hai of CSCAP (Council for Security Cooperation in the Asia Pacific) Vietnam in his speech to the Center for Strategic and International Studies Young Leaders Forum in 2006: "Our country was nearly a target of a nuclear attack by the Nixon administration in 1972. Luckily it did not happen. However, 30 years after the end of the war, Vietnamese people and the world have witnessed hundreds of thousands of children affected by orange agents [Agent Orange] massively sprayed onto Vietnam's soils. So, from the historical perspective, we, the Vietnamese people, understand the spiritual and material loss of the Japanese people in August 1945, and how the Iranians suffered from Iraqi forces['] chemical weapons in the 1980s."[73]

Statements made by Vietnamese officials in international forums over the years echo this strong aversion to all forms of WMD, which is rooted in history and in a sense of grievance at having been the victim of dioxin contamination, the consequences of which continue to this day.[74]

Over the years, Vietnam has also consistently denounced nuclear weapons on the basis that they waste precious resources that could instead be channeled into development. Vietnam's ambassador to the CD, Le Hoai Trung, reinforced this point when he assumed the presidency of the CD in January 2009; Vietnam's representatives in Vienna have expressed this view on many occasions, along with fellow NAM and ASEAN members.[75] More recently, however, the economic drivers of Vietnam's nonproliferation and disarmament diplomacy have become more pressing and complex, injecting new vigor but also greater nuance into Hanoi's diplomatic strategy. On the one hand, the huge economic, technical, and infrastructure challenges of developing nuclear power mean Vietnam needs to court partners and suppliers, and good deals may be easier to win if Vietnam is seen to be demonstrating a strong commitment to nonproliferation and nuclear security. Taking care to offer a balanced assessment of the disarmament and nonproliferation steps taken by others, including the NWS, also assists Vietnam is casting the foreign assistance net wider. But on the other hand, Hanoi is keen to maintain its strong NAM and ASEAN linkages and not to be seen to be striking out on its own: by combining their diplomatic weight, developing states are more able to resist what many regard as unfair conditions being imposed on new nuclear aspirants, such as supply arrangements that close off options for indigenous enrichment. The economic drivers of Vietnam's disarmament and nonproliferation diplomacy are thus complex, requiring Hanoi's diplomats to conduct a careful balancing act to foster good relations with developed and developing states.

Strategic drivers add another level of complexity to Vietnam's nonproliferation and disarmament diplomacy, which needs to be understood in the context of Hanoi's broader foreign and defense policy agendas. Since the end of the Cold War, the VCP has been concerned about China's rising power and has adopted a long-term strategy of trying to balance Beijing's influence through a policy of benign regional and international engagement. This approach to dealing with its powerful northern neighbor has been pursued by Vietnam since 1991, when the Seventh National Party Congress adopted the "new outlook"—a strategy designed to ensure that Vietnam is "friends with all countries."[76] As a result of this policy, Hanoi has become embedded in a network of regional institutions and has sought closer bilateral relationships with the United States and India, including in the hard security realm of military-to-military ties.[77] The VCP regards engagement and cooperation on all fronts, including nonproliferation and disarmament, as a defensive mechanism—an attempt to dissipate regional and international arms-racing dynamics, especially in the context of China's rapid military modernization program and rising maritime assertiveness; North Korea's destabilizing nuclear defiance; and questions over Myanmar's nuclear activities. The new outlook strategy of benign engagement is also seen as a way to help ensure that none of the key actors in Southeast Asia become too dominant, and all have a vested interest in maintaining peace and security in the region.

PROLIFERATION PRESSURES IN THE ENERGY ASPIRANTS

The analysis up to this point suggests that although Egypt and Vietnam may not jump on board with all of the nonproliferation initiatives that are being proposed to address the challenges created by the expansion of nuclear energy, there are no suspicions that either country is currently planning anything other than civilian nuclear programs. However, both could pose potential proliferation risks in the future if they decide to develop indigenous enrichment and reprocessing capabilities, which neither state appears to be willing to close off. But how serious are these risks? This chapter now looks to the future, at various domestic and systemic developments that might encourage Egypt and Vietnam to develop a latent or weaponized nuclear capability—outcomes that, to different extents, would put disarmament momentum in jeopardy.

Egypt

Although Egypt's nuclear program is in compliance with the IAEA, some signals do elicit concern about the possible direction of the program. In 2007, Cairo stated that it intended to leave the door for uranium enrichment open, and that it would not sign the AP, positions it has maintained since then.[78] Given that Egypt already has highly trained nuclear scientists and a large nuclear complex, the ability to create a breakout capability is somewhat of a concern, as described by Bruno Tertrais:

> It has two research reactors, including a high-neutron flux Multi-Purpose Reactor (MPR) located at the Inshas research center. The 22MWth MPR could produce 6.6 kilos of plutonium a year assuming 300 days of operation. Egypt also has since 1998 two fuel-making installations, a laboratory (Semi-Pilot Fuel Laboratory) and a full-fledged plant (Fuel Manufacturing Pilot Plant) which fabricates fuel for the MPR reactor. It also has significant uranium reserves. As is now known, Egypt has made experiments that could be useful to a military program, before and after its safeguards agreement came in force (1982). These involved the production of uranium metal, irradiation of natural uranium targets, and chemical dissolution of fuel elements. The Atomic Energy Agency (AEA) has hot cells which could be used for experimental plutonium separation, located at a dedicated facility (Hot Laboratory and Waste Management Center).[79]

Thus, as Tertrais notes, Egypt is one of the few states in the Middle East capable of creating a "full-fledged, autonomous nuclear program."[80]

In addition to Egypt's possible technical ability to develop nuclear weapons, concerns about an Egyptian military program surface because of both external and internal pressures for the country to go nuclear. Certainly, Iran's nuclear program has raised fears that Egypt could respond in turn.[81] Leaked diplomatic cables from the United States indicate that Egypt might feel "forced" into developing nuclear weapons if Iran is successful in its own program.[82] While Cairo is not particularly concerned about an Iranian attack, diplomats do not want Tehran to gain the political leverage and status that nuclear weapons will likely confer. More important, the domestic political situation in Egypt may affect the country's nuclear decision making. The most vocal critic of the Mubarak regime, the Muslim Brotherhood, pilloried the regime for its failure to balance Israel's nuclear weapons. Because experts surmised the Egyptian populace supported an indigenous nuclear weapons program (to counter Israel), Mubarak's son Gamal responded with his own nuclear strategy. Just a few months after a particularly scathing attack from the Muslim Brotherhood, Gamal announced plans for an extensive nuclear power program. While he was clear that the program would be for peaceful purposes, the proposal was well received by the public (which sees any nuclear development as countering Israel's nuclear programs).[83] In fall 2006, the Egyptian Parliament officially authorized the government to begin a nuclear power program for energy purposes, and a location for the first plant was chosen in 2010.

However, Mubarak's overthrow in February 2011 has made Egypt's nuclear future quite uncertain. Three groups are vying for power: the Muslim Brotherhood and other Islamist groups, which want to pursue an Islamist state at home and hard-line foreign policy abroad; secular intellectuals, such as former International Atomic Energy Agency director Mohamed ElBaradei, who want to pursue democratic reforms at home and a cooperative but assertive stance abroad; and the military elite, which wants to ensure a secular state, maintain its prestige and privileges, and retain the status quo internationally. After the removal of Mubarak, the military created an interim governing council (the Supreme Council of the Armed Forces) and promised both parliamentary and presidential elections quickly. The Supreme Council arranged a referendum in March 2011 on constitutional amendments and the timing of upcoming elections.

While the secular groups argued that elections should be delayed to ensure parties had the time to organize, the Muslim Brotherhood favored quick elections because they were one of the only groups already well organized. To the dismay of the secular parties and the military, the Muslim Brotherhood and other Islamist groups turned the referendum into a religious test, arguing that it was people's religious duty to vote yes and that Egypt could become a secular state if the referendum was not passed. The referendum did pass, with 77 percent of voters approving it—showing the strength of the Brotherhood and other Islamist groups. As a result, the military elite began to signal that they plan to remain a guarantor of the secular nature of Egypt, floating the idea of declaration of basic principles that would retain the military's independence and authority over foreign affairs.

How would the ascendance of different groups affect Egypt's disarmament policy? The Muslim Brotherhood has previously made it clear that they favor a military nuclear program for Egypt. As the spokesperson for the Muslim Brotherhood parliamentary caucus said in July 2006, "We are ready to starve in order to own a nuclear weapon that will represent a real deterrent and will be decisive in the Arab-Israeli conflict."[84] As a result, should the Brotherhood and other Islamist groups gain a majority in Parliament and possibly capture the presidency, they are likely to strain the nuclear nonproliferation regime and become even more vocal about the need for Israeli and NWS disarmament.

On the other hand, if a secular intellectual such as ElBaradei captures the presidency and gains strong domestic support, the nuclear weapons option would remain off the table. ElBaradei is personally committed to both nuclear nonproliferation and disarmament. However, a secular president would still face pressure for a more aggressive nuclear policy from Islamist groups in Parliament and thus may decide to counter that pressure with greater assertion of Egyptian rights to the nuclear fuel cycle. In this type of scenario, Cairo could become more rigid in insisting on steps toward nuclear disarmament (especially with regard to Israel) before making any concessions on nonproliferation.

However, if the military manages to retain control over defense and foreign policy, they likely will steer Egypt's nuclear policy on a status-quo course. The priority of military elites is to retain their privileged position within Egyptian society, and they are unlikely to allow any policy changes that could attract sanctions or heavy diplomatic pressure. In the same vein as with a secular president, however, the military could find that increased stridence on nuclear disarmament, combined with a modest nuclear power plant, may be useful in undermining Islamist critics of the failure to pursue a nuclear weapons program.

Vietnam

While all the indicators point to economic growth and associated mounting energy demands as the drivers of Vietnam's nuclear development, there is a certain degree of nervousness that, despite Vietnam's proactive nonproliferation and disarmament diplomacy, the VCP may in the future develop the capabilities that would allow it to become a nuclear threshold state (like Japan or Brazil) and may, under certain conditions, be tempted to pursue a nuclear weapons program.⁸⁵ Vietnam's efforts to raise the international profile of the Bangkok Treaty and to establish strong nonproliferation credentials are part of the government's strategy to counter these fears, but there are limits to the concessions Hanoi is prepared to make to reassure the international community that its nuclear intentions will always be benign. Crucially, Vietnam's desire not to rule out development of indigenous enrichment and reprocessing capabilities over the longer term means the potential for future breakout cannot be discounted completely. In August 2010, for example, Vuong Huu Tan, president of the Vietnam Atomic Energy Institute, stated that "Vietnam doesn't intend to enrich *as of now* because of expensive and very sensitive technology" (emphasis added).⁸⁶ If, in the future, circumstances change and this decision is reversed, it could affect how Vietnam's nuclear program is perceived by its neighbors and internationally, which in turn could have negative consequences for international disarmament momentum.

This begs the question: how likely is it that Vietnam would pursue a threshold or breakout capability in future, if the economic and technical barriers could be overcome? To answer this question, it helps to have some understanding of nuclear decision making in Vietnam, where policy is almost entirely driven by a handful of officials in the government and the VCP who exercise a virtual monopoly over political discussion. As far as it is possible for those outside the regime to determine, it appears that the reform-minded officials who have dominated the VCP since the 1990s are committed to the peaceful development of nuclear energy as their long-term goal and have no interest in developing nuclear weapons for the reasons already discussed.⁸⁷ However, political developments within the VCP that could result in a policy change cannot be ruled out altogether, especially if there is a conservative retrenchment.⁸⁸

There are a number of scenarios that may—at a stretch—convince a future Vietnamese government to pursue a nuclear weapons capability in tandem with its nuclear energy program, but none of them are likely to unfold for strategic reasons (let alone the public abhorrence of WMD and the economic and political incentives not to jeopardize nuclear supplier and cooperation arrangements, IAEA technical assistance programs, and so on). First, it could be argued that Vietnam might pursue a nuclear capability to enhance its power relative to its neighbors in Indochina and revive its past hegemonic agenda, but this appears unlikely given the peaceful trajectory of Vietnam's foreign policy and its deepening integration into ASEAN. Second, Vietnam may be tempted to pursue nuclear weapons as a strategic equalizer in the context of China's rising power, but

Beijing keeps a very careful watch on Hanoi, and the latter is more likely to respond via more energetic diplomacy: efforts to reduce bilateral tensions, ensure the major powers remain engaged in the region, and enhance ASEAN security frameworks. Third, it could be argued that Hanoi might develop nuclear weapons as a copycat response to nuclear breakout by another regional power, such as Myanmar, but again, with the trend toward closer regional integration within ASEAN and stronger extra-regional bilateral relationships, the incentives to resist copycat behavior are growing every day. Lastly—a scenario that might seem more convincing given the recent escalation of the South China Sea dispute—it could be argued that a future government may be tempted by the nuclear option in order to boost its bargaining leverage in negotiations over competing territorial claims.[89] But even in this context, nuclear weapons would not serve Vietnam's strategic purposes, which would be better accommodated via efforts to bolster its national maritime capabilities and via enhanced regional and bilateral defense cooperation.[90] This is clearly recognized by the leadership of Vietnam, which has been expanding its navy, promoting the deeper institutionalization of ASEAN, seeking closer relations with the United States and India, and taking steps to internationalize the South China Sea dispute via regional forums, including the ASEAN Regional Forum Foreign Ministers Meeting and the emerging ASEAN Defense Ministers' Meeting Plus Eight.[91] Thus, even in the context of China's continuing rise and the growing insecurities generated by the escalation of the South China Sea dispute, it is highly unlikely Vietnam will change tactics and pursue a nuclear capability unless questions arise about the future of ASEAN and the Bangkok Treaty and about the reliability of its alliances and friendships.[92]

CONCLUSION

Proliferation concerns generated by the expansion of nuclear energy to new countries certainly have the potential to stall disarmament momentum going forward, as just one of the many challenges confronting the nuclear nonproliferation and security regimes. Arguing that the nuclear intentions of nuclear energy aspirants are currently benign (as in the case of Egypt and Vietnam) is little comfort to disarmament skeptics in the NWS, who fear the future development of latent capabilities by states in volatile regions. Closing off opportunities for indigenous enrichment and reprocessing would assuage these fears, but such proposals are not popular among many developing states, including Egypt and Vietnam, which are wary of initiatives that involve any form of technology denial. It would be premature to conclude that this situation will not change in the future, especially as debates over fuel cycle arrangements, including regional options, are not well developed in either the Middle East or Southeast Asia. But given the history of the evolution of the nonproliferation regime and NAM resentments over what is regarded as a discriminatory system that benefits developed states at the expense of the developing world, the signs are not encouraging.

Where some nuclear energy aspirants are concerned (certainly Egypt and possibly also Vietnam), efforts to manage—rather than eliminate—proliferation risks may be the only feasible approach. This is not the best outcome for sustaining disarmament momentum, but the prospects are not universally bleak. In Southeast Asia, nuclear energy is being developed during a period of deepening regional institutionalization, and regional solutions are already being sought for the safety and waste management challenges posed by nuclear energy. In the future, it is possible that regional fuel cycle arrangements could also be pursued through an ASEAN initiative or by a cooperative framework launched under the auspices of the ASEAN Regional Forum (ARF). But the prospects for similar regional initiatives in the Middle East are complicated by a whole host of strategic and political constraints. Moreover, the early signs are that the U.S.-led disarmament momentum is having less impact on Egypt's willingness to demonstrate strong nonproliferation credentials than is the case with Vietnam, and it is unlikely that even sustained disarmament leadership on the part of the United States and drastic reductions in nuclear weapons by the NWS would influence this situation unless the long-standing problems of Israel's holdout status and Iran's nuclear defiance are successfully resolved. The next two chapters on the holdout states (chapter 7) and the defiant states (chapter 8) explore these challenges in detail.

Notes

1. For an overview of the challenges posed by the launch of new nuclear energy programs (in the context of many other nonproliferation challenges), see Scott D. Sagan, "Shared Responsibilities for Nuclear Disarmament," *Shared Responsibilities for Nuclear Disarmament: A Global Debate* (Cambridge, Mass.: American Academy of Arts and Sciences, 2010), 1–13. For a more in-depth discussion, see Steven E. Miller and Scott D. Sagan, "Nuclear Power without Nuclear Proliferation?" and Richard K. Lester and Rob-

ert Rosner, "The Growth of Nuclear Power: Drivers and Constraints," both in Scott D. Sagan and Steven E. Miller, eds., "The Global Nuclear Future, vol. 1," special issue, *Daedalus* 138, no. 4 (Fall 2009); and Charles Ferguson, "Potential Strategic Consequences of the Nuclear Energy Revival," *Proliferation Papers* 35 (Summer 2010).

2. Matthew Fuhrmann, "Spreading Temptation: Proliferation and Peaceful Nuclear Cooperation Agreements," *International Security* 34 (Summer 2009): 7–41.

3. Tanya Ogilvie-White, "Facilitating Implementation of UN Security Council Resolution 1540 in Southeast Asia and the Pacific," in *Facilitating Implementation of Resolution 1540: The Role of Regional Organizations*, ed. Lawrence Scheinman (Geneva: United Nations Institute for Disarmament Research [UNIDIR], 2008).

4. The linkage between nonproliferation and disarmament was stressed by President Barack Obama in his April 2009 speech in Prague. See "Remarks by President Barack Obama," Prague, Czech Republic, April 5, 2009, http://www.whitehouse.gov/the_press_office/Remarks-By-President-Barack-Obama-In-Prague-As-Delivered/.

5. "Emerging Nuclear Energy Countries," World Nuclear Association, updated January 19, 2011, http://www.world-nuclear.org/info/inf102.html.

6. "Egyptian President's Son Proposes Developing Nuclear Energy," Associated Press, September 19, 2006.

7. Sammy Salama and Gina Gabrera-Farraj, "Renewed Egyptian Ambitions for a Peaceful Nuclear Program," *WMD Insights*, November 2006.

8. On Egypt's initial goals, see Gamal Essam El-Din, "A Nuclear Falling Out," *Al-Ahram Weekly*, no. 963 (September 2009), http://weekly.ahram.org.eg/2009/963/eg3.htm; James Acton and Wyn Bowen, "Nurturing Nuclear Neophytes," *Bulletin of the Atomic Scientists* 64, no. 4 (September/October 2008): 27. On the revised goals, see "U.N. Watchdog Backs Egypt Nuclear Power Plant Plans," Reuters, June 22, 2010, http://www.reuters.com/article/idUSLDE65L0F320100622.

9. Michael Janda, "Australian Firm to Design Egypt's Nuclear Future," ABC News, June 19, 2009.

10. Gamal Essam El-Din, "A Nuclear Falling Out," *Al-Ahram Weekly*, issue 963, September 2009.

11. "Egypt: 1st Nuclear Plant Site Announced," Associated Press, August 25, 2010, http://www.jpost.com/MiddleEast/Article.aspx?id=185934.

12. Gamal Essam El-Din, "Nuclear Falling Out."

13. "Egypt," *Country Analysis Briefs*, Energy Information Administration, U.S. Department of Energy, June 2010, http://www.eia.doe.gov/cabs/Egypt/pdf.pdf.

14. "Egypt: Government Looks to Nuclear Energy to Face Increasing Power Needs," *Los Angeles Times*, August 11, 2010.

15. "Egypt," *Country Analysis Briefs*.

16. "Egypt: Government Looks"; Christopher Le Coq, "Ex-IAEA Expert on Egypt's Nuclear Power Ambitions," *Daily News Egypt* (Cairo), November 10, 2010, http://www

.thedailynewsegypt.com/energy/ex-iaea-expert-weighs-in-on-egypts-nuclear-power-ambitions-dp1.html.

17. Le Coq, "Ex-IAEA expert."

18. Jack Boureston, "Egypt," Stockholm International Peace Research Institute http://www.sipri.org/research/disarmament/nuclear/researchissues/past_projects/issues_of_concern/egypt/egypt_default.

19. "Supporting New Nuclear Countries," *World Nuclear News*, July 27, 2009, http://www.world-nuclear-news.org/newsarticle.aspx?id=25698.

20. "South Korea to Train Egyptian Nuclear Engineers," *World Nuclear News*, January 10, 2010, http://www.world-nuclear-news.org/newsarticle.aspx?id=27012.

21. "Approving the Strategy for Peaceful Utilization of Atomic Energy up to 2020," Decision no. 1/2006/QT-TTg, January 3, 2006, http://www.vaec.gov.vn. This section is based on analysis set out in Michael S. Malley and Tanya Ogilvie-White, "Nuclear Capabilities in Southeast Asia: Building a Preventative Proliferation Firewall," *Nonproliferation Review* 16, no. 1 (March 2009): 25–45; and International Institute for Strategic Studies, *Preventing Nuclear Dangers in Southeast Asia and Australasia*, IISS Strategic Dossier, November 2009, 153–54.

22. Ta Minh Tuan, "Vietnam's Nuclear Energy Development Plan until 2020," paper prepared for National Bureau for Asian Research (updated August 4, 2008), cited in IISS, *Preventing Nuclear Dangers*, 3.

23. Ibid., 3–4.

24. Ta Minh Tuan, "National Plans and Constraints: Viet Nam," presentation at the American Academy of Arts and Sciences conference on Emerging Nuclear Power in Regional Contexts: Southeast Asia, Mandarin Oriental Hotel, Singapore, November 2–5, 2010.

25. Daniel Ten Kate and Nicole Gaouette, "U.S., Vietnam Hold Nuclear Technology Talks as Suitors Vie for Contracts," Bloomberg, August 6, 2010.

26. "Vietnam Government Approves Ambitious Power Plan," *Thanh Nien News*, September 7, 2007.

27. Asian Development Bank, *Asian Development Outlook 2007 Update*, September 2007, http://www.adb.org/Documents/Books/ADO/2007/Update/default.asp.

28. Asian Development Bank, *Asian Development Outlook 2009*, http://www.adb.org/Documents/Books/ADO/2009/VIE.pdf.

29. "ADB Ups Energy Investment in Viet Nam," Asian Development Bank News and Events, September 21, 2007, http://www.adb.org/media/Articles/2007/12169-vietnamese-energies-projects/.

30. "Vietnam Boosts Nuclear Cooperation with Russia," *RIA Novosti*, May 17, 2005.

31. "U.S.-Vietnam Sign Nuclear Agreement," UPI, April 1, 2010, http://www.upi.com/Science_News/Resource-Wars/2010/04/01/US-Vietnam-sign-nuclear-agreement/UPI-79051270148580/.

32. Peter Crail, "NPT Parties Agree on Middle East Meeting," *Arms Control Today*, June 2010, http://www.armscontrol.org/act/2010_06/NPTMideast; see also William Potter, Patricia Lewis, Gaukhar Mukhatzhanova, and Miles Pomper, "The 2010 NPT Review Conference: Deconstructing Consensus," *CNS Special Report* (Monterey, Calif.: Monterey Institute of International Affairs, June 17, 2010), 11–13.

33. See, for example, disarmament expert Rebecca Johnson's commentary, "NPT Day 25: Successful Adoption of Conclusions, Recommendations and Action Plans," May 28, 2010, http://acronyminstitute.wordpress.com/2010/05/28/day-25/. Johnson argues, "Egypt has played its hand brilliantly through this conference and deserves to feel very proud of how its leadership (headed by Amb Maged AbdelAziz) has contributed to this outcome."

34. Potter et al., "2010 NPT Review Conference," 19.

35. Ibid., 14.

36. *Middle East Nuclear-Weapon-Free Zone: The Need for Practical Regional and International Approaches*, Acronym Institute for Disarmament Diplomacy, 2010, http://www.acronym.org.uk/npt/npt2010%20B10%20-%20Middle%20East%20NWFZ.pdf.

37. Cole Harvey, "African NWFZ Treaty Enters into Force," *Arms Control Today*, September 2009, http://www.armscontrol.org/act/2009_09/NWFZ.

38. Eitan Barak, "Getting the Middle East Holdouts to Join the CWC," *Bulletin of the Atomic Scientists*, January/February 2011, 58.

39. Sylvia Westall, "IAEA Governors Approve First Nuclear Fuel Bank Plan," Reuters, November 27, 2009, http://www.reuters.com/article/idUSTRE5AQ1OG20091127.

40. "Statement by Vietnam's Representative, Mr. Nguyen Duy Chien, to the Third Preparatory Committee of the 2005 NPT Review Conference," April 27, 2004; Viet Nam Ministry of Foreign Affairs, "Statement of Ambassador Le Luong Minh to the 2005 NPT Review Conference," May 5, 2005, http://www.mofa.gov.vn; Viet Nam Ministry of Foreign Affairs, "Vietnam Raises Concerns over Restrictions on Peaceful Use of Nuclear Energy", May 5, 2005, http://www.mofa.gov.vn/en/nr040807104143/nr040807105001/ns050509143601?b_start:int=0.

41. "Viet Nam Calls for Nuclear Disarmament at UN Meeting," *Viet Nam News*, April 11, 2007; "Vietnam Calls for End to World's Nuclear Threat", *Nhân Dân*, April 11, 2007.

42. Ta Minh Tuan (Institute of International Relations, Hanoi), comments noted in Chairman's Report, Second Meeting of the CSCAP Study Group on Countering the Proliferation of Weapons of Mass Destruction in the Asia Pacific, Manila, Philippines, December 2–3, 2005, http://www.cscap.org/uploads/docs/WMDSGReports/2WMDRpt.pdf.

43. "Viet Nam Calls for Nuclear Disarmament at UN Meeting," *Viet Nam News*, April 11, 2007.

44. "Vietnam Hosts Seminar on Nuclear Safeguards," *IAEA News Centre* (Staff Report), August 17, 2007.

45. According to Ta Minh Tuan, Vietnam is preparing to ratify the Additional Protocol, although it is still unclear when this will happen. Ta Minh Tuan, "National Plans and Constraints."

46. Vietnam Law on Atomic Energy, no. 18/2008/QH12, http://www.thuvienphapluat.vn/van-ban/Tai-nguyen-Moi-truong/Law-No-18-2008-QH12-of-June-03-2008-on-Atomic-energy/84395/tai-ve.aspx.

47. "Nuclear Future Poses Challenges," *Viet News*, January 19, 2011, http://www.dztimes.net/post/business/nuclear-future-poses-challenges.aspx.

48. UN Security Council, "Note Verbale," December 30, 2005, S/AC.44/2004/(02)39/Add.1; Vietnam Report to the APEC CTTF, February 26–27, 2006.

49. Roger Mitton, "Vietnam under Pressure to Join Anti-Terror Initiative," *Straits Times* (Singapore), March 29, 2007.

50. Sagan, "Shared Responsibilities," 7.

51. See the responses of James M. Acton, Jayantha Dhanapala, Mustafa Kibaroglu, Harald Müller, Yukio Satoh, Mohamed I. Shaker, and Achilles Zaluar in Sagan, *Shared Responsibilities for Nuclear Disarmament*, 14–44.

52. Todd Holzman, "Obama Seeks 'New Beginning' with Muslim World," National Public Radio, June 4, 2009, http://www.npr.org/templates/story/story.php?storyId=104891406.

53. Hassan Nafaa, "Obama's Lost Promise," *Al-Ahram Weekly*, issue 981 (January 14–20, 2010), http://weekly.ahram.org.eg/2010/981/op1.htm.

54. Ahmed Aboul-Gheit, "Address by H.E. Ahmed Aboul-Gheit, Minister for Foreign Affairs of the Arab Republic of Egypt before the Eighth Review Conference of the States Parties to the Treaty on the Non-Proliferation of Nuclear Weapons," New York, May 5, 2010, http://www.un.org/en/conf/npt/2010/statements/pdf/egypt_en.pdf.

55. Gihan Shahine, "A Question of Justice," *Al-Ahram Weekly*, issue 968 (October 15–21, 2009), http://weekly.ahram.org.eg/2009/968/focus.htm.

56. "Statement by Mr. Pham Vinh Quang, Deputy Representative of the Socialist Republic of Viet Nam to the United Nations at the General Debate of the First Committee of the 65th Session of the UN General Assembly," New York, October 6, 2010.

57. UN Security Council Department of Public Information, "Historic Summit of Security Council Pledges Support for Progress on Stalled Efforts to End Weapons Proliferation," SC/9746, September 24, 2009; "Statement by H. E. Mr. Pham Binh Minh, First Deputy-Minister for Foreign Affairs of the Socialist Republic of Viet Nam on Behalf of ASEAN at the 2010 NPT Review Conference," New York, May 4, 2010; "Statement by H. E. Dr. Le Dinh Tien, Deputy Minister of the Ministry of Science and Technology, Head of the Delegation of Viet Nam to the 54th Regular Session of the General Conference of the IAEA," Vienna, Austria, September 20–24, 2010.

58. "PM Dung Voices Concerns over Nuclear Terrorism," *Viet Nam News*, April 14, 2010; "Statement by Le Dinh Tien."

59. NPT Review Conference, "Activities relating to the Treaty on the South-East Asia Nuclear-Weapon-Free Zone," Memorandum submitted by Viet Nam, NPT/CONF.2010/18, April 12, 2010.

60. Fuel bank proposals have primarily received backing from Western countries rather than developing states, which worry that their energy needs could be held hostage by developed states if they place unreasonable conditions on the supply of nuclear fuel. See Fredrik Dahl, "Nuclear Fuel Bank Seen Winning Backing at UN Body," Reuters, November 17, 2010.

61. Alex Rothman, "Is a Region by Region Approach Really Effective in Preventing the Spread of Sensitive Nuclear Technology?" Center for Arms Control and Non-Proliferation, August 17, 2010.

62. Michael Knigge, "U.S.-Vietnam Nuclear Deal Has Experts Divided," *Deutsche Welle*, September 24, 2010; Saurav Jha, "Why a U.S.-Vietnam Nuclear Deal?" *Diplomat*, September 15, 2010.

63. This subject was discussed under "Chatham House rules" (i.e., comments cannot be attributed) at the American Academy of Arts and Sciences conference on Emerging Nuclear Power in Regional Contexts: Southeast Asia, Mandarin Oriental Hotel, Singapore, November 2–5, 2010.

64. For a thorough analysis of regional nuclear proliferation dynamics in the Middle East and East Asia, see Etel Solingen, *Nuclear Logics: Alternative Paths in East Asia and the Middle East* (Princeton, N.J.: Princeton University Press, 2007); and International Institute for Strategic Studies, *Preventing Nuclear Dangers in Southeast Asia and Australasia*, IISS Strategic Dossier, November 2009, http://www.iiss.org/publications/strategic-dossiers/preventing-nuclear-dangers-in-southeast-asia-and-australasia/read-the-dossier/.

65. For an in-depth examination of the Egyptian nuclear weapons program, see Maria Rost Rublee, *Nonproliferation Norms: Why States Choose Nuclear Restraint* (Athens: University of Georgia Press, 2009), chapter 4. Other accounts of the Egyptian quest for nuclear weapons can be found in Solingen, *Nuclear Logics*; James Walsh, "Bombs Unbuilt: Power, Ideas and Institutions in International Politics" (Ph.D. diss., Massachusetts Institute of Technology, 2001); and Robert J. Einhorn, "Egypt: Frustrated but Still on a Non-nuclear Course," in *The Nuclear Tipping Point: Why States Reconsider Their Nuclear Choices*, ed. Kurt M. Campbell, Robert J. Einhorn, and Mitchell B. Reiss (Washington, D.C.: Brookings Institution Press, 2004).

66. Bruce W. Jentleson and Dalia Dassa Kaye, "Explaining Regional Security Cooperation and Its Limits in the Middle East," *Security Studies* 8, no. 1 (Autumn 1998): 205.

67. Shai Feldman, *Nuclear Weapons and Arms Control in the Middle East* (Cambridge, Mass.: MIT Press, 1997), 216.

68. Senior official, quoted in Rublee, *Nonproliferation Norms*, 125.
69. Jentleson and Kaye, "Explaining Regional Security Cooperation," 229–30.
70. Military officer, quoted in Rublee, *Nonproliferation Norms*, 105.
71. Feldman, *Nuclear Weapons and Arms Control*, 221.
72. On the Brazilian perspective, see chapter 5 in this volume.
73. Do Thanh Hai, "Vietnam and the Proliferation of WMD," *Fighting the Spread of WMD: Views from the Next Generation*, ed. Brad Glosserman, *Issues and Insights* 6, no. 4 (Honolulu, Hawaii: Pacific Forum CSIS Pacific Forum, 2006), 7–9.
74. "Statement by H.E. Ambassador Le Hoai Trung, President of the Conference on Disarmament and Head of the Delegation of Viet Nam at the Conference on Disarmament," Palais des Nations, Geneva, January 20, 2009.
75. Ibid.
76. Douglas Pike, "The Turning Point: Vietnam in 1991", *Asian Survey* 32, no. 1 (January 1992): 74–81; Vietnam Ministry of Foreign Affairs, "Vietnam's Present Foreign Policy", http://www.mofa.gov.vn/en/cs_doingoai/cs/ns041025165700.
77. Michael R. Gordon, "U.S. and Vietnam Agree to Broaden Military Ties", *New York Times*, June 6, 2006; Grant McCool, "Vietnam Plays New Anti-terror Role," *China Post* (Taiwan), April 12, 2007; B. Raman, "China's Wake-Up Call for Vietnam and India," *Eurasia Review*, August 10, 2010; Seth Mydans, "Shared Concern about China Aligns U.S. and Vietnam," *New York Times*, October 10, 2010; Ta Minh Tuan, "The Future of Vietnam-U.S. Relations," Brookings Institution, April 14, 2010, http://www.brookings.edu/opinions/2010/04_us_vietnam_relations_tuan.aspx; "Vietnam, India Issue Joint Declaration on Strategic Partnership," *VietnamNet*, July 7, 2007, http://english.vietnamnet.vn/politics/2007/07/715169.
78. Leonard S. Spector and Benjamin Radford, "Algeria, Emirates Plan Nonproliferation-Friendly Nuclear Programs; Egypt Keeps Fuel Cycle Options Open, Rejects Expanded IAEA Monitoring," *WMD Insights*, June 2008.
79. Bruno Tertrais, "The Middle East's Next Nuclear State," *Strategic Insights* 8, no. 1 (January 2009).
80. Ibid.
81. For in-depth analysis of neighboring countries' response to Iran's nuclear program, see Dalia Dassa Kaye and Frederic M. Wehrey, "A Nuclear Iran: The Reactions of Neighbors," *Survival* 49, no. 2 (2007): 111–28. See also James A. Russell, "A Tipping Point Realized? Nuclear Proliferation in the Persian Gulf and Middle East," *Contemporary Security Policy* 29, no. 3 (2008): 521–37; and Richard Weitz, "Gulf Cooperation Council Moves Forward with Nuclear Energy Plans," *WMD Insights*, April 2007.
82. "WikiLeaks: Egypt Considering Nuclear Arms If Iran Gets Them," Associated Press, *Jerusalem Post*, December 6, 2010, http://www.jpost.com/MiddleEast/Article.aspx?id=198250&R=R3.

83. Sammy Salama and Khalid Hilal, "Egyptian Muslim Brotherhood Presses Government for Nuclear Weapons," *WMD Insights*, November 2006. See also "Egypt and Nuclear Power: Nuclear Succession," *Economist*, September 28, 2006.

84. Salama and Hilal, "Egyptian Muslim Brotherhood."

85. See "U.S. to Help Build Vietnam's First Nuclear Plant," *Agence France-Presse*, March 20, 2007, http://www.breitbart.com/article.php?id=070320153852.sl6gfarx&show_article=1&catnum=0; Chua Hearn Yuit and Yeo Lay Hwee, "The Demise of the NPT: New Players in the Proliferation Game," *Japan Focus*, May 16, 2006, http://www.japanfocus.org/site/view/1820.

86. Ten Kate and Gaouette, "U.S., Vietnam Hold Nuclear Technology Talks."

87. Ta Minh Tuan of Vietnam's Institute of International Relations (which is part of the Ministry of Foreign Affairs) has pointed out that there is no public debate about WMD in his country, and that "the government is the sole actor in this field." See Chairman's Report, *Fifth Meeting of the CSCAP Study Group on Countering the Proliferation of Weapons of Mass Destruction in the Asia Pacific*, San Francisco, February 12–13, 2007, http://www.cscap.org/uploads/docs/WMDSGReports/5WMDRpt.pdf.

88. Mark E. Manyin, "U.S.-Vietnam Relations in 2010: Current Issues and Implications for U.S. Policy," *CRS Report for Congress*, July 12, 2010, 27.

89. Although 2010 was officially named China-Vietnam Friendship Year, tensions between the two states have escalated, and Vietnam is nervously following China's naval expansion program. "PLAN Spearheads China's Ambitions for a Greater Regional Sphere of Influence," *Jane's Navy International*, October 20, 2010; "China Strengthens Maritime Patrols in Disputed Waters," *Jane's Intelligence Weekly*, October 27, 2010.

90. The government is currently increasing its national maritime capabilities, having recently ordered six diesel electric submarines from Russia. There is also speculation that Vietnam may in the future acquire a nuclear-powered attack submarine, possibly from France or Russia, which would be seen by Hanoi as a far better investment than nuclear weapons. Edward Wong, "Vietnam Enlists Allies to Stave Off China's Reach," *New York Times*, February 5, 2010; "Southeast Asia Rising," *Jane's Defence Industry*, July 17, 2009.

91. "ASEAN States Assuming a Defensive Position," *Jane's Intelligence Weekly*, October 18, 2010; Ong Keng Yong, "Enabling Effective Governance in the ASEAN Community," Remarks by the Secretary General of ASEAN at the CAPAM 2006 Biennial Conference, Sydney, October 23, 2006.

92. Some scholars regard the rising great power rivalry in Southeast Asia as a serious challenge to ASEAN integration and cooperation. See, for example, Tan Seng Chye, "Big Power Rivalry in East Asia: Will It Disrupt Regional Cooperation?" *RSIS Commentaries*, November 9, 2010.

CHAPTER SEVEN

The Nuclear Holdouts
India, Israel, and Pakistan

Devin T. Hagerty

THIS CHAPTER EXAMINES THE nuclear postures and policies of the "holdout" states, countries that have chosen not to sign the Nuclear Nonproliferation Treaty (NPT) and, more generally, maintain a posture of detachment from the corpus of rules, norms, and obligations constituting the broader nuclear nonproliferation regime.[1] Of the nine nuclear weapon states (NWS) in the world today, NPT holdouts India, Israel, and Pakistan pose perhaps the stiffest challenges for those who would rid the world of nuclear weapons. This chapter analyzes these challenges with an eye toward assessing the potential role of India, Israel, and Pakistan in the recently reinvigorated global effort to achieve universal nuclear disarmament. Its main argument is that the near- and medium-term prospects for engaging these three countries in truly meaningful disarmament negotiations are exceedingly poor.

The logic of grouping India, Israel, and Pakistan together is threefold. First, their development and continuing refinement of nuclear-weapon capabilities is tightly bound to several of the world's most enduring and intractable political-military conflicts: the Arab-Israeli standoff, the regional rivalry between Iran and Israel, the Kashmir dispute dividing India and Pakistan, and the Sino-Indian geopolitical competition. These conflicts have been at the root of numerous wars, both conventional and unconventional, and each has proved stubbornly resistant to resolution. Consequently, strategic elites in India, Israel, and Pakistan continue to perceive a compelling need for "immediate" nuclear deterrence, whereas their counterparts in Britain, France, Russia, the United States, and to some degree China tend to be motivated by the more relaxed imperatives of "general" nuclear deterrence.[2] Two decades after the Cold War's end, the persistence of regional cold wars in Asia and the Middle East is one of the greatest obstacles to the realization of universal nuclear disarmament.

Second, compared to most of the more established NWS, India, Israel, and Pakistan are still very much on the ascent in terms of the redundancy, diversity, and sophistication of their nuclear forces. Britain, France, Russia, and the United States have substantially reduced their nuclear-weapon capabilities in response to diminishing interstate security threats since the end of the Cold War. In contrast, the nuclear holdouts are considerably more potent NWS than they were twenty years ago, and this upward trend continues. Since India and Pakistan went overtly nuclear with a series of explosive tests in May 1998, both countries have endeavored to increase the number of their nuclear weapons and improve their aircraft- and missile-delivery systems. India is avidly pursuing a full-blown, albeit modest, nuclear triad, and indications are that Pakistan will attempt to keep pace. Israel's nuclear-weapon capabilities are more robust than both India's and Pakistan's, and Israel has deployed its own nuclear triad since 2003. Moreover, according to the International Panel on Fissile Materials (IPFM), "only India, Pakistan and perhaps Israel and North Korea are producing additional fissile material for weapons."[3] In sum, judging by the best available open-source evidence, the nuclear holdouts' strategic momentum is moving away from, rather than toward, disarmament, with all three nuclear establishments working hard to achieve ever-more survivable second-strike arsenals.

A third reason to consider India, Israel, and Pakistan in the same chapter is their history as opaque proliferants. Opacity in the nuclear context refers to a government's clandestine development of nuclear-weapon capabilities combined with its public disavowal of any intention to deploy nuclear weapons. The concept was developed in the 1980s to distinguish the nuclear holdouts from the five countries recognized as NWS by the NPT, Britain, China, France, the Soviet Union, and the United States, as well as to help analysts understand the political and strategic implications of this new form of proliferation.[4] Israel was the prototype opaque proliferant and remains one today. India and Pakistan abandoned the Israeli model in 1998, but because they covertly went nuclear, in defiance of the nonproliferation regime, they remain resistant to transparency in the nuclear realm. None of the three countries discloses details about the number of nuclear weapons it possesses, or how they are deployed, and all three governments believe that their deterrent postures are strengthened, rather than weakened, by preserving some measure of ambiguity. The nuclear holdouts' instinctive aversion to transparency and minimal experience with the habits and practices of compliance with arms control and nonproliferation agreements create significant obstacles for supporters of nuclear disarmament.[5]

The remainder of this chapter unfolds in the following way. The next section provides a brief overview of the nuclear-weapon and delivery capabilities, strategic postures, and historical disarmament diplomacy of India, Israel, and Pakistan. Section three describes the holdout states' reactions and responses to the vision of a world without nuclear weapons articulated by U.S. president Barack Obama during his April 2009 speech in Prague.[6] The fourth section discusses the prospects for future Indian, Israeli, and Pakistani disarmament policy and diplomacy and then offers a number of recommendations for the disarmament community.

THE HOLDOUTS' NUCLEAR PROFILES

Public knowledge of the three countries' nuclear forces and postures is imprecise at best. Analysts arrive at estimates by calculating fissile-material stockpiles and potential, combing through government statements about postures and doctrine, assessing the probable capabilities of aircraft and missile systems, and "reading the tea leaves" of media accounts that are often anonymously sourced and of questionable reliability. These pieces of information are assembled into a puzzle comprising the conventional wisdom of defense and nonproliferation analysts, but there is much that we do not know with any certainty. Furthermore, since the degree of uncertainty is directly related to the degree of nuclear opacity, estimates concerning Israel's nuclear arsenal are less certain than those regarding India and Pakistan.

India

Nuclear Capabilities and Posture. In late 2009, the IPFM reported that "India continues to produce weapons plutonium in its two production reactors, Cirus and Dhruva, at a combined rate of about 30 kilograms per year. We estimate India's stockpile of weapons plutonium produced in these two reactors to be about 700kg."[7] The IPFM's figure for India's nuclear-warhead stockpile is 60–70 kilograms, while the Federation of American Scientists (FAS) puts the number at 60–80 as of May 2010.[8] India's nuclear-delivery options are believed to include the Mirage 2000H, Jaguar IS, Mig-27, and Sukoi Su-30 MKI aircraft, as well as land-based, short- and medium-range ballistic missiles (SRBMs and MRBMs) such as the Prithvi-I, Agni-I, Agni-II, and Agni-III.[9] India is also developing a submarine-launched ballistic missile (SLBM) and air-, land-, and sea-based cruise missiles, but these will not be operational for years. India's nuclear weapons are under civilian control, with the Department of Atomic Energy/Bhabha Atomic Research Center maintaining the fissile pits and the Defence Research and Development Organisation managing the weapons' nonfissile components. These agencies "are believed to disperse their respective subcomponents over several highly secret locations to ensure that a fully constitutable nuclear capability survives a first strike as well as 'iterative' attempts to disarm India's capability."[10] India's army and air force control the country's land-based ballistic missiles and aircraft, respectively. The nuclear arsenal has "never been deployed in ready-for-use form, let alone kept on alert. Delivery vehicles do not have weapons mated with them."[11]

Declaratory Doctrine and Disarmament Diplomacy. Indian leaders have a long history of ambivalence when it comes to nuclear weapons. For much of independent India's existence, they have been reluctantly unwilling to forgo a nuclear-weapons option, while consistently championing global nuclear disarmament. The profoundly conflicted nature of India's nuclear-strategic culture was encapsulated in the late 1980s, when Prime Minister Rajiv Gandhi unveiled his June 1988 "Action Plan for Total Elimination of Weapons of Mass Destruction" before the United Nations General Assembly (UNGA) at about the same time that Indian scientists achieved the ability to fully assemble their nuclear weapons for the first time.[12] A decade later, after conducting a series of nuclear explosive tests and declaring itself a NWS, India insisted that its nuclear weapons were intended only to deter nuclear attacks by China or Pakistan, and that India would never be the first country to use nuclear weapons in a conflict.[13] India has a declaratory "doctrine of credible minimum nuclear deterrence," in which the "fundamental purpose of Indian nuclear weapons is to deter the use and threat of use of nuclear weapons" against India; "any nuclear attack on India and its forces shall result in punitive retaliation with nuclear weapons to inflict damage unacceptable to the aggressor."[14] At the same time, Indian diplomats continue to advocate the "universal and non-discriminatory elimination of nuclear weapons in a time-bound framework," to be achieved through the "negotiation of a Nuclear Weapons Convention prohibiting the development, production, stockpiling and use of nuclear weapons."[15] From the official Indian perspective today, the rest of the world is belatedly "veering around to our view that the best guarantor of nuclear security is a world free from nuclear weapons."[16]

Pakistan

Nuclear Capabilities and Posture. The IPFM's late 2009 estimate of Pakistan's uranium enrichment capacity was "a production rate of 150 kg of weapon-grade HEU [highly enriched uranium] per year [...] Our central estimate for Pakistan's current stockpile of HEU is about 2.1 [metric] tons." Pakistan also produces "10–12 kg per year of plutonium for weapons" and has manufactured "about 100 kg of plutonium" since starting its Khushab-1 production reactor in 1998.[17] Both the IPFM and FAS put Pakistan's stockpile of nuclear warheads at 70–90 kilograms.[18] Pakistan's potential nuclear-delivery platforms include the F-16 and Mirage 5PA attack aircraft, as well as land-based SRBMs and MRBMs such as the Hatf-I, Abdali, Ghaznavi, Shaheen-I, and Ghauri-I.[19] Although the various components of Pakistan's nuclear-weapon systems are tightly controlled by its army and air force, rather than civilian authorities, the warheads are not mated in peacetime with aircraft and missiles.[20] According to one credible account: "the weapons are believed to be stored unassembled with the nuclear cores separate from the rest of the weapon, and the weapon storage areas are some distance from the delivery vehicles, under normal circumstances."[21] However, it is also considered highly likely that Pakistan's nuclear weapons and their delivery systems are located close enough to one another to enable rapid deployment during a crisis.[22]

Declaratory Doctrine and Disarmament Diplomacy. Pakistan's nuclear policy is driven by its threat perceptions of a much-larger, more-powerful India. Although Pakistan also purports to follow a "strategic doctrine [...] based on minimum credible deterrence,"[23] the essential purpose of its nuclear weapons is to deter both nuclear *and* conventional attacks by an adversarial neighbor that enjoys marked superiority across the entire range of sophisticated conventional weaponry, manpower, and materiel. Because of Pakistan's conventional inferiority and limited strategic depth, it has forsworn a pledge of no-first-use (NFU) and declared in various statements "only the basic logic of its nuclear-use policy, leaving India and the rest of the world to calculate the risks."[24] According to General Khalid Kidwai, director general of the Strategic Plans Division, the apex body responsible for the command and control of Pakistan's nuclear arsenal, nuclear weapons will be used against India only "if the very existence of Pakistan as a state is at stake."[25] Kidwai has also said that if deterrence fails, Pakistan will use nuclear weapons against India under the following conditions: (1) "India attacks Pakistan and conquers a large part of its territory"; (2) "India destroys a large part either of its land or air forces"; (3) "India proceeds to the economic strangling of Pakistan"; (4) "India pushes Pakistan into political destabilization or creates a large scale internal subversion in Pakistan."[26] At a rhetorical level, Pakistan supports the same fundamental disarmament objective as India: "negotiation of a nuclear weapons convention along with a phased programme for the complete elimination of nuclear weapons within a specified time frame."[27] However, Pakistan has also made it clear that its willingness to give up its nuclear weapons is contingent upon what its diplomats have referred to as a regional "strategic restraint regime," including agreements to reduce or eliminate the disparity in conventional forces between India and Pakistan.[28]

Israel

Nuclear Capabilities and Posture. Owing to its greater degree of opacity, much less is known for certain about Israeli nuclear weapons.[29] The IPFM estimates that Israel's Dimona reactor can produce 15–18 kilograms of weapons-grade plutonium per year, and that it had produced a total of perhaps 600–740 kilograms by the end of 2009. Israel also has an estimated inventory of 100 kilograms of HEU.[30] The IPFM puts Israel's stockpile of nuclear warheads at one hundred to two hundred, while the FAS figure is eighty.[31] Unlike India and Pakistan, which are believed to deploy only fission weapons, the prevailing conventional wisdom holds that Israel also deploys fusion, or thermonuclear, weapons.[32] Israeli nuclear-delivery options likely include F-15 and F-16 aircraft, land-based Jericho-II MRBMs, and cruise missiles that can be launched from Dolphin-class submarines.[33] Approximately fifty to one hundred Jericho-IIs are reported to be stored in underground caves and silos at a missile base some forty-five kilometers southeast of Tel Aviv; their warhead-mating status and other operational details are unknown.[34]

Declaratory Doctrine and Disarmament Diplomacy. Because Israel does not admit it possesses nuclear weapons, it does not have a declaratory doctrine. At moments of high international tension, adversaries are usually left to interpret vague but forceful pronouncements by Israeli leaders concerning the retribution potential attackers might bring upon themselves.[35] Occasionally, more precise signals are sent.[36] To an even greater degree than Pakistan, Israel relies on its nuclear arsenal as the ultimate guarantor of its survival as a sovereign state. Israeli analysts frequently refer to the "existential" nature of both the threats facing Israel and the essential purpose of its nuclear deterrence posture. In the early decades of the country's modern history, Israeli decision-makers viewed the development of nuclear-weapon capabilities as a "sacred matter of national survival, the ultimate way to offset the fundamental geo-political asymmetry in conventional power between Israel and an Arab world that repeatedly threatened to destroy it."[37] The deeper context was, of course, still-vivid memories of the Nazis' attempt during the Second World War to exterminate the Jews of Europe: "Israel's nuclear project was conceived in the shadow of the Holocaust, and the lessons of the Holocaust provided the justification and motivation for the project."[38] These fears have resurfaced in recent years, as a postrevolutionary Iran whose zealously Islamist leaders regularly refer to Israel as a "cancerous tumor" moves ever-closer to achieving a nuclear-weapons capability.[39] One Israeli analyst points out that the "difference between the anti-Israeli rhetoric in Ben-Gurion's era and today's is that now, for the first time, such threats are voiced by a president of a state that is seriously pursuing a nuclear-weapon capability. Furthermore, Ahmadinejad's rhetoric accompanies Iran's increasing involvement in other parts of the Middle East, most visibly through Hezbollah in Lebanon and Hamas in the Palestinian territories."[40] Having failed miserably in several attempts to overrun Israel by conventional military means, its adversaries are now on the brink of being able to threaten Israel through a combination of unconventional and nuclear means.[41] Israel's position on denuclearization has been consistent over the decades: nuclear disarmament, most likely in the context of a Middle East zone free of nuclear weapons and all other weapons of mass destruction, is feasible only as the last phase of a "comprehensive process of regional political reconciliation encompassing both formal peace agreements and verifiable reductions in conventional and unconventional military threats."[42]

THE NEW DISARMAMENT AGENDA: REACTIONS AND RESPONSES

Broadly speaking, the three holdouts' positioning on the new push for universal nuclear disarmament has been characterized more by continuity than change.

Indian, Israeli, and Pakistani diplomats have expressed their governments' appreciation of President Obama's Prague initiative and support for many of the specific objectives he outlined in April 2009. By and large, they have voiced the "right" sentiments, partly so as not to be viewed as naysayers. However, they have also availed themselves of the opportunity provided by the post-Prague disarmament climate to air long-standing positions and the grievances underlying them. Not surprisingly, each country perceives its own nuclear-diplomatic posture, past and present, to be eminently restrained and reasonable. Although it would be an exaggeration to say that it is "business as usual" for the holdout states, a close reading of their reactions and responses to the new disarmament momentum discloses no fundamental breaks with the past. This section pays particular attention to two subjects: (1) Indian, Israeli, and Pakistani policies regarding what are currently the most salient elements of the Prague agenda for the nuclear holdouts: the long-concluded Comprehensive Test Ban Treaty (CTBT), the proposed fissile material cut-off treaty (FMCT), and—in the case of Israel—international pressure to negotiate a Middle East Nuclear-Weapon-Free Zone (MENWFZ); and (2) the material and ideational forces driving continuity rather than change in the nuclear policies and diplomacy of India, Israel, and Pakistan.

India

At the level of rhetoric, President Obama's Prague speech was warmly welcomed by Indian diplomats. During an October 2009 "thematic discussion on nuclear weapons" in the UNGA's First Committee, Ambassador Hamid Ali Rao stated: "India welcomes the renewed attention of the international community on achieving a nuclear weapon free world. World leaders, Parliamentarians, distinguished statesmen, international groups and NGOs [nongovernmental organizations] have lent their voice in favor of nuclear disarmament. [. . .] To sustain the current mood of optimism, follow up action on the ground will be needed, based on a genuine desire to take concrete steps."[43] In the same forum, Rao struck a self-justifying tone, recounting the wide range of nuclear disarmament measures India had historically put before the United Nations. These include initiatives to negotiate measures by the NWS to reduce nuclear dangers, such as the de-alerting of nuclear forces to prevent their unintentional or accidental use; a global agreement among NWS on NFU of nuclear weapons; a universal agreement on non-use of nuclear weapons against non-NWSS; a convention on the complete prohibition of the use or threat of use of nuclear weapons; and, ultimately, a Nuclear Weapon Convention "prohibiting the development, production, stockpiling, and use of nuclear weapons, and on their destruction, leading to the global, non-discriminatory, and verifiable elimination of nuclear weapons within a specified timeframe."[44]

Indeed, New Delhi has long claimed to prefer such a comprehensive "effort to achieve complete elimination of nuclear weapons," rather than what it derides as "ad hoc steps in nonproliferation, an approach whose limitations we have seen in the past."[45] Regarding the long-discussed FMCT, India depicts itself as a consistently strong supporter of efforts to negotiate a "non-discriminatory, multilateral, and internationally and effectively verifiable treaty banning the production of fissile material for nuclear weapons or other nuclear explosive devices."[46] At the same time, India has the potential to dramatically accelerate the rate at which it produces fissile material for weapons, thanks in part to the infamous (for arms control and disarmament activists) India-U.S. civilian nuclear cooperation agreement. In July 2005, India and the United States signed what amounted to a "roadmap to lift global nuclear trade restrictions on India."[47] After three years of arduous negotiations between Washington and New Delhi, inside the U.S. and Indian political systems and within the Nuclear Suppliers Group (NSG) and the International Atomic Energy Agency (IAEA), final authorization for India-U.S. civilian nuclear cooperation was signed into U.S. law in October 2008. The deal paves the way for India to purchase American (and other) nuclear fuel and technologies while still maintaining its nuclear-weapons program. New Delhi plans to import safeguarded nuclear fuel and then reprocess the spent fuel for use in yet-to-be constructed breeder reactors. India will also build reprocessing plants at the reactor sites, which it maintains "will eliminate transports of spent fuel and separated plutonium and therefore reduce the terrorist threat to its nuclear installations."[48] In principle, American companies can now compete with French and Russian enterprises to provide India with nuclear-related technology, fuel, reactors, and other equipment that will allow India to gradually increase the percentage of its vast energy needs that can be met by nuclear power.[49] However, at least some of India's future breeder-reactor activities will take place outside of the IAEA's inspection purview, which has raised concerns within the arms control and disarmament community that one effect of the nuclear deal will be to permit a significant increase in India's stockpile of fissile material for its nuclear weapons.[50]

Conspicuously absent from most of India's public statements on disarmament-related issues is its view of the CTBT, which remains a sensitive issue in New Delhi. Passage of the CTBT in 1996 generated intense pressure on India to sign the treaty and forgo the option to test nuclear explosives, which Indian scientists feared would severely limit their ability to enhance the sophistication and reliability of India's nascent nuclear arsenal. Along with the permanent extension of the NPT in 1995, the CTBT, with its controversial entry-into-force clause, is claimed to have forced India's hand on testing its nuclear capabilities and declaring itself a NWS; for the Bharatiya Janata Party (BJP) government, conducting the May 1998 series of tests was "inevitable," because its options had "narrowed critically."[51] After the tests, New Delhi declared a "voluntary, unilateral moratorium on nuclear testing" that continues today.[52] Its opposition to the CTBT remains unchanged since Prague, with Indian diplomats carefully avoiding the issue. All in all, as one analyst notes, "the Indian government is concentrating more time and resources on expanding the number and quality of its nuclear weapons and delivery platforms than on pursuing nuclear arms control and disarmament [. . .] India has not contributed proactively to either" the CTBT or the FMCT.[53] U.S. Senate rejection of the CTBT in 1999 shelved the issue for India. If the United States were to ratify the treaty, India would come under great pressure to follow suit.

The main material drivers of India's nuclear policy are its great-power aspirations, its geopolitical competition with China, and its simmering rivalry with Pakistan. If China's expressed grand strategy is the "peaceful rise," India's is captured by the favored phrase "rising above the region." New Delhi aspires to a seat at the high table of twenty-first century world affairs, along with the NPT-5, Germany, Japan, and the fourth so-called BRIC country, Brazil.[54] India's 1998 decision to go openly nuclear was fundamentally linked to New Delhi's desire to be a global power. It led to a sustained engagement between U.S. deputy secretary of state Strobe Talbott and Indian foreign minister Jaswant Singh over the CTBT and related nuclear issues.[55] Over time, Washington adapted itself to the reality that India's grand strategy included becoming a full-fledged NWS. In hindsight, 1998 destroyed the illusion that New Delhi could be coaxed out of pursuing the ultimate currency of great-power status; once the illusion evaporated, the United States and India began to relate to one another on a more equal footing.

India and China have been natural Asian competitors since they emerged as postcolonial states in the late 1940s. Both ancient civilizations were eclipsed in the age of imperialism, then reborn via nationalist movements that in turn inspired millions of people in the global South. New Delhi and Beijing chose competing paths to development, which then provided alternative models for scores of emerging Third World governments. In 1962, China trounced India in a short war whose underlying territorial disputes remain unresolved.[56] India's nuclear weapons are deeply rooted in the 1962 humiliation, which was followed two years later by China's first nuclear test. A fundamental purpose of India's nuclear arsenal is to deter another attack by China, which, while improbable, cannot be entirely ruled out. Indian leaders also believe that in any eventual territorial settlement with China, a non-nuclear India would be disadvantaged.

With their history of the 1947 partition of British India, three and a half wars, nuclear-weapons competition, numerous crises and terrorist attacks, and chronic tension over the disputed territory of Kashmir, Pakistan represents India's chief day-to-day security threat. Pakistan is also the fly in the ointment of India's great-power aspirations; what New Delhi perceives as Islamabad's chronic aggressiveness forces India to waste resources—money, manpower, military materiel—dealing with expensive irritants. When Indian strategic elites talk about "rising above the region," what they envision is a globally ascendant India that is not repeatedly dragged down, sullied, and distracted by crises and conflicts with Pakistan.[57] A second essential purpose of India's nuclear forces is to deter nuclear or conventional attacks by Pakistan.

The key term in New Delhi's rhetoric on disarmament is *nondiscriminatory*: India should be accorded the same status and privileges enjoyed by the NPT-recognized NWS. From India's vantage point, it has been a consummately responsible NWS that has broken no international laws or agreements—in contrast, Indian leaders like to point out, to China, France, and Pakistan, which have all helped other states become NWS. Practically speaking, *nondiscrimination* translates into "parity with China." Beijing has a minimum nuclear deterrent posture and a declared NFU doctrine, and it is working to assure its second-strike capability by developing a triad of air-, land-, and sea-based capabilities. New Delhi should not be constrained from following the same path. China has built up a fissile material stockpile that is much larger than India's; India should therefore continue to produce fissile material and cannot be expected to sign an FMCT that permanently freezes this asymmetry. Beijing has conducted numerous nuclear explosive tests, allowing it to modernize its nuclear arsenal and develop high confidence in its reliability. New Delhi cannot sign the CTBT lest future circumstances dictate the advisability of additional testing for the same purposes. In pursuing parity with China, India maintains, ipso facto, sufficient nuclear robustness to deter nuclear and conventional threats from Pakistan.

If the material drivers of Indian nuclear policy promote continuity in the growth of Indian nuclear-weapon capabilities, the ideational drivers hold out some hope for New Delhi's eventual participation in disarmament measures. India self-identifies as a "reluctant proliferant," a state that began its modern history as a champion of peace and disarmament but eventually was forced to meet a dangerous world on its own terms. This self-perception was evident after the nuclear tests of 1998, which Foreign Minister Singh characterized this way: "India is alone in the world in having debated the available nuclear options for the last 35 years. No other country has deliberated so carefully and, at times, torturously over the dichotomy between its sovereign security needs and global disarmament instincts, between a moralistic approach and a realistic one, and between a covert nuclear policy and an overt one. May 11, 1998, changed all that."[58] As India continues its transition from a revisionist to a status-quo power in international politics, this exceptionalist strain in the Indian strategic imagination could be harnessed to push the disarmament idea forward—as long as the principle of nondiscrimination is observed. The idea of India being a "different" kind of great power, one that leavens its realism with moral rectitude, is one that resonates among Indian strategic elites.

Pakistan

Islamabad's response to the post-Prague disarmament momentum has also been welcoming, but only at the rhetorical level. During the October 2009 UNGA First Committee session, Pakistan's representative noted the "optimism flowing from the expression of positive intentions and renewed commitment to the objective of disarmament by the major nuclear-weapon states. This has imbued the policy makers, intelligentsia, and civil society everywhere with a sense of hope." Pakistan was "encouraged by these developments" but was also "mindful of the ground realities which continue to threaten" progress in nuclear disarmament. Foremost among these, he argued, are "imbalances and asymmetries in defense spending, regionally as well as globally"; "asymmetries both in the nuclear and conventional fields that exist at the regional and sub-regional levels"; "regional disputes [that] continue to fester around the globe, particularly in South Asia and the Middle East"; the "derogation from non-proliferation norms and discriminatory exceptions, for political or strategic interests, and disregard for any equitably applicable criteria"; and the "growing trend of promoting the security of some states at the cost of others through measures adopted by a select group of states outside recognized multilateral negotiating forums." In sum, from Pakistan's perspective, "non-proliferation and peace and security are inextricably linked. A holistic approach encompassing the simultaneous pursuit of these objectives is the only solution. Progress in any one of these spheres has a beneficial effect on all of them; in turn, failure in one sphere has negative effects on others."[59]

Pakistani diplomats have wasted no opportunity since 2009 to vent their particular ire at the India-U.S. civilian nuclear cooperation agreement, which they term a "cynical and hypocritical" case of "discrimination and double standards" that has rendered the NPT and NSG a "farce."[60] More consequentially, Pakistan's actions have backed up its words. Taking advantage of the Conference on Disarmament (CD) consensus rules, Islamabad prevented discussions on an FMCT from the beginning.[61] Islamabad argues that the expected India-U.S. civilian nuclear cooperation agreement will "free up India's domestic uranium for weapons and that Pakistan would need to increase its own capability to produce fissile material." Indeed, the nuclear agreement seems already to have "accelerated Pakistan's unsafeguarded uranium- and plutonium-production capability," even though the basis for this acceleration began before the U.S.-Indian agreement.[62] Pakistani pique over India's special treatment has added vigor to its long-standing charge that the FMCT draft under consideration is discriminatory because it does not address existing stockpiles of fissile material and would thus favor countries with larger stockpiles, namely India, in Pakistan's mind. Most outside analysts, however, believe the two countries have a rough parity in their fissile-material stockpiles. As with most other nuclear-armed states, India's support for an FMCT extends only to future production of fissile material. As Pakistan's representative to the CD said in August 2010, "negotiations on a treaty that only bans the future production of fissile material will undermine our security by freezing the asymmetries in stockpiles within our region." The India-U.S. civilian nuclear cooperation agreement "will further widen these asymmetries and accentuate our security concerns. Therefore, negotiation of a mere cut-off treaty is neither possible, nor feasible and practical for regional and global security." He then stated "most categorically that Pakistan cannot compromise on its security interests and the imperative of maintaining a credible minimum deterrence."[63] After being rebuffed by the United States in its requests for a civilian nuclear cooperation deal like India's, Pakistan turned to China, which has agreed to build two additional nuclear reactors for Islamabad at its Chashma facility.[64] In turn, India has sought to mobilize opposition within the nonproliferation community to implementation of the Sino-Pakistani nuclear deal.[65]

The CTBT is not under active consideration by Pakistan, although, as one source says, "If the U.S. ratifies [the treaty], India will be under tremendous pressure to do so as well. Pakistan's stance remains tied to India's and thus Islamabad can be expected to follow suit."[66] While that may be the case, Islamabad's public statements on the CTBT and other disarmament-related measures are more cryptic and offer fewer grounds for optimism: "In truth, treaties on banning certain types of weapons, test bans, or moratoria on fissile material production have only been negotiated and agreed by certain states once these weapon systems have lost their relevance [...] or when their national defence reviews lead to certainty regarding the sufficiency and reliability of existing arsenals for future defence needs."[67] The clear subtext here is that Pakistan will keep its options open for as long as it can while continuing to increase and modernize its nuclear-weapon capabilities.

The core material drivers of Pakistani nuclear policy are Islamabad's transcendent fear of India and the Pakistan Army's dominant position in society. While Pakistani leaders no longer worry that New Delhi will somehow reverse the 1947 partition, they do retain an all-consuming dread that India might one day "cut Pakistan down to size," in a continuation of the perceived Indian divide-and-conquer strategy begun with New Delhi's liberation of East Pakistan, now Bangladesh, in 1971. Although this perception may seem far-fetched, defeats in three conventional wars and the disastrous subconventional Kargil operation in 1999, plus repeated crises stemming from the Kashmir dispute, allow Pakistan's strategic elites to dredge up ample justification for their worst-case scenarios, notwithstanding the fact that Pakistan was the initiator—directly or indirectly—of virtually all of these conflicts.

The military's paramount influence in national-security affairs adds an important domestic dimension to Pakistani nuclear policy. Although Islamabad claims that its number-one priority with respect to India is to resolve the Kashmir conflict, actually doing so would rob important political interests—especially the Pakistan Army—of their thin claims to legitimacy within the polity. Democracy in Pakistan remains skin deep. Political power is tightly held by traditional, conservative interests: the army, neofeudal landowners, big business houses, and radical Islamists. These power brokers have a vested interest in the domestic status quo, because a more equal distribution of political and economic resources would undermine their privileged positions in Pakistani society. Chronic turmoil in Indian-administered Kashmir provides these elites with the means to preserve their power, by allowing them to portray New Delhi's control of predominantly Muslim Kashmir as an insult to both Pakistan and Islam. Who better to defend the nation and the faith than the Pakistan Army and its political allies? Actually resolving the Kashmir dispute would threaten the dominance of the entrenched powers-that-be in Pakistan.[68]

The chief ideational driver of continuity in Pakistan's nuclear policy is the near-universal, almost sacred belief that nuclear weapons have repeatedly deterred Indian military aggression for the last two decades. Not only do Pakistani strategic elites often voice their certainty that nuclear weapons deterred India from escalating the 1990, 1999, and 2001–2 crises, but they tend to believe that the only thing preventing the further diminution of the Pakistan of August 1947—indeed, the only thing guaranteeing Pakistan's survival as a political homeland for South Asia's Muslims—is nuclear weapons, which have raised the costs of an Indian conventional invasion to unacceptable levels. This is why Islamabad's rhetoric is so insistent that any South Asian, and thus global, nuclear disarmament process must be "holistic," that is, accompanied by agreements on appropriate India-Pakistan conventional force balances, nonaggression and security assurances, and—most importantly—a fair resolution of the Kashmir conflict.[69]

Israel

The Israeli response to the new disarmament momentum has been extremely guarded. Part of the reason for this is, of course, that it is difficult for a country to engage in nuclear arms control and disarmament measures when it does not even admit its possession of nuclear weapons. Even substantively, though, Israel's nuclear policy exhibits few changes from the pre-Prague past. In the broadest terms, Israeli leaders continue to stress that negotiations to control or abolish weapons of mass destruction in the Middle East should logically come at the end of a process of conflict resolution and political reconciliation between Israel and its rivals, some of which persist in their refusal even to recognize Israel's legitimacy as a state and fellow United Nations member.

Israel signed the CTBT in 1996, but—like both the United States and China—

it has yet to ratify the treaty. If and when the United States ratifies the CTBT, Israel would undoubtedly come under intense pressure to do likewise, but the Israeli government seems content to bide its time until then. In the meantime, Israel remains officially "unequivocal" in its support for the treaty, which it considers "an indispensable element" of the nuclear nonproliferation regime, "especially in view of non-compliance and the cases of gross violations of international obligations related to non-proliferation in the Middle East, as well as the two nuclear explosions conducted by North Korea."[70] Not testing is part of the ambiguity deal struck between Golda Meir and Richard Nixon in 1969, under which Israel agreed not to be the first to "introduce" nuclear weapons to the region. Israel derives a rare modicum of political capital from being a CTBT signatory in contrast to its fellow nuclear holdouts, India and Pakistan.

As for the FMCT, Israel worries that the treaty represents the beginning of a "slippery slope toward premature disarmament"—in other words, disarmament *prior* to political reconciliation and conflict resolution with Israel's adversaries.[71] The IPFM argues that "Israel's approach to restrictions on fissile-material production, stockpiling, and use is to avoid the issue. Current and foreseeable policy will be to strongly oppose joining an FMCT. This was a clear point of dispute between Israel and the United States even under the Bush Administration when the United States submitted an FMCT proposal to the UN Conference on Disarmament: "Israel has been evasive and contradictory on this issue."[72] From a different perspective, Israel's position on the FMCT is cagey rather than contradictory. In August 1998, just after the Indian and Pakistani nuclear tests, the "otherwise friendly Clinton administration exerted the harshest pressure the United States had used against Israel for decades" in trying to bring Israel into the FMCT fold. The government of Prime Minister Benjamin Netanyahu opted to join the CD consensus on launching FMCT negotiations—Israel had been the last holdout—but to continue to oppose an actual treaty. In a letter to President Clinton, Netanyahu wrote: "We will never sign the treaty, and do not delude yourselves—we will not sign the treaty because we will not commit suicide."[73] Israel gambled that the FMCT process would stagnate without its opposition, and that it would be better off avoiding the international opprobrium that would come with being the sole opponent of the CD consensus. Twelve years later, with Pakistan now alone in stalling movement on the FMCT, that bet is seemingly paying off.

The idea of a MENWFZ poses the most challenging dilemmas for Israeli nuclear policy. In 1995, the NPT review conference (RevCon) passed a resolution calling for the "establishment of 'an effectively verifiable Middle East zone free of weapons of mass destruction, nuclear, chemical and biological, and their delivery systems.'"[74] The May 2010 RevCon wrestled with the question of how to move the 1995 resolution forward, with the Non-Aligned Movement (NAM) bloc ultimately inducing the United States to endorse a proposal to convene a 2012 meeting of all the Middle East states to discuss a MENWFZ.[75] The RevCon's Final Document includes the proposal, and the planned 2012 conference is to be cosponsored by Britain, Russia, the United States, and the United Nations secretary-general.[76]

The possibility of such a meeting offers Israel both perils and opportunities. On the one hand, Israel would be substantially outnumbered by its Arab rivals and Iran and thus be put on the defensive for much of the conference. Moreover, if Israel agrees to attend the gathering but does not make a positive contribution, its adversaries will have won a public diplomacy victory and will have isolated Israel even further outside the arms-control and disarmament mainstream. On the other hand, a 2012 MENWFZ parley would force countries that do not recognize Israel, such as Iran, Saudi Arabia, and Syria, to convene with it in a formal setting, thereby lending Israel de facto recognition. Also, given the long and voluminous IAEA paper trail on Iran's nuclear deceptions, Israeli diplomats would be able to shine a bright light on Tehran's efforts to acquire nuclear-weapon capabilities.

Those who think that an MENWFZ conference would inevitably impose a net cost on Israel tend to forget that it was Israeli leaders who devised the MENWFZ formula in the first place. Given the increasing global nonproliferation activism following India's 1974 nuclear test, the Israeli government realized that it was no longer sufficient simply to declare that "Israel will not be the first nation to introduce nuclear weapons to the Middle East." Instead, as Cohen states: "Israel had to propose its own non-proliferation vision as an alternative to the NPT. It had to be a positive vision of disarmament but, at the same time, a vision that would not impose tangible restrictions on Israel's nuclear capability [. . .]. It had to be a disarmament vision that imposed no prohibitions whatsoever on Israel unless some substantial political requirements regarding Arab belligerency and recognition of Israel were met."[77] This is the genesis of the fundamental connection between disarmament and regional conflict resolution that has been a staple of Israeli diplomacy for the past thirty-five years. Israel has consistently and explicitly maintained that the evolution of a stable security order in the Middle East must be an iterative process, beginning with confidence-building measures, continuing with formal political reconciliation between Israel and all of its rivals, and ending with an MENWFZ.[78]

The main material driver of Israel's nuclear policy is its struggle for security and even survival in a dangerous region. In 1948, the new state of Israel was immediately attacked by a coalition of its Arab neighbors. Over the next six decades, Israel has fought five more wars and engaged in numerous military conflicts against a variety of enemies, including several Arab states, an enduring Palestinian independence movement, and terrorist groups such as Hezbollah and Hamas, which are supported in their operations by Iran and other anti-Israeli benefactors. Today, Israeli leaders feel most menaced by Iran, whose quest for nuclear-weapon capabilities poses, they argue, "an enormous threat to the stability of the Middle East [. . .]. The possibility that terrorists would enjoy an Iranian nuclear umbrella or that they would actually receive nuclear weapons from the Iranian regime is a very real threat." Israel's perception is that "Iran's hostile policies and statements, its aggressive pursuit of missile technology, and its active involvement in support of terrorism gravely exacerbate the situation in our region. Israel, in particular, has consistently been the target of Iran's vicious anti-Semitic campaign, notably statements made by Iran's president calling for the destruction of Israel."[79] Israel's nuclear weapons represent for its leaders the ultimate insurance policy, an option of last resort to prevent their country from being defeated militarily or—at worst—put out of existence.[80]

Continuity in Israel's nuclear policies also stems from two interlinked ideational drivers. The first is the abiding national memory of the Holocaust, in which six million European Jews were systematically murdered at the hands of the Nazis. Nuclear weapons are the one and only capability that gives practical sustenance to Israelis' vow "never again" to leave themselves defenseless and vulnerable to extinction. The second driver is the strongly held conviction that nuclear weapons have, in fact, served their ultimate purpose for Israel: that a population of seven million people living in a resource-poor territory smaller than Belize, surrounded by Arab states hostile to—or only grudgingly accepting of—their sovereign identity, has managed to survive, even thrive, into the twenty-first century. Egypt and Jordan have made peace with Israel. The broader Arab world seems, in the main, to have abandoned its project to "push Israel into the sea." Israel and the Palestinians have come tantalizingly close to achieving a two-state solution to their conflict, most recently at Camp David in 2000. In sum, even Israel's bitterest Arab adversaries have reconciled themselves to the reality that Israel exists and is here to stay; Israeli strategic elites firmly believe this is attributable in great part to their possession of nuclear weapons.[81] Only Iran is left as an enemy that is implacably opposed to Israel's survival, and the Iranian pursuit of its own nuclear-weapon capabilities and MRBMs lends material weight, and thus credence, to Tehran's repeated threats to "wipe Israel off the map."[82]

FUTURE DISARMAMENT POLICY AND DIPLOMACY: PROSPECTS AND RECOMMENDATIONS

Recent history provides little grounds for optimism that India, Israel, or Pakistan will, over the next decade, assume a purposeful, proactive role in advancing the new disarmament agenda. All three governments consider their extant nuclear postures to be models of restraint, given their national security predicaments. Furthermore, they all view nuclear ambiguity as a strategic benefit and remain deeply skeptical of the value of transparency. Their responses to President Obama's Prague initiative indicate that Indian, Israeli, and Pakistani strategic elites are more concerned with protecting and advancing long-standing, deeply rooted policies than with positioning their states to be leaders of a global disarmament push. When it comes to the post-Prague nuclear agenda, the nuclear holdouts are presently playing defense rather than offense. Continuity, rather than change, is the order of the day.

The central fact of India's geopolitical situation is that China is booming. Its economy is rapidly growing, its global presence and aspirations are expanding, its military forces are modernizing and extending their reach, and an international consensus is forming that China is now the top contender for world power with the United States. Although both India and China claim to support the evolution of a multipolar world order, the structural successor to the U.S. "unipolar moment" could instead turn out to be a new form of bipolarity, with Washington and Beijing competing for influence atop the international power hierarchy.[83] In this context, India's desire for strategic parity with China portends ongoing improvements in its nuclear-weapon capabilities, both quantitative and qualitative. While Indian analysts continue to debate the requirements of "minimum credible nuclear deterrence," technological momentum within the defense-scientific establishment, newly liberated by the India-U.S. civilian nuclear cooperation agreement from significant constraints on its freedom of action, is likely to propel New Delhi toward a strategic triad with substantially more redundancy and diversity than outside observers would "objectively" deem necessary. This suggests that India will continue to keep its nuclear-testing (and thus weapons-modernization) options open, as well as quietly appreciate Pakistan's efforts to block movement in the CD on fissile-material limitations. Furthermore, if discussions ever commence on fissile-material stockpiles, rather than the more limited capping proposals that have been tabled in Geneva, New Delhi will press hard for a "nondiscriminatory" treaty—one that will establish rough parity between the Indian and Chinese fissile-material stockpiles.

Two factors might partially inhibit such a growth trajectory for Indian nuclear forces. First, India-U.S. civilian nuclear cooperation, as well as similar arrangements with other potential nuclear suppliers such as Japan, will give Indian decision makers strong incentives to resist further nuclear testing, which could jeopardize ongoing technology-transfer and supply relationships.[84] Second, there exists in Indian civil society today a modest but vocal "ban-the-bomb" movement that skillfully plays on the country's Gandhian roots to pressure the government toward disarmament.[85] Nevertheless, as one analyst argues, "Only 12 years have passed since [the] 1998 nuclear tests, which were greeted with much euphoria inside of the country by all but a small fraction of people. The tests were hailed not just as providing a mighty addition to the Indian military arsenal, but also as symbols of technological maturity, national pride, and international prominence. With so much invested in nuclearization, it clearly will take some time before the Indian public and polity can be persuaded to reverse these notions."[86]

As for Pakistan, its ever-elusive quest for strategic parity with India makes its independent engagement with a universal nuclear disarmament process highly unlikely. Islamabad's policies are likely to track with New Delhi's, but there is a strong and growing sense among Pakistani security analysts that time is not on their side as the Indian economy takes off into sustained growth and New Delhi equips itself to "rise above the region." Pakistan will undoubtedly continue to adhere to its repeatedly expressed position that embracing disarmament-related measures like the CTBT and fissile-material limitations will be impossible without "a stable balance of conventional forces to ensure strategic stability between Pakistan and India." From Islamabad's perspective, New Delhi's "massive induction of sophisticated weaponry including combat aircraft, aircraft carriers, airborne early-warning and control systems, missile defense, nuclear submarines and warships will accentuate conventional asymmetries and compel greater reliance on nuclear and missile deterrence. [. . .] Pakistan always demands and deserves parity with our neighbor."[87]

The principle of parity espoused by India and Pakistan regarding China and India, respectively, poses a broader, more generic challenge to the phased-reductions process envisioned in many of the mainstream disarmament proposals now circulating internationally.[88] The working assumption driving these approaches is that once the erstwhile superpowers, Russia and the United States, have reduced their nuclear-weapon stockpiles to somewhere around a thousand warheads, other NWSS like China, India, and Pakistan can then join the negotiations.[89] But if each of these countries, in succession, insists on the principle of parity as the price of its joining the process, progress toward disarmament is likely to be slow, because a fundamental irrationality underlies this principle. A country's minimum nuclear-deterrence and conventional force requirements should logically correlate with its interests, obligations, and potential adversaries. For the United States, with its extended-deterrence commitments, these are truly global. For Russia and China, they are more limited, but still expansive. For India, they narrow to China and Pakistan, and for Pakistan, they reduce to India. Yet the logic of parity embodied in both the Indian and Pakistani postures on disarmament suggests that there should be rough strategic equality across all of these countries, which is unrealistic and impractical. Why should Islamabad expect parity with New Delhi when India has a significantly broader threat profile than Pakistan? And why should New Delhi expect parity with Beijing, when China's interests, obligations, and potential adversaries exceed India's? Theoretically, at least, the whole point of "minimum nuclear deterrence" is that it is *not* necessary to maintain parity with one's enemy, because even a small, survivable nuclear arsenal is sufficient to deter either nuclear or conventional attacks. New Delhi and Islamabad seem to be "conventionalizing" nuclear weapons, which points not to denuclearization but to growth in nuclear capabilities.

Even if somehow the parity issue were addressed to Islamabad's satisfaction, Pakistan would have a hard time embracing nuclear disarmament measures in the absence of conflict resolution in Kashmir. Pakistan's discontent over Indian administration of the lion's share of Muslim-majority Jammu and Kashmir was a primary cause of the conventional Indo-Pakistani wars of 1947–48 and 1965, the subconventional Kargil conflict in 1999, and major India-Pakistan crises in 1990 and 2001–2. Pakistan's very raison d'être is on the line in Kashmir: New Delhi's control of the state's Muslim heartland is a continuing repudiation of the two-nation theory and thus the entire basis for the creation of Pakistan in the first place.[90] Islamabad's motivation for maintaining assured second-strike nuclear-weapon capabilities is deeply rooted in the dispute over Kashmir, where today yet another phase of anti-Indian political agitation is morphing into widespread violence with substantial escalatory potential.[91] Resolution of the conflict on terms acceptable to Pakistan is at the top of a long list of measures that Islamabad will require before it seriously considers eliminating its nuclear weapons. Other items on the list include a negotiated conventional-forces balance and a "system of security assurances, including perhaps a 'non-aggression pact'" with India[92]—all of which seem very distant prospects in 2011. Moreover, there is little anti-nuclear activism in Pakistan to dilute the pro-nuclear sentiment.

Similar circumstances prevail for Israel. With a growing threat from Iran, an Arab-Israeli peace process that is far from fruition, a Hamas-controlled Gaza, and Hezbollah entrenched in Lebanon, Israel's existential condition seems perilous to many of its citizens. One scholar writes that "the Israeli mind is tortured with questions about the country's very survival. On the surface, there is civic normalcy, but below the surface there is a certain anxiety that Israel's condition in the world is far from 'normal.' This insecurity regarding the long-term survival of the Zionist project is revealed in the way that Israelis (and non-Israeli Jews) discuss ad nauseam questions like 'Will Israel survive?' and 'Is Israel finished?'"[93] As an American commentator notes, "Israelis have never known an hour of real peace."[94] In this context, the Israeli government finds it difficult to take seriously President Obama's argument that the process of universal nuclear disarmament will strengthen nonproliferation efforts. Israel will keep its distance from the disarmament agenda. For any movement to be undertaken at all, "specific security threats and political/territorial conflicts will have to be resolved before Israel will consider surrendering its nuclear weapons."[95] A process of disarmament "clearly cannot begin in situations where some of the parties concerned still maintain a state of war with each other, refuse in principle to maintain peaceful relations with Israel, and even call for its destruction."[96] Dire external compulsions, combined with the total absence of any domestic constituency for disarmament, mean that Israel will keep its nuclear weapons well into the future.

CONCLUSION

Given that the holdouts' nuclear policies and diplomacy are closely linked to several of the world's most complex and persistent political-military conflicts, their sincere embrace of nuclear disarmament measures is likely to be dependent on the resolution of those conflicts. As evidenced by its extremely ambitious diplomatic agenda, the Obama administration understands that "progress toward the elimination of nuclear arsenals must proceed in a co-evolutionary process with improvements in political-security relations." The president "posits the need for all states that now possess nuclear weapons or rely on extended nuclear deterrence to take the steps necessary to obviate their perceived need for these weapons. This is an inherently multilateral and regional challenge to reduce threats, redress insecurities, and build political confidence."[97] In turn, much of the impetus for these conflict-resolution efforts will have to come from within the Indian, Israeli, and Pakistani political establishments, as well as from the various governments that are also parties to the Arab-Israeli dispute, the regional competition between Iran and Israel, the Indo-Pakistani rivalry over Kashmir, and the India-China territorial dispute. Although other states, international organizations, NGOs, and individual disarmament activists can and should encourage these efforts, the requisite political will and openness to compromise can emanate only from the polities most directly involved in these regional cold wars.

Notes

1. Natasha Barnes, Tanya Ogilvie-White, and Rodrigo Alvarez Valdes, "The NPT Holdouts: Universality as an Elusive Goal," *Nonproliferation Review* 17, no. 1 (March 2010): 95–113.

2. Immediate deterrence is "highly episodic, associated with crisis and confrontation;" in general deterrence, the "potential attack is more distant and less defined, even hypothetical." Patrick M. Morgan, *Deterrence Now* (Cambridge: Cambridge University Press, 2003), 80–81.

3. International Panel on Fissile Materials (IPFM), "Reducing and Eliminating Nuclear Weapons: Country Perspectives on the Challenges to Nuclear Disarmament," June 18, 2010, 7, http://www.fissilematerials.org/ipfm/site_down/gfmr09cv.pdf.

4. For an extensive treatment of nuclear opacity and its lineage, see Devin T. Hagerty, *The Consequences of Nuclear Proliferation: Lessons from South Asia* (Cambridge, Mass.: MIT Press, 1998), 39–62.

5. See the discussions of this issue in Manpreet Sethi, "Nuclear Arms Control and India: A Relationship Explored," *Arms Control Today*, September 2010, 13–20; and Claudia Baumgart and Harald Müller, "A Nuclear Weapons-Free Zone in the Middle East: A Pie in the Sky?" *Washington Quarterly* 28, no. 1 (Winter 2004–5): 45–58.

6. "Remarks by President Barack Obama," Prague, Czech Republic, Office of the Press Secretary, White House, April 5, 2009, http://www.whitehouse.gov/the-press-office/remarks-president-barack-obama-prague-delivered.

7. International Panel on Fissile Materials (IPFM), "Global Fissile Material Report 2009: A Path to Nuclear Disarmament," October 29, 2009, 16, http://www.fissilematerials.org/ipfm/site_down/gfmr09.pdf.

8. IPFM, "Global Fissile Material Report 2009," 9; Federation of American Scientists (FAS), "Status of World Nuclear Forces 2010," http://www.fas.org/programs/ssp/nukes/nuclearweapons/nukestatus.html.

9. Rajesh Basrur, "Indian Perspectives on the Global Elimination of Nuclear Weapons," in *Unblocking the Road to Zero*, vol. 2: *India and China*, ed. Barry Blechman (Washington, D.C.: Henry L. Stimson Center, March 2009), 11.

10. Vipin Narang, "Conventional Balances and Nuclear Strategy: The Sources of Nuclear Postures in India and Pakistan," paper prepared for the Annual Meeting of the American Political Science Association, Washington, D.C., September 3, 2010, 9.

11. Basrur, "Indian Perspectives," 6.

12. George Perkovich, *India's Nuclear Bomb: The Impact on Global Proliferation* (Berkeley: University of California Press, 1999), 293–95.

13. Jaswant Singh, "Against Nuclear Apartheid," *Foreign Affairs* 77, no. 5 (September/October 1998): 41–52.

14. National Security Advisory Board on Indian Nuclear Doctrine, "India's Draft Nuclear Doctrine," *Arms Control Today*, August 17, 1999, http://www.armscontrol.org/act/1999_07-08/ffja99. This policy statement was approved in 2003.

15. "India's Statement in the CD Plenary," Conference on Disarmament, United Nations Office at Geneva, August 17, 2010, http://unog.ch/80256EE600585943/(httpPages)/2D415EE45C5FAE07C12571800055232B?OpenDocument; "A Working Paper by India on Nuclear Disarmament," United Nations General Assembly, October 6, 2006, http://www.reachingcriticalwill.org/political/1com/1com06/docs/indiapaper.pdf.

16. "Statement by Prime Minister Manmohan Singh at Nuclear Security Summit, Washington, D.C.," *Hindu*, April 13, 2010, http://www.thehindu.com/news/resources/article396372.ece.

17. IPFM, "Global Fissile Material Report 2009," 13–14, 16.

18. Ibid., 9; FAS, "Status of World Nuclear Forces 2010."

19. Feroz Hassan Khan, "Pakistan's Perspective on the Global Elimination of Nuclear Weapons," in *Unblocking the Road to Zero*, vol. 3: *Pakistan and Israel*, ed. by Barry Blechman (Washington, D.C.: Henry L. Stimson Center, April 2009), 17–18.

20. Feroz Hassan Khan and Peter R. Lavoy, "Pakistan: The Dilemma of Nuclear Deterrence," in *The Long Shadow: Nuclear Weapons and Security in 21st Century Asia*, ed. Muthiah Alagappa (Stanford, Calif.: Stanford University Press, 2008), 230.

21. Robert S. Norris and Hans Kristensen, "Nuclear Notebook: Pakistani Nuclear Forces, 2009," *Bulletin of the Atomic Scientists*, September/October 2009, 85.

22. Vipin Narang, "Posturing for Peace? Pakistan's Nuclear Postures and South Asian Stability," *International Security* 34, no. 3 (Winter 2009/10): 65–67.

23. "Statement by Ambassador Zamir Akram, Permanent Representative of Pakistan at the Conference on Disarmament (CD)," United Nations Office at Geneva, February 18, 2010, http://www.reachingcriticalwill.org/political/cd/2010/statements/part1/18Feb_Pakistan.pdf.

24. Khan and Lavoy, "Pakistan," 226.

25. P. Cotta-Ramusino and M. Martellini, "Nuclear Safety, Nuclear Stability and Nuclear Strategy in Pakistan: A Concise Report of a Visit by Landau Network—Centro Volta," Pugwash Online Conferences on Science and World Affairs, Como, Italy, January 14, 2002, http://www.pugwash.org/september11/pakistan-nuclear.htm.

26. Ibid.

27. IPFM, "Reducing and Eliminating Nuclear Weapons," 67.

28. Ibid.

29. "NRDC Nuclear Notebook: Israeli Nuclear Forces, 2002," *Bulletin of the Atomic Scientists*, September/October 2002, 73–75.

30. IPFM, "Global Fissile Material Report 2009," 13–14, 16.

31. Ibid., 9; FAS, "Status of World Nuclear Forces 2010."

32. Avner Cohen, *The Worst-Kept Secret: Israel's Bargain with the Bomb* (New York: Columbia University Press, 2010), 82.

33. Ibid., 81–84; Shlomo Brom, "Israeli Perspectives on the Global Elimination of Nuclear Weapons," in Blechman, *Unblocking the Road*, 3:46.

34. "NRDC Nuclear Notebook," 74; "Israel Profile: Missile Overview," Nuclear Threat Initiative, updated November 2008, http://www.nti.org/e_research/profiles/Israel/Missile/index.html.

35. For example, during the 1990–91 Gulf War, when speculation was rife that Iraqi leader Saddam Hussein might launch chemical weapons against Israel, Israeli prime minister Yitzhak Shamir said: "all those who threaten us should know that whoever dares strike Israel will be struck hard and in the most severe way; Israel has a very strong deterrent capability." "Israel Profile: Nuclear Overview," Nuclear Threat Initiative, updated August 2010, http://www.nti.org/e_research/profiles/Israel/Nuclear/index.html.

36. Also in 1991, "then-Israeli Deputy Chief of Staff Ehud Barak told King Hussein of Jordan to pass the following message to Saddam Hussein [. . .]: 'If one single chemical warhead falls on Israel, we'll hit Iraq with everything we have got [. . .] look at your watch and forty minutes later an Iraqi city will be reduced to ashes.'" Bruce Riedel, "If Israel Attacks," *National Interest*, no. 109 (September/October 2010): 8.

37. Avner Cohen, "Toward a New Middle East: Rethinking the Nuclear Question,"

DACS Working Paper, Defense and Arms Control Studies Program, Massachusetts Institute of Technology, 1994, 9.

38. Avner Cohen, *Israel and the Bomb* (New York: Columbia University Press, 1998), 10.

39. The *Atlantic*'s May 2008 cover says it all: "Is Israel Finished?" In the lead story, "Unforgiven," Jeffrey Goldberg writes: "Iran poses the most ruthless threat to Israel's existence—no other member of the United Nations has so insistently, and in such baroque terms, threatened the destruction of another member state," http://www.theatlantic.com/magazine/archive/2008/05/unforgiven/6776/2/.

40. Cohen, *Worst-Kept Secret*, 220.

41. For a longer discussion, see Devin T. Hagerty, "Iran: The Nuclear Quandary," in Alagappa, *Long Shadow*, 306–13.

42. Devin T. Hagerty, "Virtual Nuclear Deterrence and the Opaque Proliferants," in *Nuclear Weapons in a Transformed World: The Challenge of Virtual Nuclear Arsenals*, ed. Michael J. Mazarr (New York: St. Martin's Press, 1997), 249.

43. "Remarks by Ambassador Hamid Ali Rao of India," "First Committee: Thematic Discussion on Nuclear Weapons," United Nations General Assembly, New York, October 15, 2009, http://www.reachingcriticalwill.org/political/1com/1com09/statements/15Oct_India.pdf.

44. "Statement by Ambassador Hamid Ali Rao, Permanent Representative of India, to the Conference on Disarmament, Geneva, at the General Debate of the First Committee of the 64th Session of the United Nations General Assembly," New York, October 8, 2009, http://www.reachingcriticalwill.org/political/1com/1com09/statements/8Oct_India.pdf.

45. "Statement by H.E. Mr. Hamid Ali Rao, Ambassador Extraordinary and Plenipotentiary Permanent Representative of India, to the Conference on Disarmament, Geneva, at the 2009 Session of the United Nations Disarmament Commission," New York, April 15, 2009, http://www.reachingcriticalwill.org/political/dc/statements09/15April_India.pdf.

46. "Statement by Ambassador Hamid Ali Rao, Permanent Representative of India to the Conference on Disarmament," CD Plenary, United Nations Office at Geneva, August 17, 2010, http://www.reachingcriticalwill.org/political/cd/2010/statements/part3/17August_India.pdf.

47. Mark Hibbs, "Moving Forward on the U.S.-India Nuclear Deal," *Q&A*, Carnegie Endowment for International Peace, Washington, D.C., April 5, 2010, http://carnegieendowment.org/publications/index.cfm?fa=view&id=40491.

48. Ibid.

49. Ironically, the latest chapter in this saga may significantly disadvantage American firms hoping to crack the lucrative Indian nuclear market. India's Parliament has

passed a law that "exposes firms supplying equipment to nuclear plants to liability" in case of accidents. Amol Sharma and Paul Glader, "Indian Nuclear Law Blocks U.S. Firms," *Wall Street Journal*, September 9, 2010. Indian memories of the massive 1984 Union Carbide toxic gas leak in Bhopal, history's worst industrial disaster, have made the liability issue especially controversial. As matters stand, Russian and French nuclear vendors will enjoy distinct advantages over American vendors, because they are state-controlled enterprises whose operations and liability protection are underwritten by their governments.

50. Hibbs, "Moving Forward." For another informative discussion of the linkages between India's civilian and military nuclear programs, see Ramamurti Rajaraman, "India's Nuclear Arms Control Quandary," *Bulletin of the Atomic Scientists*, March/April 2010, 27–36.

51. Singh, "Against Nuclear Apartheid," 41.

52. "India Reiterates Voluntary Moratorium on N-Testing," Indo-Asian News Service, Thaindian News, February 6, 2010, http://www.thaindian.com/newsportal/uncategorized/india-reiterates-voluntary-moratorium-on-n-testing_100315968.html.

53. George Perkovich, "The Obama Nuclear Agenda One Year after Prague," *Policy Outlook*, Carnegie Endowment for International Peace," Washington, D.C., March 31, 2010, 7, http://carnegieendowment.org/publications/index.cfm?fa=view&id=40458.

54. The BRICs are Brazil, Russia, India, and China. The acronym is generally attributed to Goldman Sachs analysts; see Dominic Wilson and Roopa Purushothaman, "Dreaming with BRICs: The Path to 2050." Goldman Sachs Global Economics Paper no. 99, October 2003, http://www2.goldmansachs.com/ideas/brics/book/99-dreaming.pdf.

55. The details are recounted in Strobe Talbott, *Engaging India: Diplomacy, Democracy, and the Bomb* (Washington, D.C.: Brookings Institution Press, 2004). Talbott recalls on pp. 3–4 that "we met fourteen times at ten locations in seven countries on three continents."

56. The total area of territory that is disputed between India and China exceeds the size of Greece.

57. Minhaz Merchant, "Rising above the Region," *Times of India*, April 7, 2010, http://articles.timesofindia.indiatimes.com/2010-04-07/edit-page/28124358_1_china-and-india-account-prime-minister-border-issue.

58. Singh, "Against Nuclear Apartheid," 43.

59. "Statement by Ambassador Zamir Akram, Permanent Representative of Pakistan to the United Nations, Geneva, in the First Committee," 64th United Nations General Assembly, New York, October 12, 2009, http://www.reachingcriticalwill.org/political/1com/1com09/statements/12October_Pakistan.pdf.

60. "Statement by Ambassador Zamir Akram, Permanent Representative of Paki-

stan to the UN and Other International Organizations, at the Conference on Disarmament," United Nations Office at Geneva, August 31, 2010, http://www.reachingcriticalwill.org/political/cd/2010/statements/part3/31_august_Pakistan.pdf.

61. Zia Mian and A. H. Nayyar, "Playing the Nuclear Game: Pakistan and the Fissile Material Cutoff Treaty," *Arms Control Today*, April 2010, http://www.armscontrol.org/act/2010_04/Mian.

62. Sharon Squassoni, "Looking Back: The U.S.-Indian Deal and Its Impact," *Arms Control Today*, July/August 2010, 51.

63. "Statement by Zamir Akram, Conference on Disarmament," August 31, 2010.

64. U.S. officials point out that years of "onward proliferation" via the A. Q. Khan network put Pakistan in a fundamentally different category than India, which Washington deems a "responsible" NWS. For details on the A. Q. Khan network's activities, see "Nuclear Black Markets: Pakistan, A. Q. Khan and the Rise of Proliferation Networks," *IISS Strategic Dossier* (London: International Institute for Strategic Studies, 2007). For Pakistan's arrangements with China, see Praveen Swami, "Pakistan's Nuclear Arms Push Angers America," *Daily Telegraph* (London), October 10, 2010, http://www.telegraph.co.uk/news/worldnews/asia/pakistan/8053775/Pakistans-nuclear-arms-push-angers-America.html. Beijing claims that the deal predates China's accession to the NSG and therefore requires no NSG approval.

65. Sachin Parashar, "To Thwart Sino-Pak N-Deal, India Lobbies for NSG Help," *Times of India* (Mumbai), August 27, 2010, http://timesofindia.indiatimes.com/india/To-thwart-Sino-Pak-N-deal-India-lobbies-for-NSG-help/articleshow/6440678.cms.

66. Squassoni, "Looking Back," 51; Moeed Yusuf and Ashley Pandya, "The Quest for Nuclear Disarmament in South Asia: A Reality Check," *Peace Brief*, United States Institute of Peace, Washington, D.C., August 6, 2010, 3, http://www.usip.org/resources/the-quest-nuclear-disarmament-in-south-asia-reality-check.

67. "Statement by Ambassador Zamir Akram in the First Committee Thematic Debate on Nuclear Weapons," United Nations General Assembly, New York, October 15, 2009.

68. This argument originally appeared in Devin T. Hagerty, "U.S. Policy and the Kashmir Dispute: Prospects for Resolution," *India Review* 2, no. 3 (July 2003): 89–116.

69. My analysis is based on numerous interviews and conversations with Pakistani politicians, diplomats, military officers, and strategic analysts in various locations for nearly twenty years. For more detail on the crises, see Sumit Ganguly and Devin T. Hagerty, *Fearful Symmetry: India-Pakistan Crises in the Shadow of Nuclear Weapons* (Seattle: University of Washington Press, 2005).

70. "Statement by Ms. Radica Radian-Gordon, Director, Arms Control Department, Ministry of Foreign Affairs, Israel, First Committee," 64th United Nations General Assembly, New York, October 12, 2009.

71. IPFM, "Reducing and Eliminating Nuclear Weapons," 42.
72. Ibid.
73. Cohen, *Worst-Kept Secret*, 232–33.
74. Alison Kelly, "NPT: Back on Track," *Arms Control Today*, July/August 2010, 23.
75. Mark Hibbs, "Reaching Consensus at the IAEA," Q&A, Carnegie Endowment for International Peace, Washington, D.C., September 13, 2010. According to Hibbs, Washington feared that "the NPT could collapse if two consecutive review conferences failed to reach a consensus conclusion."
76. Deepti Choubey, "Future Prospects for the NPT," *Arms Control Today*, July/August 2010, http://www.armscontrol.org/act/2010_07-08/choubey.
77. Cohen, *Worst-Kept Secret*, 41.
78. For a comprehensive and forceful presentation of Israeli policy in this regard, see the "Statement by Mr. Eytan Bentsur on Israel's Approach to Regional Security, Arms Control, and Disarmament," Conference on Disarmament, United Nations Office at Geneva, September 4, 1997.
79. "Statement by Radica Radian-Gordon."
80. For a speculative but well-informed discussion of possible Israeli "red-lines"—eventualities that might provoke Israel's use of nuclear weapons, see Cohen, *Worst-Kept Secret*, 77–81.
81. Ibid., 49–50.
82. Farnaz Fassihi, "Day of Anti-Israel Protest Reveals Iran's Internal Rift," *Wall Street Journal*, September 4, 2010, http://online.wsj.com/article/SB10001424052748704855104575470020696330864.html.
83. Tony Halpin, "Brazil, Russia, India, and China Form Bloc to Challenge U.S. Dominance," *Times Online* (London), June 17, 2009, http://www.timesonline.co.uk/tol/news/world/us_and_americas/article6514737.ece.
84. For an analysis of competing positions on the CTBT within India, see A. Vinod Kumar, "India and the CTBT: The Debate in New Delhi," *Bulletin of the Atomic Scientists*, November 4, 2009, http://thebulletin.org/web-edition/features/india-and-the-ctbt-the-debate-new-delhi.
85. Praful Bidwai and Achin Vanaik, *New Nukes: India, Pakistan and Global Nuclear Disarmament* (New York: Interlink Books, 2000).
86. Rajaraman, "India's Nuclear Arms Control Quandary," 35.
87. "Statement by Ambassador Masood Khan, Permanent Representative of Pakistan to the Conference on Disarmament, Geneva, at the General Debate of the First Committee, October 5, 2005," United Nations General Assembly, New York, http://www.pakun.org/statements/First_Committee/2005/10052005-01.pdf.
88. See, for example, Gareth Evans and Yoriko Kawaguchi, cochairs, *Eliminating Nuclear Threats: A Practical Agenda for Global Policymakers*, Report of the International

Commission on Nuclear Non-Proliferation and Disarmament (Canberra and Tokyo, 2009), http://www.icnnd.org/reference/reports/ent/indes.html.

89. For example, see Ivo Daalder and Jan Lodal, "The Logic of Zero: Toward a World without Nuclear Weapons," *Foreign Affairs* 87, no. 6 (November/December 2008): 80–95.

90. Hagerty, *Consequences of Nuclear Proliferation*, 67.

91. Somini Sengupta, "Kashmir Is Locked Down, but Bloodshed Continues," *New York Times*, September 14, 2010, http://www.nytimes.com/2010/09/15/world/asia/15srinagar.html?_r=1&scp=5&sq=kashmir&st=cse.

92. IPFM, "Reducing and Eliminating Nuclear Weapons," 70.

93. Cohen, *Worst-Kept Secret*, xx.

94. George F. Will, "Skip the Lecture on Israel's 'Risks for Peace,'" *Washington Post*, August 19, 2010, http://www.washingtonpost.com/wp-dyn/content/article/2010/08/18/AR2010081804691.html.

95. IPFM, "Reducing and Eliminating Nuclear Weapons," 37.

96. "The Establishment of a NWFZ in the Middle East: Explanation of Vote," First Committee of the United Nations General Assembly, New York, November 1, 2007, http://www.reachingcriticalwill.org/political/1com/1com07/EOV/L1israel.pdf.

97. George Perkovich, "The Obama Nuclear Agenda One Year after Prague," Carnegie Policy Outlook, March 31, 2010, 4.

CHAPTER EIGHT

The Defiant States
North Korea and Iran

Tanya Ogilvie-White

THIS CHAPTER EXPLORES THE possible impact of new disarmament momentum on the nuclear diplomacy of North Korea (also known as the Democratic People's Republic of Korea [DPRK]) and Iran. Both states regularly engage in nuclear defiance: openly refusing to comply with International Atomic Energy Agency (IAEA) Board of Governors and United Nations (UN) Security Council resolutions passed in response to their safeguards violations; and failing to negotiate in good faith in nonproliferation and disarmament negotiations, whether they take place within the UN purview (multilateral negotiations) or via ad hoc arrangements (bilateral or plurilateral talks). This belligerent approach to nuclear diplomacy, which is distinct from the quieter nuclear activities of Myanmar and Syria, is notable because it represents a loud and sustained rejection of international law and of expectations of appropriate behavior and thus results in an escalation of international tensions. It goes beyond nuclear noncompliance—which can be detected or undetected, intentional or unintentional, major or minor—and moves into the realm of deliberate, overt, repeated abuse of international law and norms. The core issue this chapter addresses is this: Can international disarmament impetus foster conditions that are likely to encourage North Korea and Iran to "dial down" their defiance and engage in more cooperative behavior, such as allowing greater transparency, engaging in constructive negotiations, and consistently following through on disarmament and nonproliferation commitments? Or is it just as likely, or possibly even more likely, to contribute—directly or indirectly—to conditions that result in escalation?

NORTH KOREA

The roots of North Korea's nuclear endeavors stretch back to the 1960s, when, having failed to persuade Mao Tse-tung to share China's nuclear secrets, North Korea quietly set about developing an indigenous nuclear capability, initially with Soviet assistance. The nuclear defiance that is characteristic of today began soon after Pyongyang's plutonium production facilities (three gas-cooled, graphite-moderated, natural uranium-fueled reactors; two at Yongbyon and one at Taechon) were detected by U.S. satellites in the late 1980s.[1] Pyongyang had come under increasing international pressure to allow thorough IAEA inspection of its nuclear program. Kim Il-sung (founder of North Korea and its "Great Leader" until his death in 1994) appeared to acquiesce in 1985, signing the Nuclear Nonproliferation Treaty (NPT). But North Korean reprocessing of spent fuel in 1989 and its refusal in following years to allow IAEA access to hidden waste facilities provided strong indications that Pyongyang's nuclear ambitions remained intact.[2] So began a pattern of nuclear defiance that continues to this day, with North Korea making and breaking commitments, playing cat and mouse with the IAEA and international negotiators, periodically appearing to climb down, and all the while pursuing an independent nuclear deterrent.[3]

North Korea's nuclear capabilities are shrouded in secrecy, but the information collected and released by national intelligence agencies and international verification organizations helps us piece together some of the details. According to published sources, there are two programs: a plutonium program at Yongbyon consisting of a five-megawatt reactor and a reprocessing plant, which is directed by Kim Jong-il (North Korea's "Supreme Leader" since the death of his father, Kim Il-sung, in 1994) and involves about three thousand scientists and research personnel (many of them trained in China, Russia, and Pakistan); and a more secretive uranium enrichment program, the details of which have been scarce but are beginning to emerge in open sources.[4] Data on two underground nuclear tests (conducted in North Korea's Hamgyong Province in October 2006 and May 2009) has been analyzed by the Comprehensive Test Ban Treaty Organization (CTBTO) and by numerous individual states and research institutions, which have concluded that North Korea has a crude nuclear weapons capability.[5] Significantly, Pyongyang is known to have a relatively sophisticated missile program, which would provide it with delivery vehicles. Its No-dong missiles, which are believed to have a range of 1,000–1,300 kilometers with a 700–1,000 kilogram payload, are capable of striking population centers throughout the Korean peninsula and Japan.[6] North Korea is also known to be working on longer-range systems, but U.S. experts believe that it is yet to develop a nuclear warhead that could be delivered by a missile.[7]

The current round of North Korea's defiant nuclear diplomacy began in October 2002, when the Bush administration confronted Pyongyang with intelligence relating to its secret uranium enrichment program.[8] This triggered a period of sustained nuclear belligerence: in December 2002, North Korea expelled inspectors and announced that it was restarting its five-megawatt nuclear reactor that had been shut down under the Agreed Framework;[9] in January 2003, it withdrew from the NPT; in October 2003, DPRK officials announced that the plutonium contained in eight thousand spent fuel rods from the five-megawatt reactor had been extracted (about thirty kilograms of separated plutonium, which is enough for eight to ten nuclear weapons);[10] in February 2005 it publicly declared for the first time that it had fabricated nuclear weapons; in October 2006 it conducted its first nuclear weapons test; and in 2009 it engaged in a long succession of escalatory behavior in clear violation of UN Security Council resolutions. The most defiant actions, including missile tests, the second nuclear test on May 25, 2009, and subsequent announcement that "it has become an absolutely impossible option for the DPRK to even think about giving up its nuclear weapons" were particularly disturbing, as they followed five years of painstaking negotiations via the Six-Party Talks, and a controversial decision by the Bush administration to remove North Korea from its list of state sponsors of terrorism.[11] Moreover, these actions followed a period of optimism that a policy of engagement by the Obama administration would reap rewards for the nonproliferation regime. But to the dismay of the nonproliferation community, the situation escalated further in 2010, with the sinking of a South Korean warship in March (widely believed to have been sunk by a North Korean torpedo) and the North Korean shelling of civilian-occupied Yeonpyeong Island in November—two of the most serious incidents to occur on the peninsula since the end of the Korean War in 1953.[12]

This series of confrontational activities has led to head scratching among North Korea analysts, many of whom have looked to domestic events in Pyongyang to explain the escalation. One of the most popular explanations is that Kim Jong-il's ill health and an impending power transition have contributed to the increased defiance; that the nuclear issue is being used by the leadership to shore up domestic support while Kim's third son is being prepared for the dynastic succession.[13] Others have speculated that to shore up military support for the succession, Kim Jong-il has yielded to their demands for a more aggressive nuclear posture.[14] Although no reliable information is available to confirm whether rival factions do indeed exist in North Korea, others suspect that the escalation is the result of a more general jostling among the elite, as individuals and their associated institutions attempt to outdo each other by demonstrating their hard-line credentials and thus their suitability to assume key positions in a post-Kim regime.[15]

The succession issue may well have affected the timing of recent events, but statements issued by North Korea's Foreign Ministry, which negotiators claim are the most reliable source for gauging Pyongyang's intentions, suggest that important internal and external drivers are at work, and that the escalatory series of nuclear and missile activities that took place in the first half of 2009 were long in the planning. For example, a statement released in February 2005, referred to a U.S. plot "to topple the political system in the DPRK at any cost," compelling Pyongyang "to bolster its nuclear arsenal in order to protect the ideology, system, freedom and democracy chosen by its people."[16] The statement went on to declare that "we [. . .] have manufactured nukes for self-defense to cope with the Bush administration's evermore undisguised policy to isolate and stifle the DPRK." More recent statements identify not just the United States and its allies (especially Japan) as threats to North Korea's survival, but also the other negotiating partners from the Six-Party Talks, the members of the Security Council, and even New Zealand, which participated in naval exercises off the coast of South Korea in April 2009.[17] There are also indications that Pyongyang's leaders feel as threatened by the Obama administration as they did by its predecessor: a signed commentary in *Rodong Sinmun*, the official newspaper of the Central Committee of the Workers' Party of Korea, declared that "the present U.S. administration is talking about what it calls a 'change' and 'bilateral dialogue,' but it is, in actuality, pursuing the same reckless policies followed by the former Bush administration to stifle the DPRK by force of arms."[18]

Similarly inflammatory rhetoric followed the sinking of the *Cheonan* in March 2010.[19] In response to the Obama administration's immediate declaration of solidarity with Seoul after the incident and its reaffirmation of the U.S.-South Korea alliance, Pyongyang's Foreign Ministry accused the United States of "trying to perpetrate a military provocation at any moment" and of "meddling in inter-Korean affairs in the name of the UN," and then it warned of its intention to "bolster (the North's) nuclear deterrent in a newly developed way to cope with the U.S. persistent hostile policy."[20] Exactly what form this bolstering would take was left unclear in the statement, but at the time experts speculated that a third nuclear test or further long-range missile tests were being planned. A Foreign Ministry memo, which was published on April 20, 2010, may offer some clues. The memo stated that North Korea will "manufacture nukes as much as it deems necessary," but at the same time "make consistent efforts for the denuclearization of the world including the Korean peninsula."[21] Similarly defiant statements followed North Korea's bombardment of Yeonpyeong Island on November 23, 2010. After the incident, Pyongyang called for better relations with South Korea, but in the same breath it warned that war with the South would lead to a "nuclear holocaust," and that its military was ready for "prompt, merciless and annihilatory action" against North Korea's enemies.[22]

North Korea's defiant behavior has serious consequences for the nuclear nonproliferation regime and for global security. The diplomatic consequences (the divisive and corrosive impact of belligerent statements and speeches) are significant, but in many ways they are secondary to the "unseen" consequences. Chief among these are North Korea's weapons proliferation activities, which are banned under a series of UN Security Council resolutions.[23] The fact that North Korea's trade in conventional weapons is ongoing was proved by the interception of four illicit shipments in the six months after UN Security Council resolution 1874 (2009) was adopted, including cargoes destined for Iran and Syria. Details of these shipments are provided in a May 2010 report by a UN Panel of Experts, which also noted that although no interceptions of shipments of weapons of mass destruction (WMD) or ballistic missile components have been officially reported to the UN Security Council since the adoption of resolutions 1718 (2006) and 1874 (2009), intelligence and IAEA reports suggest North Korea's proliferation activities have continued.[24] These include supplying missiles, components, and technology to certain countries including Iran and Syria and using overseas criminal networks to transport and distribute smuggled cargoes, which "may include weapons of mass destruction-sensitive goods and arms and related materiel smuggling."[25] This language reflects widely held concerns that North Korea is continuing to engage in clandestine WMD proliferation despite international efforts to stop it. Such concerns are valid because Pyongyang is known to have contributed to the illegal nuclear trade in the past (possibly assisting Syria in the construction of a clandestine plutonium reactor, which was destroyed in an Israeli strike in September 2007) and has adopted a variety of measures to overcome international efforts to constrain its illicit trade networks.[26] Moreover, although confirmation that no interceptions of North

Korean WMD and ballistic missile shipments have been reported to the Security Council could signal that sanctions are working, it is also possible that national governments that have information implicating North Korea in proliferation activities have been unwilling to divulge it.

IRAN

Iran's nuclear ambitions date back to the days of the Shah Mohammad Reza Pahlavi, who, having embarked on an ambitious nuclear energy program with U.S. assistance, set up a clandestine research organization to explore the design and manufacture of nuclear weapons. Although the work of this group was disbanded by Ayatollah Ruhollah Khomeini in 1979, some small-scale nuclear research activities (including secret centrifuge experiments) were launched in the midst of the Iran-Iraq War, with technology acquired from Pakistan. However, experts assess that little progress was made during this period.[27] A more serious nuclear revival began after Khomeini's death in June 1989, when, under the leadership of President Ali Akbar Hashemi Rafsanjani and supreme leader Sayyid Ali Khamenei, Iran's overt civilian nuclear program and undeclared nuclear activities expanded. For years, the clandestine program developed out of sight of IAEA inspectors, who inspected Iran's declared facilities but were unaware of the parallel program. This all changed in 2002, when an Iranian-dissident group—using Israeli intelligence—accused Tehran of building a secret enrichment plant at Natanz and a heavy-water production facility at Arak, exposing more than fifteen years of illicit nuclear development.[28] Nearly a decade later, despite mounting international pressure and condemnation, including numerous IAEA Board of Governors reports, statements, and resolutions, five UN Security Council resolutions, and years of diplomatic negotiations by the E-3 (France, Germany, and the United Kingdom) and subsequently the E-3+3 (the above plus China, Russia, and the United States, also known as the P5+1), Iran's enrichment activities continue. As of January 2011, Iran has installed close to nine thousand centrifuges, and if it took the decision to enrich uranium beyond 20 percent, it could be from one to three years away from a breakout capability at either the Natanz facility or a clandestine gas centrifuge facility.[29] Although the most recent estimates tend toward the conservative end of this time scale, concerns about Iran's nuclear program have not diminished, especially as it has not been possible to discount some of the reports of the program's alleged military dimensions. As Mark Fitzpatrick explains, intelligence information pointing to weaponization activities—ranging from design work for ballistic missile re-entry vehicles, with requirements highly suggestive of nuclear implosive devices, to design work for underground tests—has been troubling the IAEA and the nonproliferation community for some time.[30]

Iran vehemently denies that it is pursuing a nuclear weapons capability, despite years of defiant actions that led the former IAEA director general, Mohammed ElBaradei, to admit—after seven years of careful diplomacy and circumspection—that Iran "would like to have the technology to enable it to have nuclear weapons."[31] Its leaders and officials insist that the nuclear facilities uncovered in 2002 are part of an ongoing civilian program and deny any wrongdoing, claiming that Iran's legitimate activities were driven underground by a hostile international environment and a Western conspiracy of technology denial.[32] But these claims of peaceful intentions are becoming less convincing with the passage of time, as Iran continues to flout international demands to suspend enrichment; denies IAEA access to key facilities, documentation, and scientists; and engages in diplomatic maneuverings involving continuous obfuscations and even blatant lies. Iran's response to the June 2009 IAEA report on its activities provides the perfect example of this behavior: while the report flagged numerous serious concerns over Tehran's defiance of UN Security Council resolutions, Iranian officials announced that the report had given Tehran a "clean bill of health on the peaceful use of nuclear energy"; provided "no evidence of... prohibited activities"; and confirmed that the IAEA has been able to "continue its verification activities without any obstacle."[33] Ambassador Soltanieh went on to declare the UN Security Council resolutions "unjust and with no legal basis"—a claim Iran bases on an "inalienable right [to] utilizing nuclear energy for peaceful purposes, including [the] nuclear fuel cycle, specifically enrichment."[34] Ali Akbar Velayati, Supreme Leader Ayatollah Ali Khamenei's top adviser on international affairs, re-emphasized this position in his response to a Group of Eight (G8) announcement that Iran must either accept negotiations over its nuclear ambitions or face tougher sanctions, stating that Iran "will not retreat even one step from its peaceful nuclear activity."[35]

The lack of institutional transparency and a culture of political ambiguity in Iran make it difficult for outsiders to understand the nuclear decision-making process and to gauge the extent to which this could have changed in recent years. Most accounts suggest Ayatollah Ali Khamenei continues to be the ultimate arbiter of foreign policy and has repeatedly sided against tactical compromises suggested by Iranian negotiators. The Supreme Leader's intrinsic distrust of the United States was deepened by Bush's "Axis of Evil" speech in 2002 and again after Iran's election crisis of June 2009, which he reportedly is convinced was engineered by the U.S. and UK governments.[36] This is backed up by Khamenei's marginalization and expulsion of the reformists who had advocated a more moderate approach to nuclear diplomacy.[37] Whether this has translated into a concrete decision to actively pursue weaponization is unclear. In his public statements, Khamenei argues that Islam forbids the development of weapons of mass destruction and claims to have issued a *fatwa* (a religious decree) against it.[38] He rejects the strident nuclear advocacy of Ahmadinejad's spiritual mentor, Ayatollah Mohammad Taqi Mesbah Yazdi, who argued in a 2005 book that Iran must develop a credible deterrent "in order to be able to stand up to its enemies."[39] But as Erich Follath and Holger Stark ominously revealed in their 2010 analysis of Iran's nuclear intentions, according to Shiite faith "when faced with an existential threat, the Shiite can avail himself of the *takiya*, or sanctioned lying to serve the greater good."[40] Thus one possibility (admittedly speculative and highly controversial) that should at least be considered is that Khamenei has used—or could in the future use—the *takiya* principle to give the green light to Iran's Atomic Energy Organization to develop nuclear weapons, while at the same time making misleading declarations of peaceful nuclear intentions.

This idea of sanctioned lying provides an interesting perspective on the "dual-track nuclear policy" that the head of Iran's Atomic Energy Organization, Ali Akbar Salehi, announced in June 2010.[41] Salehi claims that Iran's strategy is "to have dialogue based on honesty as a first step and, as a second, to push ahead with our nuclear program in order to confront the pressure from enemies." As part of the first track, Iran's statements on the nuclear issue are becoming more assertive: Iran has announced that it plans to build up to ten enrichment facilities, which it claims are for peaceful purposes; enrich uranium to 20 percent (or, in fact, "to any percent it wishes," as per "Iran's legal right"—a threat it appears to have subsequently followed through); and set strict conditions for future nuclear negotiations, which will "discipline [international negotiators] so [they] will come and sit down to talks like a good kid."[42] If the talks fail and Iran's rights to indigenous enrichment are denied, Salehi has declared that Iran will retaliate by using "the Iranian people's fist to smash [international negotiators'] sticks."[43]

The second track of Iran's nuclear policy that Salehi referred to has also been in evidence in recent years, according to information made available by Western intelligence agencies to IAEA safeguards inspectors and security analysts. If this information is to be believed, Iran's leaders are combining defiant nuclear diplomacy with quiet, clandestine nuclear activities, the goal of which may be to produce a uranium implosion device.[44] Iran's development of a second enrichment facility at Fordow (near Qom), which had been tracked by Western satellite intelligence from 2006 and publicly exposed in September 2009, may be part of this second track: a determined effort to hide a parallel nuclear program, which has been at least partially successful despite advances in IAEA and national monitoring and verification activities and despite increased international intelligence sharing.[45] According to U.S. officials and the assessments of some nonproliferation scholars, there is compelling evidence that this secret facility, known as the Fordow Fuel Enrichment Plant (FFEP), is part of a military program: it is too small for civilian purposes, but as Nima Gerami and James Acton point out, it is "not too small to provide meaningful amounts of highly enriched uranium (HEU) for a nuclear weapons program"—probably enough for one weapon—worth of HEU per year, depending on the type and performance of the installed centrifuges.[46] This has inevitably led analysts, and, in fact, IAEA officials, to ask what additional secret facilities Iran might be hiding.[47] Unease has been compounded by Iran's announcement that it plans to build ten enrichment plants besides Natanz and by its refusal to identify where the new facilities will be located, despite new IAEA safeguards rules that require advance notification of nuclear facilities as soon as they are planned.[48]

EXPLAINING THE NUCLEAR DEFIANCE OF NORTH KOREA AND IRAN

Any hope that a new era of U.S. disarmament leadership would encourage North Korea and Iran to cooperate with the nuclear nonproliferation regime must be rapidly diminishing, if indeed it ever existed.[49] But that does not necessarily mean recent efforts by the Obama administration to assert moral authority on nuclear issues are having little or no effect on reining in Pyongyang and Tehran. A key foreign policy goal of the current U.S. administration, of which disarmament leadership is an important part, is to motivate states to tighten the net around states that flout their nonproliferation obligations.[50] This tightening of the net requires a major consensus-building effort between developed and developing states, as the United States in particular tries to sell its vision of a safer, more secure world, underpinned by internationally shared norms and values to all states—including China, Russia, and members of the Non-Aligned

Movement (NAM), which in the past have often been slow to criticize regime violators. A consequence of this policy is that it may further isolate and alienate North Korea and Iran, as more states demonstrate their support for the U.S. agenda by openly criticizing defiant behavior, supporting and implementing tougher sanctions against regime violators, and joining U.S.-led interdiction efforts to contain proliferation threats. Rather than convincing the defiant states of the error of their ways, U.S.-led efforts to consolidate the nuclear nonproliferation regime could have the opposite effect, leading to more desperate acts of defiance as North Korea and Iran attempt to justify and legitimize their rejection of Western-led international society to foreign and domestic audiences.

This battle for legitimacy offers a very specific explanation for nuclear defiance—one that combines domestic and systemic causes, and that focuses on constructivist notions of identity, alienation, and competing values to explain behavior. To try to understand the belligerent nuclear diplomacy of North Korea and Iran, we need to explore why they feel threatened by Western-led international society. The nuclear defiance of both states appears to be motivated on one level by a combination of the poor state of their diplomatic relations with their neighbors and with the United States—and especially by fear of U.S. conventional military superiority and nuclear intentions. North Korea, for example, justifies its nuclear defiance in response to U.S.-South Korea joint military exercises;[51] Iran increases its defiance in response to U.S. statements on its national security strategy and nuclear posture. But strategic motivations for nuclear defiance are only part of the picture—defiant behavior often appears irrational and self-destructive unless the deeper political and ideational sources of threat perceptions and vulnerability are taken into account. In the case of North Korea and Iran, both states' threat perceptions are dramatically increased by the incompatibility of their domestic structures and sources of authority with the norms that shape the institutions of global governance. Such norms are strongly promoted by Western states, many of which are driving the transition from pluralist to solidarist international society (i.e., from an international society where national sovereignty remains sacrosanct to one that is increasingly dominated by international organizations that judge, constrain, and impose standards and obligations on member states and that impose penalties for noncompliance).[52] This transition is deeply threatening and alienating to states that do not share the socially ambitious global vision on which it is based, which helps explain their defiance of its rules and obligations and their fear of states that are the most powerful engines of systemic change.

In the case of North Korea, its nuclear defiance can be understood in the context of the country's history and its national ideology of self-reliance, referred to as *Juche* ideology—a unique version of Marxism-Leninism. This national ideology was first proclaimed in 1955 by Kim Il-sung, who, after failing to conquer the south in the Korean War of 1950–53, developed the concept of *Juche* as a check against excessive Soviet or Chinese influence.[53] Over the years, the ideology has been adapted to achieve the North Korean leadership's contemporary domestic and foreign policy goals: to consolidate and legitimize the leadership, achieve economic self-sufficiency, deter external threats, and promote national unity through a strong national identity. With the collapse of the Soviet Union and declining influence of communism, *Juche* gradually morphed under Kim Jong-il from an ideology that identifies external influence as its main adversary to one that defines itself in opposition to international society more generally and specifically against what it sees as imperialist, capitalist, Western- and U.S.-dominated international society.[54] Kim Jong-il also emphasized an ideology based on a "military first" (*Songun*) principle. Buoyed by these ideologies, North Korea remains a secretive, highly centralized, authoritarian, and rigidly stratified political hierarchy. It is also extremely isolated: in terms of physical interaction with the outside world, information is tightly controlled, freedom of expression and movement are severely restricted, and societal contacts are minimal. On a normative level, North Korea's lack of integration into international society goes even deeper, as the Kim regime is considered one of the most repressive in existence—described as a "vast gulag" with a "repellent elite" capable of "extreme brutality."[55]

The tensions that exist between *Juche* ideology and the norms that underpin international society help account for North Korea's nuclear defiance. The sociocultural systems and legitimacy of North Korea, a state on the periphery of a more socially ambitious international society, are constantly under attack from international opinion and are under pressure to change. Recently, this pressure has even begun to emanate from China, which had previously been careful to distance itself from the more strident U.S. and Western criticisms of the brutal Kim regime.[56] The leadership's nuclear belligerence represents the ultimate rejection of this pressure, not just from the United States but from international society more generally. As that pressure grows stronger, as may well happen if the Obama administration achieves its goal of building greater consensus in the nuclear nonproliferation regime, the consequences may be that North Korea increases its nuclear defiance, conducting further nuclear and missile tests in order to demonstrate its independence from foreign influence and its rejection of international norms. Indeed, North Korea's response to the Security Council's unanimous decision to pass Resolution 1874 on June 12, 2009, which imposed security and economic sanctions, including a trade and arms embargo, may be a sign of things to come. Condemning the resolution as a "vile product of the U.S.-led offensive international pressure aimed at undermining the DPRK's ideology," Pyongyang declared a three-point plan: first, it would weaponize its newly extracted plutonium; second, it would commence uranium enrichment; and third, it would regard any attempt at a blockade as "an act of war."[57] This statement sheds an interesting light both on the series of escalatory events that subsequently occurred on the Korean peninsula in 2010 and on the November 2010 revelations about North Korea's uranium enrichment activities at Yongbyon.

As in the case of North Korea, it is difficult to acquire accurate information regarding Iran's nuclear intentions and motivations, but a variety of internal and external, material, and ideational forces appear to be in play. Iran's regional and global ambitions appear to be one important driver, and its leaders have long looked to scientific advancement, including mastering the nuclear fuel cycle, as one way to secure regional dominance and to achieve the international status and prestige that they regard as Iran's natural right.[58] These ambitions are mingled with insecurity and perceptions of regime vulnerability that have systemic and domestic roots: fear of U.S. and Israeli strategic dominance, including their nuclear capabilities and intentions; growing concerns over regional isolation; and an acute awareness that the ideas, values, and systems on which Iran's theocracy is based face strong ideological opposition from groups within Iran and from outside.[59] Iran's nuclear defiance could be viewed as a strategy for countering these threats, a way of attracting allies who share the same insecurities and of bolstering the theocrats' legitimacy by rallying domestic support for Iran's nuclear achievements.[60] This domestic motivation helps explain the spike in Iran's nuclear defiance following the disputed elections of June 2009, which led to a sustained period of domestic repression combined with an intractable, hard-line Iranian response to international proposals aimed at defusing nuclear tensions.[61]

In common with North Korea, many of Iran's insecurities stem from its unique theocratic system, which lacks international—and, increasingly, domestic—legitimacy.[62] This has led Tehran's clerical and political leaders to use the nuclear issue to compensate for that weakness. But unlike North Korea, which has pushed nuclear defiance to the heights of belligerence and isolated itself still further, Iran's skilled diplomats have had some success in exploiting ambiguities and inconsistencies in the nuclear nonproliferation regime and in appealing to states that (in varying degrees) share its reservations over the transition from pluralist to solidarist international society.[63] In particular, its nuclear negotiators have elicited sympathy from some NAM members, who are keen to ensure that the obligations associated with NPT and IAEA membership do not increase while the benefits become more difficult to obtain.[64] Aware of the opportunities that this provides for strengthening its diplomatic hand, Tehran's leaders have accused the United States of undermining the nuclear nonproliferation regime by engaging in "gross violations of Article IV obligations [...] depriving states parties from exercising their inalienable right," and by pursuing a "hidden agenda [...] to turn [the IAEA] into a 'UN Watchdog' with maximum intrusiveness," thus "jeopardizing the spirit of cooperation the Agency needs more than ever."[65]

Iran's nuclear negotiators are keen to ensure that the Obama administration's efforts to resume moral authority on nuclear issues do not heal divisions within the nuclear nonproliferation regime, thus reducing its opportunities to exploit them. Having spent many years attempting to justify and legitimize Iran's nuclear defiance by focusing on the "unbalanced, discriminatory, and double-standard approach" of the United States in implementing the NPT,[66] Tehran's leaders and diplomats were quick to pour cold water on Obama's disarmament leadership. "U.S. officials have recently pledged to change their approach toward nuclear weapons and have expressed their intention to move towards nuclear disarmament," Iran's deputy foreign minister, Mohammad Ali Hosseini, stated at the May 2009 PrepCom in New York, but "given the facts of the past 40 years, the international community has noticed that such pledges have never been materialized."[67] A few weeks later, these comments were echoed at the IAEA Board of Governors meeting in Vienna, where the Iranian delegation stated that "we are witnessing that there is no change in [U.S.] policies and action [...] therefore all peace loving people have to reconsider their views about dealing with such a country."[68]

It will be interesting to observe Iran's diplomatic maneuverings going forward, to see whether Iran continues to try to undermine the Obama administration's disarmament agenda, as its leaders scramble to retain the support of key NAM partners, try to perpetuate differences among the nuclear weapon states (NWS) on the implementation of sanctions and the use of force, and attempt to rally domestic opinion around the regime.[69] Developments in 2010, which some analysts predicted would be a watershed year for nonproliferation and disarmament, gave us a flavor of what can be expected. For example, Ahmadinejad denounced the April 2010 Nuclear Security Summit, which was hosted in Washington, D.C., as an event run by "stupid, retarded people who brandish their swords whenever they face shortcomings."[70] He then invited representatives from sixty countries to attend a parallel conference in Tehran, which a foreign ministry spokesman hailed as an Iranian responsibility, by virtue of its position as "a standard-bearer of nuclear disarmament."[71] At the meeting, a speech by Khamenei, read by one of his closest advisers, reiterated the Supreme Leader's position that nuclear weapons are prohibited under Islam (although, perhaps significantly, this time he only referred to their *use*—not their development or possession—as illegal); then he branded the United States an "atomic criminal" and called for its suspension from the IAEA.[72] Iranian defiance continued the following month at the 2010 NPT Review Conference, when in his opening speech, Ahmadinejad claimed that the "United States has never respected its [disarmament] commitments" and warned member states not to trust U.S. leadership on nuclear disarmament or on other "phony matters" such as the threat of nuclear terrorism.[73] Iran's diplomatic strategy at the meeting (which ultimately failed due to a lack of NAM support, leaving Iran sidelined and isolated) was to undermine the Obama administration's disarmament agenda by blocking adoption of a final document.[74] After the close of the meeting, Khamenei claimed the Final Document as a diplomatic victory for Iran (even though Iran was pulled into line by Egypt), insisting that the text calling on Israel to end its NPT holdout status demonstrated that "the Islamic Republic has been able to affect global public opinion in a way that not only peoples, but also different governments of the world stand up to the U.S. and adopt positions against it."[75] This diplomatic one-upmanship continued in the months following the Review Conference, as Iran's negotiators claimed to be abiding by their nonproliferation obligations and to be open to negotiations in good faith, at the same time as engaging in brazen acts of nuclear defiance.[76]

DEALING WITH NUCLEAR DEFIANCE

The argument that a new era of U.S. disarmament leadership could provoke North Korea and Iran to continue to escalate nuclear defiance prompts important questions over how the international community—and the United States, in particular—should respond. If, as has been argued, North Korea and Iran have been engaging in nuclear defiance to counter their declining legitimacy and increasing isolation, it follows that certain forms of domestic political and international societal change could result in greater cooperation. The remainder of this chapter explores the opportunities for external actors to directly or indirectly foster these changes and the implications of this for U.S. disarmament and nonproliferation diplomacy, for reviving the Six-Party Talks, and for renewed negotiations with Iran. It also identifies alternative strategies for dealing with the defiant regimes without legitimizing their systems of government, which may not integrate North Korea and Iran more effectively into international society but offer crucial, more immediate means for limiting the proliferation dangers associated with nuclear defiance.

One way of dealing with the nuclear defiance of North Korea and Iran would be to attempt to transform the norms and values that underpin international society so that they become more compatible with—or at least less hostile to—the ideologies that shape the regimes in Pyongyang and Tehran. This strategy would necessitate a shift back to a more pluralist type of international society that places renewed emphasis on the principles of sovereign sanctity and nonintervention, and that subjects the domestic sphere to less international scrutiny and criticism. Some scholars and practitioners would support this retreat from international solidarism,[77] particularly in the context of the serious abuses of the Bush administration, which, some have asserted, used the pursuit of solidarist international society as a cover to justify the pursuit of a self-interested foreign policy agenda.[78]

But how would a return to international pluralism shape nonproliferation policy under the Obama administration, and what would the implications be for the nuclear nonproliferation regime? *Caution, careful engagement*, and *compromise* would be the watchwords in all cases: a move away from past "disciplinarian" approaches for dealing with North Korea and Iran; an effort to soften international criticism of the regimes in question, especially on internal, domestic issues; an end to assertions that "all options are on the table" to deal with noncompliance (i.e., if not taking force off the table, at least not talking about it); and strenuous efforts to reassure Pyongyang and Tehran that hidden and overt agendas based on a desire for regime change no longer exist.[79] This would require a shift by the United States and other negotiating parties toward China's approach, which, in the case of Pyongyang, has been underpinned by a desire to prevent regime collapse, and by a desire to limit U.S. and Western dominance of international society. In terms of the mechanisms of the nonproliferation regime itself, such an approach might also include a deliberate rolling back of the nonproliferation obligations that have been growing in recent years, such as less pressure on states to bring the Additional Protocol into force; the abandonment of controversial multilateral fuel bank proposals; and a general reduction in nuclear transparency.

The above approach would help prevent North Korea and Iran from becoming more alienated and might serve the purpose of preventing further escalation. But a shift back to a pluralist approach would be regressive—a step back to the moral relativism of the past, at a time when international society is becoming more socially ambitious and the nonproliferation regime more comprehensive. A second approach would be to retain the commitment to solidarism but attempt to bring about significant change in the regimes so that they are able to integrate into international society. There are a number of ways this could be achieved, but most fall into one of the following categories: a) regime overthrow by external force or b) regime change via peaceful political, economic, and societal integration. Given ongoing and well-publicized practical problems associated with forced regime change in Afghanistan and Iraq (and the many ethical questions surrounding the Iraq invasion in particular), it is not necessary to labor the pitfalls of the first strategy here.[80] A peaceful strategy is more feasible: at the domestic level, supporting opposition movements and promoting people-to-people contacts in the hope that this will foster bottom-up regime change; and at the international level, keeping channels of diplomatic communication open in the hope that, over time, political elites will become less resistant to international norms.[81]

What are the implications of this approach for nonproliferation policy? Unfortunately, it is likely that any evidence of external interference in the fragile domestic affairs of North Korea or Iran would scupper negotiations and lead to a serious escalation of tensions. Some proponents of the regime-change approach may not consider this a negative development, given that the negotiating positions of Pyongyang and Tehran are more entrenched than ever and appear unlikely to shift significantly over the longer term, even when there are temporary lulls in defiance and when negotiations seem to offer hope of concessions.[82] Iran, for example, has made it very clear that it will not accept the P5+1 deal that has been on the negotiating table since 2006, and it is just as unlikely to accept a new deal that involves genuine and significant restrictions on its nuclear program.[83] And while Pyongyang may agree to revive the Six-Party

Talks process in return for concessions (and is, in fact, urging a revival at the time of this writing), its past actions suggest that it is unlikely to follow through on any new commitments to the extent that its nuclear capabilities are permanently compromised.[84] Renewed negotiation efforts may appear futile and wasteful in this context, but on the other hand, relying on—even assisting—current domestic political instability in Pyongyang and Tehran in the hope that it will lead to new, more cooperative regimes seems unwise. Furthermore, the risk that Iran could follow in North Korea's footsteps, ending cooperation with the IAEA and even withdrawing from the NPT (a major setback for the treaty and the nonproliferation regime in general) is too serious to ignore.

A more appropriate strategy for dealing with the defiant states would combine elements of the two approaches outlined above: the retention of the most useful aspects of a pluralist nonproliferation and disarmament agenda, without the need for regressive steps away from solidarism. Given the potential for the actions of the defiant states to further undermine the nonproliferation regime, efforts to keep diplomatic channels open are essential, even if the negotiating process is only an end in itself (i.e., preventing total alienation) rather than a means to an end (i.e., leading to agreements that ensure irreversible disarmament and full transparency and compliance). In terms of U.S. nonproliferation policy, utilizing the political leverage provided by China, Russia, and other non-Western states may be the best option in this case—states that continue to value elements of pluralist international society despite edging ever closer to solidarism, and that are perceived by the defiant states to be more attuned to their priorities and insecurities than the United States or its allies.[85] Making use of the political leverage that these states could provide would also help to overcome perceptions, strongly exacerbated during the Bush administration, that the United States and a few of its Western allies have been using the goals of solidarist international society to camouflage the self-interested pursuit of their own foreign and security policy objectives in the Middle East and Asia.

The urgent need to deal with the nuclear defiance of North Korea and Iran means that short- to medium-term strategies are essential too.[86] Attempting to reduce or prevent nuclear defiance by relying on the long-term strategies outlined above is fraught with obstacles, pitfalls, and uncertainties: they need to be combined with additional measures that limit the impact of repeated and determined nuclear defiance. Acutely conscious of this problem, Israel's hardline government, led by Prime Minister Benjamin Netanyahu, has been secretly making preparations for targeted military strikes on Iran's nuclear facilities in the hope that they can set the program back by several years.[87] But experts caution that this strategy—which Israel has used in 1981 against Iraq and in 2007 against Syria—would be an unwise choice where Iran is concerned, partly because there would be no guarantee that Iran's key facilities would be struck and their nuclear components eliminated.[88] Furthermore, the military strike option would be extremely destabilizing for the region, even though some official sources, including leaked U.S. embassy cables, report that many of Iran's neighbors fear a nuclear Iran more than they fear Israel, and Saudi Arabia's King Abdullah has allegedly urged the United States to take military action "to put an end to [Iran's] nuclear weapons program."[89] However, given the ragbag of gossip found in leaked U.S. diplomatic cables, it is probably advisable to take the latter with a grain of salt.

The reality is that there are no dependable short-term options for dealing with nuclear defiance: the least bad option is to energetically pursue nonmilitary sanctions, coordinated containment, and interdiction efforts. Even these run the risk of isolating Pyongyang and Tehran still further and, in addition, perpetuate the disciplinary approach to nonproliferation diplomacy that has riled both regimes and fed their defiant behavior.[90] But the alternative—to turn a blind eye to noncompliance—would destroy the nonproliferation regime, dramatically increase nuclear dangers (including the risk of nuclear terrorism), and put an end to any hope of a nuclear-weapon-free world. The Obama administration is aware of this dilemma and the challenges involved in the disciplinary approach, as intelligence assessments indicate that the practical impact of existing sanctions has been patchy. There is evidence, for example, that Iran has been able to bear the strain of trade embargoes and finance restrictions, due to its natural resources, its strategy of developing indigenous production networks, and the practices of entities—particularly in Asia and the Middle East—that are willing to flout sanctions and deal with Iranian banks at premium rates.[91] North Korea has shown it has a similar knack for finding loopholes, creating front companies to help it bypass restrictions, and routing trade through China and other countries that show less enthusiasm for enforcing sanctions.[92] The United States and European Union are attempting to compensate for these failures by imposing tighter, unilateral sanctions to supplement UN efforts, but they are aware that this piecemeal approach is vastly inferior to a unified international response. The success of short- to medium-term strategies is dependent on strengthening resolve to implement sanctions effectively—a situation that is clearly understood by the Obama administration, which has stepped up its diplomatic efforts to close international sanctions loopholes by engaging states that have so far been skeptical of the disciplinary approach.[93]

CONCLUSION

President Obama's rationale for embarking on a new era of disarmament leadership has been criticized for promoting an idealistic and naive belief that it will persuade North Korea and Iran to abandon their nuclear ambitions. But the administration's approach is far from idealistic; an important goal is to heal some of the divisions among NWS and non-nuclear weapon states (NNWS) by demonstrating a more balanced approach to disarmament and nonproliferation. His expectation is not that this will achieve nuclear rollback by Pyongyang or Tehran, but that it will help create conditions for a new consensus to emerge on the need for stronger enforcement of international nonproliferation obligations. As has been argued in this chapter, one of the unintended consequences of this strategy is that, if it succeeds, decision makers in Tehran and Pyongyang may engage in more and more desperate bids to shore up their domestic legitimacy and undermine signs of growing international consensus. But it would be a mistake to interpret this as a sign of failure and use it to justify beating a hasty retreat from the current U.S. approach. In particular, it would be unwise to reward provocative behavior with concessions, as has sometimes occurred in the past. It is far better to focus on building international consensus on the need for effective multilateral sanctions and interdiction, and on the longer-term opportunities to bring about regime change through people-to-people contacts and the diffusion of ideas.

Notes

1. International Institute for Strategic Studies, "North Korea's Nuclear Weapons Programme," in *North Korea's Nuclear Weapons Programme: A Net Assessment* (London: IISS Strategic Dossier, 2004), 32.

2. Hy Sang-Lee, *North Korea: A Strange Socialist Fortress* (New Haven, Conn.: Praeger, 2000), 11.

3. For years, analysts worked on the assumption that Pyongyang was pursuing a symbolic nuclear capability to use as a bargaining chip to extract economic concessions. But events since 2002 suggest that North Korea is pursuing an operational nuclear deterrent, and that it may have been on this track for some time. Tim Cook, "North Ko-

rea's Nuclear Weapons Program to 2015: Three Scenarios," *NBR Special Report*, no. 13 (May 2007), 12–16.

4. In November 2010, the U.S. nonproliferation expert Siegfried Hecker revealed that part of the uranium enrichment program is based at the Yongbyon atomic complex. The following month the U.S. State Department stated that in addition to the Yongbyon facilities, North Korea harbors "at least one other" uranium enrichment site. Peter Crail, "North Korea's Uranium Enrichment Challenge," *Arms Control Association Issue Briefs* 1, no. 36 (November 22, 2010), http://www.armscontrol.org/issuebriefs/DPRKChallenge; "NKorea Has at Least One Other Uranium Enrichment Site: US," AFP, December 14, 2010.

5. Estimates of the yield of the 2009 explosion vary (most suggest it was several kilotons). Experts agree it was significantly bigger than the 2006 test, but it was still much smaller than the first-generation tests conducted by the nuclear weapon states. Vitaly Fedchenko, "North Korea's Nuclear Test Explosion 2009," *SIPRI Fact Sheet*, December 2009, http://books.sipri.org/files/FS/SIPRIFS0912.pdf>; Dennis C. Blair, *Annual Threat Assessment of the US Intelligence Community for the Senate Select Committee on Intelligence*, February 2, 2010, http://isis-online.org/uploads/conferences/documents/2010_NIE.pdf.

6. David Wright and Theodore A. Postol, "A Post-Launch Examination of the Unha-2," *Bulletin of the Atomic Scientists*, June 29, 2009, 3.

7. In October 2010, North Korea displayed a Taepo-Dong X or Musudan missile, which has not been tested, but which is believed to have a range of 1,500–2,400 miles, sufficient to reach the major U.S. military bases at Okinawa and Guam. It is also working on a longer-range missile system, which the U.S. Department of Defense claims will have the potential to reach the U.S. mainland. U.S. Department of Defense, 2010 Ballistic Missile Defense Review (BMDR) Fact Sheet, March 3, 2010, http://www.defense.gov/bmdr/docs/BMDR%20FACT%20SHEET%20March%202010%20_Final_.pdf; Wright and Postol, "Post-Launch Examination," 3.

8. Hui Zhang, "Assessing North Korea's Uranium Enrichment Capabilities," *Bulletin of the Atomic Scientists*, June 18, 2009.

9. The Agreed Framework, signed between the United States and North Korea in October 1994, called on North Korea to freeze the operation and infrastructure development of its nuclear reactors (which were part of its suspected clandestine nuclear weapons program) in return for the provision of two proliferation-resistant nuclear power reactors and fuel oil. The agreement was under strain before North Korea restarted its reactors in 2002, due to delays in U.S. fuel oil shipments, which were held up because of resistance from Congress over funding the deal. Joseph Cirincione and Jon Wolfsthal, "Breach of Contract in Korea," *Carnegie Proliferation Brief* 1, no. 14 (1998), http://www.carnegieendowment.org/publications/index.cfm?fa=view&id=110.

10. In January 2004, a group of U.S. scientists and officials visited the spent-fuel storage site and confirmed that the fuel rods had indeed been reprocessed. Siegfried S. Hecker, Testimony before the Senate Foreign Relations Committee, January 21, 2004; Siegfried S. Hecker, "The Risks of North Korea's Nuclear Restart," *Bulletin of the Atomic Scientists*, May 12, 2009.

11. The Six-Party Talks is a stalled multilateral negotiation process, engaging China, Japan, Russia, South Korea, and the United States in diplomatic efforts to bring about the peaceful disarmament of North Korea. In each round of talks, which began in August 2003 and were suspended in April 2009 after more than five years of stop-start negotiations, Pyongyang sent mixed signals to its negotiating partners. On the one hand, it agreed to implement a series of steps to dismantle its nuclear program, and a number of these were carried out in 2007 and 2008. On the other hand, it used delaying tactics during the dismantlement process, made inflammatory statements about its negotiating partners throughout, and refused to accept key verification demands, raising suspicions that it was not genuinely committed to disarming but was using the talks to buy time for its nuclear and missile programs, acquire aid and concessions, and deepen political divisions among its regional rivals.

12. The *Cheonan* was sunk by torpedo near the western sea border with North Korea on March 26, 2010—an area where North and South Korean navies previously faced off in 1999, 2002, and November 2009. Unlike the previous skirmishes, which were relatively minor, in the case of the *Cheonan*, 46 of the 104 sailors onboard were killed in the incident. The North Korean assault on Yeonpyeong Island occurred on November 23, 2010, in the midst of a military exercise conducted by South Korean forces in the waters near the Northern Limit Line. North Korea blamed the South Korean military exercises for its attack, which killed 2 and injured 16 South Korean marines, and killed 2 and injured at least 3 civilians. More than fifty homes were destroyed in the bombardment. Melissa Hanhain, "Impact of the Cheonan Incident on the Six-Party Talks," *NTI Issue Brief*, May 17, 2010.

13. Scott Snyder, "What's Driving Pyongyang?" Nautilus Institute, *Policy Forum Online*, July 7, 2009, available on East Asia Forum, July 11, 2009, http://www.eastasiaforum.org/2009/07/11/whats-driving-pyongyang/.

14. For example, see the comments of Koh Yu-hwan, professor of North Korean studies at Dongguk University, Seoul, quoted in Blaine Harden, "North Korea Says It Will Start Enriching Uranium," *Washington Post*, June 14, 2009.

15. This is the view of Victor Cha, a North Korea expert at Georgetown University, who served on the George W. Bush National Security Council during Bush's second term. Quoted in Michael Hirsh, "Alone at the Table: Obama Is a Pro-engagement President with Nobody to Engage," *Newsweek*, May 27, 2009.

16. "N Korea's Statement in Full," BBC News, February 10, 2005.

17. "DPRK Foreign Ministry Vehemently Refutes UNSC's 'Presidential Statement,'" KCNA, April 14, 2009; "KCNA Rebukes Japan's Moves to Go Nuclear," KCNA, April 28, 2009; U.S. and SA. Korean War Exercises and Aerial Espionage against DPRK under Fire," KCNA, April 30, 2009; "DPRK Foreign Ministry Spokesman Clarifies Its Stand on UNSC's Increasing Threat," KCNA, May 29, 2009; "DPRK Opposes UN Resolution, Vows to Pursue More Nuclear Weapons," Xinhua, June 13, 2009.

18. Quoted in Park Chan-Kyong, "After Nuclear Blast, N. Korea Fires Missiles," AFP, May 26, 2009.

19. See note 12.

20. "North Korea Says It Must Bolster Nuclear Capability," Associated Press, June 28, 2010; Douglas H. Paal, "Crisis in the Koreas," *Carnegie Endowment Q&A*, June 7, 2010.

21. "Foreign Ministry Issues Memorandum on N-Issue," KCNA, April 21, 2010. Stop-start negotiations and contradictory statements have been a common feature of North Korea's nuclear diplomacy since the Six-Party talks began in August 2003, occasionally taking the edge off North Korea's provocative behavior and offering hope that the peaceful denuclearization of the peninsula is still possible. But that hope faded fast after North Korea quit the talks in April 2009. Despite the North Korean leadership's pledge in May 2010 to "provide favorable conditions for the talks resumption" and subsequent demands for the talks to be revived, many experts now believe North Korea engages in the Six-Party negotiations purely to satisfy its short-term economic and political goals and, if the talks are resumed, will not follow through on disarmament commitments (or will do so only on a temporary, limited basis). "Foreign Ministry Issues Memorandum on N-Issue"; "KCNA Snubs Call for DPRK's Dismantlement of Nukes," KFA Forum, Democratic People's Republic of Korea, February 21, 2010, http://www.korea-dpr.com/forum/?p=461; "North Korea's Kim Committed to Disarmament Talks: KCNA," AFP, May 8, 2010; Jayshree Bajoria, "The Six-Party Talks on North Korea's Nuclear Program," Council on Foreign Relations, July 1, 2009.

22. Foster Klug and Kim Kwang-Tae, "NKorea Warns War Would Bring Nuclear Holocaust," Associated Press, *Jakarta Post*, January 1, 2011, http://www.thejakartapost.com/news/2011/01/01/nkorea-warns-war-would-bring-039nuclear-holocausto39.html.

23. For details and analysis of these activities, see the chapter titled "Onward Proliferation from North Korea," in IISS, *The North Korea Security Challenge: A Net Assessment*, Strategic Dossier (London: IISS, 2011).

24. UNPanel of Experts, "Report to the Security Council from the Panel of Experts Established Pursuant to Resolution 1874 (2009)," May 12, 2010 (distributed November 5, 2010), S/2010/571, 23–27, http://www.un.org/ga/search/view_doc.asp?symbol=S/2010/571.

25. Ibid., 20, paragraph 44.

26. There is some evidence to support the Syrian nuclear connection, but reports al-

leging nuclear cooperation between North Korea and Myanmar are more opaque. Despite this, the UN Panel of Exports report of May 2010 described potential nuclear and ballistic missile trade between North Korea and Myanmar (as well as Iran and Syria) as a cause for concern. Ibid., 3. For information on North Korea–Syria nuclear cooperation, see Gregory L. Schulte, "North Korea and Syria: A Warning in the Desert," *Yale Global Online*, 28 April 2010, http://yaleglobal.yale.edu/print/6305. The uncertainties surrounding alleged nuclear cooperation between North Korea and Myanmar can be found in the secret U.S. embassy cables exposed by WikiLeaks. See "U.S. Embassy Cables: Are Burma and North Korea cooperating on nuclear weapons?" *Guardian* (London), December 9, 2010.

27. See the chapter "Political and Diplomatic History of Iran's Nuclear Programme," in IISS, *Iran's Nuclear, Chemical and Biological Capabilities: A Net Assessment*, Strategic Dossier (London: IISS, 2011), 7.

28. The Israeli intelligence services provided the group with this information but hid this fact due to concerns that if the source of the information were known, it would lead to accusations of unreliable "Zionist propaganda." Erich Follath and Holger Stark, "The Birth of a Bomb: A History of Iran's Nuclear Ambitions," *Spiegel Online*, June 17, 2010, http://www.spiegel.de/international/world/0,1518,druck-701109,00.html.

29. The "if" in this statement is very significant here—reports of an Iranian nuclear breakout capability have concerned scholars and policymakers in the West for some time, but many underestimate the perceived strategic, political, and diplomatic advantages of a latent over a breakout capability. Until recently, the serious technical hurdles that Iran's nuclear program has faced were also underestimated, but most recent breakout assessments take Iran's difficulties into account, and at least one source provides an in-depth exploration of the feasibility of different breakout options. See "Technical Assessment of Iran's Nuclear Programme," in IISS Strategic Dossier, *Iran's Nuclear, Chemical, and Biological Capabilities*, 68–75.

30. IISS, "Technical Assessment," 83–88.

31. In an interview with the BBC ElBaradei stated: "it is my gut feeling that Iran would like to have the technology to enable it to have nuclear weapons[. . . .] They want to send a message to their neighbours, to the rest of the world, don't mess with us." "Iran 'Would Like Nuclear Option,'" BBC News, June 17, 2009, http://news.bbc.co.uk/2/hi/8104388.stm.

32. "Statement by H.E. Dr. M. Javad Zarif, Permanent Representative of the Islamic Republic of Iran before the Security Council," New York, July 31, 2006; author interviews with Mansour Sadeghi (political adviser) and Reza Najafi (counsellor, First Committee) at the permanent mission of Iran to the United Nations, New York, September 5, 2006.

33. "Response of the Delegation of the Islamic Republic of Iran to Remarks Made

by Some Delegates on Implementation of Safeguards Agreement in Iran at the Board of Governors," June 17, 2009.

34. "Statement by H.E. Ambassador Soltanieh, Permanent Representative of the Islamic Republic of Iran at the Board of Governors of the IAEA," June 17, 2009.

35. "G8 Sets Deadline for Nuclear Talks," Reuters, July 8, 2009; "Iran Won't Back Down 'One Step' in Atom Row," Reuters, July 9, 2009.

36. Alex Vatanka, "Policy Disparity among Iran's Hardliners," *Jane's Islamic Affairs Analyst*, March 26, 2010.

37. Karim Sadjadpour, "Containment Policy for a Nuclear Iran?" *Council on Foreign Relations*, June 17, 2010.

38. Vatanka, "Policy Disparity."

39. Ali Akbar Dareini, "Iran Cleric Wants 'Special Weapons' to Deter Enemy," Associated Press, June 14, 2010.

40. Follath and Stark, "Birth of a Bomb," 3.

41. Farhad Pouladi, "Iran to Build 'Powerful' New Nuclear Reactor," AFP, June 16, 2010.

42. In July 2010, Iran announced it has produced around 20 kilograms of 20 percent enriched uranium and is working to produce the fuel plates needed to power Iran's research reactor. "20 Kilos of 20 Pct Enriched Uranium Ready: Iran," AFP, July 11, 2010; "Iran Can Enrich Uranium to 'Any Percent It Wishes': Atomic Chief," Xinhua, June 23, 2010; Pouladi, "Iran to Build Reactor."

43. Pouladi, "Iran to Build Reactor."

44. IISS, "Technical Assessment," 86.

45. James M. Acton, "Iran Violated International Obligation on Qom Facility," *Proliferation Analysis*, September 25, 2009.

46. Nima Gerami and James M. Acton, "What Else Is Iran Hiding?" *Foreign Policy*, September 28, 2009; Paul K. Kerr, "Iran's Nuclear Program: Status," *CRS Report for Congress*, December 29, 2009.

47. IAEA, "Implementation of the NPT Safeguards Agreement and Relevant Provisions of the Security Council Resolutions 1737 (2006), 1747 (2007), 1803 (2008) and 1835 (2008) in the Islamic Republic of Iran," GOV/2009/74, 16 November 2009, 4.

48. IISS, "Technical Assessment," 68.

49. In June 2009, Jon Kyl and Richard Perle claimed: "There is a fashionable notion, that if only we and the Russians reduced our nuclear forces, other nations would reduce their existing arsenals or abandon plans to acquire nuclear weapons altogether. This idea [...] assumes that the nuclear ambitions of Kim Jong Il or Mahmoud Ahmadinejad would be curtailed or abandoned in response to reductions in the American and Russian deterrent forces[....] This is dangerous, wishful thinking." Jon Kyl and Richard Perle, "Our Decaying Nuclear Deterrent," *Wall Street Journal*, June 30, 2009.

50. James Acton, George Perkovich, and Pierre Goldschmidt, "A Response to Jon Kyl and Richard Perle," *Proliferation Analysis*, July 7, 2009.

51. See, for example, North Korea spokesman Ri Tong-il's threat of a "physical response" to U.S. defense secretary Robert Gates's announcement of joint military exercises by the United States and South Korea in July 2010, which involved 8,000 U.S. and South Korean troops, 200 aircraft, and 20 ships, including the nuclear-powered aircraft carrier the USS *George Washington*. Justin McCurry, "North Korea Threatens 'Physical Response' to U.S. Military Exercises," *Guardian* (London), July 23, 2010.

52. The transition from pluralist to solidarist international society can be understood as a gradual shift from minimalist to maximalist international norms and institutions. In a pluralist international society, collective security mechanisms and other formal structures are created to facilitate international cooperation, but state sovereignty remains sacrosanct, and the principle of nonintervention is respected by the vast majority of its members. In contrast, in a solidarist international society, states are expected to conform to standards of behavior that stretch beyond state-to-state relations to include the conduct of domestic affairs. Barry Buzan and Richard Little, "International Systems in World History: Remaking the Study of International Relations," in *Historical Sociology of International Relations*, ed. Stephen Hobden and John M. Hobson (Cambridge: Cambridge University Press, 2001), 210–11; Hedley Bull, *The Anarchical Society: A Study of Order in World Politics*, 2nd ed. (New York: Columbia University Press, 1995); Hedley Bull and Adam Watson, eds., *The Expansion of International Society* (Oxford: Oxford University Press, 1985); and Christian Reus-Smit, "Imagining Society: Constructivism and the English School," *British Journal of Politics and International Relations* 4 (October 2002): 487–509.

53. C. Kenneth Quinones, "Beyond Collapse: Continuity and Change in North Korea," *International Journal of Korean Reunification Studies* 11, no. 2 (2002): 25–62.

54. In his theoretical study of North Korean nuclear intentions, Jacques Hymans also makes the point that the "'hermit kingdom' defines itself in opposition to a whole gamut of others beyond the Korean peninsula—not only the United States, but also Japan, China, the Soviet Union/Russia and everyone else." Whereas he explores the unit-level reasons for this via psychological approaches, I offer an explanation that attempts to capture both the systemic and domestic determinants of nuclear defiance. Jacques E. C. Hymans, "Assessing North Korean Nuclear Intentions and Capacities: A New Approach," *Journal of East Asian Studies* 8, no. 2 (May–August 2008): 262–65.

55. Amnesty International describes some of this brutality, including mass starvation and hunger caused by deliberate restrictions on food distribution; forced labor and torture in prison camps; politically motivated and arbitrary use of detention and executions; and severe restrictions on freedom of expression and movement. Amnesty International, *Amnesty International Report 2010: State of the World's Human Rights*, http://thereport.amnesty.org/sites/default/files/AIR2010_AZ_EN.pdf#page=145.

56. The Chinese Foreign Ministry has issued statements strongly condemning North Korea's nuclear tests and has supported UN Security Council sanctions (although it has not implemented these consistently and continues to provide economic support to the regime). The Chinese media have also begun to criticize Pyongyang openly for its nuclear activities. Chinese Ministry of Foreign Affairs, "Statement of Chinese Ministry of Foreign Affairs," May 25, 2009, http://www.fmprc.gov.cn/chn/pds/ziliao/1179/t564332.htm; "North Korea Should Not Offend the Chinese People," *Global Times*, June 3, 2008, quoted in Hui Zhang, "Ending North Korea's Nuclear Ambitions: The Need for Stronger Chinese Action," *Arms Control Association*, http://www.armscontrol.org/print/3726.

57. "DPRK Opposes UN Resolution, Vows to Pursue More Nuclear Weapons," Xinhua, June 13, 2009.

58. "Statement by H. E. Ambassador Soltanieh, Permanent Representative of the Islamic Republic of Iran at the Board of Governors of the IAEA," June 17, 2009; Ayatollah Ali Khamenei, Address to Foreign and Iranian Guests, June 2, 1999, quoted in Karim Sadjadpour, *Reading Khamenei: The World View of Iran's Most Powerful Leader* (Washington, D.C.: Carnegie Endowment for International Peace, 2008), 21.

59. Sadjadpour, *Reading Khamenei*, 16–31; Shahram Chubin, *Iran's Nuclear Ambitions* (Washington, D.C.: Carnegie Endowment for International Peace, 2006), 28; Vali Nasr, *The Shia Revival: How Conflicts within Islam Will Shape the Future* (New York: W. W. Norton, 2007), 212.

60. The majority of Iranian public opinion supports the regime's nuclear defiance, despite the international condemnation and associated costs. In a study conducted by the Iranian Students Polling Agency (ISPA) in January 2006, 74.3 percent responded that they supported the resumption of Iran's nuclear program, even if that led to a Security Council referral; 64 percent still supported the program if it led to sanctions; and 55.6 percent supported it even if it led to military action. Michael Herzog, *Iranian Public Opinion on the Nuclear Program: A Potential Asset for the International Community* (Washington, D.C.: Washington Institute for Near East Policy, June 2006).

61. In April 2009, the P5+1 invited Iran to participate in fresh talks on finding a diplomatic solution to the nuclear standoff, but Iran initially refused to resume negotiations unless it could dictate the terms and conditions of discussions. Since that time, Iran's position has softened only minimally, leading to what have so far been unproductive talks colored by continued defiance. On the one hand, Iranian negotiators claim they are ready to negotiate; on the other, they make it clear they are unwilling to make any significant concessions and intersperse pledges of cooperation with announcements concerning nuclear activities that are clearly in breach of UN resolutions. See "Iran Nuclear Talks: A Widening Chasm," Council on Foreign Relations, interview with Robin Wright by Bernard Gwertzman, December 8, 2010, http://www.cfr.org/publication/23574/iran_nuclear_talks.html.

62. Afshin Molavi, "Iran's 'Crisis of Legitimacy' Could Prompt Authoritarian Political Alternative," *Eurasia Insight*, August 29, 2003, http://www.eurasianet.org/departments/insight/articles/eav082903.shtml; Farnad Darnell, "The Iranian Revolution: A Process of Theocratic Legitimacy," paper presented at the annual meeting of the American Sociological Association, Philadelphia, August 12, 2005; Emile El-Hokayem, "As Iran Simmers, the Nuclear Clock Ticks On," July 2, 2009, http://www.stimson.org/spotlight/as-iran-simmers-the-nuclear-clock-ticks-on/.

63. That is, the transition from an international society where national sovereignty remains sacrosanct to one that is increasingly dominated by international organizations that judge, constrain, and impose standards and obligations on member states and that impose penalties for noncompliance. For further information, see note 52.

64. Jack Boureston and Tanya Ogilvie-White, *Seeking Nuclear Security through Greater International Coordination* (New York: Council on Foreign Relations, March 2010).

65. "Statement by Soltanieh, Board of Governors," June 17, 2009; "Statement by H. E. Mohammad Ali Hosseini, Deputy Foreign Minister of the Islamic Republic of Iran before the Third Session of the Preparatory Committee of the 2010 NPT Review Conference," New York, May 14–15, 2009; "Response of the Delegation of the Islamic Republic of Iran to Remarks Made by Some Delegates on Implementation of Safeguards Agreement in Iran at the Board of Governors," June 17, 2009.

66. For example, see "Statement by Ambassador Mohammad Khazaee, Permanent Representative of the Islamic Republic of Iran before the United Nations Disarmament Commission," April 7, 2008.

67. "Statement by Hosseini, Preparatory Committee," May 14–15, 2009.

68. "Response of the Delegation to the Iran Board of Governors," June 17, 2009.

69. See remarks of Abbas Milani, director of Iranian studies, Stanford University, in the roundtable discussion entitled "Iran's Clenched Fist Election: What's Next for U.S. Policy?" Carnegie Endowment for International Peace, June 23, 2009.

70. "Iran's Ahmadinejad Says Nuclear Summit 'Humiliating,'" Reuters, April 12, 2010.

71. "Tehran Nuclear Disarmament Conference Will Be a Success: Official," Mehr News Agency, April 4, 2010.

72. Borzou Daragahi and Ramin Mostaghim, "Iran Lashes Out at U.S. during Tehran Nuclear Summit," *Los Angeles Times*, April 18, 2010; "Iran Leader Khamenei Brands U.S. 'Nuclear Criminal,'" BBC News, April 17, 2010; "Suspend Atomic Criminal from IAEA: Iran," Al Aarabiya News Channel, April 17, 2010.

73. "Statement by Mahmoud Ahmadinejad, President of the Islamic Republic of Iran before the 2010 NPT Review Conference," United Nations, May 3, 2010, 5–6.

74. Rebecca Johnson, "NPT One Week after Consensus Adoption of Agreed Document," *Acronym Institute*, June 7, 2010.

75. "Ayatollah Khamenei Leads Tehran Friday Prayers," June 4, 2010, available in English on Khamenei's website, http://english.khamenei.ir.

76. Hashem Kalantari, "Defiant Iran Reports Nuclear Success before Talks," Reuters, December, 5, 2010; James Blitz, "Iran Nuclear Talks Fail to Make Breakthrough," *Financial Times*, December 7, 2010; "Iran Invites Foreign Diplomats to Nuclear Sites," BBC News, January 4, 2011; Hashem Kalantari, "Iran Says to Make Own Fuel for Research Reactor," Reuters, January 8, 2011.

77. For an explanation of the term *solidarism* as it is sometimes used in the international relations literature, see note 52.

78. See, for example, Jon Delury, "North Korea: 20 Years of Solitude," *World Policy Journal* 25 (Winter 2008): 75–82; Jim George, "Leo Strauss, Neoconservatism, and U.S. Foreign Policy: Esoteric Nihilism and the Bush Doctrine," *International Politics* 42, no. 2 (June 2005): 174–202; Mel Gurtov and Peter Van Ness, eds., *Confronting the Bush Doctrine: Critical Views from the Asia-Pacific* (Abingdon, UK: Routledge Curzon, 2005); Robert Jervis, "The Compulsive Empire," *Foreign Policy*, no. 137 (July–August 2003): 82–87.

79. Similar recommendations are set out in Snyder, "What's Driving Pyongyang?" 5–6; Graham Allison, Martin B. Malin, and Hui Zhang, "North Korea's Nuclear Program: Looking Forward," June 9, 2009; and Patrick Clawson and Michael Eisenstadt, "Halting Iran's Nuclear Programme: The Military Option," *Survival* 50 (October–November 2008): 13–19.

80. Some U.S. hawks have called for the use of force in response to Iranian defiance. See, for example, John R. Bolton, "Time for an Israeli Strike?" *Washington Post*, July 2, 2009.

81. For a discussion of societal engagement and cultural diffusion as a driver of regime change, see Andrei Lankov, "Toppling Kim Jong Il," *Newsweek*, April 27, 2009.

82. Some of these hurdles are discussed by Chung Min Lee, "Nuclear Sisyphus: The Myth of Denuclearising North Korea," *Australian Journal of International Affairs* 61 (March 2007): 15–22.

83. Alternative arrangements have been proposed. Jean-Louis Gergorin, for example, has suggested that negotiations could resume on the basis that Iran continue indigenous uranium enrichment on the condition of full transparency and tighter international oversight. This would limit Iran's military options, which may therefore ultimately become a sticking point. Jean-Louis Gergorin, "Iran: Breaking the Deadlock," *Survival* 51 (June–July 2009): 19–25.

84. According to Hui Zhang, Beijing lured Pyongyang to each round of the Six-Party Talks with tens of millions of dollars in incentives. Hui Zhang, "Ending North Korea's Nuclear Ambitions: The Need for Stronger Chinese Action," *Arms Control Association*, http://www.armscontrol.org/print/3726; Lee, "Nuclear Sisyphus," 19–20.

85. This approach requires very careful collaboration between the P5+1 and any additional negotiators. As the failed 2010 Brazil-Turkey initiative demonstrated, the key to ensuring diplomatic efforts are harnessed successfully (without inadvertently strengthening the hand of the defiant states) is careful and effective coordination.

86. Dealing with North Korea's nuclear defiance is especially urgent due to the risk that Pyongyang will transfer nuclear material or components to state or nonstate actors, either directly via state-controlled activities or indirectly through criminal networks. UN Panel of Experts, "Report to the Security Council from the Panel of Experts Established Pursuant to Resolution 1874 (2009)," May 12, 2010 (distributed November 5, 2010), S/2010/571, http://www.un.org/ga/search/view_doc.asp?symbol=S/2010/571; Sheena Chestnut, "Illicit Activity and Proliferation: North Korean Smuggling Networks," *International Security* 32, no. 1 (Summer 2007): 80–111.

87. Follath and Stark, "Birth of a Bomb," 11.

88. See George Perkovich, "Sanctions on Iran—The Least Bad Option," *Carnegie Endowment Q&A*, June 28, 2010, http://carnegieendowment.org/2010/06/28/sanctions-on-iran-least-bad-option/4ug.

89. See, for example, Ian Black and Simon Tisdall, "Saudi Arabia Urges U.S. Attack on Iran to Stop Nuclear Programme," *Guardian*, November 28, 2010. The text of the secret U.S. embassy cables, which was originally published by WikiLeaks, is available on the Guardian.co.uk website. See, for example, Secret Section 01 of 03 Riyadh 000649, paragraph 10, http://www.guardian.co.uk/world/us-embassy-cables-documents/150519. For a more general discussion of Arab state fears of Iran's nuclear activities, see "Iran Starts Nuclear Reaction in Arab States," *Jane's Islamic Affairs Analyst*, March 19, 2010.

90. Tehran's defiant response to the fifth round of UN Iran sanctions, imposed by the Security Council in June 2010, demonstrates this problem. A month after the sanctions were imposed, Iran's parliament passed a bill pressing the government to continue enriching uranium to 20 percent and to pursue self-sufficiency in nuclear fuel production. "Iran's Parliament Adopts Bill against Inspections," Associated Press, July 20, 2010.

91. "Iranian Economy Bears Strain of Sanctions," *Jane's Intelligence Weekly*, June 4, 2010; Brianna R. Rosen, "Iran's Plan to Combat Sanctions," *Jane's Islamic Affairs Analyst*, December 18, 2009.

92. Robert Burns, "U.S. to Hit NKorea with More Sanctions in August," Associated Press, 22 July, 2010.

93. There are some signs that U.S. efforts to encourage states to actively support the sanctions approach are beginning to work, but these successes should not be exaggerated. Although in June 2010, the United States and European Union won backing from Russia and China for a stronger UN sanctions resolution against Iran's nuclear activities, both states watered down the original text before they would accept it, and both, while

taking more steps than previously, are failing to fully implement the sanctions that they verbally and legally endorse (in common with many developing states). Richard Sabatini, "Economic Sanctions: Pressuring Iran's Nuclear Program," *NTI Issue Brief*, February 18, 2010 (updated June 24, 2010, by Cole Harvey); Louis Charbonneau, "UN Report Raises Concern about NKorea Sanctions," Reuters, June 12, 2010; "Iranian Economy Bears Strain of Sanctions," *Jane's Intelligence Weekly*, June 4, 2010.

CHAPTER NINE

The Silent Proliferators
Syria and Myanmar

Jacqueline Shire

ALTHOUGH THE NUCLEAR PROGRAMS of North Korea and Iran understandably consume the lion's share of international scrutiny and diplomatic energy in the nonproliferation realm, bubbling just beneath the surface are the intriguing cases of proliferation involving Myanmar and Syria.[1] Both nuclear programs raise questions about the limits of the nonproliferation tools available to the international community to identify emerging cases. In the case of Syria in particular such tools include preventive attack as a remedy for nuclear proliferation as well as actions available to the International Atomic Energy Agency (IAEA) both before and after preventive attacks.

By far the greatest limitation in analyzing the nuclear programs of these countries and teasing out any meaningful conclusions about the origins of their activities, their motivations, and the future direction is the dearth of well-sourced, verifiable information. Syria has effectively stonewalled the IAEA since 2007, when Israel launched its air raid on the infamous box-in-the-desert that was later established to be a plutonium production reactor close to completion. Since then, scant information has been collected about how and why Syria went about building the reactor with North Korea's assistance. Myanmar rivals North Korea for its tight control of information and near blackout of international supervision of what appears to be a very nascent nuclear effort. In the vacuum has arisen a defector report raising alarms about a possible program to develop a uranium enrichment capability, or at minimum develop expertise in nuclear fuel cycle issues.

Notwithstanding the absence of extensive media reporting, scholarly analysis, and data-rich IAEA reports to analyze, these cases raise important questions about the nature of compliance and outliers.

Neither Syria nor Myanmar is a true outlier to the international nonproliferation system in the manner of India, Pakistan, and Israel, all of which have chosen to remain outside the Nuclear Nonproliferation Treaty (NPT) by virtue of their nuclear weapons status, but which in other ways are closely wrapped into the complex multilateral system of nonproliferation treaties, rules, and norms. Nor have the nuclear activities of Myanmar and Syria risen to the level of those in Iran and North Korea, with well-established fuel cycle capabilities, and in North Korea's case, an on-again-off-again relationship with the NPT.

Myanmar and Syria remain enigmatic examples of the limits of the nonproliferation regime and at the same time of how difficult it can be to develop a nuclear weapons capability without detection and substantial foreign assistance. This chapter explores what is known about the nuclear programs of both countries, relying on a limited and imprecise set of open-source information, and attempts to draw some meaningful conclusions about their implications for both the nonproliferation regime and the current momentum for nuclear disarmament.

SYRIA: ISRAEL OPTS FOR PREVENTIVE ATTACK

On September 6, 2007, the Israeli Air Force launched an attack on what later became known as the Dair Alzour site (sometimes transliterated as Dair al Zour or Dar az Zwar, or alternatively identified as al-Kibar, the name of a nearby town), which is located in a remote area of eastern Syria along the Euphrates River.

According to an April 2008 briefing by Central Intelligence Agency (CIA) "senior intelligence officials" (currently the most detailed on-record source of information about the facility), it had been under construction since 2001. Early hints of plans for a nuclear facility arose as far back as 1997, with the information firming up but still not allowing the intelligence community to "pin it down" until sometime between 2003 and 2006.[2] In the spring of 2007, intelligence analysts finally obtained conclusive information that Syria was constructing a reactor with the assistance of North Korea.

A video produced by the CIA (which was widely disseminated online) describes the reactor site and provides details of the extent of the project and North Korea's assistance. The narrator explains that Syria was building a gas-cooled, graphite-moderated reactor that was nearing operational capability by August 2007. The reactor was "ill-suited" for research and not configured for the purpose of generating electricity but "would have been capable of producing plutonium" for weapons purposes.[3] North Korea, the CIA concluded, assisted with the construction of the reactor, which was modeled after the plutonium production reactor at Yongbyon, and as the narrator notes, it is also the only country that has built such a gas-cooled, graphite-moderated reactor in the last thirty-five years. The CIA cited procurement and official travel going back a decade indicating "sustained cooperation" between Syria and North Korea. Though more testing was likely, the reactor was judged by the U.S. intelligence community to be close to operational.[4] Almost immediately following the air raid, Syria razed the facility, removing or burying "incriminating" equipment. On October 10, 2007, Syria destroyed the remnants of the building through a "massive controlled demolition."[5]

North Korea appears to have been involved in nearly every facet of the project, including procurement, design, and construction (in one photo of the CIA presentation, the head of the fuel fabrication plant at North Korea's Yongbyon nuclear site is pictured on a trip to Syria standing next to Ibrahim Othman, the head of Syria's Atomic Energy Commission; a companion photo shows him at a meeting of the Six-Party talks).[6] North Korean officials traveled to Syria after the attack and are believed to have assisted in damage assessment. There are unconfirmed reports that North Korean technicians were killed in the attack.

IAEA reports are virtually the only other source of published data regarding the reactor site and the limited information that could be gleaned by IAEA inspectors. Between November 2008, when the IAEA released its first report on the Syrian reactor, and September 2010, the agency has issued eight such reports. For the most part these comprise a detailed chronicle of Syrian refusal to cooperate with IAEA requests for information or access to facilities beyond a very limited scope. Agency inspectors were permitted to inspect and take soil samples from the area where the reactor once stood in June 2008.

Their most significant finding during that inspection was the presence of so-called anthropogenic uranium particles. This is uranium that has been chemically processed and, according to the IAEA, is inconsistent isotopically with Syria's declared nuclear materials.

Syria's response to the IAEA inspectors begs credulity. Despite a compelling photographic record establishing the presence of a reactor at an advanced state of construction, bearing a remarkable similarity to North Korea's reactor at

Yongbyon, Syrian officials have continued to insist that the facility was a purely military one with no nuclear applications.[7] Syria has also consistently refused to provide the IAEA with documentation regarding the "past and current use" of the buildings at the Dair Alzour site, access to any salvaged equipment, and information regarding procurement activities by Syrian entities.

Syrian officials further insist that the uranium particles identified by the IAEA are from depleted uranium used in Israeli ordnance. IAEA officials and other experts dispute those claims. In February 2009, the first time it addressed directly the possibility that the uranium particles could have come from Israeli munitions, the IAEA assessed that "there is a low probability" the uranium found at the site was introduced by missiles, and that the "isotopic, chemical composition and morphology" of the particles were inconsistent with what could be expected from "uranium based munitions."[8]

The IAEA's September 2010 report summarized the information it continues to seek from Syria, including procurement efforts, access to technical documentation related to construction of the building, access to debris, munitions remains, and salvaged equipment, as well as further access to the Dair Alzour site and three other related locations.[9] There is also the nagging matter of unexplained uranium particles that turned up in samples taken in August 2008 from the Damascus Miniature Neutron Source Reactor, which the IAEA determined were "of a type not in Syria's declared inventory." At minimum, their presence indicates nuclear activity that Syria has failed to declare to the IAEA.

The Sound of Silence

In the aftermath of the attack, Syria's protests were surprisingly muted. Its ambassador to the United Nations declined to lodge a formal complaint with the Security Council protesting the air strike. A Syrian diplomat speaking that week at a meeting of the UN General Assembly's First Committee said that Israel "violates the airspace of sovereign states and carries out military aggression against them, like what happened on the 6th of September 2007 against my country."[10] A week later, Syria's ambassador to the United Nations would say only that the site was "a center for research for the desert areas, arid and desert areas in Syria."[11] There was also near-silence from Syria's Arab neighbors and scant protest from Non-Aligned Movement (NAM) countries, which might have been expected to condemn loudly Israel taking matters into its own hands rather than turning to the United Nations to address the possibility of serious NPT violations. Surprisingly perhaps, some of the loudest protests against the Israeli strike came from the IAEA director general at the time, Mohamed ElBaradei.

An Iranian Hand?

Syria's political alliance with Iran raises the intriguing possibility that its reactor construction project in the desert may have taken place, if not at Tehran's behest, perhaps with its quiet financial or political backing. After all, Iran has invested the bulk of its energies into developing a uranium enrichment capability centered on facilities for the conversion and enrichment of uranium at Esfahan and Natanz, respectively. Its heavy water reactor, which will eventually be able to produce weapons-grade plutonium in addition to its purported civilian uses, is years from completion, and Iran still has no significant reprocessing facilities. One might conjecture that Syria's reactor was a way for Iran to hedge its nuclear program, in particular if its nuclear sites were lost to an Israeli or U.S. military strike.

Much has been written about the strange-bedfellows quality to the Iran-Syria alliance. In short, the relationship between Iran and the secular, Baathist (socialist-Arab nationalist) Syria deepened throughout the 1980s following Iran's revolution. Syrian military assistance to Iran during its war with Iraq (Syria's Baathist archrival) was critical to Iran's ability to stave off defeat for nearly eight years. Israel's invasion of Lebanon in 1982 provided another pragmatic rationale for their early partnership. Scholars have noted that while tensions in the Iran-Syria relationship have come and gone over the last three decades, the alliance has generally remained strong.[12] Moderate Arab states have been concerned about the strength of the Tehran-Damascus partnership, in particular following the 2005 assassination of former Lebanese prime minister Rafik Hariri, widely believed to be Syria's doing notwithstanding official denials.[13] As recently as October 2009, Saudi King Abdullah al Saud took the step of traveling to Syria in an effort to heal the rift that has grown between Syria and its Sunni Arab neighbors. There is also information pointing to cooperation between Iran and North Korea to supply Syria with missile technology, and Syria is believed to be a transit point in shipments of Scud missiles from Iran to Hezbollah.[14] Some analysts have claimed that a July 2007 explosion at a military base near Aleppo was the result of Iranian-Syrian cooperation to produce chemical weapons, but others have expressed doubts about Iranian involvement.[15] The United States has added its own diplomatic muscle to try to split the Iran-Syria nexus, sending envoys to Damascus in an effort at reengagement and urging Russia to use its influence with Syria to further isolate Iran.[16]

Whether this political alliance extends to nuclear cooperation is another question, not easily answered based on open-source information. The German news weekly *Der Spiegel* reported in 2008 that its reporters had seen intelligence reports stating that "North Korean, Syrian and Iranian scientists were working side by side to build a reactor to produce weapons-grade plutonium" and that Iran intended to use the facility "as a 'reserve site' with the material eventually being sent back to Tehran."[17] However, former U.S. government officials note that there is no information to support the conclusion that Tehran tacitly or in any other way supported the construction of Syria's reactor.[18] In sum, while speculation about possible Syrian-Iranian collusion over the al Kibar reactor is intriguing, it remains unsubstantiated.

Nonproliferation Implications of Preventive Attacks

One of the more curious elements of Israel's strike on al Kibar has been the deafening silence from the international community, in particular the Middle East, to Israel's actions. Avner Cohen and Leonard Spector suggest that this may be due in no small part to regional antipathy toward Syria and its alliance with Iran, whose nuclear program is generally abhorred by Gulf Arab states.[19] And unlike the case of Iraq's Osirak reactor, which Israel bombed in 1981, the al Kibar facility was being built in secret, in clear violation of Syria's safeguards undertakings to the IAEA. The question of whether the international community's silence in condemning the attack chips away at established understandings of "anticipatory self-defense" in international law is an important one.

The use of preemptive military force has been explored at length by legal scholars who are careful to distinguish between anticipatory and preventive self-defense under international law.[20] In sum, anticipatory self-defense is generally defined as military action taken in response to an imminent attack, such as a U.S. attack on Japan's fleet during the Second World War in advance of Japan's attack on Pearl Harbor.[21] The notion of preventive attacks, as defined by the Bush administration in the wake of the September 11, 2001 (9/11), attacks, allows for the use of force preemptively in the event of an attack using weapons of mass destruction (WMD) by terrorists or rogue states.[22] Israel's strike on the al Kibar facility clearly falls under the latter category: the reactor was not yet operational, and there were several time-consuming and technically arduous steps between bringing the reactor online undetected, unloading the spent fuel after a period of operation, and reprocessing and ultimately weaponizing the plutonium. It can be surmised that the attack was timed to take place before fuel was loaded, so that there would be no collateral radiation damage.

Israel's actions can also be understood through the prism of Iran's nuclear program. Decision makers may have concluded that multiple opportunities were lost to strike at Iran's nuclear facilities while far less developed, and they were not willing to let Syria's reactor become a fact on the ground, in the manner of Bushehr, Natanz, or Esfahan.

The absence of an outcry from either international diplomatic circles or the legal community raises the possibility that the preventive attacks doctrine has gathered some grudging acceptance, at least with the issue of WMD, despite the controversy the doctrine generated under the Bush administration. The success of the strike and muted response also force some soul searching among the many staunch advocates of a strong nonproliferation regime, which Israel was not prepared to trust with bringing about the elimination of the al Kibar facility. Spector has compellingly argued that this is understandable—that taking its cues from Iran, Syria would have played for time and eventually operated the facility, in the process developing a stockpile of "peaceful plutonium" and a nuclear weapons capability.[23] This may well have been the result, but the international community will never know. Syria's development of al Kibar was entirely clandestine and clearly with no civilian, power-related applications, leaving far less ground to stand on with the IAEA regarding its peaceful purposes. One could also imagine a scenario in which the facility was disclosed and Security Council resolutions were adopted calling for its dismantlement under international supervision. Even allowing for the process to drag along interminably at the United Nations and various capitals, as such things do, Syria would find itself under enormous international scrutiny and would effectively have been barred from operating the facility.

Special Inspections?

The most fitting tool in the IAEA arsenal for exposing more of Syria's effort and re-establishing authority over compliance with international obligations would appear to be a special inspection. Both current and former U.S. ambassadors to the United Nations in Vienna have called for (or in the case of Glyn Davies, the current ambassador, have raised the possibility of) such inspection of Syrian nuclear facilities.[24] They are joined by a growing number of scholars and experts who argue that Syria offers a textbook example of the conditions for a so-called special inspection. Syria's comprehensive safeguards agreement with the IAEA, signed in February 1992 and entered into force in May of that year, states that a special inspection may be conducted "if the Agency considers that information made available by the State, including explanations from the State and information obtained from routine inspections, is not adequate for the Agency to fulfill its responsibilities under the Agreement."[25]

Although IAEA lawyers have concluded that the agency is on solid ground to seek a special inspection, Directors General ElBaradei and now Yukiya Amano have been reluctant to exercise that option for a number of reasons. One concern is that if confronted with such a demand, Syria could be prompted to withdraw or threaten withdrawal from the NPT (à la North Korea). A second concern is that if the IAEA were to undertake a special inspection and find nothing, its credibility would be undermined.[26] A third concern is that the IAEA could formally request the inspection; Syria could refuse; and the resulting standoff would become a major test of wills, with the risk of damaging the IAEA's authority in the event Syria refused to back down. Amano may be reluctant to go down this road if there is little hope of shedding more light on Syria's actions through forensic analysis of debris from the bombed site, and absent information that the program had progressed much beyond what is currently known.

The IAEA has only requested such inspections twice in its history—once, in the case of Romania in 1992, and a second time in 1993, when questions arose regarding the completeness of North Korea's declarations to the IAEA.[27] On balance, the first two concerns regarding the potential drawbacks of an IAEA special inspection appear to be overstated. There is always the risk that Syria could withdraw from the NPT, but Syria's actions to date do not suggest a leadership seeking the level of international isolation and condemnation that would follow such an extreme step. It is also true that the IAEA could inspect and find nothing, but any damage to its credibility is balanced by the understanding that Syria has had ample time to conceal or destroy relevant evidence of its actions at al Kibar.

More recent developments in Syria do not bode well for a near-term resolution of this issue. On June 7, 2011, the IAEA's Board of Governors adopted a resolution cosponsored by thirteen countries, including the United States and United Kingdom, that formally reported to the United Nations Security Council Syria's noncompliance with its Safeguards Agreement. The resolution contains a finding that "Syria's undeclared construction of a nuclear reactor at Dair Alzour and failure to provide design information for the facility in accordance with Code 3.1 of Syria's Subsidiary Arrangements are a breach of Articles 41 and 42 of Syria's NPT Safeguards Agreement."[28] It was adopted with seventeen votes in favor, six votes opposed (including Russia and China), and eleven abstentions.[29] When members of the Security Council took up the issue one week later, on July 14, whatever momentum the issue had in Vienna quickly dissipated. Diplomats in New York, after hearing a technical briefing of the IAEA's assessment of the Dair Alzour site, failed to reach agreement on a resolution. Russia and China questioned the rationale behind Security Council involvement, with China's envoy saying, "We should not talk about something that does not exist. There are a lot of things that happened in the past—should we discuss all of them?"[30]

One interesting wrinkle in the IAEA's referral to the Security Council was identified by Mark Hibbs, who has written extensively on the agency and its internal politics. He notes that the conclusion by the IAEA that the Dair Alzour facility was "very likely" a reactor was based primarily on intelligence information provided to the agency by governments and less so the agency's own investigative and inspection work on the ground. Hibbs suggests that the absence of a common understanding of safeguards noncompliance in this context may have prompted some states "to allow extraneous political considerations to take precedence over what should have been a safeguards judgment. Instead of contributing to a common resolve to put Syria on notice, many of these states abstained or voted no."[31]

The Security Council's decision to shrug off the report from Vienna (more officially, waiting for the IAEA's next report on the matter), comes as no surprise. The referral by the IAEA collides with a Security Council agenda already packed with contentious nonproliferation cases (Iran and DPRK), alongside growing domestic political turmoil in Syria, which has been repeatedly condemned by the international community yet shows no signs of abating. The appetite among Security Council members for punishing Syria for building a nuclear reactor and failing to declare it to the IAEA is near nil in the context of the region's political upheaval. The Syria nuclear issue is likely to remain before the Security Council for the indefinite future without significant action.

MYANMAR

Examining Myanmar's nuclear program and developing meaningful conclusions about the capabilities and intentions of the country's leadership is difficult for a number of reasons, not the least of which is the closed nature of Myanmar's government. The problem is compounded by Myanmar's lack of transparency with the IAEA, by the very small number of journalists, scholars, and experts who make a close study of the country, in particular its missile and nuclear programs, and also by a degree of misinformation that takes root in the analysis and can be difficult to separate from the little that is well sourced and credible. As discussed further below, the developing narrative of Myanmar's nuclear history includes a number of allegations that have not withstood closer scrutiny.

Though Myanmar has very little in the way of any nuclear infrastructure, it has aspirations for civilian nuclear technology and is clearly investing some time and energy into procurement and research activities that could have nuclear weapons-related applications. Adding to the suspicions of the international community are the claims that this is happening with the support of its relatively new ally in the region, North Korea. The latter's well-established willingness to sell missile and nuclear technology (though not yet, to any one's knowledge, actual fissile material) makes this partnership especially troubling.

Background

Concerns about Myanmar's nuclear intentions surfaced almost a decade ago with word of its agreement with Russia to build a small, light water research reactor for civilian purposes. The deal was announced during a July 2001 trip to Moscow by Burmese foreign minister Win Aung and several other cabinet officials. Russian foreign minister Igor Ivanov called Myanmar a "promising partner in Asia and the Pacific region."[32] The agreement caught the attention of not only nonproliferation officials in Washington but also the International Confederation of Free Trade Unions, which protested the reported barter payment for the reactor with Burmese timber, fish, and rice and Myanmar's reported use of forced labor in those industries.[33] Both Myanmar and Russia have insisted that the research reactor would be under safeguards. Given its small size, it would not present a proliferation threat. Yet questions inevitably arose as to why a country at Myanmar's level of economic development would need a research reactor other than for status reasons.[34]

The reactor project languished for several years, apparently over Myanmar's inability to finance the reactor's construction under terms that were acceptable to Russia. It was reenergized in 2007 when Russia again announced plans both to build a ten-megawatt light water research reactor and to provide up to 350 students with training in related Russian technology institutes.[35] To this day, the reactor has not been built, and construction remains unlikely.

There have been other reasons to worry about Myanmar's nuclear intentions. There were reports, for example, that Pakistani nuclear scientists had traveled to Myanmar on a mysterious research project. After the 9/11 attacks, CIA director George Tenet asked Islamabad to allow the CIA to interview the two Pakistani scientists, Suleiman Asad and Muhammed Ali Mukhtar. Pakistan insisted that they were unavailable for questioning; according to unconfirmed reports, they were in Myanmar and not reachable.[36] In November 2003, the *Far Eastern Economic Review* reported suspicious North Korean deliveries near a purported reactor site, although this report, and other more lurid allegations from defectors, could not be confirmed.[37]

In other respects, Myanmar gives at least the outward appearance of supporting international nonproliferation norms and rules. In the 1960s and 1970s it signed a spate of arms control treaties including the Partial Test Ban Treaty, the Seabed Arms Control Treaty, the Outer Space Treaty, and the Biological Weapons Convention. It signed the Treaty of Bangkok, establishing a Southeast Asian Nuclear-Weapon-Free Zone in 1995, and the Comprehensive Nuclear-Test-Ban Treaty in 1996. Myanmar's diplomats have also participated actively in multilateral negotiating venues including the First Committee of the UN General Assembly and the Conference on Disarmament in Geneva. Myanmar joined the NPT in 1992 and maintains a traditional comprehensive safeguards agreement in addition to a so-called Small Quantities Protocol (SQP), which is the custom for countries that maintain no significant nuclear activities but might retain some nuclear material for medical or industrial applications. Under the SQP, the IAEA agrees to forgo the implementation of traditional safeguards, though it has warned Myanmar that its decision to enter into an agreement to purchase a research reactor requires the full implementation of safeguards.

As in the case of Iran, it is in the fine print of Myanmar's safeguards relationship with the IAEA that its safeguards credentials begin to fray. It has refused to sign the Additional Protocol (AP), which would expand its reporting requirements to Vienna and give the IAEA broader inspection rights (though as noted in the case of Syria, the IAEA maintains its ability to call for a special inspection even in the absence of the AP). Myanmar also refuses to implement a small but important element of its safeguards agreement, known as Code 3.1 of the safeguards subsidiary arrangements. The updated version of Code 3.1 requires states to provide design information for nuclear facilities during the design and construction phase. Myanmar's decision to enter into an agreement for the construction of a research reactor argues strongly for implementation of regular safeguards (as opposed to the SQP) and acceptance of Code 3.1.

The IAEA has not been shy about expressing its reservations about Myanmar's stated intention to produce its own medical isotopes via the research reactor, arguing that such a reactor would be a waste of resources absent the necessary infrastructure and technical know-how. "The IAEA doesn't want countries like Burma to end up with stranded research reactors[....] Without a supporting environment (these facilities) will over time pose a safety and security risk."[38]

A Contentious History with North Korea

The history of North Korea–Myanmar relations is a complicated one and beyond the scope of this chapter. In brief, the two countries initially established diplomatic relations in 1974 only to have them interrupted in 1983 following a brazen act of terrorism by North Korea against a visiting South Korean presidential delegation to Myanmar.

On October 9, 1983, North Korean agents detonated a bomb at a wreath-laying ceremony at the Martyrs' Mausoleum in Rangoon (Yangon) attended by a visiting delegation from South Korea that included President Chun Doo Hwan and several senior cabinet officials. Chun survived the blast because his car was held up in traffic, but nineteen people were killed, sixteen of them South Korean, including four South Korean cabinet ministers and two senior advisers. Myanmar quickly determined that North Korea was responsible for the attack. President Chun said at the time, "I cannot control the raging anger and the bitter grief at this atrocity." He added, "We will not be the only ones to point to the North Korea Communists, the most inhumane group of people on earth, as the perpetrators of the brutal crime to harm me as the head of state of the republic." The Burmese government announced barely a month later that it had "firmly established" North Korean agents were responsible for the bombing and gave its diplomats forty-eight hours to leave the country.[39]

Relations with North Korea were quietly restored in April of 2007 after diplomatic contact and trade gradually resumed. Some experts suggested that the two were an example of "outposts of tyranny getting together," having been driven by sanctions and political isolation to seek alliances with those in similar straits.[40]

Suspicious Cargos and Procurement

The narrative of Myanmar's nuclear (and missile) program development is replete with reports of dubious procurement and cargo deliveries, which add to the atmosphere of suspicion surrounding their activities but provide little in the way of hard information. In June 2009, Japan arrested a North Korean and two Japanese nationals for attempting to export missile-related equipment to Myanmar via Malaysia. The equipment consisted of a magnetometer, used to measure magnetic fields and relevant to missile guidance and control (experts note that the equipment also has nonmilitary applications in the geophysical sciences).[41] Li Gyeong Ho, the ethnic Korean director of the trading company, was eventually given a seven-month ban from exporting any items by Japan's Ministry of Economy, Trade, and Industry.[42]

On May 23, 2007, only a month after North Korea and Myanmar reestablished diplomatic relations, the *Kang Nam I*, a North Korean vessel, docked at the Myanmar port of Thilawa. The crew claimed it was having engine trouble and needed to take shelter from a storm. Government officials were quick to state that the ship's cargo was carefully inspected and nothing incriminating found.[43] A few months earlier, the *M.V. Bong Hoafan*, another North Korea vessel, docked in Myanmar, and again no suspicious cargo was reported. On June 17, 2009, only five days following the adoption of UN Security Council Resolution 1874 (which imposed a new round of sanctions and called on countries to interdict North Korean ships suspected of carrying illicit cargo), the *Kang Nam I* left a North Korean port.[44] The U.S. Navy began tracking the ship, which based on South Korea media reports was believed to be headed to Myanmar via Singapore carrying missiles and other proscribed items.[45] The Obama administration was not so sure, and fearing a possible trap, opted to watch and wait rather than to demand a boarding and risk embarrassment over a cargo that contained no significant proliferation-relevant items.[46] Ultimately, North Korea blinked, with a nudge from Myanmar (which declared on June 30 that it was not interested in having the ship dock at its ports), and the ship turned around, arriving back in North Korea a few days later. (It was also reported that the Obama administration "applied diplomatic pressure" on Myanmar's military leaders to bar the ship from its ports).[47]

The *Kang Nam* episode amounted to a test of the international community's resolve to implement Resolution 1874 and appears to have succeeded in deterring North Korea from proceeding with a potentially unlawful export. The UN Panel of Experts established by Resolution 1874 concluded, "While no inspection had been conducted, the Security Council measures served to deter the delivery of what was believed to be a proscribed cargo in compliance with the terms of the resolution."[48]

Debunked Reporting

Over the past several years, scattered reports of secret nuclear facilities have emerged from defectors. They reported hundreds of Burmese students being sent abroad, mostly to Russia, for training in engineering and the sciences. They also noted a great deal of tunneling activity into mountains, a reactor being built in parallel to the one planned in cooperation with Russia, and the construction of a uranium ore-processing facility. In August 2009, the *Sydney Morning Herald* published a report detailing the testimony of two defectors who alleged the construction of a secret military reactor at Naung Laing built with assistance from North Korea.[49] The stunning allegations made headlines around the world and captured the attention of the nonproliferation community, which quickly went to work identifying and assessing commercial satellite imagery of the alleged nuclear facility.[50] Shortly after the report, diplomats close to the IAEA were quoted saying with "near certainty" that it is not a reactor, but a "nonnuclear industrial workshop or machinery center."[51] Testimony by a subsequent defector confirmed that the facility (which looked like a reactor on satellite imagery) is, in fact, an industrial building holding precision machine tools, some of which may be relevant to Myanmar's nascent missile program.[52]

Over the summer of 2009 there was a flurry of reporting suggesting tunnel construction projects being supervised by North Korean engineers. While in Bangkok for the Association of Southeast Asian Nations (ASEAN) Regional Forum, Secretary of State Hillary Clinton stated, "we know that there are growing concerns about military co-operation between North Korea and Myanmar, which we take very seriously."⁵³ Analysis by independent analysts at the Institute for Science and International Security (ISIS), however, acknowledged the existence of mountain tunneling or underground storage facilities but concluded that in at least some cases they were related to dam construction and are "likely not nuclear industrial facilities."⁵⁴ In January 2010, ISIS released another report assessing claims of a uranium mine and mill that were advanced in at least two reports between 2007 and 2009. Based on a careful analysis of satellite and ground photos, ISIS concluded that the alleged refinery or mill is more likely a cement plant, and that the alleged mine is probably a quarry.⁵⁵

The most detailed recent revelations about Myanmar's nuclear (and missile) program have come from a single defector, former Burmese Army major Sai Thein Win. His information was analyzed by a former senior IAEA safeguards official, Robert Kelley, in a report for the dissident Burmese group Democratic Voice of Myanmar.

Kelley describes Win as an educated individual who is able to "separate information into what he knows well and what is hearsay." He reportedly has excellent knowledge of Myanmar's "special military programs," in particular its missile activities. Much of Win's evidence of Myanmar's nuclear activity is in the form of photographs, which Kelley acknowledges can be manipulated. Nevertheless, he concludes that "there are so many and they are so consistent with other information [...] that they lead to a high degree of confidence that Myanmar is pursuing nuclear technology."⁵⁶

Shift in U.S. Policy

The Bush administration's approach to Myanmar rested heavily on the use of sanctions to target the ruling junta and its policies, in particular sanctions on individuals, financial assets, and arms trading.⁵⁷ On July 29, 2008, President Bush signed the Tom Lantos Block Burmese JADE (Junta's Anti-Democratic Efforts) Act of 2008, legislation originally introduced by the late congressman Block, which closed loopholes allowing the import of certain Myanmar-origin gems.⁵⁸ The Obama administration, sensitive to growing concerns about Myanmar's military relationship with North Korea, announced a new policy toward the regime in a September 2009 statement by Assistant Secretary Kurt Campbell.⁵⁹ Campbell noted that neither sanctions nor engagement alone were sufficient to improve conditions in the country and move it closer to democracy, and that the United States was prepared to begin a direct dialogue with Myanmar aimed at improving relations and addressing democracy and human rights issues and Myanmar's compliance with UN Security Council resolutions 1874 and 1718.[60] It is not clear yet how successful the Obama administration has been in seeking both engagement and further sanctions, a policy that some have termed "pragmatic engagement."[61] When Aung San Suu Kyi was released from fifteen years of house arrest in November 2010, the State Department spokesperson hinted at Washington being prepared to have a "different kind of relationship" with Myanmar.[62] At the same time, Suu Kyi raised the possibility of rolling back sanctions that are seen to be detrimental to the Burmese people. Regional powers China and India are opposed to sanctions, with India in particular reluctant to use its influence to press for democratic reform in favor of building on growing economic ties with Myanmar.

In the End, What Does Myanmar Really Have?

In a carefully worded 2010 State Department report to Congress on the status of compliance with arms control treaties and agreements, Myanmar is singled out for "concern" about its "interest in pursuing a nuclear program, including the possibility of cooperation with North Korea."[63] The report highlights the possibility of North Korean assistance to establish a nuclear research center but notes that the United States "lacks evidence to support a conclusion that Myanmar has violated its NPT obligations or IAEA safeguards." For its part, the IAEA is seeking answers from Myanmar about reports of transshipments, alleged procurement, and possible cooperation with North Korea. According to media reporting, the head of the IAEA's safeguards division, Herman Nackaerts, wrote to Myanmar in late 2010 asking to visit several sites.[64]

When examined in totality—the media reporting, expert analysis, credible defector documentation—it is impossible to escape the conclusion that Myanmar is pursuing, however clumsily and perhaps inexpertly, an effort to acquire at least some of the tools and knowledge to advance a nuclear program. The military junta is dedicating resources to developing intellectual capital in the nuclear area, as well as some rudimentary elements of the fuel cycle. It is also likely that North Korea is assisting this effort to some degree, though the extent of that assistance is not clear. While it is possible that North Korea's assistance to Myanmar is greater than is currently understood, it is also possible that North Korea has been reluctant to take its assistance to Myanmar beyond a certain basic level. If the latter is true, this could point to at least some degree of self-imposed restraint on its proliferation activities.

ANALYSIS

The unresolved and uncertain nature of nuclear activities in Syria and Myanmar have a subtle but nagging impact on broader efforts to strengthen momentum toward disarmament and to shore up the nonproliferation regime in general. Though neither country dominates debate in regional or multilateral negotiating venues, they serve as close-at-hand examples of the limits of the nonproliferation regime's ability to detect and thwart noncompliance. This is especially true in the case of Syria. Although the IAEA Board of Governors as of 2011 has not found Syria to be violation of its safeguards obligations, many analysts argue that the construction of the al Kibar reactor and Syria's refusal to cooperate with the IAEA investigation are grounds for such a finding.[65]

The impact of the Syria and Myanmar cases on broader disarmament objectives is uncertain and not yet easily quantified. Israel's reliance on the use of preventive attacks to address a proliferation threat certainly undermines confidence in the nonproliferation regime—a confidence that must be securely and firmly established if the world is ever to approach an advanced stage of disarmament. But it is also important not to overstate the impact of Israel's actions, especially in the context of the region and the broader international community's tacit acceptance of those actions.

The dramatic increase in interest among countries in the Middle East and Southeast Asia in nuclear power is another field in which proliferation concerns and suspicions are played out. Vietnam and Indonesia are moving ahead with plans to build nuclear reactors, and other countries in the region have expressed varying degrees of interest in nuclear power (though Thailand, for now, appears prepared to continue relying on natural gas). In general the increase in nuclear power in Southeast Asia is explained by the area's rapid growth and development and its need for nonfossil fuel-based energy. But the growth in nuclear power must be accompanied by a corresponding growth in a culture of awareness and support for strong nonproliferation norms and laws, and wherever possible agreement by nuclear-powered countries to forgo enrichment and reprocessing. In the Middle East, Iran's nuclear program is seen as a factor in the interest of its neighbors in at least exploring their nuclear power options.

The United Arab Emirates (UAE) is the farthest along, with contracts in place with a South Korean consortium for the construction of four reactors by 2020. Perhaps most significantly, the UAE has signed the IAEA's AP and in its nuclear cooperation agreement with the United States has agreed to refrain from any enrichment and reprocessing activities. What is not clear, however, is whether other countries in the region will follow the UAE's lead in relinquishing so readily all rights to the fuel cycle.

The IAEA is continuing to come to terms with its role in both the Syria and Myanmar cases. As discussed above, the agency has written to Myanmar seeking answers to basic questions as a first step in probing the country's activities. In Syria, the picture is more complex, with the agency unwilling yet to take the step of demanding access under a request for a so-called special inspection, and more recent referral of the issue to the Security Council, which is preoccupied now with Syria's brutal crackdown on protesters. Syria's continuing refusal to address the al Kibar issue and the IAEA's apparent reluctance to demand answers via a special inspection have contributed to a sense of a prolonged and not easily broken stalemate.

The two cases also raise issues related to regional power and influence. Among the uncertainties of the Syria case is how, if at all, Syria's neighbors (with the exception of Israel) are reacting to the al Kibar matter. While superficially, at least, states are quick to raise the nuclear double-standard accusation with respect to Israel and the nuclear ambitions of other countries, not far under the surface is real wariness about any countries in the region obtaining a nuclear capability. (The WikiLeaks cables published by the *Guardian* and other publications offer an example of this, especially in the case of Iran.)[66]

Myanmar is surrounded by larger, more powerful countries that are often frustrated by its seeming immunity to their influence, and this complicates the interests of disarmament and nonproliferation, usually falling further down bilateral priorities related to economic interests (in the case of China) or counternarcotics issues (in the case of Thailand). Myanmar's strongest supporter, China, has privately expressed its frustration with the ruling junta. A 2008 cable from the U.S. embassy in Myanmar reports China's ambassador privately noting that Beijing had effectively given up defending the regime and acknowledging that the generals had made a bad situation worse.[67] Rather, the Chinese are focusing on preventing political turmoil that could undermine economic interests. This kind of pragmatism is also evident in statements by Thailand's former prime minister, who, on the margins of the ASEAN summit in December

2010, said that he was unable to confirm that Myanmar is developing a nuclear program.[68] China, Thailand, and India have also been united in opposing a formal UN inquiry into human rights abuses and possible war crimes called for by the United Nations' special *rapporteur* on human rights.[69] These disparate but pressing issues among bilateral and regional relationships underscore the challenges for achieving compliance with international nonproliferation norms and rules.

If "silent proliferators" such as Myanmar and Syria are not to be allowed to undermine larger disarmament objectives, other nonproliferation tools grow in importance. Expanding adherence to the AP, concluding a verifiable fissile material cut-off treaty (FMCT), encouraging spent fuel take-back arrangements, and preventing wherever possible the establishment of enrichment and reprocessing facilities are all vital to promote greater confidence in the ability of the nonproliferation system to sniff out emerging cases of proliferation, especially in regions with growing nuclear power capabilities.

CONCLUSION

The cases of both Syria and Myanmar beg for greater transparency and clarity. In the absence of a clear motive for either country to develop a nuclear weapon independently, and given their close relationships with nuclear-minded allies and neighbors (Myanmar–North Korea and Syria–Iran–North Korea), one possible interpretation is that the nuclear activity in Myanmar and the attempted construction of a plutonium production reactor in Syria reflect a larger objective of Iran and North Korea to diversify their nuclear activities, in the process spreading risk beyond their borders in the hopes of achieving greater returns based on a relatively small investment. But this conclusion is premised on assumptions that cannot yet be supported by information in the public domain.

Other scholars have suggested that Syria's pursuit of WMD is the logical outgrowth of its adversarial relationship with Israel and that rather than focusing on a punitive response, primarily via sanctions, the United States would do better to seek a long-term solution through a comprehensive settlement of the Arab-Israeli conflict.[70] Although it is true that no country's pursuit of a weapons capability can be understood in a vacuum, it is also the case that such a settlement has long been the goal of successive U.S. administrations, each approaching the issue with renewed vigor and commitment to attaining a lasting peace. The elusiveness of that goal has dogged the international community, which continues to insist that countries abide by a set of rules and norms that include a broad-based ban on the production of WMD.

Syria's apparent willingness to wade into the world of secret procurement and reactor construction with North Korea cannot be overlooked or explained away on the basis of its adversarial relationship with Israel or Israel's possession of nuclear weapons. Neither can Myanmar's decision to invest enormous resources in suspicious procurement and facility construction be justified by its adversarial relationship with neighbor Thailand or other regional concerns.

The other lesson to draw from both cases, and the al Kibar reactor in particular, is that they have not brought the international nonproliferation system screeching to a halt, hamstrung or tripping over itself by yet another case of noncompliance. There was no mention of Syria or Myanmar in the Final Document capping the May 2010 NPT Review Conference. And as discussed above, an important tool that the IAEA has yet to deploy in either case is the possibility of a special inspection. The ongoing standoff between Syria and the IAEA makes this a logical next step, while the situation in Myanmar calls for continued monitoring and scrutiny of suspicious procurement. An unresolved issue remaining is Israel's decision to preempt the process contained in the NPT to address noncompliance and the corresponding lack of protest from both the region and broader international community. Ultimately, the unambiguous nature of Syria's noncompliance and the surgical nature of the strike are likely to mute any residual concern about ramifications for the nonproliferation system, but this issue bears further consideration.

Notes

1. Burma's official name was changed to "Union of Myanmar" in 1989. In 2005 the seat of government was moved from Rangoon to Naypyitaw.
2. "Background Briefing with Senior U.S. Officials on Syria's Covert Nuclear Reactor and North Korea's Involvement," April 24, 2008, http://dni.gov/interviews/20080424_interview.pdf.
3. Video of the full CIA presentation can be seen in two parts via VOA at http://www.youtube.com/watch?v=4ah6RmcewUM and http://www.youtube.com/watch?v=A9HL3NVLZy0&feature=channel.
4. Ibid., minute 5:00 of video (part 1).
5. Ibid.
6. Ibid., minute 5:45 of video (part 1).

7. IAEA Board of Governors, "Implementation of the NPT Safeguards Agreement in the Syrian Arab Republic," November 19, 2008, http://isis-online.org/uploads/isis-reports/documents/IAEA_Report_Syria_19Nov2008.pdf.

8. IAEA Board of Governors "Implementation of the NPT Safeguards Agreement in the Syrian Arab Republic," February 19, 2009, http://isis-online.org/uploads/isis-reports/documents/IAEA_Report_Syria_Feb_2009.pdf.

9. IAEA Board of Governors, "Implementation of the NPT Safeguards Agreement in the Syrian Arab Republic," September 6, 2010, para. 7, p. 3, http://isis-online.org/uploads/isis-reports/documents/Syria_report.pdf.

10. "UN Says Syrian's Bomb Target Comment Mistranslated," Reuters, October 17, 2007, http://uk.reuters.com/article/idUKN1737434720071017.

11. "Syria Air Strike Target 'Removed,'" BBC News, October 26, 2007, http://news.bbc.co.uk/2/hi/7063135.stm.

12. Jubin Goodzari, *Syria and Iran: Diplomatic Alliance and Power Politics in the Middle East* (New York: St. Martin's Press, 2006), 3.

13. Julien Barnes-Dacey and Margaret Coker, "World News: Saudi King to Pressure Syria over Iran Alliance," *Wall Street Journal*, October 7, 2009; and "Syria: Saudi King Arrives for Talks," *New York Times*, October 8, 2009.

14. Kenneth Katzman, "Iran: U.S. Concerns and Policy Responses," *Congressional Research Service*, July 23, 2010, http://books.google.com/books?hl=en&lr=&id=LoU9pz97OCoC&oi=fnd&pg=PP1&dq=Iran:+U.S.+Concerns+and+Policy+Responses&ots=N_RQGU47QT&sig=fXyXpt_RdSuqd2yTOheoNv2LWlc#v=onepage&q&f=false.

15. Robin Hughes, "Explosion Aborts CW Project Run by Iran and Syria," *Jane's Defence Weekly*, September 26, 2007; Markus Binder, "Explosion at Syrian Military Facility: A Chemical Weapons Accident?" *WMD Insights*, November 2007, http://www.wmdinsights.com/I20/I20_ME1_ExplosionAtSyrian.htm, and also at St. Louis Terrorism Early Warning Group, http://sltew.org/%28S%28f1shqmzxgorobbzqhixdsm55%29%29/default.aspx?act=newsletter.aspx&category=TEW+Related+News+%28HAZMAT%2FChemicals%29&Startrow=85&MenuGroup=Home&NewsletterID=878.

16. Jay Solomon, "U.S. Reaches out to Russia and Syria to Isolate Iran," *Wall Street Journal*, March 4, 2009; Howard LaFranchi, "U.S. Courts Syria as Linchpin to Altered Relations with Iran," *Christian Science Monitor*, March 5, 2009.

17. "Syria Turning toward the West? Assad's Risky Game," *Der Spiegel*, June 23, 2008, http://www.spiegel.de/international/world/0,1518,561409,00.html.

18. Discussion with former U.S. government officials.

19. Leonard Spector and Avner Cohen, "Israel's Airstrike on Syria's Reactor: Implications for the Nonproliferation Regime," *Arms Control Today*, July/August 2008, http://www.armscontrol.org/act/2008_07-08/SpectorCohen.

20. Sean D. Murphy, "The Doctrine of Preemptive Self-Defense" (for the symposium

Brave New World: U.S. Responses to the Rise in International Crime), *Villanova Law Review* 50, no. 3 (October 2005): 699–748. Some scholars refer to the notion of "preventive self-defense" as "preemptive" self-defense. See also Niaz Shah, "Self-Defence, Anticipatory Self-Defence and Pre-emption: International Law's Response to Terrorism," *Journal of Conflict and Security Law* 12 (2007): 95–126.

21. Mary Ellen O'Connell, "The Myth of Preemptive Self-Defense," American Society of International Law: Task Force on Terrorism," August 2002, 9, http://www.asil.org/taskforce/oconnell.pdf, as cited in Yoram Dinstein, *War, Aggression and Self-Defense* (Cambridge: Cambridge University, 2001).

22. *National Security Strategy of the United States of America* (Washington, D.C.: White House, 2002); "Text of Bush's Speech at West Point," June 1, 2002, http://www.nytimes.com/2002/06/01/international/02PTEX-WEB.html?pagewanted=all.

23. Leonard S. Spector, "Sterry R. Waterman Lecture: Slowing Proliferation: Why Legal Tools Matter," *Vermont Law Review* 34, no. 3 (Spring 2010): 619–32.

24. Jay Solomon, "U.S. Considers Push for U.N. Action in Syria," *Wall Street Journal*, August 6, 2010. See also Gregory L. Schulte, "Investigating the Rubble of Syria's Secret Reactor," *Nonproliferation Review* 17, no. 2 (July 2010): 403–17.

25. Comprehensive Safeguard Agreements (CSAs) are contained in "The Structure and Content of Agreements between the Agency and States Required in Connection with the Treaty on the Non-Proliferation of Nuclear Weapons," information circular INFCIRC/153, IAEA, http://www.iaea.org/Publications/Documents/Infcircs/Others/infcirc153.pdf. The full text of the safeguards agreement between the Syrian Arab Republic and the IAEA can be found in "Agreement of 25 February 1992 between the Government of the Syrian Arab Republic and the International Atomic Energy Agency for the Application of Safeguards in Connection with the Treaty on the Non-Proliferation of Nuclear Weapons," information circular (INFCIRC/407), July 1992, http://www.iaea.org/Publications/Documents/Infcircs/Others/infcirc407.pdf.

26. Mark Hibbs, "Reaching Consensus at the IAEA," Q&A with Mark Hibbs, Carnegie Endowment for International Peace, September 13, 2010, http://carnegieendowment.org/publications/index.cfm?fa=view&id=41551#4.

27. Fiona Simpson, "IAEA Special Inspections after Israel's Raid on Syria," *Bulletin of the Atomic Scientists*, February 10, 2008, http://www.thebulletin.org/web-edition/features/iaea-special-inspections-after-israels-raid-syria.

28. IAEA Board of Governors Resolution (GOV/2011/40), June 7, 2011.

29. Julian Borger, "Arab Spring: Syria Nuclear Programme: IAEA Votes to Refer Damascus to Security Council," *Guardian*, June 10, 2011.

30. "UN Nuclear Agency Brings Syria to Security Council," Reuters News, July 14, 2011.

31. Mark Hibbs, "The IAEA and Syria: A New Paradigm for Noncompliance?" Carn-

egie Endowment for International Peace, June 17, 2011, http://www.carnegieendowment.org/2011/06/17/iaea-and-syria-new-paradigm-for-noncompliance/270.

32. Bertil Lintner, "Myanmar Joins the Nuclear Club: Russia Muscles in on China's Turf with a Reactor for Myanmar," *Far Eastern Economic Review*, December 27, 2001.

33. "Labour Union Slams Russia-Myanmar Nuclear Deal," Reuters, July 24, 2001.

34. International Institute for Strategic Studies (IISS), *Preventing Nuclear Dangers in Southeast Asia and Australasia*, ed. Mark Fitzpatrick, Strategic Dossier (London: IISS, September 2009) 105–6, http://www.iiss.org/publications/strategic-dossiers/preventing-nuclear-dangers-in-southeast-asia-and-australasia/read-the-dossier/.

35. Amy Kazmin and Catherine Belton, "Russia to Build Nuclear Reactor for Myanmar," *Financial Times*, May 15, 2007.

36. Douglas Frantz, James Risen, and David E. Sanger, "Nuclear Experts in Pakistan May Have Links to Al Qaeda," *New York Times*, December 9, 2001. The Burmese government later denied that the two scientists were in Myanmar at the time. See "Myanmar Rebukes Journalists, Says Reporting without Checking Facts," BBC News, June 10, 2004. It is also important to note that these two scientists are not to be confused with Sultan Bashiruddin Mahmood and Chaudry Abdul Majeed, the two retired Pakistani scientists who reportedly met with Bin Laden, and whom the U.S. intelligence community concluded had little of value to offer terrorists.

37. Bertil Lintner and S. W. Crispin, "Dangerous Bedfellows," *Far Eastern Economic Review*, November 20, 2003, 22; Fitzpatrick, *Preventing Nuclear Dangers*, 110–11.

38. Mark Hibbs, "IAEA Probes Myanmar Data, Discourages New Research Reactors," *Nuclear Fuel*, August 10, 2009.

39. "Burma Says Agents of North Korea Set Blast That Killed 21," Associated Press, *New York Times*, November 5, 1983.

40. Seth Mydans, "2 Diplomatic Outcasts Find Common Ground: Myanmar Restores Ties with North Korea," *International Herald Tribune* (*New York Times* global ed.), April 27, 2007.

41. David Albright, Paul Brannan, and Andrea Scheel Stricker, "Smugglers Assist North Korea-Directed Illicit Trade to Myanmar," Institute for Science and International Security (ISIS), July 14, 2009.

42. "Administrative Sanction under Foreign Exchange and Foreign Trade Law," Japanese Ministry of Economy, Trade and Industry (METI), June 2010, http://www.meti.go.jp/english/press/data/20100618_07.html.

43. "Myanmar Says North Korean Ship Docked near Yangon to Take Shelter from Storm," Associated Press, May 23, 2007.

44. United Nations Security Council Resolution 1874 (2009), "Security Council, Acting Unanimously, Condemns in Strongest Terms Democratic People's Republic of Korea

Nuclear Test, Toughens Sanctions," June 12, 2009, http://www.un.org/News/Press/docs/2009/sc9679.doc.htm.

45. "U.S. Destroyer Tracks North Korean Ship Suspected of Heading to Burma," *National Post*, June 23, 2009, A15.

46. David Sanger, "Is Freighter a Transport for Arms or a Floating Trap? Wary of a Confrontation with North Korea, U.S. Is Vigilant but Cautious," *New York Times*, July 2, 2009.

47. James Hookway, "U.S. Pushes on Myanmar—At ASEAN Summit, Clinton Reiterates Worry about North Korea's Nuclear Plans," *Wall Street Journal Asia*, July 23, 2009.

48. "Report to the Security Council of the UN Panel of Experts Established Pursuant to Resolution 1874 (2009)," 30, http://www.fas.org/irp/eprint/scr1874.pdf.

49. Desmond Ball and Phil Thornton, "Burma's Nuclear Secrets," *Sydney Morning Herald*, August 1, 2009, http://www.smh.com.au/news/world/burma8217s-nuclear-secrets/2009/07/31/1248977197670.html?page=fullpage#contentSwap2.

50. See Jeffrey Lewis, "Big Odd Myanmar Box," blog post at Arms Control Wonk, August 3, 2009, http://lewis.armscontrolwonk.com/archive/2407/big-odd-myanmar-box.

51. Mark Hibbs, "IAEA Probes Myanmar Data, Discourages New Research Reactors," *Nuclear Fuel*, August 10, 2009.

52. Geoff Forden, "Now It Can Be Told: Inside BOB," blog post at Arms Control Wonk, June 3, 2010, http://forden.armscontrolwonk.com/archive/2720/now-it-can-be-told-inside-bob.

53. Tim Johnston, "Clinton Highlights Danger of North Korea-Myanmar Alliance," *Financial Times*, July 22, 2009.

54. ISIS Imagery Brief, "Imagery Brief of Tunnel Complexes and Unidentified Building in Myanmar," ISIS, August 3, 2009, http://isis-online.org/uploads/isis-reports/documents/Burma_tunnels_3August2009.pdf.

55. Robert Kelley, Andrea Scheel Stricker, and Paul Brannan, "Exploring Claims about Secret Nuclear Sites in Myanmar," ISIS) Imagery Brief, January 28, 2010, http://isis-online.org/isis-reports/detail/exploring-claims-about-secret-nuclear-sites-in-myanmar/. For an excellent summary and review of these allegations, see David Albright, Paul Brannan, Robert Kelley, and Andrea Scheel Stricker, "Burma: A Nuclear Wannabe, Suspicious Links to North Korea and High-Tech Procurements and Enigmatic Facilities," ISIS, January 28, 2010, http://isis-online.org/isis-reports/detail/burma-a-nuclear-wanabee-suspicious-links-to-north-korea-high-tech-procureme/.

56. Robert E. Kelley and Ali Fowler, "Nuclear Activities in Burma," Democratic Voice of Burma, May 25, 2010, http://www.dvb.no/burmas-nuclear-ambitions/burmas-nuclear-ambitions-nuclear/expert-analysis/9297.

57. Martin Crutsinger, "Bush Imposes Economic Sanctions on Officials of Myanmar's Government," Associated Press, September 28, 2007.

58. White House, "President Bush Signs H.J. Res. 93, the Renewal of Import Restrictions on Burma, and H.R. 3890, the Tom Lantos Block Burmese JADE (Junta's Antidemocratic Efforts) Act of 2008," July 29, 2008, archived Bush administration website, http://georgewbush-whitehouse.archives.gov/news/releases/2008/07/20080729.html.

59. Kurt M. Campbell, "U.S. Policy toward Burma," Special Briefing, U.S. Department of State, September 28, 2009, http://www.state.gov/p/eap/rls/rm/2009/09/129698.htm.

60. UNSCR 1874 was adopted on June 12, 2009, following North Korea's second nuclear test, and establishes an embargo on all military-related trade to and from North Korea (with an exception only for the importation of some small arms). UNSCR 1718 was adopted in October 2006 following North Korea's first nuclear test.

61. Priscilla Clapp and Harn Yawnghwe, "Prospects for Rapprochement between the United States and Myanmar: A Response," *Contemporary Southeast Asia* 32 (December 2010).

62. "U.S. Official Arrives in Myanmar to Meet Suu Kyi, MPs," Reuters, December 7, 2010.

63. U.S. Department of State, "Adherence to and Compliance with Arms Control, Nonproliferation, and Disarmament Agreements and Commitments," July 2010, http://www.state.gov/documents/organization/145181.pdf.

64. Jay Solomon, "Myanmar's Links with Pyongyang Stir Nuclear Fears," *Wall Street Journal*, December 18, 2010.

65. See, for example, James M. Acton, Mark Fitzpatrick, and Pierre Goldschmidt, "The IAEA Should Call for a Special Inspection in Syria," Proliferation Analysis, Carnegie Endowment for International Peace, February 26, 2009, http://www.carnegieendowment.org/2009/02/26/iaea-should-call-for-special-inspection-in-syria/4x2.

66. Ian Black and Simon Tisdall, "Saudi Arabia Urges U.S. Attack on Iran to Stop Nuclear Programme," U.S. Embassy Cables, *Guardian*, November 28, 2010, http://www.guardian.co.uk/world/2010/nov/28/us-embassy-cables-saudis-iran.

67. Ewen MacAskill, "China 'Fed Up' with Burma's Footdragging on Reforms," U.S. Embassy Cables, *Guardian*, December 9, 2010, http://www.guardian.co.uk/world/2010/dec/09/wikileaks-china-impatience-with-burma.

68. "Thai PM Says Myanmar Adamant It Has No Nuclear Weapons," Thai News Service, December 14, 2010.

69. Tim Witcher, "Myanmar Junta Casts Shadow over UN Chief's Asia Tour," Agence France Presse, October 24, 2010.

70. Murhaf Jouejati, "Syrian Motives for Its WMD Programs and What to Do about Them," *Middle East Journal* 59 (Winter 2005): 52–61.

CONCLUSION

The Nuclear Dragon
One Eye Open, One Eye Closed

Tanya Ogilvie-White and David Santoro

THIS VOLUME BEGAN WITH a simple puzzle: What forces are driving and stalling current nuclear disarmament momentum? Recently, a combination of factors has brought the idea of eliminating nuclear weapons back onto the international security agenda. The growing realization that many of the Cold War constraints are long gone; that the proliferation of nuclear technology is occurring rapidly throughout the world; and that one day a catastrophic nuclear terrorist attack could be perpetrated have made a world free of nuclear weapons appealing to many countries, big and small. This global disarmament project, however, has already proved daunting in its infancy—a clear reminder that, in the colorful words of Michael Howard, the nuclear dragon is not dead but at best is sleeping. Commitment to slaying the nuclear dragon once and for all entails overcoming considerable obstacles of all kinds. Because nuclear disarmament momentum is for the first time creeping inside key governments, most notably inside the U.S. government, and because it is not developing in response to any specific historical event, there is a clear need to depart from the traditional debate between nuclear disarmament devotees (or "idealists") and cynics (or "realists") and to provide what Michael Quinlan called a "cool and careful examination" of the topic. This has been the goal of this volume, which has focused specifically on identifying and analyzing the state-level political opportunities and challenges affecting current nuclear disarmament momentum.

To address this puzzle, we adopted a country-based approach, with states divided into nine different groups. These groups included states that are the drivers of current nuclear disarmament momentum (the "optimistic nuclear weapon states" (NWS), the "advocacy states," and the "rollback states"); states with possible stalling effects on momentum (the "pessimistic NWS," the "threshold states," and the "nuclear energy aspirants"); and states with a primarily negative impact on momentum (the "holdout states," the "defiant states," and the "silent proliferators"). As is apparent from the chapters included in this volume, these categories are not always clearly and easily defined. South Africa, for example, is a rollback state and at times has played the role of advocacy state, but if the current trend in its nonproliferation and disarmament diplomacy continues unabated, it may be more accurate in the future to place it among the categories of states that could stall disarmament momentum. Equally, Japan is a threshold state that plays an important advocacy role; its nuclear capabilities combined with concerns about its nuclear future led us to place it among the states that have a potential stalling effect, yet it is important to acknowledge Japan's role (especially its civil society role) in keeping the disarmament goal alive. Despite these complexities, we consider our analytical framework to be a useful organizing device in terms of dividing states according to their past and present nuclear policies and their nonproliferation and disarmament diplomacy.[1]

It is now time to stand back from our analytical framework and take stock of our findings more generally. Plainly, what are the current opportunities and challenges to further progress toward a world free of nuclear weapons? What have we learned about the current condition of the nuclear dragon?

THE NUCLEAR DRAGON HAS ONE EYE CLOSED

An important finding of most of the chapters that make up this volume is that current nuclear disarmament momentum is already having a positive impact on the nuclear nonproliferation and nuclear security regimes, which has been a key goal of U.S. and UK disarmament leadership. There have been a number of encouraging developments, from the April 2010 Nuclear Security Summit to the December 2010 endorsement of the International Atomic Energy Agency (IAEA) fuel bank proposal, and numerous other signs of growing international cooperation. These successes, however modest, are likely to generate strong incentives for the United States and United Kingdom to continue their leadership roles, at least in the short term. Without doubt, we can conclude that the nuclear dragon now has one eye closed: (1) nuclear weapons are declining both in numbers and in roles, and (2) there is growing political space for nuclear disarmament in nuclear discussions. These developments are mutually reinforcing and thus will help to keep nuclear disarmament momentum alive.

Declining Roles and Numbers of Nuclear Weapons

NWS and other states no longer revere nuclear weapons and extended deterrence to the extent they once did. Because the world has changed considerably since the end of the Cold War, these states have been losing some of their confidence in the weapons they once believed would foster international peace and stability and prevent major war. In today's security environment, nuclear deterrence is increasingly showing its limits: the United States (and others) are realizing that nuclear deterrence would likely be largely ineffective against terrorists prepared to die for their cause and of much more limited effectiveness in a world with many more nuclear powers. A key factor in this reassessment of nuclear deterrence stability, as David Santoro points out in chapter 1, is that "new and want-to-be entrants to the nuclear club, unlike 'the original members,' are arguably fundamentally unsatisfied with the current international status quo." Moreover, relations between major powers have improved significantly, so much so that nuclear deterrence now seems to be much less the key organizing principle of the international system than the newly coined concept of "strategic stability." Santoro observes that the choice of this concept (first used in the 2010 U.S. Nuclear Posture Review [NPR]) over the traditional concept of deterrence is an indication that the United States now emphasizes "the potential for cooperation over the potential for conflict in major power relations." And although deterrence (and extended deterrence) certainly continues to have important relevance in today's world, there is growing recognition that it can be achieved using non-nuclear means, notably ballistic missile defense (BMD) systems. As is clearly stated in the new NPR, "non-nuclear elements will take on a greater share of the deterrence burden."[2]

One of the consequences of this shift in thinking is that some nuclear-armed states have been gradually pushing their nuclear weapons into the background. A combination of strategic and financial constraints has led the United States, the United Kingdom, France, and Russia to undertake major reductions in their nuclear forces over the past twenty years. All the NWS recognized by the Nuclear Nonproliferation Treaty (NPT) have signed the Comprehensive Nuclear-Test-Ban Treaty (CTBT), and although the United States and China have not yet ratified it, they have so far honored the testing moratorium. Moreover, the NPR commits the United States to refrain from developing new nuclear warheads and to seek CTBT ratification. Four of the NWS have also made clear that they are no longer producing fissile material for weapons purposes. As Santoro explains in chapter 4, China is the only NWS that has been swimming against the tide, working consistently over the past two decades to expand and modernize its small nuclear arsenal. China is also the only one not to proclaim an end to fissile material production, even though it is believed to have stopped. But unlike the other NWS, China has always been committed—at least officially—to a no-first-use (NFU) policy, and pressure has been growing on the other NWS to follow suit. To date, the latter have refused to adopt a full-fledged NFU, although the United States and the United Kingdom have taken steps to further circumscribe the role of their nuclear weapons. The new NPR, for instance, states that "the fundamental role of U.S. nuclear weapons [...] is to deter nuclear attacks on the United States, [its] allies, and partners" and that the United States will continue to "reduce the role of nuclear weapons in deterring non-nuclear attacks, with the objective of making deterrence of nuclear attack on the United States or [its] allies and partners the sole purpose of U.S. nuclear weapons."[3] All this demonstrates that threatening adversaries with nuclear annihilation, however it is finessed in the language of nuclear doctrine, is not considered a sensible policy option to deal with most current state and nonstate threats.

Similarly, there have been positive developments outside the NWS. Maria Rost Rublee, for instance, explains in chapter 5 that some in Japan have begun to question the value of U.S. extended nuclear deterrence. She notes that in an October 2009 survey, 61 percent of Lower House members of the ruling Democratic Party of Japan wanted to end reliance on U.S. nuclear protection. Brazil—the other threshold state that Rublee discusses—has adopted a constitution that prohibits the manufacture and possession of nuclear weapons, bars the allocation of funds to nuclear-weapon-related activities, and makes a president who secretly orders a nuclear-weapon program subject to impeachment. This aspect of Brazil's nonproliferation policy is regarded as a model for other countries to follow, in that it puts in place a strong domestic constraint on possible future temptations and should reassure neighbors of peaceful nuclear intentions. It sets an important precedent for new nuclear energy aspirants. As Tanya Ogilvie-White and Rublee note in chapter 6, the fact that Vietnam's 2008 Atomic Energy Law specifically prohibits "researching, developing, manufacturing, trading in, transporting, transferring, storing, using, or threatening to use nuclear or radiation weapons" is also an encouraging development, but it stops short of Brazil's prohibition and faces significant implementation hurdles.[4]

Growing Political Space for Nuclear Disarmament in Nuclear Discussions

There is a growing belief, most notably in the United States and United Kingdom, that the pursuit of nuclear disarmament is necessary to generate progress on the nuclear nonproliferation and nuclear security fronts. The political space for nuclear disarmament, once solely occupied (at the state level at least) by individual and coalition advocacy states, has grown in recent years and now includes the United States, the United Kingdom, and other key governments. It is currently rare for formal and informal diplomatic discussions on nuclear nonproliferation and nuclear security not to mention moving toward a nuclear-weapon-free world as a fundamental part of the package for dealing with nuclear dangers. The idea is that nuclear nonproliferation/security and nuclear disarmament are not alternatives but two sides of the same coin, which, as leading nonproliferation expert Joseph Cirincione has stressed, needs to be flipped over and over again to help strengthen international peace and security.[5]

The first section of this volume, which dealt with the state-level drivers of current nuclear disarmament momentum, explored this development in some detail. As Santoro notes in chapter 1, the 2010 U.S. NPR states that "we are pursuing arms control efforts [. . .] as a means of strengthening our ability to mobilize broad international support for the measures needed to reinforce the nonproliferation regime and secure nuclear materials worldwide."[6] This echoes the widely praised speech that former UK foreign secretary Margaret Beckett delivered at the Carnegie Endowment for International Peace in 2007. There, she asserted that "any solution [to today's nuclear problems] must be a dual one that sees movement on both proliferation and disarmament—a revitalization, in other words, of the grand bargain struck in 1968, when the Nonproliferation Treaty was established."[7] That is why both governments have clarified their negative security assurances (NSA), making it perfectly clear to all states that while nuclear disarmament will proceed, nuclear proliferation should simultaneously be stopped (the United States has also promised to increase U.S. support to nuclear-weapon-free zones [NWFZ]). As a result, the NPR reads that "the United States will not use or threaten to use nuclear weapons against non-nuclear weapons states that are party to the NPT and in compliance with their nuclear non-proliferation obligations." According to the NPR, U.S. NSAs also apply in the case of biological and chemical weapon use, but it is potentially reversible depending on the evolution and proliferation of biological weapons. The 2010 UK Strategic Defence and Security Review (SDSR) echoes this pledge almost exactly.

Much of the political space for disarmament discussions, which has facilitated the important disarmament leadership of the United States and the United Kingdom, was carved out by the advocacy states during the 1990s and sustained during the fraught years of the Bush administration. As Marianne Hanson explains in chapter 2, the sustained focus on disarmament by individual states, such as Norway and New Zealand, and by advocacy coalitions, such as the New Agenda Coalition (NAC), laid the foundations for today's disarmament successes. Although advocacy states have very different perspectives on the wisdom of nuclear power, their shared belief in multilateral nuclear disarmament has led them to put their differences aside and work together to encourage progress toward a nuclear-weapon-free world. Crucially, these states have helped keep nuclear disarmament on the global agenda after the terrorist attacks of September 11, 2001 (9/11), caused the United States to redouble its nonproliferation and counterterrorism efforts. As Hanson observes, the 2006 Report of the Blix Commission was "another key example of how advocacy states—in this case Sweden—sought to keep alive a focus on nuclear weapons dangers when great powers were either not fulfilling their commitments to disarmament or were diverted by other issues." She also stresses that, through the Seven-Nation Initiative (7NI), Norway "sought to salvage something from the failed [2005 NPT Review] Conference." This determination and ability to keep the disarmament agenda alive, even when the NWS and other states are stalling on or backtracking from their disarmament obligations has made a very significant contribution over the past twenty years and is likely to continue to do so into the future. As Stephen F. Burgess and Togzhan Kassenova explain in chapter 3 and Rublee in chapter 5, some states are especially well placed to play this role, none more so than South Africa and Kazakhstan, which both renounced their nuclear weapons, and Japan, which is determined to ensure that memories of the horrific nuclear attacks on Hiroshima and Nagasaki never fade.

In addition to keeping the disarmament goal alive, the advocacy states have helped build bridges between the NWS and non-nuclear weapon states (NNWS) by espousing realistic incremental and multilateral approaches to disarmament, and this has facilitated constructive debate. As Hanson observes, the politically charged rhetoric that often colors Non-Aligned Movement (NAM) statements on nuclear disarmament has been noticeably absent from statements of the NAC, whose call "was not for unilateral U.S. disarmament, but rather for phased, balanced, and verifiable moves toward the eventual elimination of nuclear weapons—in other words, a cautious approach to a global project." Hanson goes on to explain that, crucially, the expert reports that have been funded and supported by advocacy states "have all accepted that the security concerns of the NWS would need to be effectively addressed during any moves to zero"—an acknowledgement that has brought NWS and NNWS closer together and led to the launch of some ground-breaking disarmament initiatives. The UK-Norway project on the verification of nuclear warhead dismantlement is one example—a unique NWS-NNWS initiative.

Coalitions such as the NAC and the 7NI have changed the political landscape of disarmament negotiations, with long-term implications for middle power diplomacy. The NAC's political impact has been especially visible, leading to diplomatic successes that have increased the diplomatic clout of its members and encouraged more and more NNWS to join forces to replicate and build upon their achievements. In her chapter on the threshold states, Rublee describes how in 2000 Brazil reaped many of the benefits of its nuclear disarmament leadership through the NAC, because the group was "widely credited with fostering the success of the 2000 NPT Review Conference (RevCon), which produced the 'Thirteen Practical Steps' toward nuclear disarmament." Hanson reveals that these diplomatic benefits have been shared by Norway with the launch of the 7NI, as well as Australia and Japan with the launch of the International Commission on Nuclear Non-Proliferation and Disarmament. It would not be surprising, therefore, if these middle power groupings continued to grow in number and strength, spurred on by the significant (though still limited) nuclear disarmament progress over the last few years.

This leads to the question of what else the advocacy states could do to harness disarmament momentum going forward. Probably the most profound impact they could hope to have would be to promote a shift in thinking on nuclear deterrence among nuclear-armed states. However, despite their diplomatic successes, much of the analysis in this volume reveals the important limits on what individual and coalition advocacy states are likely to be able to achieve in the current international security environment. For example, as Rublee explains in her chapter on the threshold states, the German-led initiative to press the North Atlantic Treaty Organization (NATO) to remove U.S. tactical nuclear weapons stationed on European territory has so far failed to produce any tangible results, although it has made the issue a topic of ongoing alliance discussion. The reason is that some NATO Member States continue to see deterrence value in those weapons in the face of a resurgent Russia still smarting from the loss of its Baltic states. In their chapter on the rollback states, Burgess and Kassenova chart the decisions of South Africa and Kazakhstan to unilaterally abandon their nuclear weapons, but they made the important point that these actions were self-interested. In South Africa's case, nuclear rollback coincided with the collapse of that country's perceived existential threat from the Soviet Union; in Kazakhstan's case, it stemmed from a dominant belief among decision makers that nuclear possession would undermine rather than enhance their country's security. The analysis provided in virtually every chapter of this volume leads to the conclusion that the complete abandonment of nuclear deterrence by nuclear-armed states would have to be preceded by a similarly radical transformation of their threat perceptions. For instance, as Santoro mentions in chapter 4, "Paris will not start contemplating the elimination of its nuclear weapons unless the security environment changes considerably," and this is true of other states. To be fair, as mentioned above, this process of threat reassessment has already begun (because the international security environment has changed considerably since the end of the Cold War and since 9/11). But the transformation of the international security environment is still at an early stage, and most importantly, the advocacy states have far less impact on its evolution than the major powers and other nuclear-armed states.

Working within these limits, there is still potential for new initiatives that could keep expanding the political space for disarmament discussions. One such opportunity—so far not fully exploited—is to utilize the valuable experience gained by the rollback states, not necessarily in the hope that this would influence current nuclear-armed states, but with the goal of strengthening nonproliferation and disarmament norms and incentives among NNWS—especially the nuclear energy aspirants. An important point that Burgess and Kassenova make in chapter 3 is that such states offer scholars and practitioners a unique opportunity to study how nuclear disarmament—from beginning to end—can actually take place, which is a valuable role the rollback states could play in the future. But in the shorter term they could also turn themselves into active leaders of the current momentum as living examples that (1) nuclear disarmament is not just a pipedream, and (2) there is international status and prestige attached to nuclear nonproliferation and disarmament leadership in addition to moral authority. South Africa and Kazakhstan are in the ideal position to play this role, and as Burgess and Kassenova reveal, President Nazarbayev has embraced this opportunity, using it as a "trump card" in Kazakhstan's foreign policy. But they also note that although South Africa played a very constructive disarmament role under Mandela, this began to change after Thabo Mbeki became president in 1999. Encouraging South Africa back into a period of sustained nuclear disarmament leadership could strengthen the nuclear nonproliferation/security regimes and provide a boost to current momentum for a nuclear-weapon-free world.

THE NUCLEAR DRAGON HAS ONE EYE OPEN

While there have been important successes in the current nuclear disarmament drive and many opportunities on which to build, the contributors to this volume all caution that sustaining the momentum will be very challenging. In other words, the nuclear dragon still has one eye open, which means the possibility of a nuclear revival still exists despite the progress being made in nuclear disarmament. Sustaining current momentum will depend on bringing other nuclear-armed states (the pessimistic NWS and holdout states) into the fold, which promises to be a fierce struggle, given their positions on the question. It also requires, among other things, significant strengthening of the nuclear nonproliferation/security regimes—especially the ability to deal with noncompliance—and broad agreement among nations of the world that the most sensitive aspects of the nuclear fuel cycle (enrichment and reprocessing technology) be restricted. As the contributors of this volume explain, these challenges are likely to be immense.

Continuing Belief in Nuclear Deterrence

The most serious obstacle to nuclear disarmament is the persistent belief among decision makers in many states (from optimistic NWS to silent proliferators) that nuclear deterrence works and is still necessary in today's world. The roles and numbers of nuclear weapons are declining, but they continue to be regarded as having political and strategic value. Claiming that they do not is fanciful and feeds the disarmament skepticism of what Quinlan termed the "dismissive realists." The analysis set out in this volume makes this point very clearly, as even the United States and the United Kingdom—two NWS that are spending significant political and economic capital on their nuclear disarmament leadership—have made it clear that while nuclear weapons now play a reduced role in their defense and security policies, they still serve an important purpose and will continue to do so for the foreseeable future. The United States makes no secret of the fact that although it is much less relevant today than during the Cold War, the primary function of its nuclear arsenal is still to serve in the traditional role of deterring major powers (specifically Russia and China); the United Kingdom admits that there is no obvious strategic role for its nuclear forces at present but that Trident is being maintained as an insurance policy against potential future threats; and the NFU pledges that many nuclear disarmament advocates hoped would be adopted by the United States, the United Kingdom, and NATO in 2010 did not materialize (and were never a serious consideration). In short, the combination of cuts in numbers and roles for nuclear weapons and proactive disarmament leadership—although a positive development in terms of disarmament progress—does not signal a fundamental loss of faith in nuclear deterrence by the optimistic NWS. Far from it. Both the United States and the United Kingdom remain convinced of the value of their nuclear weapons for national and extended deterrence and regard the maintenance of their nuclear capabilities as a strategic responsibility to their own populations and to those of their allies. Likewise, although nuclear deterrence and extended deterrence are being questioned by some NATO partners and other U.S. allies, the significance of that questioning should not be exaggerated: policy changes are highly likely to be slow and incremental.

Belief in nuclear deterrence is also very strong among the pessimistic NWS and the holdout states, where a lack of disarmament leadership (and, in the case of China, India, and Pakistan, nuclear expansion) makes the commitment to nuclear weapons appear even more entrenched. As Santoro points out in chapter 4, Nicolas Sarkozy of France is particularly blunt in his statements on the value of nuclear deterrence, declaring that it "is not going to give up on its nuclear deterrent, whether or not this will disappoint you." Moscow and Beijing may be less blunt, but the former is modernizing its nuclear weapons systems, and although the latter adheres to a declaratory policy of "defensive deterrence," it is expanding and enhancing its small nuclear arsenal, and there are growing doubts over the seriousness of its NFU pledge. These developments are generating stronger proliferation pressures among the holdouts, as India aspires to strategic parity with China, and Pakistan aspires to strategic parity with India. As Hagerty argues in chapter 7, although all three holdouts have voiced support for the Obama administration's disarmament agenda, strategic momentum in these states "is moving away from, rather than toward, disarmament, with all three nuclear establishments working hard to achieve ever-more survivable second-strike arsenals." Hopes that proactive disarmament leadership from the United States and the United Kingdom might be able to rein in these powerful arms-racing dynamics appear far-fetched, to say the least, because they are being generated by worst-case scenario thinking.

Belief in the political value of nuclear weapons among all nuclear-armed states (and states that aspire to a nuclear-weapon capability) means that the disarmament diplomacy of the advocacy states and coalitions often falls on deaf ears. Since the beginning of the nuclear age, the development of nuclear-weapon capabilities has been associated with status and prestige—a fact that has increased their appeal to states that have sought (and retained them) to reinforce their diplomatic weight. Although decision makers in the United Kingdom, for example, now recognize that there are significant diplomatic costs associated with nuclear-weapon possession, this has not undermined the persistent belief that Trident enhances the United Kingdom's international influence. Not surprisingly, this is also a major factor in the nuclear-weapon retention (and, in many cases, expansion) of the pessimistic NWS and holdout states, and in the nuclear ambitions of the defiant states and silent proliferators. And as Rublee and Ogilvie-White note in chapters 5 and 6, in the future it could also create proliferation pressures among threshold states and the nuclear energy aspirants. Challenging the prestige value of nuclear status has been a major preoccupation of the advocacy states over the years, as Hanson recounts in chapter 2, but their efforts have been hampered by the strong political support for nuclear weapons in most (if not all) nuclear-armed states and the growing support for the nuclear option in some NNWS. This places strong constraints on nuclear disarmament momentum, including in the optimistic NWS, where influential domestic constituencies oppose the disarmament agenda. In the United States, for example, there is strong domestic opposition to the CTBT, and there are calls from some influential quarters for nuclear warhead modernization. These dynamics slow momentum and risk stalling it altogether.

Skepticism about the Current Nuclear Disarmament Drive

There is significant skepticism among key NWS and NNWS over the motivations behind the current Western-led disarmament drive. As Santoro explains in chapter 4, this is the case in Russia and China, where there are doubts about the sincerity of the Obama administration's disarmament leadership and questions over whether it is motivated by a desire to weaken the nuclear-weapon capabilities of adversaries and strengthen the U.S. conventional advantage. These doubts are likely to become a more serious obstacle to nuclear disarmament if a follow-on treaty to the New Strategic Arms Reduction Treaty (New START) is negotiated. A likely scenario is that Russia will insist that further negotiations are contingent on multilateral efforts, in the knowledge that further reductions will become complicated (and, at the very least, significantly delayed) by the inclusion of the other NWS in the process, notably China. Concerns over growing U.S. conventional superiority may also be encouraging key states to swim harder and faster against the disarmament current, by either quietly or overtly developing, expanding, or enhancing their nuclear and other weapons of mass destruction (WMD) capabilities to serve in the role as strategic equalizers. This dynamic could be one of the negative unintended consequences of current nuclear disarmament momentum, as China, the defiant states, and silent proliferators look to WMD to enhance their position relative to the United States, with potential unintended effects on neighbors and regional rivals. In this context, the expansion of sensitive fuel cycle technologies to unstable regions, as discussed by Ogilvie-White and Rublee in chapter 6, is a genuine proliferation risk, especially where intractable regional disputes remain unresolved and cooperative security mechanisms are weak, as in the Middle East.

Suspicion regarding the motivations driving current nuclear disarmament leadership extends to the United Kingdom and the advocacy states—a sign that it is not limited purely to concerns about U.S. conventional superiority. As Ogilvie-White suggests in her discussion of the defiant states, the current nuclear disarmament drive is perceived by some states as being part of a broader Western-dominated security agenda, which is transforming the institutions of global governance and challenging the legitimacy of states that do not conform to international norms. Resistance to this dynamic, which has been observable for some time in nonproliferation and disarmament forums, increased during the Bush administration, has failed to dissipate since, and may even be intensifying. According to Ogilvie-White's analysis, this may also be partly responsible for some of the quieter clandestine nuclear activities discussed in Jacqueline Shire's chapter on the silent proliferators. Resentment over Western-dominated security agendas and questions over what is driving them are also generating skepticism over the current nuclear disarmament agenda among NAM states more generally. South Africa, for example—a rollback state that is in a position to demonstrate vital disarmament leadership—has retreated from balanced NAC positions toward harder-line NAM positions on nonproliferation and disarmament and, as Burgess and Kassenova explain in chapter 3, is wary of Obama's nuclear disarmament agenda, which it questions as genuine. Overcoming this wariness will not be easy because it is linked to a whole host of related issues, including long-standing accusations of Western technology denial at the expense of the developing world.

Within the NWS, including among influential figures in the United States and the United Kingdom, there is skepticism about whether there is genuinely a connection between nuclear disarmament and nuclear nonproliferation, and there are doubts that current momentum will yield any positive results for the regime. This skepticism is especially strong among the pessimistic NWS, particularly France, which, as Santoro explains in chapter 4, has been outspoken on this issue, declaring itself "categorically opposed" to a nuclear-weapon-free world. Among decision makers in Paris, there is no conviction that nuclear disarmament momentum will help alleviate proliferation challenges, especially those involving the holdout states, defiant states, and silent proliferators, where nuclear policies are tied to extremely complex and long-running regional disputes. Hagerty raises some of these doubts in his discussion of the impact of current nuclear disarmament momentum in South Asia and the Middle East, where proliferation pressures are strong, nuclear transparency is lacking, and there is strong official opposition to key elements of the nuclear disarmament agenda, such as the CTBT and an FMCT. To be fair, few if any of the nonproliferation experts and political leaders who are driving current nuclear disarmament momentum are under the illusion that it will help stem regional proliferation dynamics in the most volatile regions, at least not in the short to medium term. It is widely recognized that the focus must be on addressing the underlying causes of disaffection, defiance, and regional instability, via bilateral and multilateral initiatives in which nuclear proliferation is just one of many issues on the agenda. This has been recognized for some time, however, and the regional initiatives that have been launched, such as the troubled Six-Party Talks process, demonstrate the difficulties of trying to resolve multiple interrelated disputes simultaneously. It is a fraught, long-term undertaking that requires patience, resilience, and determination. And as Ogilvie-White and Shire point out in their analyses of the defiant states and silent proliferators, such efforts need to be combined with effective international collaboration to counter and interdict suspicious cargoes. Ogilvie-White also argues that there should be a third longer-term element to the strategy: consistent efforts by states and international organizations to nurture grass-roots support of international norms.

There is a risk that failure to make significant progress in dealing with the difficult cases could destroy nuclear disarmament momentum and revive the nuclear dragon—a problem that would be exacerbated if expectations are unrealistic. Rather than focusing on the pace of change (or lack of it) among states that are the outliers of the nuclear nonproliferation regime, a better measure of success of the current approach to nonproliferation and disarmament is to explore its impact on the threshold states and nuclear energy aspirants. These NNWS could stall or accelerate current momentum, depending on their nuclear activities and diplomacy. For example, as Rublee points out in chapter 5, there are proliferation concerns over Brazil's lack of transparency at the Resende facility, its rejection of the AP, and its plans for nuclear-powered submarines. But at the same time, Brazil is a member of the NAC, has played an important role in developing regional nuclear nonproliferation mechanisms in Latin America, and has assisted international efforts to engage Iran in nuclear negotiations. Similarly, Japan's reprocessing program sets an unhelpful precedent in the nuclear nonproliferation regime, and the fact that Japan continues to rely on the U.S. nuclear umbrella reinforces perceptions that nuclear weapons enhance security. But Japan has also been one of the most consistent advocates of nuclear disarmament and plays a crucial role in keeping disarmament momentum alive, including during periods of doubt and uncertainty. The threshold states, therefore, are in a position to prod the nuclear dragon back into action or to help send it to sleep. Ensuring that they help achieve the latter is a realistic goal of the current disarmament drive, although still a significant challenge. The same can be said of the nuclear energy aspirants: the nuclear activities of each and every one of them will have an impact on the nuclear nonproliferation regime and the prospects for nuclear disarmament. A realistic goal of the current nonproliferation and disarmament agenda is to persuade states embarking on nuclear energy programs to adopt transparency measures that increase confidence in their peaceful nuclear intentions. This is not an easy undertaking given NAM wariness over any initiative that could be seen as discriminatory or as undermining sovereign rights, but nevertheless this is an area where progress is possible, and where—at the regional level, at least—serious discussions are yet to begin.

SLAYING THE NUCLEAR DRAGON: NEXT STEPS

What are the next steps for nuclear disarmers? How can they move forward in their quest to slay the nuclear dragon? The conclusions of this volume suggest that there are five main areas where further research is required to give nuclear disarmers the necessary energy and ammunition to make progress toward a nuclear-weapon-free world. There is a need for studies on the following topics: (1) how to further reduce roles and numbers of nuclear weapons; (2) how to bring all nuclear-armed states into the disarmament fold; (3) how to clarify the terms of the NPT bargain; (4) the politics, current and future, of nuclear disarmament dynamics; and (5) postnuclear military strategy.

Further Reducing Roles and Numbers of Nuclear Weapons

More in-depth research is needed into the conditions that would allow all nuclear-armed states to make NFU pledges. Indeed, multilateral NFU pledges would be the ideal declaratory policy so long as there are nuclear weapons in the world. So far, only China and India proclaim NFU pledges. While it could be argued that the United States and the United Kingdom have both recently made some progress toward such a policy, France and Russia have refused bluntly to make any moves in that direction. What is the way forward? What would be the implications for other nuclear-armed states, in particular the holdouts? These questions need to be addressed thoroughly to allow progress toward a world free of nuclear weapons. The debate has so far tended to focus only on the advantages and drawbacks of NFU, broadly understood.[8] The research community now needs to go beyond this debate and ask the question of how a multilateral NFU by all nuclear-armed states can be realistically achieved and sustained over time—an exercise perhaps best done, as a first step, in Track-II (i.e., informal) diplomatic forums.

Similarly, in addition to thinking about innovative ways to allow the CTBT's entry into force and the conclusion of an FMCT (as both treaties would institute a qualitative and quantitative cap, respectively, on nuclear-weapon development), substantial research efforts are needed to explore options for progress on the next steps for nuclear reductions. As Santoro explains in chapter 1, the NPR makes it clear that the next arms control negotiations between the United States and Russia should include tactical nuclear weapons (TNW) and nondeployed nuclear weapons. Yet, as he points out, the challenges to address those weapons, "which will be intertwined with BMD and conventional weapons issues, are likely to be long and intense [...] because there is no prior experience in arms control history to deal with such weapons." New START, which has restored a transparency and predictability framework for the United States and Russia, can with its ten-year term certainly serve as a basis on which progress can be built toward the next treaty. The research community, therefore, could help drive this process forward by describing ways in which headway could be made.

Bringing All Nuclear-Armed States into the Disarmament Fold

Although it is only fair for the United States and Russia to lead the nuclear disarmament process because they have by far the largest arsenals, progress toward a nuclear-weapon-free world will only be successful if it is a collective enterprise. In particular, reciprocal moves on the part of other nuclear-armed states, notably the other three NWS, are essential. As Santoro stresses in chapter 4, China has yet to join the process of nuclear reductions because at the moment, "Beijing [...] believes that the levels of [New START] are still much too high for China to rapidly jump on the nuclear disarmament bandwagon." A key task for the research community is to find solutions for how China can be brought into the disarmament fold. This is particularly imperative because China is the only NWS that, in Santoro's words, "is both enhancing and expanding its nuclear arsenal," and, most importantly, because China is rapidly becoming more central than ever to maintaining global strategic stability, as noted in the new U.S. NPR. The absence of success on this front, therefore, could slow—or maybe even stop—current nuclear disarmament momentum. So far, this puzzle has not received much in-depth analysis, even in Track-II diplomatic forums where Chinese scholars are actively participating. This urgently needs to be remedied.

Similarly, although both the United Kingdom and France have conducted (unilaterally) important nuclear reductions since the end of the Cold War, the question of how they can further participate in the nuclear disarmament process is open. As Santoro explains in chapters 1 and 4, while the United Kingdom has carved itself a role as "a facilitator" of current momentum and is likely to continue efforts in that direction, it is very unclear what role France will end up playing: "Sooner or later, [the French] will reach a point when they will no longer be able to take any more 'concrete' steps toward nuclear disarmament." So what could Paris do in order to get further involved in the process? In the same way, in the medium to longer term, will London's actions be sufficient to show the United Kingdom's continuous enthusiasm to move toward a world free of nuclear weapons? What other actions will it have at its disposal to show that it is committed to remaining proactive on the matter? All these questions need to be addressed if any progress toward a nuclear-weapon-free world is to be sustained over the long term.

Last but not least, slaying the nuclear dragon will require the research community to find solutions to the thorny question of how other non-NWS nuclear-armed states (most notably the holdout states) can also be brought into the disarmament fold. It will be extremely challenging because, as Hagerty clearly points out in chapter 7, they are currently "moving away from, rather than toward, disarmament." Nevertheless, without tackling such hard questions, current momentum is unlikely to be sustained for very long: a careful analysis of the options available to move forward, however limited they may be at present, is therefore absolutely critical.

Clarifying the Terms of the NPT Bargain

Current nuclear disarmament momentum is based on the premise that progress toward a world free of nuclear weapons will in response yield results on the nuclear nonproliferation and nuclear security fronts, and vice versa. It is a nice, balanced, and arguably very logical idea, which is at the very core of the NPT bargain. Yet, it is unlikely to remain a solid foundation of current momentum if the terms of this bargain are not more thoroughly defined or clarified. At the moment, every time the NWS make advances toward nuclear disarmament, they are congratulating themselves and expecting—sometimes explicitly requesting—NNWS to reciprocate by subscribing to additional nuclear nonproliferation and nuclear security agreements or arrangements. NNWS, for their part, tend to argue that the nuclear disarmament steps taken by NWS are certainly progress in the right direction but that they are far from sufficient for them to be more active in nuclear nonproliferation and nuclear security. At the 2010 NPT Review Conference, for instance, the pressure was high for NNWS to agree that the IAEA Additional Protocol (AP) should be made the new "gold standard" of safeguards, notably in view of the positive developments that had taken place in nuclear disarmament. Yet, this failed to produce any results because many NNWS suggested—explicitly or implicitly—that the disarmament efforts were not yet "enough" for them to endorse the AP.

The questions then shift: What is "enough"? What nuclear disarmament progress is "enough" for "substantial advances" (another phrase that needs to be defined) on nuclear nonproliferation and nuclear security? In the same way, what advances on nuclear nonproliferation and nuclear security are "enough" for "substantial progress" toward nuclear disarmament? Plainly, to use Cirincione's image one more time, what does it mean, in concrete terms, to flip the nuclear coin over and over again? Can NWS and NNWS agree on benchmarks to be met in both areas? If so, what would these be? What criteria would one use to define them? Without a doubt, identifying benchmarks for progress (toward nuclear disarmament *and* toward nuclear nonproliferation and nuclear security) would certainly be extremely challenging, but it would equally be immensely helpful: it would give a brand-new meaning to the concept "NPT bargain." The bargain would then have more clear-cut requirements, both for NWS and NNWS, which, in addition to having more of a sense of being bound in a fight against common dangers, would be likely to provide a stronger incentive to produce results—and produce them quickly. In particular, it would help dispel the belief held by many NNWS that the current nuclear disarmament drive is, in fact, a mere illusion that conceals an NWS-/Western-led hidden agenda aimed at imposing stronger nuclear nonproliferation and nuclear security obligations on them—a belief that Ogilvie-White describes at length in chapter 8. Clarifying the terms of the NPT bargain, therefore, is a very important question that the research community needs to address thoroughly in order to help make progress toward a nuclear-weapon-free world.

Studies on the Politics, Current and Future, of Nuclear Disarmament Dynamics

One of the core conclusions of this volume is that although the idea of nuclear disarmament is clearly in the air, stark skepticism remains, notably about the desirability and feasibility of an actual world without nuclear weapons. Current momentum, therefore, will not be sustained very long without the help of in-depth studies by reputable and knowledgeable experts who seek and propose viable solutions to the political and technical issues raised by the skeptics (or the "dismissive realists," to use Quinlan's phrase again). Only with solid and convincing findings would the skeptics begin to open up to the idea that a nuclear-weapon-free world is both desirable and feasible. Some excellent work is being undertaken in this area (especially through the disarmament commissions discussed by Hanson), but the problem remains that the task is immense and studies are surprisingly thin on the ground, especially outside the United States.

What do future studies need to focus on exactly? A pivotal question is how to strengthen and enforce the nuclear nonproliferation and nuclear security regimes. In this regard, as Ogilvie-White and Shire suggest in chapters 8 and 9, it is doubtful that current nuclear disarmament momentum will be sustained for much longer without the relatively near-term resolution of current proliferation crises, be it in the defiant states or the silent proliferators. Launching further studies on how to improve responses to current noncompliance cases is therefore a priority. But it is also paramount for the research community to focus more of their efforts on demonstrating how it would be possible to effectively prevent and counter states tempted to "break out" from the future nuclear-weapon-free world and develop nuclear weapons.[9] In other words, will nuclear breakout be preventable without nuclear deterrence? How so? How should major powers and other governing organizations respond? Research on these questions has been underway for some time, but detailed and convincing answers are needed if the world is to do away with nuclear weapons at some point in the future.

Studies on Postnuclear Military Strategy

Last but not least, to have any hope of sustaining disarmament momentum over the longer term, the research community needs to make a convincing case that appallingly destructive conventional wars would not dominate a postnuclear international system. For decades, strategists have argued that nuclear weapons play a vital war-prevention role; that they make major conventional war between the great powers much less likely and should therefore be retained. This issue lies at the very heart of the disarmament debate, and yet it has received relatively little attention in the scholarly literature. In the UK 2006 White Paper, Tony Blair made a "Quinlanesque" point: "those who question the decision [to replace Trident] need to explain why disarmament by the UK would help our security [. . .] They would need to argue that the UK would be safer by giving up the deterrent."[10] To make this case, scholars and disarmament activists in the nongovernmental organization community need to address difficult questions about what types of defense and security arrangements are needed to promote peace and security in disarming and disarmed worlds. For example, on the road to eliminating nuclear weapons, as stockpiles decline, what defense and security options are open to the NWS? Could a "part-time" or virtual nuclear deterrent be credible? What types of alliance commitments can replace extended deterrence? How can collective security be strengthened? In a world without nuclear weapons, what types of non-nuclear forms of deterrence could be relied on to prevent major conventional war? And how would a non-nuclear world deal with the emergence of an aggressive great power? These and other important questions related to the study of military strategy in a postnuclear world need our undivided attention. It is an area of research in which academics have the potential to influence nuclear decision makers, many of whom are open to ideas about a world without nuclear weapons but are unconvinced that a non-nuclear future would be peaceful and stable.[11] So far, with a few notable exceptions, work has tended to focus on the legal and regime requirements of a nuclear-weapon-free world, which is, of course, important but is deeply unsatisfying for those at the sharp end of defense and nuclear decision making.[12] The latter want reassurance that military threats—both conventional and unconventional—can be deterred and populations protected from the scourge of major war. If they can be convinced that this can be achieved without nuclear weapons, then the nuclear dragon's days will genuinely be numbered.

Notes

1. In terms of future studies, this volume provides useful secondary source material (along with other studies on disarmament dynamics) to help in the task of building a theory of nuclear disarmament. In their chapters on state responses to disarmament momentum, the authors have identified important disarmament drivers, distinguishing between material and ideational pressures and constraints. This type of analysis has been helpful to proliferation theorists in the past and is likely to provide useful material for disarmament theorists.

2. *Nuclear Posture Review Report* (Washington, D.C.: Department of Defense, 2010), xiii.

3. Ibid., 15, 17.

4. Vietnam Law on Atomic Energy, no. 18/2008/QH12, June 3, 2008, http://www.dissertationsgratuites.com/dissertations/Law-On-Atomic-Energy/192481.html, and "Nuclear Future Poses Challenges," *Vietnam News*, January 19, 2011, http://www.dztimes.net/post/business/nuclear-future-poses-challenges.aspx.

5. Joseph Cirincione, "Toward a Nuclear-Free Future," *Yes! Magazine*, September 23, 2009, http://www.yesmagazine.org/peace-justice/toward-a-nuclear-free-future.

6. *Nuclear Posture Review Report* (Washington, D.C.: Department of Defense, 2010), vii.

7. "Remarks by Margaret Beckett, Secretary of State for Foreign and Commonwealth Affairs, United Kingdom," Carnegie International Nonproliferation Conference, Washington, D.C., June 25, 2007.

8. See, for instance, Scott Sagan, "The Case for No First Use," *Survival* 51 (June–July 2009): 163–82; and Morton Halperin, Bruno Tertrais, Keith Payne, K. Subrahmanyam, and Scott Sagan, "The Case for No First Use: An Exchange," *Survival* 51 (October–November 2009): 17–46.

9. Recent studies that address these questions and could usefully be taken further include, among others, the following: Barry M. Blechman and Alexander K. Bollfrass, eds., *Elements of a Nuclear Disarmament Treaty* (Washington, D.C.: Simson Center, January 22, 2010); and George Perkovich and James M. Acton, eds., *Abolishing Nuclear Weapons: A Debate* (Washington, D.C.: Carnegie Endowment for International Peace, 2009). These studies build on the early work on monitoring, verification, and breakout that was undertaken under the auspices of the Canberra Commission. See, for example, Andrew Mack, "Nuclear 'Breakout': Risks and Possible Responses," Working Paper 1997/1, Department of International Relations, Research School of Pacific and Asian Studies, Australian National University, Canberra, 1997, http://ips.cap.anu.edu.au/ir/pubs/work_papers/97-1.pdf.

10. *The Future of the United Kingdom's Nuclear Deterrent* (London: Ministry of Defence, 2006).

11. This point was made by Tanya Ogilvie-White during a debate on the future of Trident. It prompted the United Kingdom's first sea lord and chief of naval staff, Admiral Sir Mark Stanhope (who has operational control of Britain's nuclear deterrent and was presenting the official case for replacing Trident) to vigorously agree that future disarmament momentum hinges on studies of postnuclear military strategy, the goal of which should be to explore how peace and security can be achieved in a nuclear-weapon-free world. Admiral Sir Mark Stanhope, Frank Barnaby, and Tanya Ogilvie-White, "A New Trident: Is There Still a Need for the Nuclear Option?" Debate at the Spectator/RUSI Conference on the Future of Defence Procurement, QEII Conference Centre, London, November 9, 2010.

12. Notable exceptions include James M. Action, *Deterrence during Disarmament: Deep Nuclear Reductions and International Security*, Adelphi Series (London: IISS, April 2011); Commander Robert Green, *Security without Nuclear Deterrence* (Christchurch, N.Z.: Astron Media, 2010); Ward Wilson, "Stable at Zero: Enforcing the Peace in a World without Nuclear Weapons," in Blechman and Bollfrass, *Elements of a Nuclear Disarmament Treaty*; and Ward Wilson, "The Myth of Nuclear Deterrence," *Nonproliferation Review* 15, no. 3 (November 2008): 421–39.

CONTRIBUTORS

STEPHEN F. BURGESS is a professor in the Department of International Security Studies, U.S. Air War College. His three books are *South Africa's Weapons of Mass Destruction* (with Helen Purkitt, 2005), *Smallholders and Political Voice in Zimbabwe* (1997), and *The United Nations under Boutros Boutros-Ghali, 1992–97* (2001). He has published numerous articles and book chapters on African and South Asian security issues, including two on U.S. Africa Command. He helped to lead in the organization and execution of the Air Force Africa Command Symposium held in March and April 2009 at Air University, which focused on air power. Since 1999, he has taught courses on international security, peace and stability operations, and African regional and cultural studies. He is also the resident expert on Pakistan and Afghanistan in the department. He is an associate director of the U.S. Air Force Counterproliferation Center. He holds a Ph.D. from Michigan State University and has been a faculty member at Vanderbilt University, the University of Zambia, the University of Zimbabwe, and Hofstra University.

DEVIN T. HAGERTY is a professor in the Department of Political Science at the University of Maryland, Baltimore County. He chaired the department from 2008 to 2011. His main research interests are India-Pakistan security issues, nuclear proliferation and arms control, and the Iranian nuclear program. He is the author of *The Consequences of Nuclear Proliferation: Lessons from South Asia* (1998), coauthor, with Sumit Ganguly, of *Fearful Symmetry: India-Pakistan Crises in the Shadow of Nuclear Weapons* (2005), and editor of *South Asia in World Politics* (2005). He has also published in *International Security, Security Studies, India Review, Current History, Australian Journal of International Affairs, Asian Survey*, and numerous other journals and edited volumes. His most recent publication is "Iran: The Nuclear Quandary," in *The Long Shadow: Nuclear Weapons and Security in 21st Century Asia*, edited by Muthiah Alagappa (2008). He was awarded a Ph.D. in political science by the University of Pennsylvania in 1995.

MARIANNE HANSON is an associate professor of international relations at the University of Queensland, Australia. Her research focuses on international security, the role of law and ethics in world politics, nuclear arms control, and human rights. Her recent publications include "Arms Control," in *Introduction to International Relations: Australian Perspectives*, edited by Richard Devetak, Anthony Burke, and Jim George (2nd ed., 2011), and "Nuclear Weapons in the Asia-Pacific: A Critical Security Appraisal," in *Critical Security in the Asia-Pacific*, edited by Anthony Burke and Matt Macdonald (2007). She has also published several journal articles in such journals as *International Relations*, *International Journal of Human Rights*, and *Nonproliferation Review*. She is an Australian member of the Council for Security Cooperation in the Asia-Pacific (CSCAP). She is director of the Rotary Centre for International Studies in Peace and Conflict Resolution at the University of Queensland.

TOGZHAN KASSENOVA is an associate in the Nuclear Policy Program at the Carnegie Endowment for International Peace (CEIP) and a Stanton Nuclear Security Fellow. Prior to joining CEIP, she was a senior research associate at the University of Georgia's Center for International Trade and Security (CITS) in Washington, D.C., and a postdoctoral fellow at James Martin Center for Nonproliferation Studies in Monterey, California. She serves on the UN Secretary-General's Advisory Board on Disarmament Matters and on the Steering Committee of the Fissile Material Working Group. She is a member of the Council for Security Cooperation in the Asia Pacific (CSCAP) and a nonresident fellow of Pacific Forum-CSIS. Her expertise is in WMD proliferation issues, strategic trade controls and implementation of UN Security Council Resolution 1540, and nuclear energy. She is the author of *From Antagonism to Partnership: The Uneasy Path of the U.S.-Russian Cooperative Threat Reduction* (2007). She has published widely in scholarly and policy journals, including *Nonproliferation Review*, *Disarmament Forum*, and *China and Eurasia Forum Quarterly*. She is a native of Kazakhstan.

TANYA OGILVIE-WHITE is a senior lecturer in International Relations at the University of Canterbury, New Zealand, and a consulting fellow at the International Institute for Strategic Studies (IISS), London. While on study leave in 2010–11, she was a research fellow at (IISS), London, under the Stanton Nuclear Security Fellowship Program. She is a member of the Council for Security Cooperation in the Asia Pacific (CSCAP) and an international partner of the Fissile Material Working Group (FMWG), and she is an associate editor of *Asian Security*. Her recent publications include "Nuclear Intelligence and North-South Politics" (*International Journal of*

Intelligence and Counterintelligence, 2011); (with Jack Boureston) "Expanding the IAEA Nuclear Security Mandate" (*Bulletin of the Atomic Scientists*, 2010); (with Michael S. Malley) "Nuclear Capabilities in Southeast Asia" (*Nonproliferation Review*, 2009); "International Responses to Iranian Nuclear Defiance" (*European Journal of International Law*, 2007); and "Non-Proliferation and Counter-Terrorism Cooperation in Southeast Asia" (*Contemporary Southeast Asia*, 2006). In 2007, she received the Michael Leifer Memorial Award for her research on Southeast Asia. Her article "Is There a Theory of Nuclear Proliferation?" (1996) won the inaugural CNS nonproliferation prize.

MARIA ROST RUBLEE is a senior lecturer in the School of Politics and International Relations at Australian National University. She is author of *Nonproliferation Norms: Why States Choose Nuclear Restraint* (2009), winner of the Alexander George Book Award for best book published in political psychology, which is awarded by the International Society for Political Psychology. Her work uses social constructivism and social psychology to understand how material and normative factors interact to shape elite and civil society conceptions of "security." She has published articles in a variety of journals, including *International Studies Review*, *Nonproliferation Review*, and *Comparative Political Studies*. Her current projects include an examination of civil society's impact on Japan's nuclear policy, succession politics and nuclear policy in Egypt and Libya, and a book manuscript exploring the use of norms as policy tools in international security. She serves on the editorial board of *International Studies Perspective*, is a member of CSCAP-New Zealand, and is a frequent consultant to the U.S. government on security issues. She received both her M.Phil. and Ph.D. in political science from George Washington University.

DAVID SANTORO is a nonproliferation and disarmament senior fellow at the Pacific Forum CSIS. He is also a research affiliate at the Center for International Security and Arms Control (CESIM). Previously, he held research positions in France, Australia, Canada, the United States, and the United Kingdom. He was most recently a research associate at the International Institute for Strategic Studies (IISS), under the 2010–11 Stanton Nuclear Security Fellowship Program. His main research interests are centered on nuclear issues against the backdrop of major power relations. In addition to his work on nuclear disarmament, he is leading a project on the role of the permanent members of the UN Security Council in addressing proliferation after it has been detected and is developing a project on Asian-Pacific perspectives on U.S.-China nuclear relations. His first book, *Treating Weapons Prolifer-*

ation—*An Oncological Approach to the Spread of Nuclear, Biological, and Chemical Technology* was published in 2010. He has also published in several journals and edited volumes.

JACQUELINE SHIRE is the U.S. member of the Panel of Experts on Iran sanctions established pursuant to UN Security Council Resolution 1929. Prior to that, she was a senior analyst at the Institute for Science and International Security (ISIS) and a consultant for ABC News on nuclear proliferation. She began her career at the State Department's Bureau of Political-Military Affairs with assignments to the UN Special Commission on Iraq (UNSCOM) and to the Conference on Disarmament in Geneva. Recent publications include "Taking Back the High Ground: How the Obama Administration Is Setting a Bold New Course in Disarmament and Nonproliferation" (*Georgetown Journal of International Affairs*, 2010); "Iran's Growing Weapons Capability and Its Impact on Negotiations" (*Arms Control Today*, 2009), and an op-ed, "Slowly but Surely, Pyongyang Is Moving" (*Washington Post*, 2008).

INDEX

ABACC (Brazilian-Argentine Agency for Accounting and Control of Nuclear Materials), 154–55
Acton, James 5, 10, 32, 154, 158, 177, 257
Additional Protocol, 93, 102–3, 109, 155, 163, 189, 264, 290, 320
African National Congress, 86
Algeria, 89, 189
al Kibar, 284–86, 295–96, 298
Amano, Yukiya, 91, 286
Article IV, NPT treaty, 177, 261
Article VI, NPT treaty, 11, 58, 64, 92–93, 122, 177
ASEAN. *See* Association of Southeast Asian Nations
Association of Southeast Asian Nations (ASEAN), 196, 199, 200–201, 204, 209–11, 292, 296, 302
Australia, 7, 57–60, 62–63, 66, 68–69, 71, 75–76, 196, 310

ballistic missile defense (BMD), 13, 16–19, 40, 120, 126–27, 130, 136–37, 139–42, 306, 318
Beckett, Margaret, 31–32, 40, 308
Belarus, 6, 25
Biological and Toxin Weapons Convention (BTWC), 13, 195
Blair, Tony, 28, 41–42, 322
Blix Commission, 65, 309
BMD. *See* ballistic missile defense

Board of Governors, IAEA, 26, 105, 196, 249, 254, 261, 286, 295
Brazil: and Additional Protocol, 195; advocacy by, of disarmament, 57, 62, 310; agreement of, with Turkey and Iran, 94; as BRIC country, 228, 317; and Egypt, 203; and Japan, 151–60, 163, 166–69, 171–78; and Non-Aligned Movement, 90–91; as nuclear threshold state, 6–7, 208, 307, 317
Brazilian-Argentine Agency for Accounting and Control of Nuclear Materials (ABACC), 154–55
Brown, Gordon, 29, 33
Browne, Des, 32
BTWC (Biological and Toxin Weapons Convention), 13, 195
Buffett, Warren, 25
Bush, George W., 309, 315; and Australia, 59; and China, 140; and France, 120; and Iran, 256, 263; and Myanmar, 293; and North Korea, 251–52, 263; and Obama administration, 16, 35; and preventive attacks, 284; reversals by, of arms control agreements, 13–14, 56, 64; and Russia, 126; and solidarist agenda, 263, 265; and South Africa, 90, 95

Cameron, David, 31, 52
Canada, 7, 57, 59, 60, 64, 69, 71, 75–76, 152

[330] INDEX

Canberra Commission, 58–61, 63, 68, 75–76
CD. *See* Conference on Disarmament
Chemical Weapons Convention (CWC), 58–59, 195
Cheonan, 252
Cherbourg speech, 119, 121, 123, 134
Chile, 57, 66, 69, 152
Chilton, Kevin, 22
China: and Comprehensive Nuclear-Test-Ban Treaty, 24, 132, 233, 306; as de jure nuclear weapon state, 5–7, 11, 118; development of nuclear weapons by, 138–39; and Egypt, 202; and France, 135; Indian rivalry with, 222, 228–29, 230, 232, 237, 241, 313; and International Commission on Nuclear Non-Proliferation and Disarmament, 68; and Japan, 165–66; military modernization program of, 130–31, 139, 142, 205, 229, 307; and Myanmar, 296–97; and North Korea, 250, 259, 264–66; and nuclear security center, 25; as pessimistic, 5, 6, 7, 11, 103, 118, 128–32; position of, on disarmament, 131, 138, 141–42, 143–44, 219, 220, 239, 313, 319; as potential U.S. target, 13, 140; and pressure on Iran, 91; pride of, in nuclear weapons, 138–39; Russian relations with, 136–38, 139–41, 143; triangle with United States and Russia, 38, 141, 315; and United States, 25, 38, 40, 129, 139–42, 166, 314–15; and UN Security Council, 287, 294; and Vietnam, 193, 205, 209–10
Chu, Steven, 26
Clinton, Hillary, 23, 26, 292
Clinton, William, 12, 234
Cold War: and advocacy states, 58–60, 74–75; and China, 139; and France, 120–21, 133–35; and Kazakhstan, 85; and Russia, 123–24; and South Africa, 87; threat of global annihilation, 1, 3; and United Kingdom, 27, 40–41; and United States, 12, 37, 39, 313
Comprehensive Nuclear-Test-Ban Treaty (CTBT): and advocacy states, 71, 77; and Brazil, 167, 171; and Bush administration, 13; and Central Asian nuclear-weapon-free zone, 102–4; and China, 132, 140–41; and Egypt, 195–96; and France, 121–22, 143; and holdout states, 226; and India, 228–29; and Japan, 161; and Kazakhstan, 96, 108–9; and Obama administration, 15, 22–25; and Pakistan, 232–34, 238; ratification of, 306; and Russia, 126; and South Africa, 88; and United Kingdom, 27, 32; and United States, 39, 314
Comprehensive Nuclear-Test-Ban Treaty Organization (CTBTO), 96, 104, 250
Conference on Disarmament (CD): and Brazil, 153; and FMCT negotiations, 24; functionality of, 71; and Israel, 234; and Japan, 160; role of, 77; and Vietnam, 199, 204; mentioned, 2, 32, 57, 171, 231, 238, 289
Council for Security Cooperation in the Asia Pacific (CSCAP), 204
CSCAP (Council for Security Cooperation in the Asia Pacific), 204
CTBT. *See* Comprehensive Nuclear-Test-Ban Treaty
CTBTO. *See* Comprehensive Nuclear-Test-Ban Treaty Organization
CWC (Chemical Weapons Convention), 58–59, 195

D'Agostino, Thomas, 22–23
Dair Alzour, 280, 282, 287
Danon, Eric, 122
de Klerk, F. W., 87
Democratic Party of Japan (DPJ), 166, 169–71, 173–75, 307
Democratic People's Republic of Korea (DPRK), 249–52, 260, 287
DPJ. *See* Democratic Party of Japan
DPRK. *See* Democratic People's Republic of Korea

Egypt: and Comprehensive Nuclear-Test-Ban Treaty, 24; and joint declaration to UN, 62; and nonproliferation diplomacy, 201–3; nuclear aspirations of, 152, 188–91, 193–95, 198, 205–8, 210–11; and South Africa, 85, 88, 90–91, 94
ElBaradei, Mohamed, 91, 207–8, 255, 283, 286
Ethiopia, 89
Evans, Gareth, 59, 65, 67, 76

First Committee, 23, 57, 61, 84, 199, 226, 230, 282, 289
First World War, 9
fissile material cut-off treaty (FMCT): and Australia, 71; and China, 132 140–41; and France, 121–22; and Kazakhstan, 104, 108; and nuclear holdouts, 226–29, 231, 234; and optimistic nuclear weapon states, 14–15, 24–25, 27, 32; and Russia, 126; and silent proliferators, 297; and United States, 140–41
FMCT. *See* fissile material cut-off treaty
Fordow, 91, 257
Fox, Liam, 29–30, 42

France: as nuclear-armed state, 5–7, 11; and nuclear holdouts, 219–20, 229; and nuclear reductions, 306, 313, 316, 318–19; as pessimistic, 118–23, 132–35, 142–44; and United Kingdom, 42–43; and Vietnam, 192–93
Freedman, Lawrence, 4, 34
French-UK Nuclear Cooperation Agreement, 30–31
fuel-swap deal, 168, 173

Gates, Robert, 22
G8, 57, 123, 173, 255
General Assembly, 61–63, 70–71, 89, 104, 106, 131, 152, 194, 199, 222, 282, 289
Germany, 38, 64, 69, 133, 152, 167, 171, 228, 254
GICNT (Global Initiative to Combat Nuclear Terrorism), 105–6
Global Initiative to Combat Nuclear Terrorism (GICNT), 105–6
Gorbachev, Mikhail, 126
Gottemoeller, Rose, 23

Hague Code of Conduct against Ballistic Missile Proliferation (HCOC), 122
Halperin, Morton, 21
Hamas, 225, 236
HCOC (Hague Code of Conduct against Ballistic Missile Proliferation), 122
HEU. *See* highly enriched uranium
Hezbollah, 225, 236, 240, 283
highly enriched uranium (HEU), 25, 87, 91, 97, 105–6, 121, 157–58, 164, 223–24, 257
Hiroshima, 3, 60, 106, 159–62, 309
Howard, Michael, 2, 8, 304

IAEA. *See* International Atomic Energy Agency

IAEA fuel bank, 105
ICJ (International Court of Justice), 62–63
ICNND. *See* International Commission on Nuclear Non-Proliferation and Disarmament
IISS (International Institute for Strategic Studies), 32, 66
Il-sung, Kim, 250, 259
India: and China, 139; and Comprehensive Nuclear-Test-Ban Treaty, 24; and Myanmar, 294, 297; and no-first-use pledge, 318; as nuclear holdout state, 6, 8, 14, 219, 220–24, 226–35, 237–41, 313; nuclear tests of, 61; as rollback state, 90–91, 94–95, 103; and threshold states, 159, 164, 172; and Vietnam, 193, 205, 210
Indonesia, 24, 57, 66, 103, 189, 295
INF. *See* Intermediate-Range Nuclear Forces
Initial Gate, 30
Intermediate-Range Nuclear Forces (INF), 12, 124, 128, 137
International Atomic Energy Agency (IAEA): and Brazil, 153, 155–58; and Brazilian-Argentine Agency for Accounting and Control of Nuclear Materials, 155; and Egypt, 191, 206–8; funding of, 25–26, 93; and Hans Blix, 65; and India, 227; and Iran, 91, 94, 164, 173, 235, 249, 254–57, 261–62, 265; and Japan, 160, 163–64; and Kazakhstan, 102–3, 105, 107–8, 109; and Myanmar, 279–80, 288, 289–90, 292, 293, 294, 295–96; and North Korea, 168–69, 249, 250, 253; and nuclear disarmament, 57, 94, 305, 320; and Nuclear Security Summit, 25; relationship of, with United States, 25, 261–62; and South Africa, 87, 91, 96–96, 109; and Syria, 279–80, 281–83, 284–87, 295–96; and Vietnam, 193, 196–97, 199–200, 209
International Commission on Nuclear Non-Proliferation and Disarmament (ICNND), 68–69, 71, 75, 170–71, 173
International Court of Justice (ICJ), 62–63
International Institute for Strategic Studies (IISS), 32, 66
International Panel on Fissile Materials (IPFM), 153, 220–24, 234
IPFM. *See* International Panel on Fissile Materials
Iran: aspirations of, for nuclear power, 35, 103, 206–7, 254–58, 260, 279–80, 295, 297; and Comprehensive Nuclear-Test-Ban Treaty, 24; criticism by, of Obama administration, 261–62; French views on, 123, 134, 135; history of nuclear aspirations of, 254; influence of, on South African nuclear policies, 94–95; and International Atomic Energy Agency, 91, 94, 164, 173, 235, 249, 254–57, 261–62, 265; and Mahmoud Ahmadinejad, 105, 168, 173, 225, 256, 262; nuclear defiance and resistance of, to nuclear disarmament, 2, 6, 8, 69, 123, 167–68, 196, 249, 257–58, 260, 262, 267, 287, 317; and Nuclear Nonproliferation Treaty, 21; as potenial U.S. target, 13; and Syria, 283–85; tensions and rivalry of, with Israel, 219, 225, 235–37, 240–41, 260, 262, 265–66; trade of, with Brazil, 168–69, 172–73; trade of, with North Korea, 253; use by, of Japan for nuclear justification, 164
Iraq, 13, 14, 65, 90, 95, 136, 140, 155, 254, 264, 266, 283–84

Ireland, 7, 57, 62, 70, 85
Israel: and Brazil, 174; and
  Comprehensive Nuclear-Test-Ban
  Treaty, 24; and Egypt, 194–95, 198–99,
  202–3, 207–8; as holdout state, 6, 8,
  211, 219–21, 240–41, 262; and Nuclear
  Nonproliferation Treaty, 88, 94, 280;
  opacity of nuclear capabilities of,
  224–26; response of, to disarmament,
  233–37, 240–41; South African views
  on disarmament of, 94–95; strike
  of, on al Kibar, 284–85, 295–96; and
  Syria, 279, 282–83, 297–98; tensions
  and rivalry of, with Iran, 219, 225,
  235–37, 240–41, 260, 262, 265–66

Japan: attidude of, toward convention,
  71; and challenges to disarmament,
  162–66, 307, 317; and India, 228, 238;
  and International Atomic Energy
  Agency, 160, 163–64; and North
  Korea, 251–52, 291; and preemptive
  military force, 284; studies on effects
  of nuclear weapons in, 106; support
  of, for disarmament, 57, 60–61, 68–69,
  159, 169–71, 173–77, 305, 309, 310, 317;
  as threshold state, 6, 7, 151–52, 176,
  177–78, 204, 205; as U.S. ally, 20, 252;
  and Vietnam, 193, 196, 208
Jong-il, Kim, 250–52, 259
Juche, 259

Kargil, 232, 239
Kashmir, 219, 229, 232–33, 239–41
Kawaguchi, Yoriko, 68, 170
Kazakhstan, 6–7, 85–86, 96–110, 162,
  309, 311
Kelley, Robert, 293
Khamenei, Sayyid Ali, 254–56, 262
Khomeini, Ruhollah, 254

Ki-moon, Ban, 104–5
Kissinger, Henry, 1, 14, 56, 68, 101
Kyl, Jon, 18, 23, 46, 48, 54
Kyrgyzstan, 102, 136

Lavrov, Sergey, 126, 128
LDP. *See* Liberal Democratic Party
Liberal Democratic Party (of Japan; LDP),
  169, 171, 173
Libya, 6, 13, 15, 189
Life Extension Programs, 21
low-enriched uranium, 25, 91, 94, 106,
  156–58, 162, 169
Lula, Luis, 158–59, 168–69, 171–75, 184–87

Main Gate, 30
Mandela, Nelson, 88, 90, 95, 311
Mbeki, Thabo, 90, 95, 311
McCain, John 14, 23
MDA (Mutual Defense Agreement), 27
Medvedev, Dmitry, 126, 133
Merkel, Angela, 133
Mexico, 57, 62, 69, 90, 152
Middle East, 135, 233–34, 316; and Brazil,
  174; Bush policies in, 265; cold wars
  in, 220, 230, 315; and disarmament
  diplomacy of Egypt, 203, 206; fuel-
  cycle arrangement for nations in, 211,
  315; and Iran, 225, 236, 266; and Israel,
  225, 284; nuclear energy aspirants in,
  6, 188–89, 295; Nuclear Weapon Free
  Zone, 88, 94, 194, 202, 226, 235; WMD
  free zone, 194–95, 202
Middle Powers Initiative, 64
Minty, Abdul Samad, 88, 90–95
Missile Technology Control Regime
  (MTCR), 87, 153
MTCR (Missile Technology Control
  Regime), 87, 153
Mubarak, Hosni, 190, 194, 203, 207

Mullen, Michael, 17
Mutual Defense Agreement (MDA), 27
Myanmar, 6, 8, 205, 210, 249, 279–80, 288–98

NAC. *See* New Agenda Coalition
Nagasaki, 3, 106, 159, 160–62, 309
NAM. *See* Non-Aligned Movement
Nasser, Gamal, 202
Natanz, 254, 257, 283, 285
National Nuclear Security Administration, 22
NATO. *See* North Atlantic Treaty Organization
Nazarbayev, Nursultan, 99, 103–6, 311
negative security assurances, 21, 89, 107, 119, 308
Netanyahu, Benjamin, 234, 265
Netherlands, 69
New Agenda Coalition (NAC), 7, 61–67, 85, 88–90, 93–95, 109–10, 153, 165–67, 194–95, 309–10, 315–17
New START, 2, 16–19, 22–23, 25, 37, 39, 92, 103, 127–28, 141, 198, 315, 318–19
New Strategic Concept, 19, 38
New Zealand, 7, 57, 62–64, 70, 85, 197, 252, 309
Nixon, Richard, 18, 204, 234
NNWS. *See* Non-Nuclear Weapon States
no-first-use, 129, 169, 170, 173
Non-Aligned Movement (NAM), 4; as advocate of disarmament, 3, 57; and Egypt, 194–95, 198–99; and Iran, 91–92, 259, 262; and Israel, 282–83; and Middle East Nucear Weapon Free Zone, 234–35; and New Agenda Coalition, 62–63, 309; and North Korea, 259; and Nuclear Nonproliferation Treaty benefits, 261; and rights of enrichment, 26; and South Africa, 88, 90–95, 109, 315; and Syria, 282–83; and Vietnam, 195–96, 201, 204; wariness of, to West and to verification, 315, 317
noncompliance, 249, 258, 263, 266, 287, 295, 312, 322
Non-Nuclear Weapon States (NNWS), 309–10, 311, 317, 320–21; and Brazil, 155, 178, 203; and Bush administration, 35; and Chemical Weapons Convention, 58–59; and China, 129; and France, 119, 121; and fuel cycle, 177; and Japan, 61, 178; and Kazakhstan, 96, 98, 102, 107; and New Agenda Coalition, 62, 310; and Nuclear Nonproliferation Treaty, 35, 93; pursuit by, of disarmament, 58, 197–98; and *The Road to 2010*, 33; and South Africa, 85, 88, 91; support of, for nuclear weapons, 314; tensions of, with Nuclear Weapon States, 35, 43; and United Kingdom, 27, 43; and United States, 43, 140; and Verification Research, Training, and Information Centre, 32; and Vietnam, 196
North Atlantic Treaty Organization (NATO), 19, 28, 38, 41–42, 60, 64, 69–70, 77, 120, 124, 133–37, 143, 167, 310, 313
North Korea: Brazil's diplomatic relationship with, 167–68; and China, 139; and Comprehensive Nuclear-Test-Ban Treaty, 24; as defiant state, 6, 8, 69, 205, 220, 234, 249–54, 257–60, 262–67; and Iran, 283–84; and Japan, 161, 164, 165, 170, 252; and Juche ideology, 259; and Kazahkstan, 96–97, 99, 104, 108; and Kim Jong-il, 250, 251–252, 259; and Myanmar, 288, 289, 290–95, 297–98; and Nuclear Non-

Proliferation Treaty, 21, 280, 286; as potential U.S. target, 13; and Syria, 279, 280–82, 283–84, 297–98; U.S. tensions with, 35, 252–53, 258, 259–60, 262–63, 266, 267
Norway, 7, 32, 34, 57, 66–67, 69–72, 75, 77–78, 81–83, 104, 108, 309–10
NPR. *See* Nuclear Posture Review
NPT. *See* Nuclear Nonproliferation Treaty
NPT Preparatory Committee, 64, 122
NPT Review Conference, 60, 64, 89, 92, 122, 153, 154, 161, 171, 194, 262, 310, 320
NSG. *See* Nuclear Suppliers Group
nuclear fuel cycle, 8, 68, 94, 151, 164, 177, 189, 208, 255, 260, 279, 312
nuclear industry, 66, 100, 159, 162
Nuclear Nonproliferation Treaty (NPT), 2, 11, 57, 87, 118, 152, 194, 219, 250, 280, 306
Nuclear Posture Review (NPR), 12–15, 17, 20–22, 31, 35–38, 128, 140, 142, 306–8, 319
Nuclear Security Summit, 25, 92–93, 95, 105, 199, 200, 262, 305
nuclear sharing, 131
Nuclear Suppliers Group (NSG), 90, 109, 153, 156, 227, 231
nuclear terrorism, 2, 35, 41, 93, 95, 262, 266
nuclear test, 86, 90, 97, 121, 131, 164, 167, 229, 235, 251, 253
Nuclear Threat Initiative, 25, 67, 105
Nuclear Weapon Free Zone (NWFZ), 27, 88, 96, 108, 119, 121, 129, 200, 308; African, 26, 88–89, 195; Central Asian, 26, 96, 102–3, 109; Middle East, 88, 94, 202; Northeast Asian, 173; Southeast Asian, 26; South Pacific, 26, 89
Nuclear Weapons Convention (NWC), 70–72, 224

Nuclear Weapon States (NWS), 4–6, 11, 77, 304–10, 312–16, 319–20; and Africa, 89–90; arsenal reductions by, 15, 131–32, 188; and Brazil, 153–56, 167; China as, 130–32; and Egypt, 208; and enrichment, 176–77, 188, 210; France as, 121–22, 134; holdout, 219–20; India as, 222, 226, 228–29; and Iran, 261; and Japan, 165, 170, 173; and Kazakhstan, 100; New Agenda Coalition pressure on, 61–64, 85, 89–90; no-first-use policy of, 21, 131, 170, 173, 222, 226; Non-Aligned Movement pressure on, 57–59, 85; and nuclear weapons ban, 70, 74; optimistic, 11; pessimistic, 118–19, 142; Russia as, 137; and Seven Nation Initiative, 67; and South Africa, 85, 89–90, 92–96; and START treaties, 15, 19, 128; types of, 4–6, 11; United Kingdom as, 42–43, 134; United States as, 21, 26–28, 31–33, 35–36, 39; and Vietnam, 195–98, 200, 203–4
Nunn, Sam, 1, 14, 68, 100–101
NWC. *See* Nuclear Weapons Convention
NWFZ. *See* Nuclear Weapon Free Zone
NWS. *See* Nuclear Weapon States

Obama, Barack, 118, 237, 266–67, 313–15; and Brazil, 166, 168–69, 173–75; and Bush policies, 35; and China, 140–42; and Comprehensive Nuclear-Test-Ban Treaty, 23–24, 39, 141; and congressional hawks, 22–23, 39; and Egypt, 198; and India, 226; and international pluralism, 263; and Iran, 168, 257, 261–62; and Israel, 240; and Japan, 166, 170; and Kazakhstan, 105; and Myanmar, 291–92, 293–94; and New START treaty, 16–19, 37, 39, 92, 198; and North Korea, 251–52, 257,

[336] INDEX

Obama, Barack (*continued*)
259; and nuclear security summit, 25; nuclear-weapon-free-world agenda of, 1, 2; and Nuclear Weapon Free Zone, 26, 89; and Pakistan, 226; and Russia, 126; and South Africa, 94–95; speech of, on nuclear weapons, 2, 34–35, 43, 90–91, 101, 151, 174, 221, 226; and United Nations, 122–23; and U.S. nuclear policy, 15–20, 36–37, 67–69, 76–77; and Vietnam, 199; *Wall Street Journal* editorials' effect on, 56

Organization for Security Cooperation in Europe (OSCE), 104

OSCE (Organization for Security Cooperation in Europe), 104

Pakistan, 223–24, 230–33; and Central Asia, 103; and China, 132, 139, 228, 239; and Comprehensive Nuclear-Test-Ban Treaty, 24; and fissile material cut-off treaty, 132, 238; as holdout state, 6, 8, 219–21, 226, 234, 237, 241, 280, 313; and India, 222, 229, 238–39, 240; and Iran, 91, 254; and Myanmar, 289; and North Korea, 250; and nuclear tests, 61, 170; status symbol of nuclear weapons to, 159; and terrorism, 301n36

Perkovich, George, 5, 32, 154, 158, 175–77

Perry, William, 1, 14, 23, 56, 68, 101

plutonium: disposal of, 161; in Egypt, 206; in France, 121; in Japan, 162–64, 166, 176, 178; in India, 221, 227; in Iran, 283, 284; in Israel, 224; in Kazakhstan, 97, 105; in North Korea, 161, 250–51, 253, 260; in Pakistan, 223, 231; in Syria, 279, 281, 285, 297; U.S.-Russia separate disposition agreement regarding, 25

Polaris, 27
Prague speech, 85, 90, 151, 226
Proliferation Security Initiative (PSI), 197
Prompt Global Strike, 18
PSI (Proliferation Security Initiative), 197

Quinlan, Michael, 4–5, 42, 304, 312, 321

Rafsanjani, Akbar Hashemi, 254
Reliable Replacement Warhead (RRW), 13, 21–22
Republic of Korea, 25
Resende, 156–58, 317
Resolution 1540, UN Security Council, 66, 197
RNEP (Robust Nuclear Earth Penetrator), 13
Robust Nuclear Earth Penetrator (RNEP), 13
Rokkasho, 163
Romania, 66, 286
RRW (Reliable Replacement Warhead), 13, 21–22
Rudd, Kevin, 68–69, 81
Russia, 123–28, 131, 135–38, 265, 313, 318, 319; and Africa, 89; and central Asia Nuclear Weapon Free Zone, 103; and China, 140–41; and Cold War's end, 12; and France, 133, 134; and India, 227; and International Commission on Nuclear Non-Proliferation and Disarmament, 68–69; and Iran, 91, 254, 257–58; and Japan, 161; and Kazakhstan, 96–97, 100, 106, 107–8, 109; and Myanmar, 288–89, 292; and NATO, 82n45, 134, 310; and North Korea, 250; and Nuclear Security Summit, 25–26; as Nuclear Weapon State, 5, 11; as pessimistic, 6, 7, 11, 118,

132, 142–43; as potential U.S. target, 13, 314; reductions to nuclear arsenal of, 32, 77, 93, 140–41, 219–20, 239, 306; and RevCon, 235; and START treaties, 12, 14, 15, 16, 17, 18, 92, 140, 314; and Syria, 283–84, 287; and United Kingdom, 41; and United States, 13, 16, 18, 19, 20, 38, 40, 82n45, 140–41, 314–15; and Vietnam, 192–93, 218n90

Samore, Gary, 20, 24, 105
Sarkozy, Nicolas, 119–21, 123, 133–34, 313
SDR (Strategic Defence Review), 27–29
Second World War, 1, 3, 8, 12, 27, 36, 120, 225, 284
Security Council: and Brazil, 159, 172; and France, 134; Iranian defiance of, 6, 249, 254, 255; and Joint Declaration, 172; and Kazakhstan, 100; and Myanmar, 291–92, 294; North Korean defiance of, 249, 251, 252, 253–54, 260, 291–92; and Obama, 15–16, 122–23; Resolution 1540, 66, 197; Resolution 1874, 291–92; and Russia, 137; sanctions against Iran, 94, 168, 255; and Sarkozy, 123, 134; and Syria, 282, 285, 287, 296; 2009 Summit, 15, 122–23, 200; and U.S. intervention against Serbia, 136; and Vietnam, 196, 197
Semipalatinsk, 99, 102, 104, 106
Seven Nation Initiative, 7, 62, 65–69, 309–10
Shultz, George, 1, 14, 56, 101
Six-Party Talks, 167, 251–53, 263–64, 281, 316
Slovenia, 62
Small Quantities Protocol (SQP), 289–90
SORT (Strategic Offensive Reductions Treaty), 14

South Africa, 6–7, 57, 62, 66, 85–96, 108–10, 152, 155, 172, 195, 203, 305, 309, 311, 312, 315
Southeast Asia, 6, 66, 188–89, 200–201, 205, 295, 301
Soviet Union, 3, 12, 27, 41, 85–86, 97, 100, 102, 108, 133, 193, 202, 220, 259, 311
Sputnik, 27
SQP (Small Quantities Protocol), 289–90
Stockpile Management Program, 21
Strategic Defence and Security Review, 30, 308
Strategic Defence Review (SDR), 27–29
Strategic Offensive Reductions Treaty (SORT), 14
strategic stability, 33, 38, 44, 128, 132, 142, 238, 306, 319
Sweden, 7, 57, 62, 65, 70–71, 85, 309
Syria, 6, 8, 13, 189, 235, 249, 253, 266, 279, 280–87, 290, 295–97

tactical nuclear weapons (TNW), 12, 17–19, 38, 68–69, 86, 124–28, 130, 143, 310, 318
Tajikistan, 102
Tanzania, 89
Tauscher, Ellen, 23–24
Thirteen Practical Steps, 64, 66, 90, 122, 153, 169, 310
TNW. *See* tactical nuclear weapons
Tokyo Forum, 61, 63, 160, 170, 181–82
Trident, 16, 27–31, 41–43, 143, 313–14, 322
Trident Value for Money, 30
Turkey, 69, 91, 94, 168, 172–73
Turkmenistan, 102

UK-Norway Initiative, 32, 66–67, 310
Ukraine, 6, 25, 136

United Kingdom: and Blair, 28, 41, 42, 322; and Brown, 29, 33; and Cameron, 31; as de jure nuclear weapon state, 5, 118; and France, 42–43, 121, 135, 143; and Kazakhstan, 100; nuclear development in, 41, 42–43; as optimistic, 7, 11–12, 26–32, 34, 40–44, 197, 305, 306–7, 308–9, 312–16, 318–319; and Seven-Nation Initiative to Strengthen Adherence to Nuclear-Nonproliferation and Disarmament Agreements, 66, 67; and Syria, 287

United Nations: Atomic Energy Commission, 3; and China, 297; and Egypt, 194; and France, 119; and India, 222, 226, 297; and Israel, 233; and Kazakhstan, 100, 103, 104; and Non-Aligned Movement, 57; Nuclear Security Summit, 25, 93; Special Committee against Apartheid, 87; and Syria, 282, 285–86; and Thailand, 297; and Vietnam, 197. *See also* Security Council

United States, 31–32, 77, 78n3, 257, 258, 265, 296; and Australia, 68; and ballistic missile defense, 18; and China, 129, 131, 138–42, 143, 237; and Comprehensive Nuclear-Test-Ban Treaty, 24, 233–34; and Egypt, 194, 198, 206; and France, 135; and India, 227–28; and Iran, 168, 254, 255–56, 261–62, 283–84; and Israel, 234; and Japan, 61, 164–66, 169–70, 173–74; and Kazakhstan, 99, 100, 102, 103; and Middle East, 235, 297; and Myanmar, 293–94; and New Agenda Coalition, 61, 65; and New Zealand, 62–63; and North Korea, 252, 259, 263; as nuclear abolition driver, 4, 5, 11–15, 20–22, 34–40, 43–44, 56–58, 118, 197, 305–9, 312–18, 321; and Nuclear Security Summit, 25–26; as Nuclear Weapon State, 219–20; and Pakistan, 231–32; and Russia, 19–20, 82n5, 123–24, 126–28, 131, 136–38, 143, 239, 318–19; and South Africa, 86, 89–95; and Syria, 287, 297; and United Kingdom, 26–27; and Vietnam, 192–93, 197, 205, 210

U.S. Congress, 27, 33
U.S.-India Civil Nuclear Cooperation Agreement, 24, 90, 193, 231, 296
U.S. Strategic Posture Commission, 164
Uzbekistan, 102

verification, 5, 13–14, 16–17, 32, 68, 73, 94, 96–97, 104, 108, 176, 250, 255, 257, 310
VERTIC (Verification Research, Training, and Information Centre), 32, 66
Vietnam, 6, 8, 188–89, 191–210, 295, 307

weapons of mass destruction (WMD), 20, 65, 86, 88, 95, 105, 129, 133–34, 197, 204, 209, 222, 253–54, 284–85, 297, 315; free zone, 194–95, 202
White House, 20, 22, 43, 53, 105, 118, 126, 140
WikiLeaks, 296
WMD. *See* weapons of mass destruction
World War II. *See* Second World War

Xiaoping, Deng, 139

Yongbyon, 250, 260, 281–82

Zedong, Mao, 138, 150
Zimbabwe, 89
Zuma, Jacob, 95

www.ingramcontent.com/pod-product-compliance
Lightning Source LLC
Chambersburg PA
CBHW011753220426
43672CB00017B/2942